CECIL KUHNE

NEAR DEATH
IN THE
MOUNTAINS

Cecil Kuhne is the editor of three previous anthologies on adventure travel, *On the Edge*, *The Armchair Paddler*, and *Near Death on the High Seas*. A former whitewater rafting guide, he has also written nine books about rafting, kayaking, and canoeing. He lives in Dallas.

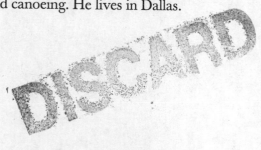

ALSO EDITED BY CECIL KUHNE

Near Death on the High Seas

On the Edge

The Armchair Paddler

NEAR DEATH
IN THE
MOUNTAINS

NEAR DEATH
IN THE
MOUNTAINS

TRUE STORIES OF
DISASTER AND SURVIVAL

EDITED BY
CECIL KUHNE

VINTAGE DEPARTURES
Vintage Books
A Division of Random House, Inc.
New York

A VINTAGE DEPARTURES ORIGINAL, JULY 2008

Copyright © 2008 by Cecil Kuhne

All rights reserved. Published in the United States by
Vintage Books, a division of Random House, Inc., New York,
and in Canada by Random House of Canada Limited, Toronto.

Vintage is a registered trademark and Vintage Departures
and colophon are trademarks of Random House, Inc.

Permissions appear at the end of the book.

Cataloging-in-Publication Data is on file
at the Library of Congress.

ISBN: 978-0-307-27935-4

Book design by Rebecca Aidlan

www.vintagebooks.com

Printed in the United States of America
10 9 8 7 6 5 4 3 2 1

CONTENTS

PREFACE

Struggling through thin air to reach a snowcapped and wind-whipped summit has to be about more than just admiring the view on top. At such altitudes breathing becomes difficult, and the climber is operating in an atmosphere as inhospitable as that of the deep-sea diver. Any endeavor in which a single misstep can send you hurtling backward into darkness to your death is not easily or quickly explained.

Interestingly enough, the collection of books we call mountaineering literature constitutes the most literate among adventure pursuits. This accounts for the sizable and avid population of armchair mountaineers who enjoy reading about alpine travails but who are perfectly content not to leave their living rooms. The whole genre of books has the comfortable feel of an English mountaineering club, full of tweed-jacketed climbers sitting around in overstuffed leather chairs, pipes ablaze, talking about their next journey to the Hindu Kush.

But, believe me, the alpine dangers out there are *very* real. Heading toward the crest of a jagged peak with, at most, a rope and a pack full of carabiners and pitons is not for the faint of heart. These protections against falling are illusory, for one false move and you may be gone forever. There is always the possibility that your companion will slip and bring you down with him. Or, even worse, that you are able to stabilize yourself while your colleague dangles helplessly in midair and the pitons above you start to pop out of the rock wall like buttons on a cheap suit. Do you take the knife and cut the poor soul free to save your own life?

The collection before you, I believe, represents the finest climbing memoirs in the field, and the writers convey their passions in ways that are irresistible. They describe the beauty of high places, to be sure, but, more important, they explain their obsession to reach the top in ways that the rest of us can relate to but never fully comprehend. The stories here include peaks from around the world. Many are renowned, like Everest, but others are less familiar but equally challenging, especially when the weather suddenly turns ugly, which it is apt to do when humans are present.

And when climbers fall, as sometimes happens, there is no sudden awakening for them from a bad dream. Often their tattered bodies are never recovered. Other dangers also await. One particularly haunting story included here concerns a young woman who was the daughter of a famous mountaineer and who died of high-altitude sickness while attempting to scale the mountain for which she was named.

When the famous British mountaineer George Mallory was asked why he wanted to climb Mount Everest, he replied, "Because it is there." Perhaps in the end all other answers are hopelessly superficial.

Cecil Kuhne
Dallas, Texas

FOREWORD
Eiger Dreams

JON KRAKAUER

The sunshine came on October 8, along with a promise from the meteorologists that there would be no precipitation for at least five days. We gave the Nordwand the morning to slough off the post-foehn accumulation of snow, then hiked through crotch-deep drifts over to the base of the route, where we set up a hastily patched-together tent. We were in our sleeping bags early, but I was too scared to even pretend to sleep.

At 3 a.m., the appointed hour to start up the wall, it was raining and some major ice and rockfall was strafing the face. The climb was off. Secretly relieved, I went back to bed and immediately sank into a deep slumber. I awoke at 9 a.m to the sound of birds chirping. The weather had turned perfect once again. Hurriedly, we threw our packs together. As we started up the Nordwand my stomach felt like a dog had been chewing on it all night.

We had been told by friends who had climbed the Nord-wand that the first third of the standard route up the face is "way casual." It isn't, at least not under the conditions we found it. Although there were few moves that were technically difficult, the climbing was continuously insecure. A thin crust of ice lay over deep, unstable powder snow. It was easy to see how Ragone had fallen; it felt as though at any moment the snow underfoot was going to collapse. In places where the wall steepened, the snow cover thinned and our ice axes would ricochet off rock a few inches beneath the crust. It was impossible to find anchors of any kind in or under the rotting snow and ice, so for the first two thousand feet of the climb we simply left the ropes in the packs and "soloed" together.

Our packs were cumbersome and threatened to pull us over backward whenever we would lean back to search out the route above. We had made an effort to pare our loads down to the essentials, but Eiger terror had moved us to throw in extra food, fuel, and clothing in case we got pinned down by a storm, and enough climbing hardware to sink a ship. It had been difficult to decide what to take and what to leave behind. Marc eventually elected to bring along a Walkman and his two favorite tapes instead of a sleeping bag, reasoning that when the going got desperate, the peace of mind to be had by listening to the Dead Kennedys and the Angry Samoans would prove more valuable than staying warm at night.

At 4 p.m., when we reached the overhanging slab called the Rote Fluh, we were finally able to place some solid anchors, the first ones of the climb. The overhang offered protection from the unidentified falling objects that occasionally hummed past, so we decided to stop and bivouac even though there was more than an hour of daylight left. By digging out a long narrow platform where the snow slope met the rock, we could lie in relative comfort, head-to-head, with the stove between us.

The next morning we got up at three and were away from our little ledge an hour before dawn, climbing by headlamp. A rope-length beyond the bivouac, Marc started leading up a pitch that had a difficulty rating of 5.4. Marc is a 5.12 climber, so I was alarmed when he began to mutter and his progress came to a halt. He tried moving left, and then right, but an eggshell-thin layer of crumbly ice over the vertical rock obscured whatever holds there might have been. Agonizingly slowly, he balanced his way upward a few inches at a time by hooking his crampon points and the picks of his axes on unseen limestone nubbins underneath the patina of rime. Five times he slipped, but caught himself each time after falling only a few feet.

Two hours passed while Marc thrashed around above me. The sun came up. I grew impatient. "Marc," I yelled, "if you don't want to lead this one, come on down and I'll take a shot at it." The bluff worked: Marc attacked the pitch with renewed determination and was soon over it. When I joined him at his belay stance, though, I was worried. It had taken us nearly three hours to climb eighty feet. There is more than eight thousand feet of climbing on the Nordwand (when all the traversing is taken into consideration), and much of it was going to be a lot harder than those eighty feet.

The next pitch was the infamous Hinterstoisser Traverse, a 140-foot end run around some unclimbable overhangs, and the key to gaining the upper part of the Nordwand. It was first climbed in 1936 by Andreas Hinterstoisser, whose lead across its polished slabs was a brilliant piece of climbing. But above the pitch he and his three companions were caught by a storm and forced to retreat. The storm, however, had glazed the traverse with verglas, and the climbers were unable to reverse its delicate moves. All four men perished. Since that disaster, climbers have always taken pains to leave a rope fixed across the traverse to ensure return passage.

We found the slabs of the Hinterstoisser covered with two inches of ice. Thin though it was, it was solid enough to hold our ice axes if we swung them gently. Additionally, an old frayed fixed rope emerged intermittently from the glazing. By crabbing gingerly across the ice on our front points and shamelessly grabbing the old rope whenever possible, we got across the traverse without a hitch.

Above the Hinterstoisser, the route went straight up, past landmarks that had been the stuff of my nightmares since I was ten: the Swallow's Nest, the First Ice Field, the Ice Hose. The climbing never again got as difficult as the pitch Marc had led just before the Hinterstoisser, but we were seldom able to get in any anchors. A slip by either of us would send us both to the bottom of the wall.

As the day wore on, I could feel my nerves beginning to unravel. At one point, while leading over crusty, crumbly vertical ice on the Ice Hose, I suddenly became overwhelmed by the fact that the only things preventing me from flying off into space were two thin steel picks sunk half an inch into a medium that resembled the inside of my freezer when it needs to be defrosted. I looked down at the ground more than three thousand feet below and felt dizzy, as if I were about to faint. I had to close my eyes and take a dozen deep breaths before I could resume climbing.

One 165-foot pitch past the Ice Hose brought us to the bottom of the Second Ice Field, a point slightly more than halfway up the wall. Above, the first protected place to spend the night would be the Death Bivouac, the ledge where Max Sedlmayer and Karl Mehringer had expired in a storm during the first attempt on the Nordwand in 1935. Despite its grim name, the Death Bivouac is probably the safest and most comfortable bivouac site on the face. To get to it, however, we still had to make an eighteen-hundred-foot rising traverse across the Second Ice Field, and then ascend several hundred devious feet more to the top of a buttress called the Flatiron.

It was 1 p.m. We had climbed only about fourteen hundred feet in the eight hours since we'd left our bivouac at the

Rote Fluh. Even though the Second Ice Field looked easy, the Flatiron beyond it did not, and I had serious doubts that we could make the Death Bivouac—more than two thousand feet away—in the five hours of daylight that remained. If darkness fell before we reached the Death Bivouac, we would be forced to spend the night without a ledge, in a place that would be completely exposed to the avalanches and rocks that spilled down from the most notorious feature on the Nordwand: the ice field called the White Spider.

"Marc," I said, "we should go down."

"What?!" he replied, shocked. "Why?"

I outlined my reasons: our slow pace, the distance to the Death Bivouac, the poor condition the wall was in, the increasing avalanche hazard as the day warmed up. While we talked, small spindrift avalanches showered down over us from the Spider. After fifteen minutes, Marc reluctantly agreed that I was right, and we began our descent.

Wherever we could find anchors, we rappelled; where we couldn't, we down-climbed. At sunset, below a pitch called the Difficult Crack, Marc found a cave for us to bivouac in. By then we were already second-guessing the decision to retreat, and we spent the evening saying little to each other.

At dawn, just after resuming the descent, we heard voices coming from the face below. Two climbers soon appeared, a man and a woman, moving rapidly up the steps we had kicked two days before. It was obvious from their fluid easy movements that they were both very, very good climbers. The man turned out to be Christophe Profit, a famous French alpinist. He thanked us for kicking all the steps, then the two of them sped off toward the Difficult Crack at an astonishing clip.

A day after we had wimped out because the face was "out of condition," it appeared as though the two French climbers were going to cruise up the climb as if it were a Sunday stroll. I glanced over at Marc and it looked like he was about to burst into tears. At that point we split up and continued the nerve-wracking descent by separate routes.

Two hours later I stepped down onto the snow at the foot of the wall. Waves of relief swept over me. The vise that had been squeezing my temples and gut was suddenly gone. By God, I had survived! I sat down in the snow and began to laugh.

Marc was a few hundred yards away, sitting on a rock. When I reached him I saw that he was crying, and not out of joy. In Marc's estimation, simply surviving the Nordwand did not cut it. "Hey," I heard myself telling him, "if the Frogs get up the sucker, we can always go into Wengen and buy more food, and then go for it again." Marc perked up immediately at this suggestion, and before I could retract my words he was sprinting off to the tent to monitor the French climbers' progress through binoculars.

At this point, however, my luck with the Nordwand finally took a turn for the better: Christophe Profit and his partner got only as far as the Rote Fluh, the site of our first bivouac, before a large avalanche shot past and scared them into coming down, too. A day later, before my Eiger luck could turn again, I was on a jet home.

NEAR DEATH
IN THE
MOUNTAINS

The short-lived escape of World War II prisoners in order to scale a mountain is not your typical climbing tale. When Felice Benuzzi and two of his fellow Italian inmates fled a British POW camp in equatorial East Africa to ascend the 17,000-foot heights of Mount Kenya, they did so, they said, to escape the boredom of prison.

The suspense of this unusual journey was two-sided. Would the Italians successfully climb the mountain, and what would the prison guards do when they discovered their escape?

NO PICNIC ON MOUNT KENYA

FELICE BENUZZI

The Mountain

Our problem demanded consideration. From where we were the north face of Batian looked formidable. We knew that the peak had been climbed, but wondered from which side the ascent had been made. Would it look more feasible from other aspects? Was there any standard route to the summit, and if so where was it? In order to answer these questions we should have to make a detour all round the base of the peak, but we did not know if this could be accomplished in one day and we had promised Enzo to be back soon after noon. Moreover, we had very little food left and Enzo's condition would not allow us to move the base camp nearer to the peak even if we had been able to locate a more promising route. We had not the faintest idea, of course, that there was a hut on the far side of Batian, a thousand feet higher than our base camp and at the very start of the standard route. For all these reasons we resolved to attempt the ascent from the north.

Having reached this decision, it remained to be seen whether a plan could be worked out in detail.

Two ridges buttress the mass of Batian on the north side, running left and right from the appalling Northey Glacier: the northeastern which is very long and unbelievably jagged and the northwestern which is shorter, steeper, and smoother on the whole but with a few very doubtful-looking pitches.

We agreed that if there was any possibility of scaling Batian from our side, this could only be done by bestriding, or traversing, the northwest ridge. This ridge has been climbed only once, under summer conditions by climbers of world-wide fame, Shipton and Tilman.

This being settled, we were faced by a further poser—how best to get on to the northwest ridge which has at its base a rock-tower with a roughly conical top, called by Shipton the Petit Gendarme.

Faced by the same problem, Shipton and Tilman abandoned the idea of an approach from the northern side and decided to make for the gap in the ridge behind the Petit Gendarme, attacking from the south. Their decision proved wise as they were successful. Had we known that these two English aces had declared that any attempt to approach the ridge from the north was hopeless, we should have made other plans; as things were, we proposed to try a route where Shipton and

Tilman saw no hope. We decided in the end to traverse Dutton Peak and a black tooth behind it, reaching Petit Gendarme from a gap between "Black Tooth" and Petit Gendarme itself. It looked difficult but not impossible.

To get a closer view we decided to try out the first stage of the proposed route there and then, a plan which would have the advantage of giving us a practice climb.

We descended from the rocks to a large saddle just north of Point Peter, marked by a rock shaped like a molar tooth. As this saddle has no official name on Dutton's map and as it is mentioned many times in this story I shall call it, as we did, "Molar Saddle."

After eating a piece of chocolate we got round Point Peter on a scree and found an easy couloir, covered with hard snow. After half an hour of gentle climbing we reached a gap some fifty or sixty feet below the summit of Dutton Peak from which we looked down to César Glacier. Had we known that we were so near the top of a named peak, and one not often climbed, we should have attempted to scale it; but as we did not know this and as our attention was wholly absorbed in studying our approach to Petit Gendarme, we were quite content to sit in the gap, dangling our feet above César Glacier and eating another piece of chocolate in lieu of lunch.

We guessed that a traverse on the north face of Dutton Peak would bring us to the "Black Tooth" and to the very foot of Petit Gendarme. From thence, with our "eyes of faith" as Mummery used to say, we thought we could see a possibility of carrying on, although the difficulties seemed to increase toward the higher rocks.

As it was getting late, we left our lofty observatory and scrambled down until we reached the foot of Point Peter. With regret we decided not to make an attempt on it. Enzo would get anxious if we stayed out longer and Guiàn was getting worried about him.

On the scree below the rocks of Point Peter were the last lobelias, mostly dry and dead. We broke and bent some of them to mark the route when we should return to make our actual attempt on Batian.

At 2 p.m. we were back at the "Molar" pass whence we slid down a long scree to the upper tarn.

The colors of both tarns had changed, as we were now looking at them from a different angle, but the impression of complete peace and beauty was the same as from above.

After having drunk at the cool waters of the upper tarn, we walked along its shore toward the lower one.

"Dreamland," murmured Giuàn, struck, as I was, by the sheer perfection of the landscape. Between the tarns and round about the lower one was a veritable flower garden made up of numerous tropical alpine species, many of them in bloom: groundsels with violet-gold inflorescences, giant groundsels, some of them with a plume-like crest of young mauve leaves, finger-like lobelias, mosses of all sorts and colors, cushions of ivory-white dwarf helichrysum, scabiosae, anemones, and many others which I do not know by name. An occasional blue-grey granite rock or a tuft of the long tussocky grass scattered among what appeared to be well-ordered flowerbeds added effectively to the harmony of the setting. Between the upper and the lower tarns, the newborn Nanyuki would be murmuring, and beneath its crystal clear water one could count the stones on the bottom.

I could not help recalling what I had read about the masterpieces of the wise gardeners of ancient China, said to have been experts at making miniature wonder-gardens. Again, a poor modern city dweller, I had been reminded of human craft and artificiality by an example of Nature's own supreme taste as shown in the selection and blending of color and forms.

This sheer loveliness of plant life had a background which at first sight contrasted strangely, so cold and harsh did it look, for between reddish rocks on the left and grey-blue walls on the right hung the snout of César Glacier. The savage seracs forming a huge frozen waterfall ended in tongues and curls and embroideries of green shaded ice protruding from the main mass; but on looking again from the fairy garden in the foreground to the ice and rock-world behind, I soon found that this apparent discord merged in the placid mirror of the tarns, which reflected both glacier and flowers, blending colors, smoothing contrasts as an accord links and welds seemingly contrasting musical notes.

When we arrived back at the camp, we found that Enzo had been busy. He had doubled the ropes supporting the tent roof, dug a ditch all round the tent, and had made a cup for me of the empty jam tin, as I had mislaid my own mug. He had also carried out several minor works in *his* base camp to show that though ill, he was in no way a passenger but still an active member of the party.

The camp looked more comfortable, but unhappily we could do nothing about our greatest problem, that of food. Our rations being almost at an end, we divided the last tin but one of corned beef for our dinner, put the last drops of olive oil on it, and ate it with a few buttered biscuits. Following the advice of Giuàn, we had reserved our butter to be eaten at the higher altitudes. He had been right, as now we really craved for it more than for any other food.

It is true that the quantity we ate left very much to be desired, but we comforted ourselves with the thought that our eyes had feasted on unforgettable scenes to compensate us for what our mouths had lacked.

The day was ending in a crescendo of beauty.

Beyond the real mountain of rock and ice appeared a

phantom shape, a fairy mountain of those huge rounded heaps which the scientists call "cumuli" but which the Venetian painters of the seventeenth century used to call "heroic clouds." At first they were so dazzling white that the eye could not withstand the glare, but later, as the sun set behind a mist-bank overlying the Laikipia plateau, they slowly changed color, forming at last a crimson halo round the bloodred crags of Batian, while the rosy glaciers overhanging the invisible tarns faded slowly in sympathy.

February 3

This day, according to plan, was wholly devoted to rest and to final preparations for our attempt on Batian.

We got up late, having slept soundly for twelve hours on our grass palliasse in the narrow tent. The night had been so cold that the water in our bottles was still frozen solid at 9 a.m., though the bottles had been well covered and had been placed inside our rucksacks.

This ice was the best answer to a question I had put to myself: was it or was it not foolish to sleep without keeping a watch? As a rule, dangerous beasts like lions and leopards do not frequent very high altitudes, but there are exceptions.* As keeping watch without a fire was not possible I decided that it

---

* One of the points of Kibo crater on Kilimanjaro is named Leopard Point in commemoration of a leopard carcase found there at nineteen thousand feet; the carcase of a second leopard was discovered not far below that of the first in 1943 (*Kilimanjaro Crater* by E. Robson—*East Africa Standard*, 19th Nov. 1943); on Ruwenzori, E. A. T. Dutton found leopard pug marks at a great height (*Kenya Mountain*, p. 55); on Mount Kenya P. Ghiglione found leopard spoor in the lobelia and giant groundsel belt (*Le mie scalate nei cinque continenti*, p. 162) and in the high Mackinder's Valley "Campi ya simba" at some fifteen thousand feet owes its name according to native tales (Dutton, p. 55) to a night call paid there by a lion.

would be perfectly safe to trust to luck insofar as mountaineering felines were concerned.

In order to get boiling water for breakfast coffee and for shaving, we experimented again and again with dry lobelia and giant groundsel wood, but we could not get it to burn. The reason we could not is still a mystery to us, as all parties on Mount Kenya whose records I have read managed to get giant groundsel to burn. It might be that native porters are experts at making out a fire from anything, and every party which climbed before us was served by native porters.

Thus we ate two tiny biscuits with plenty of butter and meat extract, and shaved with cold water. But still we did not give up hope. If giant groundsels and lobelias did not like the idea of being burnt by us we should have to try other fuel, as Enzo reckoned that the alcohol left for the boiler would be just enough for breakfast on "Batian day." Therefore we burnt dry grass heaped between two boulders under our closed cooking pot. The grass curled, blackened, and smoked furiously without showing a flame, but it did develop heat. After more than an hour the water in the cooking pot started boiling, and for lunch we were able to have good tea with our last tin of corned beef.

Unexpectedly ambitious hopes of being able to cook "game" arose with our discovery of the rats. Actually the discovery had been made by Enzo but had not been credited by us.

This is what happened: as I was returning from washing and shaving at the ice-fringed brook, I found Enzo busy fastening our rucksacks halfway up the stems of giant groundsels near the tent. I commended him:

"It gives an impression of order and tidiness wholly worthy of a base camp commanded by you."

"There's nothing to laugh at," he answered. "There is a

reason apart from order and tidiness and I bet you could not guess what it is."

I tried first "moisture," then "danger of a sudden snowfall, subsequent thaw, and deluge." Finally I guessed "animals" scoring from a shot in the dark. "Marmots" was my next guess and, at last, "rats."

Enzo answered with a mysterious "Might be."

"What do you mean by 'might be'? Either they are rats or they are something else, perhaps shrews or ground squirrels."

"I don't know what they are. They seem to be rats."

"Rats?" I repeated, wondering what rats could live on at this altitude. Enzo, misunderstanding my doubts and knowing that as a rule neither I nor Giuàn took his remarks at face value, retorted:

"I don't see why you have to make such a fuss about it. Whatever the animals are, they live under the boulders."

Triumphantly, Giuàn intervened, "How did you see them if they live under boulders?"

"When they come out, like they did yesterday when you were both away. They have dark-brown fur and a white stripe running from the neck to the base of the tail. The fur is very thick indeed."

"Fur-bearing animals then!" I said, still wondering if it was one of the yarns Enzo sometimes liked to spin, or if I could believe him.

"Exactly. I was wondering how many of them I should want to make a cape for my wife."

Giuàn and I ended the interview with a hearty laugh and decided that Enzo was joking.

But after lunch when we were all three sitting quietly near the tent basking in the weak sun, Enzo sewing the flag, Giuàn fastening a new cord to his ice axe, and I oiling my boots, Enzo suddenly pointed to the next boulder. It was a gesture of pride which reminded me of that made by a conjurer when he produces the white rabbit out of his silk hat, points at it, and remarks with theatrical modesty, "Voilà!"

There it was, and Enzo, who had been proved right, smiled in a self-conscious manner. His description proved exact. The animal's tail was rat-like, not furry like a squirrel's. It sat on its hind legs, its forefeet close to its breast, and looked at us in the half-suspicious and half-concerned manner with which an old solicitor's clerk looks over his glasses at an intruder in his office.

It did not stay long and at the first movement it dashed off.

Anyhow, rats formed the main topic of our conversation in the afternoon and we left it to Enzo's well-proved ingenuity to discover the proper bait and to make a trap to catch some, not in order to make a cape for Enzo's wife—of which Giuàn's and my wife would have been rightly envious—but merely to provide us with something to eat, as we were at the end of our rations. True, neither my companions nor I had any particular craving for rat meat ordinarily, and as a matter of fact we had never tasted it; but we felt at that moment that we could have eaten not only one but several, bones, skin, and all.

Our day of rest and preparation passed in a flash. Washing, darning, mending, checking over ropes and crampons, putting spare hobnails into the soles of our boots, which had lost a lot of them owing to the continuous wading, oiling boots, and other odds and ends took a lot of time.

Enzo had at last sewn together the three sections of our flag which we had carried separately. In order to prevent it from being seized in case we were caught during our escape, the flag had been divided between us as follows: Enzo had carried the red section, using it as a bag for our biscuits, Giuàn the green sewn into the lining of his cap as a business-like protection against ultraviolet rays, and I had concealed the white with the royal arms inside my shirt.

I wrote on a sheet of drawing paper a message with our names (but without our prisoner-of-war numbers as this would have been against our rules) and put it into the—alas!—empty brandy bottle and sealed it with candle wax, while Enzo tackled the matter of the flagpole, to be carried inside my rucksack.

The five-foot pole, which Enzo had carried fastened to the tent poles or had used as a walking stick, was cut in half. On top of the lower half he fixed a mortise made of an empty corned-beef tin, into which the tenon of the upper pole could be slipped when we planted the flag. On the upper part of this pole Enzo sewed the flag and at the very top he fastened four wire rings through each of which we could pass a string to support the whole affair.

It looked business-like and not at all "improvised," and we were proud of it.

Both parts of the flagpole, complete with flag, fitted well into my rucksack, leaving only a few inches protruding.

At dinner we tightened our belts, and immediately afterward we went to sleep while it was still light.

February 4

I do not know how I managed to wake at the agreed hour and rouse my companions.

It was 2 a.m. when I got out of the tent and the sky was amazingly starry.

Tent and boots were frozen hard, and we had to wait a long time before Enzo was able to melt the lump of ice in our cooking pot over the weak flame of the boiler, and to announce "Breakfast ready!"

It was at length the breakfast for the day. With slow delight

we swallowed the almost-solid brew of cocoa, Ovaltine, powdered milk, and plenty of sugar, followed by two biscuits for
each of us, with butter and meat extract.

Enzo shook hands with us, perhaps slightly moved. We
told him not to worry if we did not return at dusk because we
should possibly have to bivouac on the mountain.

We anointed our hands and face with the antisunburn
cream prepared for this purpose by Giuàn, put on our mitts,
and set off shortly before three o'clock feeling in good form
and in high spirits, joyfully aware that the day had in store the
climax of our trip, whatever it might be.

The swamps were frozen hard. The ice crackled under the
nails of our boots but it held. The giant groundsels seen in
the beam of the torchlight had a ghostly appearance.

With slow and steady steps we followed the Nanyuki
upstream and passed between the two pitch-black tarns. High
rose the overwhelming bulk of Batian, black and threatening,
the cauldron of the north glaciers only slightly less dark in
color.

On the upper shore of the top tarn we rested. The water
was so still that we could see the stars of the zenith reflected
motionless in it. We lay down and solemnly, as if performing a
strange ritual, we drank in small, slow draughts the ice-cold,
black, and starry water.

It was ten past four by the time we started the wearisome
ascent of the scree which the day before we had descended in
one cheerful slide. Steadily, our nailed boots rasped the loose
stones with a grinding noise and the light-cone of our torch
slowly gained height.

The "Molar" was at first silhouetted against the stars as if it
were a feature of a far horizon, but gradually its size increased
until it stood out as a bulwark against the sky, which still bore
no sign of the dawn.

As soon as we reached the saddle we were met by an icy gale. The *Flying Dutchman* reared its storm-battered breakwater into the night. It appeared even more fairy-like than when seen in the light of day, separated from us not by a valley but by centuries. Two bright stars seemed to us to be riding lights on her invisible masts, eternal lights for her motionless voyage through time.

Although it was only twenty minutes to six we were quite ready to rest and to nibble a biscuit, but the wind blew so cold that our fingers became stiff as soon as they were out of the mitts. Accordingly we went on, ascending the scree east of Point Peter where the broken lobelias showed us the way.

As we reached the rocks which marked the beginning of the actual climb, the dawn broke rapidly beyond the jagged outline of the northeast ridge. We ate a tiny biscuit each and as soon as it was light enough we started.

We progressed rapidly, aiming at the gap below Dutton Peak which we had reached in our reconnaissance two days before.

The morning was fine. Not a single cloud appeared to mar the sky which was of that deep blue-violet shade it assumes only when it is seen from over sixteen thousand feet. It occurred to me that if I looked westward over the Aberdares from the edge of the ridge dropping down to César Glacier, at this hour and in this glorious weather I might be able to recognise Lake Baringo or even Mount Elgon.

Giuàn agreed to my proposal, and we moved off our main route on the crest of the ridge between Point Peter and Dutton Peak. We saw neither the Lake nor Mount Elgon owing to a thick bank of mist covering everything below eight thousand feet, but our efforts were rewarded by a view which I shall always remember as one of the most amazing of the whole trip.

On the undulating silver-grey sea of mist was cast the

dome-shaped shadow of Mount Kenya surmounted by the tooth-like form of Batian, all in a dull brown-violet hue. The peculiarity of this natural shadow play was that from the very summit of Batian's image there rose a second shade-cone pointing to the west, together with an exactly similar, complementary light-cone pointing to the east. It was a phenomenon of reflection I am still not able to explain.

We stared, forgetting for a moment that we were due to climb Batian. It was as though a giant with magic scissors had cut a wedge from the shade of the mountain and, pivoting this on its apex, had turned it 180 degrees filling the empty space with silvery wool.

We turned, and after following the crest of the ridge for a while reached the gap below Dutton Peak where we immediately roped on.

A mountaineer when writing his memoirs usually refers to the rope, to which he often owes his life, as "trusty." I fear that I must deny our rope the customary adjective. From the very beginning it looked so untrustworthy that we thought it better to link ourselves together with a double length. We hoped that two "untrustworthys" added together would make, against all rules of arithmetic, one "trusty." I cannot blame our poor sisal ropes for being unreliable, because it was our fault for bringing them. They had been manufactured for the purpose of fastening bedding nets to bunks and were satisfactory when used thus.

Guiàn led, and by 8 a.m. we were climbing steadily.

It was great fun traversing the north face of Dutton Peak more or less on the contour with the white, cracked surface of César Glacier at our feet far below. At last, after months of preparation, we were climbing Batian, the goal of our dreams. It was almost too good to be true.

The rock, although exposed, was sound, and the holds

even when small were safe. The rocks of Batian (nepheline-syenite as discovered by Gregory) seemed to offer the same degree of reliability as the granite of the Mont Blanc group and Giuàn, whose last climb in the Alps had been a severe ascent of the Grandes Jorasses, was delighted to find many similarities so far as the rock was concerned.

On our route across the face we were forced to cross a few couloirs filled with very hard ice. There our camp-made ice axes proved their worth gloriously.

We left the contour so as to reach a small lower terrace offering a foothold for both of us. Here I left the first of our red-painted paper arrows, brought to show us the way back in case we were surprised by mists.

So far everything had gone well. We both felt in good fettle and in high spirits, and only the sisal ropes worried us. They seemed to have been made deliberately in such a manner that they clung to every minute irregularity of the rocks, owing to their coarse, hairy texture. They continually got entangled and alternately Giuàn and I, according to who was managing the belay at the moment, cursed them roundly.

From the terrace we had to regain our height, and it was only possible to do this by scaling an oblique crack leading to a ledge some thirty feet above. Giuàn managed it in good style with "pressure grips" technique and soon shouted that on the ledge he had found a good belay and that I could follow him.

I started, but halfway up the crack my arm muscles weakened and I felt that I would have to yield. As I expected, my left hand gave way and for a moment I dangled above César Glacier, supported only by the grip of my right hand on a tiny hold. As I felt I could stand the strain no longer, I shouted to Giuàn, "Give me rope," and let myself glide—or, better, fall—toward the terrace, which was some twelve feet below me and slightly to my left. I managed to push myself—I had almost written "my body," but at this stage of my story it would have had too gruesome an implication—toward the left and I actually landed on the terrace.

The anticlimax of the incident came soon. My knees started trembling pitifully and I had to sit down.

Giuàn had no clear idea as to what had happened because, as he was facing the rock, he had not seen me. Apart from this the rope had become entangled for the hundredth time on some small projection on the rocks.

"Have you got enough rope?" he asked from above. "Are you coming?"

"Coming," I answered, partly because I had no breath left to give him a longer explanation which would have been unavoidable had I said "No" or "Not yet"; and partly, I have to confess, because I felt ashamed. Why this was so I do not know. Who can fathom completely his own feelings? There was, I imagine, some loss of face for having failed in a pitch which my companion had overcome brilliantly, if not easily; but there was also, I know, more than a prick of conscience for having dared to attempt more than my training should have allowed me to undertake. A good mountaineer may take justifiable risks, but is never foolhardy.

Anyhow, I started again breathing deeply and regularly and summoning all my energy.

"Pull the rope," I said to Giuàn.

While resting on the terrace I had noticed high above the left (upper) lip of the crack a little fingerhold. Thanks to my height—blessed again be my parents!—I managed to catch hold of it with my left hand, thus avoiding the necessity of continuing to work by pressure in the crack. In a few minutes I was sitting on the ledge near Giuàn.

"You're looking rather pale," said my friend and doctor, and I explained what had happened.

After a good rest we went on.

Following the contour we reached a black rock-rib which we had noticed on our reconnaissance climb. It would lead us to the "Black Tooth" between Dutton Peak and Petit Gendarme. Behind the rib there was a narrow gully which we ascended vertically. A few pitches were ice covered but offered no other difficulty. I myself was not in the same mood as I had been when we set out. Something had gone wrong with my conscience and I was mentally no longer at ease. I felt as though I had wronged someone and was guilty of a crime.

At ten o'clock we were on the ridge dividing Northey from the César-Josef Glaciers and very soon afterward we reached the rocks on the ridge we had called among ourselves "Black Tooth." We found no cairn and wondered if by chance we were the first to have reached this sequestered and unimportant feature of Mount Kenya's north face. Now I think that it must have been climbed by other people during reconnaissances on this side of the peak.

We sat there for a quarter of an hour studying the next move like chess players not knowing that, though they were far more skilful at the game, Shipton and Tilman had classed as "hopeless" every attempt on the summit from this point, even during summer conditions on the rocks.

We were mesmerized by the formidable, glistening white ice-cliffs of Northey Glacier. No, definitely here was no bread for our teeth. It looked as if they could be overcome only with first-class crampons, ice axes, pitons, and ropes, after first-class training and first-class food; a mere dream for escaped prisoners!

We studied again the northwest ridge itself, the route we had planned originally. It was an awe-inspiring view and technically very difficult, sprinkled with ice and snow as it was, under the existing winter conditions. The first five hundred feet or so from the gap behind Petit Gendarme seemed not too bad, but higher up it looked rather grim, although we were too far below to be able to see details clearly even with the binoculars. Still, whatever route we decided to try, we had first to reach the gap behind Petit Gendarme.

To do so we first descended from our observatory in the direction of Northey Glacier and without meeting any difficulty we reached by a detour the gap between "Black Tooth" and Petit Gendarme. Had we had better and longer ropes it would have been quicker to have made a rappel straight down from "Black Tooth."

At 11 a.m. we were at last attacking the rocks at the foot of Petit Gendarme, in other words the very body of Batian.

The first rope-lengths were rather easy although the rocks were rotten and offered no sound belay. Soon we met much damp snow, covered now and then with a thin frozen crust. At every belay I left an arrow.

First we kept trying to swing to the left in the direction of the gap, our immediate aim, but the rocks became smoother and soon they offered no holds at all. Thus we climbed vertically, hoping to find higher up a traverse to the left.

More and more snow plastered the slabs. Had it been frozen to any depth it would have offered us in exchange for the relatively light labor of step-cutting a good and quick way up; but it was not and Giuàn had to clean it off, and as I was as a rule directly below him, little snow avalanches hit me regularly. If I looked up to give him another foot of rope from my belay, the snow would fall on my face, and if I bent my head it landed on my neck and went under my clothes and down my spine. I comforted myself by trying to imagine that it was an agreeable change from our camp showers, but I could not find it agreeable for all that.

A sad disappointment was the discovery that the rocks

under the snow plaster appeared to be smooth slabs as devoid of holds as those we had already decided not to try toward the gap. Presently I could give no more belay to Giuàn. We were already risking too much, or as the Italian proverb has it "pulling the Devil by his tail." Had Giuàn fallen he would have dragged me with him and vice versa.

Nevertheless, we continued to advance by inches, hoping to strike a possible line of traverse toward the gap or an ascent line toward the arête between the gap and the top of Petit Gendarme. It was distinctly a tough struggle. In some places I was able to leave an arrow, fixing it with a piece of snow crust. After all, we had to consider our return journey.

I wondered if we had reached five thousand meters, which would have been an achievement in itself for every Alpine climber as the highest peak of the Alps, Mont Blanc itself, is only 4,883 meters.[1]

Giuàn was faced with a peculiarly awkward pitch, and the minutes dragged on into a quarter of an hour without any appreciable gain. My fingers were already numbed with cold. I managed to move the ropes, which were our very theoretical safeguard, only with great difficulty.

At 12:30 p.m., to my horror, I noticed rags of mists coming from the south. In no time they enveloped the upper part of northwest ridge, while other tongues, blown by an increasingly strong wind, passed through the gap we had so far failed to reach and condensed on our side of the mountain. Soon they enveloped Northey and César Glaciers, Dutton Peak, "Black Tooth," everything.

---

[1] 5,000 meters = 16,404 feet. As Shipton determined Dutton Peak as about 16,100, and I had the impression that we were some three hundred feet higher than this—as a matter of fact I could see it between my legs—I am inclined to think that we were near the 5,000-meter mark.

The temperature dropped. An icy storm brought more and more misty clouds. I started shivering. Giuàn's ghostly grey figure alternately disappeared and reappeared on the rocks above my head.

He seemed unable to advance. He too was probably considering the situation from this new point of view.

"Hello!" I shouted to him.

"Hello!" came his answer, half-drowned by the whistling of the wind.

"How are you going on?"

"Not at all."

I didn't answer.

"I see no possibility," he carried on after a while, "of going an inch further, nor perhaps of getting back." I still do not know—and neither does he—how he had managed to climb as far as he had.

I cannot remember the exact words we shouted to each other in the roar of the storm, but it was a very short conversation which, as a novelist would say, held life and death in the balance.

We decided to retreat, if possible.

While Giuàn, inch by inch, made his sorrowful and awkward way down, the temperature seemed to me to rise again, and it started snowing and hailing together. Not only would any attempt to climb further have been unpardonable lunacy, but the prospects of a safe retreat began to appear rather problematic.

For the following forty minutes—and it took Giuàn that long to reach the spot where I still clung to the rock—the storm was dead against us. Slowly my numbed fingers, cut and bruised during the past week by bamboo and rock, retrieved the rope which separated me from my friend. Fortunately the wind was so strong that the falling snow did not immediately cover the rocks. Had it done so the red arrows I had left would have been hidden and we should have been hopelessly lost.

When Giuàn joined me at last on my precarious perch, his eyebrows, moustaches, and blanket suit were frozen with ice and his lips were almost white. According to my reading, people in similar circumstances shake hands. We had neither the inclination nor the time to do so at that moment.

The wind dropped a little but the snow fell more steadily and more thickly. Snowflakes whirled round us, snow heaped on every irregularity of the rocks and plastered the wool of our caps, jackets, and trousers with an icy crust.

Thus we started the descent, doubly difficult as we were retracing our steps not only because of the blizzard but also owing to the fact that we had been technically defeated by the rocks.

Clinging to my small holds, I peered down into the fury of the elements, trying to locate a red arrow in all this white hell. At last I saw one, a welcome sign of life in this dead world. Slowly and with great effort we reached it. "Shall we have the strength to attempt Lenana tomorrow in order to hoist our flag there at last?" I asked myself. "Shall we be able to descend from Batian today?" was the question I was afraid to ask myself.

Our fingers were frozen from continuously cleaning the snow from our holds. The sisal ropes were as hard as iron rods and their icy fibres stung our hands like needles.

The few rope-lengths down the slabs of Petit Gendarme amidst the whirling blizzard were as long as miles, and even now as I am writing this I can scarcely believe that all these things happened to me. Sometimes I am inclined to think that I only dreamt it.

When at last we reached the gap between Petit Gendarme and "Black Tooth," we felt exhausted in every muscle and nerve. We sat down awhile, relaxing and compelling ourselves to swallow a piece of toffee and the handful of sultanas which my mother had sent me in her Christmas parcel and which I had kept for "Batian day." Only I know how often I had resisted the temptation to eat them before this.

At 2:50 p.m. we unroped and started crossing the easy rocks round "Black Tooth." Fortunately we managed to find the red arrow marking the point where we should start the descent of Dutton Peak north face. We roped on again and started our traverse back. It was 3:30 p.m. Only three and a half hours of daylight remained.

Descending the more difficult rocks—and descending in mountaineering is as a rule more difficult than climbing—we realised at every step how weary we were. Every hold had first to be cleared of snow with hand or foot and tested thoroughly for its stability. Several times we had to cut ice off the rocks or to cut steps in an ice-couloir.

It had almost stopped snowing but the mists were so thick that we could see no further than twenty or thirty feet. The whole face of the mountain which we had crossed the morning before seemed totally new to us.

When I was lucky enough to find an arrow, we made for it and remained there until I had discovered the next one. It was a nerve-racking job. Frequently having mistaken some reddish-looking spot on the rocks for an arrow, we went astray and had to retrace our steps. I cannot remember how many times I concluded that we were irretrievably lost on that hostile, snow-covered face. I remember only that when at last I saw the terrace where I had made the "landing" in the morning, the episode seemed to me to have happened weeks, not hours before.

We roped down to the terrace on a rappel, avoiding the ominous crack, and there we rested a little.

Looking at the crack Giuàn remarked, "I can't understand how I managed it this morning."

"You're telling me!" I answered.

The mists cleared.

The sight of the gap below Dutton Peak was as welcome to us as is the flash of a lighthouse to the crew of a boat endangered in stormy waters. Even so, we were more than an hour in reaching it.

Once there, we unroped. We had got out of a tight corner.

Before leaving for good the scene of our unsuccessful struggle, we glanced back. Batian's northwest ridge looked grand, ice-sprinkled, and partially enveloped in clouds. Perhaps it looked even more superb for being inviolate.

We consoled ourselves by thinking that at least we *had* stretched out our hands toward that magnificent goal, and though we deeply regretted having been defeated we felt sure that in our condition we could not have done more.

In one of those abrupt changes of weather which occur so often on high mountains, the mists were now lifting en masse toward the setting sun. César and Joseph Glaciers glistened at our feet, all their crevasses covered by new snow.

Point Peter, also newly whitened by snow, scintillated in the flashes of sunlight like a giant sugar loaf. "It would prove a good climb," I thought, for those who love mountains are incurable dreamers—even before they have recovered from one defeat they begin unconsciously to plan a new attempt. I chased away such thoughts. Every crumb of our energy—and it seemed that only very little was left—must be stored for Lenana.

I wondered then, perhaps for the first time that day, how Enzo had fared; whether it had snowed at the base camp too and whether he had been worried at seeing the fury of the blizzard on the peak.

Making a bundle of our frozen ropes, we started to descend the easy rocks. We had neither the time nor the energy to roll them up in a business-like manner. We slid and jumped downhill until we reached the more-or-less level going of the scree where the last lobelias grew. As soon as the last of the rocks lay behind us we felt ready to collapse.

So long as we continued climbing on all fours, our muscles and nerves had carried out their functions almost automatically; but we had been engaged in actual rock climbing for almost twelve hours, not under the easiest conditions, and now we felt the anticlimax and exhaustion were near.

We ate a bit of toffee but I could hardly swallow mine. I craved liquid food like soup or milk.

While resting we discussed my proposal for bivouacking near the "Molar" and attempting Lenana on the morrow, as I assumed that we should never be able to make the long march thither from our distant and low base camp. Giuàn turned down this foolhardy idea on the grounds that after the day's strain we should literally freeze at night and that we must look after Enzo. I had to give in, but my hope of climbing Lenana was vanishing.

However, the next forty minutes' march around the base of Point Peter to the "Molar Saddle" showed me how right Guiàn had been to turn down my proposal. Every step was sheer misery. My ears were humming and a nervous hiccup shook me at every few steps. Giuàn was not much better. Feeling his pulse he said that he had a bit of temperature.

In a hollow of the "Molar" I hid the ropes and crampons. If we were to use them for Lenana we should pass here and pick them up. Then we tried to slide down the scree toward the tarns, but our lassitude did not allow us to keep our balance. It was getting dark and late.

Hoping to find a shorter way from the scree directly to the

lower tarn, I got into a ravine of big rocks where we had to climb on all fours once again. Giuàn, who from the beginning had been against trying to take this shortcut, grumbled angrily behind me at this extra exercise in semidarkness, but we were too weak to argue.

It was almost completely dark when at last we reached, after our useless detour, not the lower but the upper tarn.

A few clouds scurried westward and the last shimmer of daylight cast a gruesome, dim light over the tarn, revealing a broad ice belt round its margin and a few large ice plates floating in the center, reminding me of the description of some horrid skin disease. Among the flower gardens, which erstwhile had fascinated us with their true expression of beauty, we stumbled sullen and worn-out, without enthusiasm, without strength. In the fading light the giant groundsels seemed monsters trying to grasp us with their tentacles.

I shivered and hiccuped. Before me I saw nonexistent dancing lights.

Now and then Giuàn behind me murmured, "Oh dear!" I wondered again how we should be able to make a fresh start for Lenana tomorrow. It seemed impossible. We must have a whole day of rest. Our strength could not be restored with food, for almost none was left.

As we descended, following the outlet of the lower tarn, the Nanyuki, the mists closed in more and more. It was already inky dark, but by the light of our torch I could see the mistrags performing their *danse macabre*. Soon the fog became thicker and thicker and the mist in front of my torch was a whitish wall. We could not see more than a yard or two. It was frightfully cold. Every leaf of groundsel, every grass-culm, every stone was dripping moisture.

"How long have we to go before reaching the tent?" asked Giuàn.

"Not much longer," I answered, adding to myself, "if we ever find it at all."

Presently I heard a strange sound, like the chiming of bells. Yes, I positively could hear bells.

"Giuàn!"

A grumble answered me.

"Do you hear?"

"Hear what?"

"Bells."

"Bells?"

"Bells."

"You are mad."

Was I getting mad? And yet I had heard them distinctly, like the cowbells of the herds in the open Alps in summer, or the bells of the little churches with steep-roofed towers emerging from clusters of houses in the highest villages of the valleys. The chiming seemed to invite me to sit and rest but I rebelled against its soft suggestions. Stopping to rest would have meant perhaps . . . well, after all I think now that it was only the deep-rooted instinct of self-preservation that dragged us along this night.

Later a thought flashed through my half-numbed brain: "Could we by any chance have passed the erratic boulders where our tent was?"

A glance at my watch showed me that we could not have done so, but in order not to lose the way we kept closer to the brook, and where it passed through swamps we walked right in the water, wherever it seemed to be running fastest.

We were cold, exhausted, and wet, and it was still not the end of our day. Lucky are mountaineers who, after an unsuccessful climb in the Alps, can at least find a hut in which to dry their clothing and a fire at which to warm themselves.

Our feet splashed in the water of the brook or squelched in

the marshy grass. We fell and rose again. Luckily the torch never failed. How we managed to carry on I scarcely remember. All I know is that I must have been delirious as I "saw" and "heard" people. I knew exactly who they were: characters from the last books I had read before escaping. There was Thomas Buddenbrook of Thomas Mann's novel, his pale face with its small pointed beard and a small Russian cigarette between his lips; and there were two characters from Charles Morgan, Piers, Lord Sparkenbroke after an attack of angina pectoris, just back from the threshold of his Platonic world, and Mary. Though characters of different authors, they talked together of distant and supreme topics, of Death and Love and Time.

There at last was the row of erratic boulders. We called Enzo. We screamed with all the power of our lungs. No answer came.

It occurred to me that there were two rows of boulders and that the tent was behind a rock in the second row. We carried on.

Things danced before my eyes. Now and then Giuàn sobbed. Every step was an exertion which it seemed impossible to repeat. We marched and marched and the second line of boulders did not appear.

My heart was sinking into my boots; I realised that the row we had seen was the *second* row, and that we had passed the first unnoticed, owing to the fog.

I turned back. Giuàn followed automatically, without even asking why I was retracing my steps.

Those last minutes were the worst. I only remember that it was long, almost unbearably long before I reached the boulders again.

"Were they the first or the second line?"

I did not know but I began to realize how a man goes mad.

"Enzo," we screamed again.

No answer came.

Moisture-dripping groundsels stood around us. None of the boulders had a familiar shape. Which row was it? And where was the other one? On the left or on the right?

I started following the row, casting at every boulder a beam of light and looking for footprints. Everything seemed strange and new.

Then I saw—yes, I saw, it was not a mirage—the tent. It was almost invisible, low and small, seemingly crouched under the big boulder; and yet for us it meant everything.

"Enzo!" we shouted with renewed energy.

There was a grumbling answer from inside the long low bag which started tossing and at last ejected a crawling Thing wrapped in a blanket. Enzo. He was perfectly right in having gone to sleep as we had told him that we were probably going to bivouac on the mountain.

"Is there a drop of alcohol left for making tea?"

"Only enough to boil one pot of water."

"Please make tea."

He lit the boiler while Giuàn staggered toward the tent, crawled in on all fours, turned over, and fell asleep.

I tried to take off my puttees, sodden with water inside and covered with a crust of frozen mud outside. Puttees, hands, legs, all together trembled and shook. It was the last hard job of the day.

"What time is it?" asked Enzo.

"Ten to nine," I answered. We had been out for almost eighteen hours.

Enzo did not question me anymore.

He had seen the flagpoles still protruding from my rucksack. He knew we were beaten. He knew that in our condition we could not attempt Lenana on the morrow. He saw clearly that his agony would continue for more than another forty-eight hours. He had not eaten a bite the whole day. He had been mountain-sick and terribly hungry. He knew that after Lenana we should have to march back practically without food. His condition could not improve and he had only to wait, and to wait is one of the most horrible things on earth as every prisoner knows; but he did not grumble.

I had not known him before our escape. On our trip I had found him funny, crazy in a way, quick-tempered, full of the spirit of adventure. I had found him amusing. Now I appreciated him fully. He was worth his salt.

February 5

By silent agreement the day was devoted to rest.

Our boots were so soaked that we could not put them on and our clothes were still damp, though we had not taken them off during the night. We felt exhausted and frightfully hungry.

When I washed and shaved at the ice-fringed brook, I saw in the mirror a strange worn-out face which almost frightened me. "If we were attacked by buffaloes," I thought, "we should not even be able to climb the boulders as we had planned."

After having had the last of our porridge and two biscuits each (size 1 × 2 inches) with butter and meat extract, the whole ration allotted for the day, we took careful stock of the remaining food: three little bags of salt, coffee, and tea; the bottom of the bag (a part of a pajama-leg sewed at one end) of our "climbing-food": consisting of a few pieces of chocolate, toffee, and a dozen sultanas; four teaspoons of sugar; some four ounces of barley sugar; half a pound of rice; ten biscuits; a heaped knife-top of meat extract; some five or six ounces of butter.

On paper it looks a lot, but we could have devoured the whole in one meal. Instead it had to last us for at least four days.

At 10 a.m. I made a sketch of the base camp with Batian in the background. While I was drawing, a new storm started raging on the peak. Enzo, who had seen "our" blizzard the day before, remarked that that had been more severe; but whether this was so, or whether he said it to flatter us, I do not know.

Before dark we were already lying in the tent, waiting for sleep to put an end to hunger and cold.

February 6

It was 1 a.m. when we got up after only a few hours of sleep. On the last flickering flame of the boiler, Enzo melted the lump of ice which had formed in the cooking pot. When the water was getting warm the flame died out. The alcohol was finished.

In the warm water Enzo washed the inner side of the bags which had contained Ovaltine, powdered milk, and cocoa, added the four teaspoons of sugar, a few leaves of tea, and served almost cold.

It proved a delightful mixture. In addition we had one biscuit each and the last of the meat extract.

At 1:50 a.m. Giuàn and I started. The torch cast a dim, failing light, perfect symbol of the strength of our party.

The night seemed to me colder than the one preceding our attempt on Batian, and if the same rules as regards weather were applicable to Kenya as in the Alps, this presaged a fine day.

Though we had started one and a quarter hours earlier than on "Batian day" we only reached the lower tarn at three.

We lost our way several times among the boulders, and after having made a longer detour between the two tarns owing to the weak light shed by our torch, we arrived at the upper tarn only forty minutes earlier than on the previous day.

We were amazed when we saw the whole surface of the tarn covered with ice. In the light of the stars it was a wonderful sight. More wonderful, although not entirely necessary as we were not at all thirsty, was the new experience which followed. With the point of our ice axes we opened a hole in the ice and, lying on the smooth surface, we sucked a drink of water through the hole.

The ascent of the steep slope below "Molar Saddle" was particularly hard. To avoid repeating the error made as we came down from Batian when we found ourselves in a ravine on the left side of the valley, I erred in the opposite direction, as happens not only while mountaineering. We struck so far to the right that we finished on the front moraine of Joseph glacier.

As soon as we became aware of my new mistake, we climbed down a steep gorge and up the far side to the scree. This new waste of time upset us thoroughly. We wanted to reach the top of Lenana at 10 a.m., as on the day before the storm on the peaks had started at this hour, and we feared that it might repeat itself.

Scarcely had we started up the scree when the torch decided to call it a day and the fading light died out completely. In pitch-black darkness we scrambled on, often sliding down several yards in the attempt to make one step up.

It was a long, tiring job, and we were very relieved to reach the "Molar" at last. From the cache I produced the crampons and ropes and slowly we started descending the side of Mackinder's Valley. The stars shone brightly, giving us some light, but as neither of us had been here

before we had to conduct this night march on terra incognita
with care.

There was a nip in the air which pierced the very bones.
We were over fifteen thousand feet up and it was the hour
before dawn, the coldest of the night.

The sky was clear; the Southern Cross hung glorious over
Point Piggott and Magellan's Cloud was setting on the western horizon, but not even from this altitude could we see the
polar star.

We reached two little pools on the moraine of Northey Glacier. Beyond them the ground proved rocky and we thought it
better to sit down and to await daylight.

By and by the gloomy forecastle of the *Flying Dutchman*
grew paler and paler and round the pools we could distinguish the lobelias, looking in the first dim light of day like
funerary torches or stones in an Arab cemetery.

At last the sky between Sendeyo and Lenana blushed rosy.
There was no breath of wind. An abysmal silence reigned.

Always, and more especially on mountains, have I watched
daybreak with deep awe. It is an age-old miracle which repeats
itself again and again, every day the same and every day different. It is the hour of Genesis.

Then, on the high bowsprit of the *Flying Dutchman* there
rose a flag of flame-color, while her petrified bulwarks showed
faintly rose. A breeze passed over the rocks and rippled the
surface of the pools slightly.

It was day and we could start marching again.

The morning was glorious and as we walked straight
toward the rising sun the whole of Mackinder's Valley was
bathed in golden light.

The curled pinnacle near the summit of Lenana twinkling
on the horizon above the violet-shaded Gregory Glacier
looked cheerful and inviting.

We passed close to the foot of the formidable-looking northeast ridge, making our way between boulders of all sizes and shapes. I particularly remember one of them of the exact size and shape of a grand piano.

On our left the valley got narrower and at its head we saw the unbroken blue-green mirror of a tarn.* The brook formed by its outlet roared down the valley, recalling to my memory the noises, as of another world, made by trains which run through some Alpine valleys.

Frequently we looked at the western face of Sendeyo (our *Flying Dutchman*) not yet touched by the sun and appearing gloomy and terrible, and wondered if ever a bold climber had scaled those fascinating rocks from this side.†

We did our best to keep along one contour at the base of the northeastern face of Batian, but soon we realised that we should have to lose some height as one of the pillars supporting the gigantic walls had its base below our altitude. While descending slightly, we could not help being attracted by the features of this northeast wall. It was still virgin ground as no party had managed to reach Batian's summit from this side. Only on July 31, 1944, did Arthur H. Firmin, Nairobi, and Peter Hicks, Eldoret, in a brilliant climb make the first ascent of the northeast face.

Dutton compared this sight to gigantic organ pipes. I, not having read Dutton's book at this time, recalled a forlorn valley-top under the sheer four-thousand-feet drop of the west face of Jof Fuart in the western Julian Alps, where from time immemorial the herdsmen had called a place like this *lis altaris*: "the altars." Not by mere chance is the mountain climber

---

* Campi ya Simba Lake.
† The rocks were scaled on the 16th of February 1945 by Olimpio Gabrioli and J. W. Howard.

induced to think of organ pipes or of altars as he looks up those towering rocks; it is a religious feeling which fills his heart.

As we reached the edge of the buttress which had forced us to lose height, we found ourselves facing another little marvel, recalling homely mountain customs. At almost a man's height, the rock showed a niche, rounded as though carved by man's tools. At the foot of the niche and round it, the rock was covered by helichrysums clinging in a compact cushion and enjoying the sun. One could hardly believe that the flowers had grown there spontaneously; they seemed to have been put there, in homage to an invisible Madonna in a wayside shrine, by some wanderer who saw in the majesty of the mountain a sign of the Creator's might.

Gaining height again we set foot on the moraine of a small glacier bearing the name of the discoverer of Mount Kenya, Krapf. Later we crossed the scree which comes down from Point Thompson and soon found a large, almost horizontal ledge of rocks, partially split by ravines and resembling an ancient road. It led straight to a flat saddle which I think is Flake Col, although on Dutton's map it bears no name at all.

We did not make for the col but scrambled up easy, partially ice-covered rocks, aiming toward the ridge of Lenana itself. Only our desire to be on the summit of Lenana by ten o'clock lent us speed. We felt very weak and every step was a real effort.

At 8 a.m., six hours after leaving the base camp, we were on the top of the ridge. We sat down, basking in the sun and finishing the contents of our climbing-bag, crumbs of chocolate, toffee, and sultanas.

We were generously compensated for the lack of food by the magnificent view. At our feet lay Nithi Valley between two gentle slopes dotted with rocks and groundsels and showing several shimmering pools.

Further down we noticed the Hall tarns glittering with water and the clear-cut drop above the dark-green Lake Michaelson; further on a seemingly boiling sea of clouds cloaked the plains, but two dark ridges protruded looking like whales among the waves. I believe they were Mount Ithungani and Mount Fangani. Almost at the uttermost limit of vision on the northeastern horizon rose a black table-topped mountain such as may be seen commonly in Ethiopia. We wondered if it was Marsabit, the paradise of big game hunters.

The eastern face of Batian presented a totally different but an equally beautiful sight. It was an unbelievable bright yellow ochre in color. Any painter portraying it would be blamed for exaggeration, but perhaps no painter in the world could reproduce *this* yellow.

After a short pause for resting and sketching, we followed the crest toward the summit. The rock has a reddish color totally different from Batian, and its "behaviour" insofar as this affects the climber is quite different as well. On Batian's north side we had found on the whole solid, reliable rock, sometimes even too smooth. Lenana had craggy rotten rock. As soon as the climber grasps it whole vertical slabs tend to break away with a slight pull.

Since reading Gregory's *Rift Valleys and Geology of East Africa*, I have learnt that the differing behaviour of the rocks on the two peaks corresponds to a different geological origin. Batian like Nelion, Piggott, Dutton, and Peter is derived from the plug of rocks of plutonic origin (nepheline-syenite) which choked the crater of the decaying volcano. Lenana, like Sendeyo (as noticed so far as I know for the first time by E. E. Shipton), is of volcanic origin and its rock is a type of lava discovered by Gregory himself and by him named kenyte.

Once we had reached Lenana's "handle" we tried to circumvent it from the glacier side, but we were so weary that we found the rocks too difficult and had to make a little detour to the east. Here we should have found, according to Dutton's map, Kolbe Glacier; but owing to the general retreat of all glaciers on Kenya, as well as on Kilimanjaro and Rwenzori, we did not see even a remnant of it.

By this route we reached the shoulder above the handle.

Giuàn showed me some stones he had collected. They bore strange oblong crystal plates ("rhomb-porphids") looking like stamps. While he was trying to increase his new stamp collection he noticed a pair of sunglasses with the once-white glare refractor yellowish and weather stained. The owner of these glasses was not popular with us. Instead of blessing him for losing something which might have been of use to us—as a rule everything is of some use to a POW and the exceptions to this rule have still to be found—we blamed him for having lost only his glasses. Could he not have mislaid, for instance, a tin of sardines or of meat or cheese? We should have devoured it on the spot, as in the refrigerator at 16,300 feet it would have kept for several years.

After advancing a few yards along the broad shoulder, we saw the cairn marking the top not far from us.

I waited a while for Giuàn who was still busy collecting "stamps"—or hoping that the owner of the glasses or someone else might have dropped something edible—and together, filled by an odd feeling almost of solemnity we reached the point whence one could ascend no farther.

We shed our rucksacks and ice axes and sat down, looking around. It was 10:05 a.m.

A great peace hung over the broad expanse. Under the dark velvety sky the wonderful scenery of the country at our feet had a strange radiance.

This was the climax of eight months' preparation and of two weeks of toil. It was worth both.

If a touch of bitterness marred our bliss it was the thought

that we stood on Lenana and not on Batian. And there HE
towered, separated from us by a broad ice saddle, above the
pedestal of his yellow buttresses. The climb from this side certainly would not be the same as our vain attempt.

Some three hundred feet below the peak of Lenana and to
the south, we noticed an iron hut, a sure indication that this
was on the standard route used by those who wished to climb
Batian. It stood near a frozen pond.

The actual climb from the southeast seemed far shorter
than that on the north side, as the beginning of the vertical
ascent was there at a lower level than it was on the southeast.

"The standard route is probably a difficult climb," we
remarked, studying the face, "but at least the climber who
tries it has probably been assisted by porters, has eaten
enough and has slept in the hut, some two thousand feet
higher than our base camp. He has usually read accounts of
previous climbs even if he is not led by an experienced guide.
When he is on the rocks he is reassured by the knowledge that
others have already managed it, men maybe with greater technical skill and knowledge, but always men of flesh and blood
like himself."

Yes, we were delighted to be on Lenana, but at the same
time sorry not to be on Batian.

After resting a while we scrambled around the rocks trying
to find at least a remnant of the cross, gift of the Pope, placed
on Lenana on January 30, 1934, by the fathers of the Conso-
lata Mission of Nyeri, as we had read in P. Cagnolo's book.
We found none and were at a loss to explain how a big cross,
a photograph of which we had seen in the book, could have
disappeared in ten years. We did not know then that the cross
still exists and is well preserved, and that it had not been left
on the very summit of Lenana, but on the south ridge some
hundred and fifty feet below.

Like Giuàn, who in looking for "stamps" had found the glasses, I looking for the cross found another trophy, a wooden tent pole top once painted red and bearing the letters J.H.H–F.L.V. and the date 11.IX.37. I still keep it as a souvenir, and in many a transfer from one prisoner of war camp to another in East Africa it has caused astonishment to the officers searching my kit. At first glance nobody can make out what the blessed thing is as it bears some resemblance to a hand grenade.

It was getting late and distant mist banks were approaching rapidly. Mist to the south had prevented us from seeing Kilimanjaro, which has been observed from here several times by more fortunate parties. The mist was tossing and tumbling like surf but now and then when the curtains parted we had a quick vision of quiet tarns in remote valleys or of jagged rocky peaks.

Presently it was almost on us. Fragments of cloud would reach the rocks at our feet only to burst and dissolve like a pricked soap bubble.

It was time to hoist the flag.

We stuck the lower pole into the stones of the cairn, and fitted the upper part onto which the flag had already been fastened, into its tin mortise; then we tied the four strings onto four rocks, roughly north, south, east, and west. It looked solid and steady, not at all "improvised" as the paper had it when describing the discovery of the flag by a party of climbers from Nairobi only a week later. Neither was it "flying upside down (signal of distress?)" as imagined by the author of the article in the same paper.

We asked ourselves how long the flag would remain there, as after all we had hoisted it in order that it should be found. We certainly did not suspect that at the very end of the winter climbing season, only a few days later, Lenana would be visited once again by a party which would discover it with the aid of binoculars from the Camp at Thompson Lakes.

Even while I was sitting on a rock and sketching the scene of the flying colors at the climax of our trip, the mists arrived above us. The breeze at first blew gently, only stirring the colors slightly, but soon increasing in strength it spread out until they were flickering, tossing, flying.

If anyone wonders what it meant to us to see the flag of our country flying free in the sky after not having seen it so for two long years, and having seen for some time previous to this only white flags, masses of them, I can only say that it was a grand sight indeed.

We left the note with our message and names in the sealed brandy bottle, picked up the rucksacks and ice axes, and plunged into a raging battle of floating and swirling mists.

We had intended to enjoy a prolonged rest at the pools where we had awaited the dawn because from there we should have a last view of Northey Glacier and northwest ridge, but as the mists were by now covering Batian also, we had to travel at high speed. Quickly descending the rocks of Lenana to a pond, which I imagine is that called Harris Tarn on Dutton's map, we shot down a long scree to the bottom of Mackinder's Valley.

There we had a breather which we needed badly, then slowly we started the ascent of the ravine toward our immediate goal. Behind us Lenana had long since disappeared in a grey cloak and the beauties of Batian's northeast face were already obliterated.

By the time we reached the pools only the snout of Northey Glacier protruded from the cover of the clouds. It looked like a white dragon enveloped by smoke from its own throat. The northwest ridge was quite invisible. As it was only half past twelve we decided to enjoy a good rest at any rate.

We had just settled down at a spot selected to give a view

which included the lobelia-fringed shore of one pool with the seracs of Northey Glacier in the background, when the mists suddenly closed down further and it started snowing.

It was not a snowstorm like that which finally encompassed our defeat on Batian. It started gently and gently it carried on without a breath of wind. It was such a quiet and kind snowfall that we thought it could not last long. Thus we decided to take shelter and to wait for it to cease. Shelter was soon found under the overhanging brow of a big boulder, but as far as the rest of the program was concerned—well that was another matter.

Patience is a virtue which becomes a well-trained POW more than any other, and we did not feel the lack of it. Thus we made the best of a bad job, put on every rag of clothing we had with us, and just started to wait. We did not like the idea of moving on and of reaching the base camp so soaked once more that we should have to pass another night with wet clothes on.

We ate every crumb we could find in the bottom of our climbing-food bag, we divided one biscuit between us and spent half an hour in eating it, while in the meantime I explored the inside of the Bovril bottle as industriously as any ant with my knife point. The reward of my microscopically accurate work was worth the toil as we each got a thin film of meat extract on our half biscuit, in itself only the size of a postage stamp.

The storm showed no sign of slackening. Snow accumulated slowly, steadily, stubbornly, on the ice fringe of the pools, on the boulders, on every stone, even on top of every lobelia.

Mist rose everywhere as if emanating from the soil. Of the wild scenery of Northey Glacier nothing was visible. By and by we heard the grumbling roar of falling seracs, ending with the whistle of minor ice fragments thrown far into the air, but the silence which followed seemed the more awe inspiring. Of the great work of destruction which weather and time carry on ceaselessly on the ice fields of the mountain we could see nothing, but the sound was enough.

Hours passed by.

We were frozen but did not feel at all unhappy. For a while we even sang some of our alpine songs to pass the time.

The white hoods on top of the lobelias increased in size. The plants looked stranger than ever and recalled to our memory, unconsciously busy on food topics, visions of cream-covered chocolate cones. We felt like Charlie Chaplin in *The Gold Rush*.

We hoped that before dusk the weather would clear and allow us to reach our base camp. From Nanyuki we had noticed that in the dry season the mists usually cleared toward the hour of sunset but after the heaviest storms and during the rains.

At last it stopped snowing but the mists did not seem to have the faintest intention of lifting. We set off anyhow and warmed up on the ascent toward "Molar Saddle."

Once there we stopped. As we had decided to get rid of every ounce of useless weight, we made a bundle of all the ropes but one to be used in the passage of the gulley, added the crampons and even the remaining paper arrows and put everything in the hole of the "Molar" situated at the side of Mackinder's Valley. I scribbled a few lines on a piece of paper and put it into the Bovril bottle: "Mountaineering tools made in Prisoner of War Camp used during an outing on Mount Kenya. Good luck to any who may find and use them." So far as I know they are still there, covered by the stones I put on them, for when Alpini Lt. Col. G. Sora of Spitzbergen fame climbed Nelion in January 1945 he had not time to dig for them, and nobody else knows anything about them. I do not think that treasure hunting is much practised on Mount Kenya, and only a treasure hunter or a dentist would think of excavating in the "Molar."

In the meantime the mists had cleared above Mackinder's Valley, and as though from a stormy sea the *Flying Dutchman* bade us farewell. She looked even finer than when we had first seen her. The ghostly rags of whitish mists against the dark background of stormy sky suited her to perfection. Billowing clouds hung round her like slowly lifting cannon smoke after a fight in buccaneering days, while the lazily drifting clouds above her castles looked like trailing and battle-torn sails under the tattered Jolly Roger.

I looked back at this strange mountain with a pang of regret. The word "end" already hung above our adventure.

We ran down the scree toward our tarns and met the mists ascending, like cotton-wool clouds in a children's theater, from Hausburg Valley.

Flashes of sunlight made the ice-covered surface of the tarns sparkle when we reached them. It was like a last smiling farewell: "Good-bye, little prisoners! Don't forget us!" Had they not faithfully reflected our mood every time we had passed?

Before leaving them forever we collected some flowers which we meant to bring back when we returned to our own home, whenever that might be. The sun lit up the ice-sprinkled surface of the tarns as I saw them for the last time, and thus they are engraved in my memory.

We loved them for they had given us the memory of an inexhaustible store of beauty, on which we could draw during the years behind the barbed wire which would follow our adventure. I shall never see them again, but I shall never forget them.

The Nanyuki tumbled foaming along as we followed its course on our way back toward the inevitable barbed wire. We were strangely moved, sad and happy at the same time.

Presently we approached the rows of erratic boulders, and there was the would-be white towel flying from a giant groundsel, and soon between two rocks we saw the pale and worn-out face of Enzo with his grey beard. He had been watching.

Giuàn and I agreed to pull his leg for as long as possible. We did our best to assume the most doleful expression pretending that not even on this occasion had we been able to hoist the flag.

But it cut no ice. As it was still early—not more than 6 p.m.—he had guessed that Lenana at least had yielded to our weak efforts. Enzo was no fool.

Giuàn and I had to summon all our strength, and there was little enough of it, in order not to spoil the game.

On the grassy stretch beside the boulders, Enzo met us and immediately tried to get behind me to make sure that the flagpoles were no longer protruding from my rucksack. As he turned I turned too, always facing him.

At last Giuàn and I made several steps to the rear and presented arms with our ice axes to the "Base Camp Commander."

"Sir," I addressed him, and he saluted in military fashion, "please strike your dirty banner, as from 10:30 a.m. today far better colors, our colors, have been flying from the top of Point Lenana."

We had tried to joke, but the joke did not last. Enzo was no longer able to conceal his feelings. He bit his lips, clenched his teeth, and, if I am not wrong, two good hearty tears ran down his sunken cheeks as with one leap he embraced us both.

With less emotion but with the same cheerfulness, we celebrated the achievements of the day by skipping our dinner.

Postscript: After a successful ascent of Mount Kenya and their return to the POW camp, the three Italians waited patiently for World War II to end.

Walter Bonatti is an Italian mountaineer who pioneered many of the most difficult routes in the world, and particularly those of the Alps. One of his most notable achievements was the solo ascent of a never-before-climbed path up the southwest pillar of the sheer and majestic heights of France's Aiguille du Dru in 1955, when he was twenty-five years old. Beware: his description of the experience is not for the faint of heart.

THE MOUNTAINS OF MY LIFE

WALTER BONATTI

The Southwest Pillar of the Dru

The Dru, like the Grand Capucin, is, in my opinion, the perfect mountain. One might say its history is the story of mountaineering itself, and so of great interest. The French had ascended the grandiose west wall in 1952; but their route—with all due respect—was so much to the side of the huge face it served merely to highlight the dazzling emptiness and the challenge of the precipitous southwest pillar. For me it was as if the perfect route on the perfect mountain was still lacking—a definitive and elegant route that would serve as the perfect debut for my career as a solo climber.

It was certainly a presumptuous idea. But it was also electrifying to have decided to confront alone a climb that, at that time, was considered the last great unattainable legendary challenge of the Alps.

My attempt on the Dru began on August 18, 1955, and for the next five days it was like living in another world, like entering an unknown dimension, like being in a mystical, visionary state in which the impossible did not exist and anything could happen. On the other hand there were moments of extreme uncertainty when I felt utterly drained and incapable of action. What enabled me to find the strength to resume climbing was the awareness that I had been struggling at the limits of the possible for days in order to solve my personal problems: anyone who had deliberately chosen the Dru to reconcile himself with his own being and with his life could certainly not fall into passivity and just let himself die. There were some places, such as the zone of huge overhangs, where the rock deceived me. For example, a crack that suddenly became too wide for the type of piton I had with me, or an unexpected concavity where it seemed the Dru had swallowed the rock for a joke, leaving in its place a huge featureless flaring funnel. Or a crack that at the last moment revealed itself to be a solid vein of quartz. This certainly would have been no problem if I had been carrying certain gadgets like expansion bolts, or spits, which some people had started to use at that time, and which were eventually used to put up other new routes on the same face.

With spits there is no doubt I could have climbed straight up the smooth featureless slabs without problems and with no particular risk. But I had been conditioned, as was entirely appropriate, by the rules of this game of mine, which in this case seemed particularly rigid and pitiless. I had to go right back to the bottom of the unclimbable sections and search there for other solutions—such as the extreme, improvised maneuvers of the pendulum-swing into space, which was later to become famous. On that occasion I had to hold on with my hands to a rope caught between some protruding spikes above an overhang, not knowing what I would find above it.

However, with regard to "super" climbing methods, I would like to add something that has always been perfectly clear to me and is deeply rooted in my own views on the subject.

Let us go back to those days in the fifties when spits first appeared in mountaineering circles, and people started to use them more frequently. I believe it was then that the great technical degradation of alpinism began.

Using this type of piton (which demands a preliminary drill hole in the rock and is characteristic of the whole business) is to employ a tool that, unlike a normal piton, cancels the impossible. And it therefore also cancels adventure. One might say it is tantamount to cheating in a game one has chosen to play voluntarily. By acting in this way, one no longer conquers the impossible but eliminates it. The motivation to confront the impossible and test one's mettle against it is destroyed. Insight is no longer required, nor is judgment.

The use of spits destroys the commitment and the emotional response of traditional alpinism. With expansion bolts the intelligent search for a logical route is bypassed and one loses the critical assessment of difficulty. The terms "paragon" and "standard" become invalid. What emerges is a degenerated, sterile ascent, little more than an athletic feat. As such, it is a convenient and easy way to achieve success—but, judged from a traditional standpoint, obtained by a hoax. What follows is self-deception and a confidence trick played on the good faith of those who follow our exploits and derive meaning from them, but do not know the facts.

I think everyone should confront a mountain in a particular and precise way, obeying natural impulses, and be driven by precise, personal motives. Right from the start my own motivation has been mostly of a thoughtful, introspective nature, ending in an assertion to myself about myself. But for such an affirmation to have any value to me, I must adopt precise reference points. Therefore I did not adopt the "super" methods so I could conquer the "impossible" at all costs. Instead, I opted for the classic concept of mountaineering that developed in the thirties, and accepted its traditional and rather limited technical methods. I chose those limited technical methods quite deliberately.

It was the ethos of the classical alpinism of the thirties that inspired me. It was a choice perfectly suited to my temperament and needs. I always sought, and still do seek, to carry the tradition further without distorting it, respecting the rules of a game that has real meaning precisely because it will accept no subterfuge. These rules do not include winning at all costs. My climbs assume the value of affirming a principle that is opposed to growing degradation.

First Attempts

My first attempt on the Dru had taken place two years earlier with Carlo Mauri, at dawn on August 15, 1953, the year before the ascent of K2. Mauri and I were wearily climbing the Snow Cone under the west wall of the Dru. In the complete silence of dawn, dun colored, squat in perspective, and still hidden from the sun, the Dru made me think of a gigantic sleeping monster. The air was freezing and still. Carefully and quietly, as if not to break the spell, we roped up and began the great adventure.

From the very beginning it was tough going, a difficult vertical buttress about 130 feet high leading to the entrance of a huge dark icy couloir, which looked anything but inviting. Here the Dru is accustomed to give vent to all its fury, collecting and channeling everything that comes off three thousand feet of sheer peak by force of gravity. Very steep slopes of green ice alternate with slabs of granite, polished by stone-falls. The fear of being taken unawares by one of these stone-falls forced us to climb as far to the right as possible over difficult but less exposed rocks.

For the first half of the couloir our route was the same the French had taken to reach the west face, but the remainder belonged purely to the southwest pillar. When we reached the point where the Frenchmen had crossed to the left, across the inviting "lower terraces" of the west face, we went on climbing up the ever-narrowing couloir and gained height, not without a little apprehension.

In the early afternoon a storm broke. A cascade of water poured all over us. We waited for the chaos to subside, with our backs to the sheer face of the Flammes de Pierre and our heads just sticking out of the rubberized sacks that were our only bivouac equipment. What terrors surrounded us! We had reached the center of a wide amphitheater of ice where the deep gorges of the Dru converge with those of the adjacent Flammes de Pierre. Below us a narrow slimy gut of black ice dropped away down a 1,300-foot slope to the glacier. It was a gloomy funnel, freezing and oppressive, hollowed out by erosion but also marked by the savage fury of frequent stone-falls. Around us we could see nothing but glimpses of walls, which culminated in the sheer gray massif of our pillar. It seemed to rise up to infinity beyond the clouds. Only to our left, toward the north, was there a narrow strip of sky, and this made the funnel seem even deeper. The sun, when it appeared, only briefly illuminated the inside of the icy gut;

otherwise no more than a fleeting cold light reached us. We felt as if we were hanging from the walls of a deep well.

A sudden flash lit up the mountain. The attendant thunderclap shook the rocks beneath us. A second thunderbolt followed, then a third, and then many more, accompanied by thick hailstones. The route was inundated by brawling white cascades of water. It was an impressive spectacle, which quickly transformed the area before our very eyes. It made us vitally aware how savage this mountain could be.

Rain and hail pelted down by turns, and at times there were blasts of snow. Time passed. Night fell. The storm continued in this way all night and all next morning. Toward midday, the rain finally stopped, the clouds lifted, and we resumed our climb. The idea of giving up had never even entered our heads. We reached the longed-for compact rock where our pillar actually started. We were at about 9,700 feet; 2,200 feet of overhangs lay between us and the summit.

The pillar of the Dru is unique. Its smooth rocks of protogenic yellow-brown granite are only rarely fissured, but are furrowed by deep cracks that outline enormous slabs with compact faces and sharp, regular edges. The lower part is mostly composed of pale rock, an incontestable sign of recent stone-falls; it is not excessively vertical at first sight, but this is only because of its deceptive perspective. By contrast, the higher part, which is the real crux of the pillar's "problem" and which I will refer to as the red slabs, is more than just impressive. Here the face is incredibly compact, smooth, and of a reddish color. It is almost completely vertical, interrupted only by smooth bulges. The whole wall is then crowned by a barrier of enormous roofs and overhangs, some of them jutting out several yards. We were out of luck: we had scarcely climbed a hundred feet from our bivouac when it began to rain again. Just like the day before, it went on almost constantly all afternoon and far into the night.

We were worried because we had already eaten two days' food and still were only at the beginning of the pillar. For the first time the specter of retreat appeared, but this was exorcised by the radiant dawn that followed. Our fears of the night before were swept away, so we decided to go on. After three difficult pitches, a surprise awaited us on a terrace: a heap of old wooden wedges and a still-intact packet of dried figs. We had no idea how long ago they had been left there. All around there were no other signs of passage; there were no pitons winking in the rocks above, which had every appearance of being a tough nut to crack. We found it hard to believe someone had already attempted the southwest pillar. Probably this was the highest point reached by our mysterious predecessors.

We climbed thirty feet to a second small terrace, then another eighty feet up open corners.* We then turned a rough cleft on the left, where a huge slab leaning out a little from the face seemed about to collapse at any moment.

Finally, we reached a comfortable, airy gallery right on the line of the pillar and stopped, intimidated by what had come into view: an enormous protruding, precarious series of slabs surged up on the smooth face. On both sides it fell away into an appalling abyss. This really should not have startled me as much as it did, since its form had been clearly visible from the valley below. In fact from Montenvers this granitic structure curiously resembled a lizard stretched out on the pillar in the act of climbing to the summit.

Here our morale received a severe blow. Added to the fatigue caused by the cumulative effects of three days of bad weather was the knowledge that we had just now reached only the beginning of the real problem. I admired Mauri, who conquered his pride and was the first to have the honest courage to pronounce the fateful words: "Let's go back!"

* Open corners are corners with an angle greater than ninety degrees.– TRANSLATOR

One more sad glance at the elusive "lizard," a silent salute to the red slabs, which seemed to rise even higher, and we slid into the void in a series of abseils, which soon took us to a terrace at the base of the pillar. That was enough for the day; we would go down the rest of the way tomorrow, when the night frost had stopped the stone-falls. For some hours, stones had been bounding down the funnel, to be swallowed by the great couloir.

At the beginning of summer in 1955, after the K2 affair, I returned to the Dru for a second attempt on the splendid southwest pillar. This time there were four of us: Mauri, Oggioni, Aiazzi, and myself. At dawn on July 24, 1955, still on the Snow Cone before attacking the Dru, we were running like madmen toward a huge rock to take shelter from an unexpected stone-fall roaring down the couloir. After this traumatic start, the rest of the day went by industriously. That evening, however, just as we were about to reach the first slabs of the pillar, it started to rain. We wondered if the Dru might be angry with us. The reality was that, apart from our modest barometer/altimeter, we had nothing else to give us any sort of reliable weather forecast. We had to bivouac early. We could scarcely find room for all four of us on a tiny ledge. After the rain, it snowed all night, and a continual fusillade of falling stones and ice bounced down the funnel, often coming very close.

There was no talk of retreat next morning. Indeed, at about ten o'clock, taking advantage of a brief clear spell, we decided to go on and wait for better weather as high up as possible, where we would be safe from stone-falls. After a couple of hours of strenuous climbing up dripping wet slippery slabs, we reached the famous "ledge of the mysterious wedges"; and there, soaked to the skin, we wriggled into our bivouac sacks again, because in the meantime snow had started to fall in large flakes. We spent the whole afternoon there; our only diversion was to let the snow pile up on our sleeping sacks and then shake it all off suddenly. Another night came, and we were dozing off when suddenly the mountain shook beneath us and a terrifying roar split the air. We felt we were falling with the mountain, which seemed to be collapsing all around us. The cataclysm lasted several minutes, during which we stayed rooted to the spot. We passed the rest of the night buried in snow, lost among the overhangs.

Only at dawn the next day were we able to work out what had happened: a stone-fall of monstrous proportions had broken away above us, and after grazing our bivouac ledge it had rushed down the couloir, dredging it out and devastating it. The west side of the Dru had been subject to massive stonefalls for some years, almost as if to remodel itself and restore lost equilibrium to its overhangs. We owed our survival to the previous morning's inspiration to get as far away from the couloir as possible.

It went on snowing. Alas, the time had come to retreat again.

At first light we were already on the move, preparing to go down; there was an interminable series of worrisome abseils over the rubble left by the night's stone-fall. The great collapse had completely changed the whole rock face. The little terrace where we had spent the first night had almost been destroyed. The slope of hard ice had been totally swept away. In its place was now a soupy mess of pulverized stone mixed with ground-up ice. Looking down the couloir, we saw that everything visible through the mist was affected. Rocks of every size, which the stone-fall had scattered along its course, were precariously balanced, ready to fall at any

moment or be knocked off by other stones falling from above.
This was the dramatic scene through which we had to lower
ourselves.

The discomfort of our saturated clothes added to the
trouble the hemp ropes gave us—they were soaking wet, they
were stiff, they were constantly twisted, they refused to run
freely over our shoulders during the abseils, nor would they
run through the piton rings when we tried to recover them.
Many times we risked being left without any ropes at all
because we couldn't pull them down. Volleys of stones grazed
us throughout this frustrating exercise, often dangerously
invisible in the mist.

As Oggioni was sliding down the rope toward me, he was
struck on the head by a ricochet. He was crouched against the
rock, blood running freely down his neck and left arm. I
reached him with four pull-ups on the doubled rope, which he
had let go. The blow had stunned him, but as it was impossible to stop there, I bandaged him as best I could and we continued our descent.

At two in the afternoon, after eight interminable hours of
abseiling, we finally reached the Dru glacier. A chaotic jumble
of blocks and detritus littered the glacier for three hundred
yards. This collection of boulders of all sizes scattered everywhere testified somberly to the size of the terrifying landslide
for the rest of the summer.

Only on the next day, before we left Montenvers, did the
clouds lift enough to let us glimpse the Dru, pitiless and trans-
figured in its thick white shawl.

The Solo Ascent

This new rebuff induced a great spiritual depression. The Dru
had become the most important goal of my life. One day,

quite suddenly, I thought of returning to the Dru, but this time I would tackle it alone.

On August 11, 1955, I was at Montenvers. Yet again this area bestowed its customary blessing: for four days it rained cats and dogs.

Finally, on the fifteenth, it was clear. At two in the morning I set off for the base of my mountain by the feeble light of a pocket flashlight. An uncertain dawn, a few gusts of the sirocco, a few drops of rain. Finally the sun. In contrast to previous excursions the great couloir looked remarkably snow filled, although the remains of the rock-fall of the past twenty days still showed impressively. I hesitated for a long time at the sight of so much snow, but at nine I made up my mind.

In the couloir, everything was uniformly ice coated, difficult, and dangerous. Wherever the snow had not been able to take hold because the surface was too sheer, the rock was encrusted in hard ice or, worse still, covered by a thin and treacherous film of verglas, the result of the icy drizzle of a few hours before.

The effort was immediately exhausting. I was pulling behind me an enormous and very heavy sack, in which there were provisions for five days, an alcohol stove, bivouac clothing, a first-aid pack, seventy-nine pitons (I had lost the eightieth along the way), two hammers, fifteen carabiners, three stirrups each with three rungs, two 130-foot ropes (one of nylon, at last, and another of silk given to me by a friend), a dozen pieces of cord, six wooden wedges, an ice ax, a camera, and, finally, a walkie-talkie. (A friend was going to climb to the foot of the Dru at least once to see how I was getting on.)

All this gear was in one huge cylindrical sack, which weighed more than sixty pounds. I was tied to this heavy burden by a rope, and every so often I had to pull the sack up to me. If the face was not quite vertical, friction made the sack even heavier, or it became so jammed I had to go down again to free it. This procedure was neither simple nor effortless, but on the other hand it was the only system that could guarantee I had everything I needed for an exploit of this sort. Occupied in this way, I spent seven hours in the couloir, but gained no more than five hundred feet in altitude. Once again, the Dru decided to drive me away. The reason was utterly predictable: it snowed. I had been defeated for the third time. But I would try again.

Twenty-four hours of bad weather drove me back to Montenvers. When it cleared, I took off once more for the heights with a new plan: to avoid the couloir, which was now too snowed-up and dangerous, and make for the Flammes de Pierre gap on the normal route of the Dru. Then, by a series of abseils for about eight hundred feet down steep gullies on the other side, I would reach the infamous icy funnel from which the southwest pillar rose. If I couldn't reach it from the west, I would get there from the south by coming down from above.

I lightened my sack by sacrificing a good part of the food. I also discarded the walkie-talkie, which actually had been an affront to my mountaineering ethics. In truth it had not been my idea to take it up there in the first place, but now I had no more doubts about the compromise this gadget represented. I left it behind.

That afternoon I reached the deserted Charpoua hut. Paola Ceresa, a friend of mine from Turin, came with me, and in the early evening we went on up to the edge of the Charpoua glacier, where I left my enormous sack and made a brief reconnaissance. This lower part of the glacier was in such poor condition that I could find a way over it only with difficulty.

I found the twilight hour in those gloomy surroundings

rather oppressive, because of the many worries that always fill one's thoughts with turmoil on the eve of any great undertaking. To tell the truth, I felt like a prisoner of my own decisions.

I envied Ceresa, who would be leaving this place tomorrow, and I also envied all men who did not feel, as I did, the need to confront such trials in order to prove themselves. Filled with these thoughts as I was returning to the hut, I saw on the snow a poor butterfly, carried up by the warmth of the day. Now the frost was numbing it, and with one last beat of its wings it lifted itself, but then fell again at my feet. Poor little thing; how sorry I was for it. Something inside me identified with the unfortunate insect. I came to see in it my own destiny. Impelled by these emotions I could do no less than lift the dying butterfly from the snow and carry it with me safely to the hut, protected by the warmth of my hand.

After an anxious, sleepless night, the hour of departure came as a liberation. It was four in the morning of August 17. The great adventure had begun. I closed the creaking hut door behind me and, to overcome my misgivings, nearly ran toward the Dru.

Dawn broke as I reached the equipment left there the previous evening. Crossing the chaotic glacier was again complicated and I had to pull the sack up after me. The passage took a long time, and at times I had to take to the rocks.

The abundant snowfall of the past few days had converted the pleasant granite spires of the Flammes de Pierre into steep snowy slabs more comparable to the feared northern slopes of the range. My slow progress up the wall, burdened as I was by the sack, made me think of the convicts of days gone by, who dragged a ball and chain with every step they took.

By eleven thirty in the morning I reached the gap. I felt a surge of emotion as I answered Ceresa's calls, which reached me very clearly from the far-off hut. I was sadly leaving behind me not only the warm sun and my friend's voice, but also part of myself, the part made of small things and unrealized dreams. But my search for inner peace compelled me to be here.

On the far side of the gap lay the unknown, but the void was the thing that hit me when I looked over, an abyss of cold, fleeting shadows dominated by the sharply outlined profile of the southwest pillar. In the half-hour rest I allowed myself before starting the descent, I was dominated by the mental torment of this decisive moment. Until then, with every step I had taken, I still had the opportunity to turn back; beyond the gap this would no longer be possible. At best it would mean two thousand feet of abseils down the icy gut, to the foot of the eastern side of the Dru.

About midday I finally decided to pass the two 130-foot ropes round a spike after knotting them together; then, tying the sack to the doubled rope, I lowered it into the void the whole length of the line. Then it was my turn. One final shout toward Charpoua, one last hesitation, and I let myself slide into the chasm.

The heavy snow cover on the face and the heavy sack forced me into complicated maneuvers and, at times, restricted me to descents of no more than thirty feet. This increased the number of pitons I had to fix in the rock and then abandon. At one point when I had to plant one of these abseil pitons I found myself in a truly absurd position. I was wedged into a narrow chimney that the afternoon thaw had turned into an icy shower, and I found myself a little askew, bent over and stretching out, supporting my weight by pushing sideways against the two opposing sides of the chimney. Then, holding the piton with my left hand to stop it from slipping out of the crack in which I was trying to fix it, I used the hammer with my right hand—one, two, three blows! The fourth, which was harder than the others, glanced off the tar-get and smashed the tip of my ring finger against the rock. The pain made me feel faint and the blood gushed out in a flood; I clenched my teeth and with a few more inept hammer strokes fixed the piton well enough to support me, hooked myself onto it, and let go the abseil rope. The blow had been so strong it had completely removed the tip of my finger plus a third of the nail and the nail bed beneath it. At least an hour passed before I could stop the bleeding and resume my descent with the finger bandaged.

About seven in the evening, after one single abseil of about one hundred feet down an overhanging slab, I finally set foot on the ice slope of the great funnel, now completely snow covered. In vain I tried to recover the doubled rope; it had absorbed enough water from the melting snow to be com-pletely sodden, and absolutely refused to run through the loop of cord that held it to the piton one hundred feet above me. Time passed fruitlessly. The only solution was to climb right up to the anchorage to which the rope was attached. This operation would demand me pulling myself up the rope by using my arms with the help of Prusik knots. Before I had the chance to accomplish this, night fell. Another perilous bivouac awaited me in this intimidating glacial funnel of the Dru.

With a series of hammer blows I dug out a little step in the hard ice. I could have done with the ice ax, but I had left it at the gap where I could pick it up going back down the normal route.

This first bivouac of mine was appalling. I was soaked through, my hand was injured, I had no ropes, and I was smack in the middle of the funnel of the Dru, a sitting duck for anything falling from above. But that wasn't all. I was also short of food. The previous evening I had been forced to throw away more than half of what little food I had to begin with, thanks to a piton that had punctured the plastic flask of fuel-stove alcohol, which had leaked inside the sack and spoiled the food. I had nothing left but two packets of biscuits, a tube of condensed milk, four little cheese triangles, a small tin of tuna, a tin of liver pâté, a few lumps of sugar, some dried fruit, a small flask of cognac, and two cans of beer. Not a tempting start for this climb, especially considering that the loss of fuel meant I could no longer melt snow to relieve the thirst that was already making my lips burn.

Another anxious, sleepless night. Endless hours in a place as lonely as a tomb.

The next morning started better. The rope had been dangling from above all night and had drained off before it froze. It came down at the first tug, which was just what I had hoped for.

Without any great difficulty I reached the first rocks of the pillar and could begin the real climb. Here, however, I was in a zone of shadow, where every nook and cranny and even the smallest cracks were blocked by snow and ice. This new problem continued for three hundred feet or so, up to where the mountain was more exposed to the sun and so had shed its snowy mantle. These difficulties were worse than on my earlier attempts, and progress was slow, both because of the complicated maneuvers necessary to safeguard myself and because the sack repeatedly got stuck and was difficult to retrieve. I also had a lot of pain from my injured finger.

It was afternoon when I reached the ledge of the mysterious wedges, which was completely full of snow. This time, instead of outflanking the infamous rough cleft again on its left, I went straight at it and got up almost in a single bound. I found myself on the little terrace from which Mauri and I had retreated two years earlier. On the walls of the daunting "lizard" above I could see no sign of anywhere to rest; it was not yet evening but I'd had enough for the day. I cleared the terrace of snow and settled down for my second night in the open, breaking off some icicles to relieve my thirst.

I reflected on everything I had lived through in the last two days, and I contemplated what was in store for me. The sun seemed to set more slowly this time. The first lights of Montenvers appeared, and then the flashlight signals of my friends. "All's well!" I answered with my weak little torch. The night wore slowly on in silence.

A third dawn. A third rough beginning. Mastering the lizard involved difficulties that were extreme at times. I could only overcome a tremendous sheer overhanging cleft by trusting myself completely to wooden wedges, and, since I had only three of the right size, I had to go down and retrieve one every time I fixed another. Using this system, I had nearly reached the exit at the top of the lizard. No more than a few feet from the top, I found myself in a very exposed position in a smooth flaring chimney converted into an ice flow by alternating freezing and thawing of the abundant snow higher up. Belayed on a lone piton I had fixed in the only ice-free crack available, I patiently and very carefully hammered very small but firm notches for my feet in the green ice that covered the rocks of the chimney. A little higher up, where the chimney narrowed dramatically and was blocked by an overhang, the situation grew desperate. It would be overwhelming to have the whole venture fail due to a casual obstacle like this, which was not even typical of this sort of face. For a while I clung there, pondering the problem. Annoyed and determined, I let instinct take over and started an extreme move that turned into a furious struggle.

With precise taps of the hammer I almost completely freed the whole length of the base of the cleft, which was completely blocked by ice—but no large crack came to light. I planted a wedge there, clipped the rope in, and hung a stirrup on it. Summoning all my strength, I put my entire weight on this piece of wood and stretched up until my muscles cramped. It was useless. I still couldn't manage to wedge myself into the overhanging bottleneck to recover my breath and repeat the acrobatics. I knew from experience how a piton or a wedge fixed in an iced-up crack does not stay firm for more than two or three minutes. I quickly placed a second, haphazard wedge as high as possible in the same verglas-clad cleft. I then repeated the operation, hooking on the rope and the stirrup and committing all my weight to it; finally I overcame this impossible obstacle. A little higher up, while I was crawling like a snake on the demanding rock face, a tinkle from below told me the second wedge and the stirrup attached to it had popped out. With a shiver, I watched it slide down the rope that connected me to the sack.

On the conquered lizard, I could finally warm myself in the sun and rest, lying on my back on one of its huge scales; above, the red slabs, smooth and vertical, were waiting for me.

As if in a dream I suddenly heard a shout, very far off but quite clear; there was no doubt it was Ceresa's voice. I could not make him out, but he had to be on the moraine of the Dru glacier.

"Everything's fine!" I shouted back, but that call of his had awakened a flood of memories, gloomy thoughts, and the realization of how far I was from the world of men. Two and a half days had passed since I had run off from the Charpoua hut. Hearing my friend's voice made it seem that an eternity had passed. I had even been startled to hear my own voice replying to his calls. Only now did I realize that for the past two days I had lived and acted without saying a word, in absolute silence. It scared me a little.

Before resuming the climb I allowed myself one of the two cans of beer. Holding the ice hammer by its long thin pick, I gave the can a sharp blow. A jet of beer exploded in my face. I tried in vain to plug the hole and stop the precious liquid from escaping: the point of the hammer remained totally jammed in the tin, and when the unwelcome spray stopped, the beer was unfortunately almost all gone. The terrible burning caused by the beer on my injured hand and chapped face was worse than the fury I felt.

Using short rope-lengths to make recovering the sack easier, I climbed another one hundred feet or so without much trouble. The rock was sound, dry, and almost warm, because it was in full sun, but a menacing change in the weather was brewing. I had just started a difficult artificial pitch when the storm broke violently. I climbed rapidly down to the sack, and then farther down to a ledge, arriving there completely soaked.

The rain and hail pelted down against the wall; lightning flashes split the black sky. I stayed quiet as a mouse on the ledge, wrapped in my bivouac sack waiting for the storm to end, as far as possible from all the ironmongery that I feared might attract the lightning. The storm proved an odd blessing: I satisfied my thirst by sucking the water that ran in torrents down the face.

As in the *Alpine* Symphony of Strauss, the storm died, calm returned, all was quiet; the sun reappeared, but it was almost evening and its weak rays were no longer strong enough to dry my sodden clothing.

A freezing bivouac followed; then another dawn, the fourth, which heralded a day of intense but almost monotonous climbing up the terrible red slabs. From the very beginning I had repeated the same sequence with greater or lesser difficulty: I would climb a short pitch, belay myself to a piton, climb down the rope, recover the pitons I had previously fixed, climb back up again, and finally haul the sack up to me, which frequently caught on rough places. I had to descend to free it once, twice, or even more on every pitch. In the end, my climb amounted to at least three ascents and two descents. My hands were bleeding from the constant wear and tear of hanging on to the rocks, climbing up and down ropes, and hauling up the sack.

I often caught myself talking unconsciously, putting into words everything passing through my head. I even found myself talking to the sack as if it was a human climbing partner. Actually that's just what it was: a patient, generous, valuable companion—quite apart from being a safe support if I should fall. In fact, since the previous morning, among the various strange maneuvers I had improvised as need arose, I had worked out a system in which the sack had a very important role, which I call the Z system, for self-belaying. From then on I used nothing but this system, which is a little too complicated to explain here.

The fourth sunset surprised me on a good ledge in the heart of the red slabs just below the formidable barrier of roofs and overhangs. Its most dominant feature was a gigantic apse that precluded all possibility of going on. Exhaustion set in: all my limbs were hurting, especially my injured finger, but above all I was oppressed by uncertainty and anxiety about what was above me. When I got into my sleeping sack it was already dark.

The sharp edge at the center of the pillar, only a few yards from me, blocked the light signals that my friends at Montenvers were certainly sending. Nor could I answer them. But even had it been possible to send a signal, I would have known I was lying that evening if I had sent my customary "All's well!"

The sack had been damaged by the friction on the rocks,

and threatened to come apart. While I was mending it with a piton and some string, I fell asleep.

An unpleasant night. But the dawn, as always, gave me new energy. However, my hands were so sore and swollen I couldn't touch anything without spasms of shooting pain. The tip of my ring finger was throbbing as if it were infected; the inactivity of the night had reduced me to this state. To restore enough feeling in my hands to resume climbing, I had to force myself to do warm-up exercises, clenching my teeth in pain.

The sun was already high by the time I was ready to set off. Once I had gained another thirty feet I could see the problem. All around, the rock was smooth, concave in the center and with a monstrous overhanging eave. It really did resemble the apse of a cathedral. One solution, an extreme one, was to climb straight up its huge black roof, which jutted out at least twenty feet directly above me. The presence of some threateningly unstable blocks hanging from this roof, coupled with the fact that I was alone, made the risk too great. I would have to try my luck to the left.

I climbed some easy rocks, which brought me to the foot of an enormous, vertical, compact red slab at least 160 feet high. I attacked the slab, following a crack that gave every appearance of being suitable for my pitons, but after some sixty feet things changed. The crack became too wide to take pitons and at the same time too narrow for the damaged wooden wedges I still had left. With a drill and some expansion bolts there would have been no problem. I would have been able to climb straight up anywhere I liked in perfect safety. Instead I was bound by my self-imposed rules, which then seemed harsh and pitiless. It had been the same when I had climbed the lizard. I had to abandon this crack and look for another solution. (Subsequent climbers of the pillar, finding themselves in quite different conditions from those I encountered and using more suitable pitons, were able to climb either the huge black roof or up the crack in the 160-foot red slab as they chose. Obviously, no one will ever repeat my original route the same way I climbed it because they are now well aware of the dangers and traps.)

I heard a noise in the air, and a small, single-engine plane appeared in the sky to my left and flew around the Dru very close to the cliff. It was clearly looking for me. (When I got back I discovered it was Monsieur Toussaint, the proprietor of the Montenvers hotel.) With one foot on a stirrup and one hand clutching the piton holding me up, I leaned out into space as far as I could, waving my other arm, my other leg. I was suddenly enveloped in a white cloud, and I could hear the plane departing. Had the pilot seen me? I was overcome by a strange sensation, as if the plane, which I could still hear in the distance, were a living part of me that was now leaving. I suddenly felt absolutely alone and torn apart. I wished the plane had never come.

It was midday. Once I had climbed down from the crack it was as if I had not gained a single foot since the morning. In fact I was still at the same level as the little terrace where I had spent the night. I reexamined the problem and a new possibility suggested itself.

It would not be easy, but was perhaps the only possible solution. By a series of pendulum-swings to the right through space, I could reach a well-marked crack and climb it. Above that, I should be able to go on more or less directly, until I had got out of this unclimbable zone. The existence of this crack would undoubtedly guarantee I could fix my pitons and so be able to conquer the great overhanging face.

A pendulum traverse is a maneuver that consists of attaching the rope to a piton planted as high as possible, which allows you to swing horizontally once you have climbed down to your starting point. In this way you can swing across and reach part of a smooth, compact face otherwise insuperable by traditional means. The series of pendulum-swings I was about to start would let me "fly" across 130 feet, in successive sections, in a gradual ascent from the point where I was.

With two swings, and without complications, I arrived right under the fall line* of the huge black roof, then still farther to the right in the direction of the well-marked crack. But here the trouble started. I tried and tried again, in vain, to go straight up, far enough to fix a piton sufficiently high to allow me one wide swing. No such luck. I would have to divide the swing into two shorter sections a little lower down. I forced the first of these sections.

After I had pulled the pendulum rope across to me and thrust myself out a couple of yards farther to reach a small ledge from which I could carry out the final conclusive swing, I was dismayed to discover an immense cavity between myself and the fissure. It was as if the Dru, at this point, had sucked in the rock to leave in its place an enormous, smooth, flared hollow, which by a cruel trick of perspective revealed itself only now. And to think the lower end of the crack was no more than fifty feet higher on my right.

But the crack was beyond the unsuspected abyss, unreachable. What could I do now? I couldn't go back and reverse the moves that had brought me here by pendulum-swings; I had burned my bridges behind me by recovering the rope time and again after swinging across. Nor was it possible to abseil, because just below my feet the wall receded so much it disappeared for at least three hundred feet. I felt drained of all physical and moral energy; for at least an hour I could not

* The line down a slope or cliff taken by a falling stone. —TRANSLATOR

move, and stayed where I was, glued to the single piton that supported the sack and myself in total isolation, above an abyss that almost made me feel sick.

But little by little I found the strength to stir myself from despair. Perhaps what restored my energy was the realization that I had been fighting desperately for five days at the limits of the possible to prove myself. I had spontaneously chosen the Dru to reconcile myself with my entire life and soul. I could not just sit there and wait for death.

Above the unexpected concavity that separated me from the point where the fissure of my salvation began, and exactly where I had hoped to arrive with my last pendulum, I could see a rock outcrop projecting about forty feet above me. It was shaped like a hand with the fingers spread. I thought I might be able to lasso it with a rope and hoist myself up. But the granite fingers looked unreliable and I realized they would not support me. So I improvised a system of knots to act as tentacles on the end of the rope, like the bolas used to capture animals on the Argentinean pampas. This arrangement, which would not pull directly on the rock fingers, should reduce the danger of the anchorage giving way. If I kept throwing, sooner or later one of those "prehensile" tentacles should stay hooked up in the gap between the rock flakes. Or at least I hoped so.

I tried again and again. After a dozen throws the rope seemed to catch quite solidly. I gave it a trial tug: the rope gently unhooked itself. I tried again several times until the knotted octopus hooked on again. This time it resisted when I pulled.

But I was pulling it sideways: Would the knots and loops slip off their holding places when I was hanging vertically under the outcrop? It was best not to think about it—there was no way to test it, and in any event there was no other solution. I took the final precautions before launching myself into space.

I could not adopt my improvised Z self-belay system for

this acrobatic performance, so I tied the sack to the other end of the rope I had thrown over the outcrop. This was the only safety measure, real or imaginary, that I could take. But to allow me to recover the sack from above once I got there, it could not stay attached to the piton. On the contrary, it had to be freed and balanced on the ledge. So this is what I did.

As far as the second rope was concerned—the one that might give me at least some possibility of a belay—I tied one end to my waist and threaded the other end through the ring of the piton for half its length, then tied the other end around my waist as well. This loop would allow me to swing down away from the ledge for sixty feet or so, but I made some hitches in it to reduce it to about forty feet. This was quite enough to reach the outcrop. Naturally, I would have to pull myself up on the other rope hanging from the rock fingers. If I fell while climbing, before I was checked by the rope to hang in space, I would plunge down the entire height I had then gained, plus an extra forty feet, which was the distance the loop would allow below the piton. After such a great fall there would be little chance the piton to which I would be attached could stand the strain.

Everything was ready. Now I had to throw myself into the abyss, hanging with my hands to the rope stuck in the outcrop over there. One last nerve-racking pause, then, before doubts eroded my self-control, I closed my eyes for a second, held my breath, and let myself slide into space, hanging on to the rope. For a moment I felt myself falling, then my headlong flight slowly lessened and almost at once I felt myself swinging back: the anchorage held! In those few moments a hundred thoughts tumbled over one another, etched on my mind with absolute clarity for the rest of my life. I allowed myself to swing back and forth on a dizzy seesaw but, before I began to twist around, I started to hoist myself hand over hand up the rope. The danger increased with every foot I climbed, because the oscillations I imposed on the rope inevitably shook its knotted attachment repeatedly, harder and harder as well as more and more quickly: I had no idea how firmly it was stuck.

It was a tremendous effort, driven by the instinct of survival. When I had to let go of the rope and grab the outcrop I had another moment of hesitation. I was scared it would all collapse on top of me like a house of cards; but even as I was thinking this I found myself crawling over its rough projections, making myself as light as possible. It had worked.

I let the agitation subside, then recovered the sack from where it sat on the ledge below. I pulled the rope toward me and the gigantic pendulum of the blue cylinder in the abyss filled me with awe. That had been me just a few minutes ago! Then I untied one end of the rope loop round my waist and pulled on the other to retrieve it. I felt a great sense of relief only when I saw the rope pull away from the piton, where it might easily have become stuck.

I put one of the two ropes back in the sack, tied myself to the end of the other one, to which the sack was attached, and resumed normal climbing. I went up over unstable blocks for a few feet, then managed to plant a safe piton. I hooked the sack to it and, after arranging my Z system for security, managed with difficulty to master a flaring overhang. This was the section that preceded the famous crack I had set out to reach, and that I had thought of right from the start as an ace in the hole to solve the problems posed by the huge apse.

But once I arrived there was no crack! In its place was merely a vein of compact quartz. The vertical groove that ran up almost parallel to this quartz-filled crack was also devoid of cracks. This complete mistake was utterly disconcerting.

I was once again plunged into the depths of despair, but this didn't last too long. With a furious lunge, and levering with my legs and shoulders in the flaring chimney, my impetus took me up a few feet, but it was absolutely impossible to plant a piton. By using a short bottleneck in the chimney and stretching into it, I managed to fix a wooden wedge in its depths. I attached a rope and hooked on a stirrup and was then able to regain my breath. I knew perfectly well this maneuver was very dangerous, even crazy. I was furiously struggling at the extreme limits of my powers, in totally free climbing and constantly on the point of slipping off into space. But I went laboriously on, always with the vain hope that I would be able to fix a piton. Then the worst happened—there was no more rope. It was impossible to stop, so I had to immediately dismantle the loop of the Z system that secured me. I don't know how I did it, but though I was only just held in the chimney by my shoulders, and my muscles were in spasm, I unhooked this loop from the carabiner. Once this was done I had completely lost my already precarious protection, though I now had the whole length of the rope, 130 feet, at my disposal, and could go on climbing. But my troubles were not over because, a few feet higher up, the rope became caught and stopped me in my tracks just as I arrived under a small projecting roof. I floundered, and tried pulling on the rope, even with my teeth, but there was no sign of it coming free. My strength was running out; I couldn't keep going any longer. But then I had an incredible, wonderful surprise, just as I was at the end of my tether. In this dazzling chaos of sensations I discovered the rock around me was soft and crumbly, almost like chalk, so soft I could even cut into it with my fingernails.

Holding on with my elbows and buoyed by a great surge of adrenaline, I unhooked a small piton from my belt, and then the hammer. I hammered pell-mell wherever and however I could on the little iron nail, which, incredibly, sank halfway into what should have been solid granite. Without even thinking about it, I hooked myself onto this insecure anchorage long enough to get my breath back and regain a little energy. Then I fixed more pitons, one after another, until they formed an arc of small protruding hooks. Since they might well come out as easily as they went in, I tied them all together with cord that I knotted into a loop and in this way achieved a reasonably firm anchorage.

While I was carrying out this maneuver in such a precarious position, a stirrup slipped from my belt where it had been hanging. Weary of overhangs, my eyes refused to follow its fall. But hearing served: several seconds passed before I heard it bounce off the face, far below me.

I unroped and, carefully holding the rope fixed to the arc of pitons with one hand, I climbed down again to the big sack, which I untied from its piton and pulled up after I had returned to the odd group of anchorages.

With this unforeseen, crazy unhooking of the rope, done without the benefit of even the most minimal protection, I felt I had conquered the huge apse, which was the crux of the entire climb. Now, heading left this time, I got back to the elegant verticality of the pillar by means of another two pendulum-swings over easy stretches. Combining all the moves I had made throughout the day, I had finished up tracing an almost complete circle around these overhangs.

The face above, as a whole, now presented itself as a little more laid-back than previously, and the route became more and more obvious, unfolding itself up a series of corners and cracks. Once the worst was past, I realized I was leaving bloody handprints on the rocks. The pain wasn't too bad, however, perhaps because my hands were a little numb after all the hard work they had done.

It was almost dark when I reached a good ledge where I could spend my fifth bivouac. Late that night, I clearly heard shouts from below, confirmed by a couple of faint flashes of light from the same direction. It had to be my friends climbing up to the Charpoua hut. I shouted back, and to show them where I was I set fire to a piece of paper. They replied. From their shouts I thought I understood they would climb up to meet me the next day. (I was to learn later they thought I was already on my way down the normal route, because that's what it looked like from their position.)

I felt I had come back to life, after being so far away from it for so long. Nothing had actually changed: the pain in my hands, the burning thirst, the black shadows of the harsh face—they were all still there. But within me I felt the rebirth of human sensibility, with which I had had no rapport for days. This was enough to make me understand the intensity of what I had just experienced. Until just a few hours ago my measure had been the mountain, whose elements—rock, cold, space, stasis, durability—I had absorbed until they became part of me. The mountain and myself: one single, indivisible entity.

For the first time, I felt I had the southwest pillar of the Dru within my grasp, and had also crossed some far-off, invisible boundary. I realized I had surmounted a barrier separating me from my innermost soul, and had finally chosen my own true destiny. In the sheer exaltation of the moment I found myself in tears; then I sang with pure joy.

The sky grew paler; the sixth day of struggle was about to start. All my energy was concentrated on the last obstacle between me and the summit, but my hands would no longer respond to this last desperate appeal. They were so swollen that I could neither clench my fists nor open them. I forced myself to move them again, gradually at first. This brought on spasms of acute pain. Every wound oozed, producing not blood but clear serum.

Voices reached me distinctly; then three figures appeared on the gap of the Flammes de Pierre. I replied with deep emotion

to their shouts and questions. I recognized only the voice of
Ceresa; the other two were speaking French. It was clear even
from their fragmented calls that they were very worried about
me. I concluded they were anxious because it must have been
disconcerting to see, from the normal route (to be precise, from
the gap of the Flammes de Pierre), a lone figure climbing up a
huge, vertical slab of granite more than three thousand feet
high. To allay their fears I started to climb again, though my
hands were not too mobile. Ceresa shouted they were climbing
to the summit of the Dru and would wait for me there.

A slanting edge to the left took me almost onto the direct,
narrow, central line of the southwest pillar. A little higher up,
this spur also leaned back and the difficulties lessened. By
midday I was less than three hundred feet from the summit.
The rock was now very easy, so much so that it induced me to
lighten the sack and abandon everything that was no longer
necessary. Among other things I was about to get rid of were
the thirty or so pitons and the two stirrups, but at the last
moment I instinctively put them back in the sack, unwittingly
allowing myself to master the last deception of the Dru. In
fact, just above me, a deep notch completely separated the
southwest pillar from the summit of the Dru. A new face presented itself on the far side of the notch, consisting of compact
overhangs for at least another 150 feet. This was a surprise,
which at other times might perhaps have been my coup de
grâce, but now I attacked this obstacle in an almost furious
manner, face-to-face, as if I now had in my heart the mathe-
matical certainty that nothing could keep me from reaching
the summit.

My hands had stopped hurting; the pitons and the stirrups
again came into play in an almost brutal manner. A huge slab
of granite weighing at least one hundred pounds unexpectedly broke away, helped by a piton I was trying to fix, and hit

me a glancing blow, numbing my left leg, but my hands did not lose their grip. I felt as if I had supernatural strength and kept going, even overcoming vertical slabs and notable overhangs in free-climbing.

Then the face really did lean back again. It became more and more fissured and covered by protruding blocks. Beneath me my friends reappeared on the normal route. They could see I was almost at the top, so they stopped to wait for me six hundred feet below the summit. At exactly 4:37 in the afternoon I reached the summit of the Dru. I left the celebrations for a more suitable occasion and confined myself to a quick glance around. At last I could lighten the sack and carry it on my shoulders. I started my descent by abseiling, then finally leaped down to join my friends. The French climbers Gerard Gery and Lucien Berardini had climbed up with Ceresa. It was a really sympathetic gesture on their part. Berardini had been one of the four conquerors of the west face of the Dru in 1952.

Night overtook us near the gap of the Flammes de Pierre, where I retrieved my ice ax. A sixth bivouac was inevitable, but this one was like a wonderful party with friends.

—Translated by Robert Marshall

Postscript: After Walter Bonatti successfully tackled the ascent of the Dru, he went on to achieve great distinction in the mountaineering world. He was awarded the French Legion d'Honneur for saving the lives of two climbers after an accident in the Alps.

Climbing Mount McKinley, the highest peak in North America, is a daunting feat even in summer, but doing so in the dead of an Alaskan winter simply boggles the mind. In 1967 seven climbers set off to do exactly that, and three of them—Art Davidson, Dave Johnston, and Ray Genet—actually made it to the summit. Their story of perseverance in the worst imaginable conditions is without a doubt one of the most captivating reads in the annals of mountaineering literature.

MINUS 148°

The Winter Ascent of Mt. McKinley

ART DAVIDSON

Denali in Winter

What would *Mount McKinley be* like in winter? I became intrigued with the idea of climbing McKinley, or Denali as we liked to call it, in winter when I climbed the mountain in the summer of 1965 with my friend Shiro Nishimae and the Osaka Alpine Club.

While Shiro and I watched huge cornices soften and crumble in the July sun, we tried to imagine the winter storms that packed snow into these massive formations. Shedding our jackets on the lower glaciers, we wondered what the temperature would drop to in February. Climbing through the sun-lit days of June, we shuddered at the thought of the winter darkness.

No sooner had Shiro and I come down from Denali in summer, than we wanted to go back in winter. It would be like a journey to an unexplored land. No one had lived on North America's highest ridges in the winter twilight. No one knew how low the temperatures would drop or how penetrating the cold would be when the wind blew. For thousands of years Denali's winter storms had raged by themselves. No one had ever watched the fleeting light of the winter sun filter into the mountain's basins and cols. It was this mystery, this uncertainty of what we'd find that made us want to climb Denali in winter.

Meteorologists told us to expect temperatures of minus sixty degrees and winds up to 150 miles per hour. In December, the days would have eighteen hours of darkness. McKinley pioneer Bradford Washburn said that above eighteen thousand feet the thin air would reduce our mental capacity by 50 percent. Much to our surprise, Dr. Terris Moore of the University of Alaska calculated that the difference between geographic and barometric altitude meant that a winter ascent of McKinley would be equivalent to climbing to 23,500 feet in the Andes or Himalayas.

For some reason, Shiro and I thought we'd have no trouble finding others to join us. In turning us down, one veteran climber said our chances of success were about zero. Another declined, saying the combination of cold, wind, darkness, and altitude could be the harshest ever encountered. Others asked why try something so miserable, with so little chance of success? Why risk losing your hands and feet?

Shiro and I persisted in our belief that Denali could be climbed in winter—and climbed safely. By the fall of 1966,

we'd found six other climbers who agreed. Each strengthened
the team in their own way. Gregg Blomberg, who designed
specialized mountaineering gear, would be our leader. Dr.
George Von Wichman, an orthopedic surgeon, was our expedition's doctor. John Edwards was an Alpine entomologist
who had climbed in Europe as well as in his native New
Zealand. At six foot seven, Dave Johnston was a force of
nature; like Shiro and I, he had already climbed Denali in summer. Ray Genet, from Switzerland, wore a red bandana on his
head, had a black beard, and liked to be called Pirate; he
lacked high mountain experience, but possessed great physical
strength and determination. Then there was Jacques Batkin,
the Frenchman everyone called Farine; he was noted for pio-
neering long, difficult winter ascents in the Alps; with Lionell
Terray three years earlier, he had climbed Mount Huntington,
the most difficult ascent in Alaska at the time.

On January 30, 1967, we said good-bye to family and
friends on Don Sheldon's airstrip in Talkeetna. When we
landed on the Kahiltna Glacier, it was twelve below zero.
There was no wind and a silent world of ice and snow lay
before us.

Our second full day on the glacier began with everyone in
high spirits. When the sun lifted above a ridge and flooded
our tents with its pale light, we were eager to start off. In the
sunlight we felt warmer, though the temperature still hovered
around fifteen below. We shouldered sixty- to seventy-pound
packs of food we'd cache two and a half miles up the glacier.
We'd return for personal gear, then head up the glacier again
to arrive late at the new camp, perhaps after dark. We had
established the route the day before. There were no signs of
crevasses. The winter storms must have filled them in. The
entire glacier was windpacked and the hard snow made perfect walking. It appeared safe to go unroped.

Or so it seemed, until we couldn't find Farine.

"Farine, Farine," Gregg's voice was cracking. He was out of breath. His eyes were glazed. He was yelling into a hole in the glacier . . . "Farine . . ." There was no answer.

Gregg turned to us with a frantic sigh. "Oh God, I don't know if I can face a body."

Gregg and Pirate anchored themselves thirty feet from the crevasse. Two ropes ran from them into the hole. Dave fastened Jumar ascenders, small clamps that grip a fixed line, to the rope he would descend. He tied into the other rope for protection. Flicking on his headlamp, he disappeared down the hole.

Fifty feet down there was an ice shelf. Below that the crevasse narrowed and disappeared into the darkness of the subglacial rocks. Dave found Farine lying unconscious on the shelf. Only six feet above him, Dave's rope jammed. He yelled and swore at me to lower him. I shouted at Gregg and Pirate to give him slack. With the rope freed, Dave reached Farine. With startling speed he tied the hauling line around his limp body. While he worked, I could hear Dave talking to his friend; "Come on, Farine baby . . . you'll make it . . . Won't be long. We'll get you out of here."

Farine reached the top of the hole, but there he snagged on the sharp lip of the crevasse. While Pirate and Gregg pulled on the rope, I grabbed Farine under his shoulders to draw him up over the edge. Within seconds he slid out onto the flat snow. I loosened the hauling rope around his huge chest. His face was bloody, his lower lip torn.

I couldn't detect any breathing, but he might still be alive. We slipped Farine into a sleeping bag to save all the warmth left in his body. His eyes were open, staring blankly. George couldn't find a pulse.

Kneeling over Farine, I wiped some blood away from his

mouth with my finger and began mouth-to-mouth respiration. While Gregg held Farine's nostrils shut, I breathed deeply into him. There was a rasping noise. The air passage sounded blocked. I pressed my mouth harder to Farine's so no air would escape; I breathed and breathed and breathed. While I tried to force breath back into his body, George massaged his heart and applied rhythmic pressure to his chest. Dave had clambered over the edge of the crevasse and moved in to relieve George. There was still no sign of life.

I breathed with all the strength in my lungs. Dave pressed harder. George shone the flashlight on Farine's face again. There was no movement of the pupils, no reaction. There was no pulse. His face was purple. George pronounced him dead.

We were crushed. All the joy had been sucked out of us. Seven of us crowded into a four-man tent. The air was thick with moisture from our breathing.

As the hours passed, we began trying to talk our way through what had happened. We were angry at ourselves for being fooled by the winter conditions. We had prepared for the cold. We had prepared for the wind. But we hadn't anticipated how they could combine to create a condition none of us had ever seen. To our horror, we realized that instead of filling in crevasses, the wind-driven snow had covered them with a crust that concealed their presence. The cold helped bind this thin, hardpacked layer in place, with no trace of the crevasse below.

When Gregg finally spoke he tried to sound matter-of-fact. He said we had to decide whether we were going to abandon the climb. His feelings were clear: "This isn't Everest guys. It's not a once-in-a-lifetime deal. We could take our gear and return another time. Reaching the summit now would be meaningless for me."

He asked how I felt. "I want to go on more than ever." I

tried to remain calm. "We've got to reach the summit. Farine wouldn't have wanted us to quit."

"No. I don't understand," Gregg shot back. "I guess I climb for different reasons. I climb to be in the mountains . . . for the joy of the wind, the sun, and the cold. All the joy of this climb left me with Farine's death. I don't climb for something like this."

"None of us climb for this," I answered. "But we have to accept the risk that someone, maybe ourself, might be injured or killed."

"You don't understand, Art. I'm the leader. I'm responsible. I can't risk taking you guys up higher after this happened. God, what if someone else died."

"Gregg, we simply won't have another accident. And this one is as much my fault as it is yours, or anyone's."

Pirate tried to comfort Gregg by saying that Farine would have been the last one to put on a rope. "You saw him that first day . . . sure of himself . . . by himself. . . He was happy that way. It wasn't your fault, Gregg."

Gregg asked each of us how we felt, what we wanted to do.

Dave said he wanted to go on, but added that he thought his reasons were selfish. He didn't think he could afford trying again. He grew quiet for a moment, then said he wanted to continue for Farine's sake, to complete the climb for his friend.

Pirate made no attempt to conceal or apologize for his desire to reach the summit. "On construction jobs, I've had friends killed only a few feet from me. The work goes on. We should keep climbing."

George's unusual quietness and drawn face revealed his deep hurt. He appeared reluctant to complete the climb and acknowledged in a roundabout way that he was more inclined to return to Anchorage. He even suggested we might continue without him.

John, who hadn't been at the scene of the accident, said, "Look, we're all in shock. Let's wait a day or two before making a decision."

Shiro agreed with John that we shouldn't decide that night, but, in no more than a whisper, added that he wanted to go on.

We avoided talking about Farine himself by speaking in more general and abstract terms. Gregg said you couldn't equate a life with a climb, no climb was worth it. Dave said he hoped he'd die climbing, doing what he loved, and be left in the mountains. George said, "There's no joy or satisfaction in climbing to compensate for death." Pirate mumbled, "We all go sometime. Dying is a part of climbing. It's a part of life."

We woke the next morning to see a storm front sweeping in from the south. Dark clouds were forcing their way up the Kahiltna. The summits of McKinley and Foraker were obscured by lenticular caps. Camp had to be moved because the tents were pitched under a slope that might avalanche after a heavy snowfall. There was no time to dwell on the previous day.

We retreated down glacier with snow flying into our faces. As we passed Farine's body, we quickly marked it with a bamboo pole so we could find him again if the storm covered him with snow. Moving on, our emotions were caught between anguish for Farine and our apprehension over the storm and for the campsite we hadn't found yet.

It began snowing harder and everything became white. The ground and the sky appeared the same. In ropes of two we groped and wandered in a desultory manner, looking for snow packed into the hard consistency needed for igloo blocks. We'd lose sight of the others, only by calling out could we rejoin them. For several horrible minutes we all just clustered together in the driving snow, no one speaking, no one knowing what to do.

Several voices, muffled by the storm, said we ought to pitch the tents. Someone growled that the tents would rip apart if the wind grew much stronger. Again we set off in pairs to find snow soft enough for our saws to cut, yet firm enough to hold when set in an igloo wall. We stumbled about. We poked the points of our ice axes hopefully at the frozen surface. We cursed the blizzard. Frantic visions of Farine's bloody face darted through my mind.

At length, we found snow that would make good blocks. Gregg and two others headed back to yesterday's camp for food. Four of us started building an igloo. Shiro took the key position in the center of the circle we had scribed for the first row of blocks. I cut the blocks several yards away. As soon as I had one ready, Dave's long arms would reach for it and pass it to George.

The faster we worked, the less we thought of Farine. Hours passed. The whiteout became thicker. It began to grow dark. Every few minutes we yelled and listened for a reply from the three who had gone for supplies. One of our calls was finally answered by a high-pitched cry that reached us through the roar of the storm.

The blowing snow and caring for Farine's body kept us holed up for several days. By the time the storm passed, we had decided to go on.

February 15: The Climb to 17,200 Feet

I put off getting up as long as I could.

Inside the tent it was minus thirty-eight. Each time we brushed against the tent walls we were showered with ice crystals. My clothes were so cold it hurt my fingers to touch them. During the night, Dave's tossing in his sleep had woken me several times. Now he complained. "Didn't sleep worth a damn . . . half-cold all night."

Getting a stove going was frustrating: spilling gas on bare hands, fumbling with matches, watching a sputtering flame go out, cleaning the orifice, pumping up the air pressure, striking another match. Dave reached for our cooking kit and, mumbling through his beard, tried to persuade a stubborn stove to melt snow into the water we needed for hot drinks.

Once we'd eaten, Pirate and Shiro hustled us out of the tents into a breeze, which brought the wind-chill temperature down to about minus fifty. We didn't have any breath to spare for talking as we clomped slowly up the ice to Windy Corner. We tried to avoid breathing too deeply, because the dry, cold air caused a burning sensation in our lungs.

By late afternoon, we reached a basin at 14,400 feet that is just below the snow and ice wall rising to the crest of the West Buttress. We selected a campsite that we thought would be out of reach of avalanches sweeping down from above. We wanted to build two igloos before dark, but the surface snow was soft, and we had to dig down a few feet to find wind-packed snow we could cut into blocks. Working by the light of our headlamps, we finished the first igloo by seven o'clock. Tired and needing a good meal, we decided to call it a day.

By morning, a south wind had picked up. Snow began falling before we set the last blocks in the roof of our second igloo. For three days the blizzard pelted our basin with more than two feet of snow.

Although the storm restrained us from starting up the wall, we were able to fetch the food we'd cached at Windy Corner. Bundled up in sweaters and parkas and hidden behind woolen balaclavas and goggles, we leaned into the blustery wind. I liked the feel of the wind whipping our clothing and the rope that tied us together. I liked quickly shifting my stance to counter an unexpected gust.

It struck me that the physical strain of climbing in this storm was a relief from the emotional strains down below. On the Kahiltna, tormented by the hidden crevasses and the accident that took Farine's life, and uncertain about continuing the climb, we had begun bickering with one another. This blizzard was something we could size up and pit ourselves against. It was bringing us together.

When we stepped out into the flying snow each morning, we became invigorated. We filed back to the igloos each evening with a satisfying sense of fatigue. Although falling snow and clouds obscured the summit, the end of our climb seemed within reach, maybe just a few days away.

Darkness

By the end of February, we had established a well-provisioned camp with two igloos at 14,400 feet and had dug a snow cave for our high camp at 17,200 feet. The night of February 27 found us hunkered down in the cave. One of John's ears, the tip of Dave's nose, and the end of Gregg's foot were showing signs of frostbite. Otherwise, we were in pretty good shape. A break in the weather would give us a chance to go for the summit.

The next morning, Shiro woke at first light to check the weather. The temperature was minus forty-three. It was clear, but windy.

"Maybe wind will die down," Shiro said, "and we have chance for summit later in morning."

We ate with barely saying a word. We dressed slowly and eventually went out to relieve ourselves. The wind seemed to be slacking off. There was not a cloud in the sky.

"Hell, let's go for the summit," said Pirate, pacing restlessly in front of the cave.

"We could climb up to Denali Pass and turn back if it's too windy," said Dave.

Our sleepy camp suddenly buzzed with excitement as we hustled to get our gear ready. George said he was too tired from the previous day to give it a try. John, too, was worn out, and his ear had swollen up during the night.

Pirate suggested we go extremely light, but was overruled by Shiro who insisted we take sleeping bags, foam pads, and a stove in case nightfall or an accident forced a bivouac.

Shiro was the first to have his gear packed, and he selected enough food to last five days in case a storm caught us. By ten o'clock everyone was ready. Shiro motioned to Dave, Pirate, and myself and said in his usual unassuming way, "You three go first. I'll come along with Gregg."

I tied into the rope behind Dave and Pirate, cinching several loops tightly around my waist. We shouldered our packs and grabbed our ice axes. Each of us wore goggles to cut the reflection of the sun off the ice; Dave, I noticed, had put on Farine's Himalayan glasses.

John and George shook hands with us and said that they hoped we'd make it. They waved as we set out across the basin at a brisk, smooth pace. As the angle of the ice increased we climbed with slower, more calculated steps. The wind had all but disappeared.

Through the dark lenses of our goggles the sky appeared a deep, tranquil blue. The basin receded below us; Shiro and Gregg moved as tiny dark figures on the whiteness of the ice. Behind them the sharp white forms of the Kahiltna Peaks, Foraker, and Crosson cut the sky, and to the north and west patches of low gray clouds drifted across the flat tundra. Our crampons gripped the ice, which rose steeply above us to Denali Pass.

Cautiously, we climbed diagonally up the steep final hundred yards of ice below the pass. Finally reaching the level ice at the pass, we decided to wait for Shiro and Gregg, still a quarter of a mile below.

We had begun stepping in place to warm our toes by the time Gregg and Shiro appeared over the rim of the pass; they climbed the gentle slope to our resting spot very slowly. Anxious to be off again, Dave, Pirate, and I urged them to quickly cache the emergency gear and set the pace on up the route. Shiro looked tired. Gregg hesitated. "I don't know," he said, looking down toward our ice cave. "I feel strong enough, but my heart's just not in it today."

I wondered if the memory of Farine was bothering him. I drew him aside and spoke quietly. "Gregg, after all the two of us have gone through to get this far, we've got to go for the summit together."

"No, you and Dave and Pirate can climb faster than I can," he said. "Besides, we've got only three sleeping bags here, and it's going to get dark before you return. It's really safer for everyone to have a bag, so you guys take mine. I'll make it tomorrow." Gregg turned back to the group.

I wondered whether Gregg really wanted to go down. He was right in saying that it would be safer if all five of us didn't continue. In an emergency the food we brought up would last longer if fewer people had to depend on it. The summit was close. But our safety was more important to Gregg than reaching the summit himself. We were silent for a moment. Shiro spoke first.

"I think I'll feel stronger tomorrow," he said. "I'll come up with Gregg and maybe John and George. Looks like the weather should stay good."

It didn't seem fair that either Shiro or Gregg go down. In the end we shook their hands, slapped their shoulders affectionately, and left them behind.

Dave remained tied into the middle of the rope, with Pirate at the opposite end from myself; they had asked me to take the lead. I set a pace considerably slower than I knew we could climb because I wanted to conserve our strength for later.

I led slowly up the ice, around scattered outcroppings of rock, over slight rises of wind-packed snow, all the time keeping close to the crest of the ridge. The next time I halted to rest, Gregg and Shiro had disappeared; they were either hidden behind some rocks or had already started down. The ice around us had a harsh and ragged feeling to it; the wind-carved drifts were not delicate and elegant as they had been down on the Kahiltna.

"How's the pace I'm setting?"

"OK, Dad."

Minutes and hours slipped away as we gradually gained altitude. The sky above held clear and breezeless. I turned from the ridge to cut left across a basin. My eyes usually focused on the ice a foot or two in front of my feet, because the flat afternoon light made it difficult to see all the ups and downs of the ice. Suddenly a crevasse gaped in front of me. Our procession came to an abrupt halt. My heart pounded faster; I'd come within a step of casually walking over the edge.

The crevasse stretched the length of the basin, and we searched thirty to forty yards in each direction without finding a place we could easily cross. We would have to jump across a two-foot gap onto an ice platform of questionable strength.

Dave put me on belay. I tiptoed down the ramp, trying to keep as many crampon points as possible on its narrow edge. I stepped along the snow bridge, studied the platform for a moment, then swung one leg across the dark gap taking care not to jar the ice when my boot touched the other side. The platform held; I scampered across and up the other side of the crevasse.

Negotiating the crevasse had taken about forty-five minutes. The sun was now hidden from our sight behind the crest of the ridge, and toward the southwest the sky was filling with the first pastel yellow of evening. We hurriedly angled back to the ridge, but because of the altitude I soon had to gauge down our pace to allow two breaths between each step. Every thirty steps I'd pause to count out fifteen breaths before continuing.

Ahead of us Archdeacon's Tower arched gracefully into the sky. The scattered clouds we had seen drifting over the tundra had begun packing up against the foothills. Another bank of clouds had socked in around the base of the range to the south and west. They weren't alarming because we had often watched storms gather and then spend their force at lower elevations while McKinley's upper reaches remained clear.

I began forcing our pace up the ridge. Not a word had been said about the approaching darkness. Yet it was obvious we would soon have to decide whether to climb on after the sun set or hightail it back to the cave. We climbed steadily, but just as steadily the white glare of the sun diminished to yellow, then to orange as the sun slipped into the dusky haze above the horizon. In the emptiness of the thin air the sky seemed especially enormous.

Our ridge gave way to a basin rimmed with smaller ridges. Archdeacon's Tower rose off to our left. A higher ridge, perhaps the summit ridge itself, appeared in the distance. Pirate shouted for me to hold up a second.

"Man, we're getting close!" Dave said.

"Yea, and it's getting dark," I replied.

"Hey, Art, why don't you take off your dark glasses?"
Pirate laughed.

Sure enough, with the goggles off the sky was lighter.
However, the sun remained an orange ball suspended beyond
Foraker. If we went on, we probably wouldn't reach the
summit before nightfall. I asked Dave what he thought. He
said a night out wasn't going to kill us. Pirate growled his
agreement.

A few minutes after we had begun climbing again, we
gained the crest of a low rise, then headed across a small basin
toward the crest of another rise. The landscape rolled and
rose around us like a sea of enormous, frozen swells. Each of
us concentrated on the contours and variations of the ice; we
needed to inscribe them on our minds to help guide us down
in the dark. The only other markers we'd have were marks
our crampons left in the snow and ice, and we'd have to find
those with the light of our headlamps.

I climbed more slowly than ever up the slope of ice that hid
the summit ridge. When I reached the crest, only a broad
plateau lay between us and the ice wall that rose straight to the
final ridge. Suddenly, all the ice lay clear and sharp before us!
Our remaining uncertainty vanished! We were going to reach
the summit! For the first time in all the years I had been climbing, tears rolled down my cheeks as I looked toward the
summit.

Dave climbed up to me with a big grin on his face. He
grabbed my arm and shook it in his excitement. Pirate
reached us out of breath, mixing growls and laughter with his
gulping for air. In our minds we had already climbed to the
summit. I wiped the tears from my cheeks before they had a
chance to freeze.

The vastness of the mountains half obscured by clouds
reflecting an orange-gray light gave an unearthly quality to

everything we could see. The incredible stillness, immensity, and remoteness of the world that only the three of us inhabited gave me the notion that we were stopping for a moment in a fairy tale. Something magical about the ice and rock and sky seemed about to disappear. I tried to grasp an impression of the forms and colors around us, because I knew this moment would suddenly vanish, to be recalled only with the vagueness of a dream half remembered, or a memory from childhood.

We stretched our legs, which had stiffened during the minutes we had rested. I led us quickly across a plateau covered with wild ice drifts, unsettling evidence of the power of the wind's architecture.

Once we were on the ice wall, our progress became almost imperceptible. I was breathing four or five times between each step. After fifteen steps I would have to pause for about half a minute. I angled up to the left to skirt several *bergschrunds*. The ice beneath our crampons changed from a soft pink to a delicate purple as the sun set.

For the moment we didn't think of reaching the summit—it was too far away—but only of making it up the wall. Between steps I fixed my eyes on the ridgeline at the top of the wall. Step followed step, and suddenly, there was the summit ridge, then we rested several minutes before starting off again. Because the ridge rose much less steeply than the wall, I could set a faster pace.

Pirate called for another rest stop; I figured he must really love his father to lug that radio up here. Dave nudged me to start on again. Perhaps we should have taken time to put on our headlamps because we were climbing the ridge in the last moments of twilight, nearly an hour after the sun had sunk below the horizon.

Except for a faint blue which lingered in the west, the sky

had become completely dark by the time we neared the top of the ridge. A rest stop now came every seven or eight steps. Behind me, Dave and Pirate were dark forms swaying against the grayness of the ice like dim shadows. No one spoke; occasionally the rope tugged me gently from behind.

The ridge ended; it simply faded into a shallow depression. To my left and right I could barely make out the lines of slightly rising ice against the sky. While I wondered which direction to head, Dave came up beside me. He said it rose to the right. I asked him to go ahead.

Close together, grabbing up coils of rope in our hands, the three of us crept along the ice crest. A stiff breeze came up from the south face, which now fell away to our right and in front of us. The crest wasn't knife-edged, but we treated it as if it were because in the darkness we were unable to see the ice beneath us. Dave stopped by an aluminum pole sticking out of the ice.

It took me a moment to realize that this was the summit. We grabbed one another in a three-way hug. We shouted and slapped one another's shoulders. We had made it!

We had looked forward to the view from the summit, but there was only darkness in every direction. After a few moments, Dave spotted a faint glitter of greenish lights way to the south. "Wow!" he sighed. "The lights of Anchorage look like specks of phosphorescence in a black sea."

I gazed off into the quadrants of the black sky, trying to imagine the wild landscape that was hidden in the darkness. It was hard for me to picture where the ridges and glaciers ran.

Pirate asked who had put the pole here. I shrugged and tried not to think about it. I said, "Look, isn't it funny that there are no stars out?" A high haze must have developed since the sun had set. Dave called my attention back to the lights by saying he noticed that curious effect of vision, which made them appear brighter when we didn't look directly at them but slightly off to one side. Faint as it was, the cluster of lights gave off an illusive warmth. The green glow was almost pretty. I dreaded the thought that in a few days I'd be back among those lights. Nevertheless, I began thinking fondly of people I'd see again.

"Yup," Pirate barked, "there's my gal's porchlight!"

"This breeze must be about twenty knots," said Dave.

The wind rising from below had begun to chill us through our parkas. We retreated seventy-five feet back along the crest to the little hollow. On level ice again, we put on our head-lamps. Dave read off the time: three minutes after seven. He checked the thermometer: minus fifty-eight. I said "Let's be moving."

Pirate set the radio on the snow. All his twisting of dials, shaking, and rattling, cursing couldn't coax out even a healthy static—it was too cold.

Dave dug a small pit in the ice to bury an assortment of mementos people had asked him to place on the summit; he tossed in a seal of the State of Alaska, and a cross from the diocese of Hudson Stuck, first climber to this summit. Then, to my amazement, I watched Dave pull out of his pocket something that I thought had been lost long ago. As he placed Farine's hat in the ice, the inevitable images flicked through my mind. What were Dave and Pirate thinking? I didn't know.

While Pirate tinkered with the radio and Dave fumbled in his pack to find a flag from John's mountaineering club, which had once been taken to the summit of Mount Everest, I grew anxious to descend. I urged them to hurry up. Pirate told me to take it easy. I felt an irrational urgency to start down. When Dave said I was acting almost paranoid, I realized I was sort of frightened. But of what? It seemed we shouldn't stay here any longer than necessary. We had a long, difficult descent ahead of us.

Pirate finally gave up on the radio. Flashing my headlamp toward him, I saw how disappointed he looked. Suddenly I saw him, not as our tough old Pirate, but as a kid thinking of his home a long way off.

Dave said, "OK, Art, lead us down."

I started down the ridge, my headlamp illuminating about ten square feet. Beyond this area everything was black. As expected, the route was traceable only by the marks our crampons left in the snow on our way up. Wherever the snow thinned I had to search for tiny nicks in the ice. Over and over I warned myself to forget the summit, to forget my relief. It's just beginning, I told myself. I tried to bolster up all my powers of concentration.

We stepped over the edge and down the ice wall, where only tiny niches revealed where our crampons had bit into the ice. If I lost the trail, we might wander to the right, where the ice was too steep for us to climb, or stumble across one of the *bergschrunds.* Each of us was well aware that, should anyone slip, we would all tumble down through the darkness to the basin five hundred feet below.

About a third of the way down the wall, my eyes began watering from staring at the ice; I stopped to rest both eyes and legs. Looking out into the unbroken darkness which surrounded us, I was seized by the sensation that nothing at all was out there, that the night was empty and there remained only our three headlamps in the blackness which seemed complete.

We continued down with extreme caution. As the ice became less steep, we moved more quickly. We didn't stop when we reached the bottom of the wall, but quickened our pace across the plateau. Once I lost sight of our tracks. I thought "Thank God for the rope!" Since I was connected to Dave, who was still on the route, I could retrace my steps back to him and pick up our previous tracks again. We moved on.

My legs were beginning to feel weak and shaky. I asked if I was going too slowly. Dave and Pirate assured me they didn't want to go any faster. I began resting every few minutes. Several more times I lost the trail; each time I was able to return to where Dave had stopped and find it again. In many places the marks in the ice were barely visible even when we stared directly at them. Weariness was overcoming our ability to concentrate.

When we reached the crevasse that stretched across the lower basin, I was suprised that we crossed it much more quickly than we had in the daylight. We wound down the ridge and among the outcroppings of rock. Our memory of the route told us we were almost at the spot where our bivouac equipment was cached. We stumbled onto the sleeping bags covered with the parachute and weighted down with rocks.

Should we descend all the way to our cave or sleep at Denali Pass until dawn? Dave wanted to go on. Pirate, fully bushed by this time, said he would just as soon rest the few hours until it would be light. I argued that we shouldn't risk the steep ice in the dark while we were so tired. Dave insisted we get it all over with, but in the end I persuaded him that it would be safest to spend the night at the pass.

Soon we were lost in the dreamless sleep of exhaustion.

March 1: −148°

Note: The expedition is split between Denali Pass and the 17,200-foot camp. With no means of communication, each group has no way of knowing what is happening to the other group. The narrative follows Dave, Pirate, and Art at Denali Pass. Diary entries written by Gregg, Shiro, George, and John follow their actions.

Denali Pass: Art, Dave, Pirate

The wind woke us. The wildly whipping parachute billowed and snapped with reports like those of a bullwhip or rifle. The wind blasted against the rocks we were nestled among with a deafening eruption of noise; crosscurrents in the storm fluctuated its pitch to a groan or a prolonged whine. A dull, aching pressure along my backside was the cold, pressed into me by the wind.

I twisted in my sleeping bag to grope for the loose section of parachute thrashing me from behind. The moment I caught it my hands were pierced with cold; groggy with sleep, I'd forgotten that the nylon, like everything else outside our sleeping bags, was about minus forty. The cold sank into my fingers while the parachute, jerking and cracking erratically, resisted my attempts to anchor it. As soon as I managed to gather the slack material under me, the weight of my body holding it down, I shot one hand under an armpit and the other into my crotch for warmth. I was out of breath from the effort.

Drawn tighter, the parachute made less noise, and I was able to relax for a few moments. My fingers, aching inside from being deeply chilled, began to gradually rewarm with strong tingling sensations. I pressed the length of my body against Dave to be warmer on that side, and I felt Dave shift inside his bag, trying to press against me. I snuggled close to him and lay quietly for a long time, hoping I'd fall asleep again, as if not thinking about the wind and cold would make them disappear.

I couldn't sleep, and the wind only grew more vicious. I

tried to ignore the cold along my backside, away from Dave, but when the first shiver ran through my body I turned to check the sleeping bag where it touched my back. To my horror it was no thicker than its shell, two pieces of nylon. The wind had pushed the down away.

The parachute began cracking again. "Oh, hell," I mumbled. The cracking meant a portion of the parachute had broken loose again. Feeling I didn't have the strength for another attempt at anchoring it, I curled up in my bag, shivering occasionally, waiting for something to happen; I didn't know what. After what seemed like several minutes but was probably only a matter of seconds, I heard Pirate trying to tie down the parachute.

"Art." Pirate's voice sounded far off and unfamiliar. "Help me hold it." I felt Dave get to his hands and knees and begin wrestling with the parachute, which was now pounding his head and back as it billowed and cracked back in rapid succession. Yanking and cursing, Dave managed to pull part of it around him again, only to have it whip off as soon as he settled down into his bag.

"Look, we gotta get outa here!" Dave yelled.

"Where? We'd never make it down!" I said, grabbing onto the piece of parachute that Pirate was clinging to. "Maybe it's a morning wind that'll die down."

"Morning wind?" Dave looked at me with disbelief. "It's a bloody hurricane, you fool! I'm checking the other side of the rocks."

"Awwghaaaaa. . . ." Pirate growled, staring up into the wind.

Instead of getting completely out of his bag, Dave tied the drawstring at the top tight around his middle. With his legs still in the sleeping bag and his arms free, he lurched toward the crest ten feet away. I was horribly apprehensive. If he lost his grip on the rocks he could easily be blown off the mountain. On the other side we'd never hear him again if he called for help. How far was he going? Maybe he'd be hidden behind a rock where we wouldn't be able to find him if we needed his strength. Besides the logic of my fear, I recoiled emotionally against Dave's leaving because it seemed to break a fundamental law of survival—stay together.

"Dave," I cried. "Wait! I think it's safer here."

"Stay if you want!" he hollered back. "This wind's bad, and I'm gettin' out of it!"

"Where are you going?" Dave didn't hear me. "It's exposed over there!" He had disappeared over the crest.

Since my mittens were too bulky to grip the parachute, I pulled thick wool socks onto my hands; my fingers were nearly numb already. I was astonished as I looked up to see Pirate holding the parachute with his bare hands. Just as I yelled at him to get something over them, one of my socks started to slip off. Pulling it back on, I shifted position, and the wind seized the wind parka I had been sitting on. One moment the parka had been under me, then I saw it whirling through the air, fifty, a hundred feet up, sailing in the direction of McKinley's summit.

With Dave gone, his loose end of the parachute caught the wind, and this threatened to rip the entire piece of nylon from our grip. We gave up trying to wrap the parachute around us; the pull on our arms wrenched our whole bodies as we clung to it to keep it from escaping. The parachute was our only shelter.

"My hands are bad!" Pirate's voice was weak, almost a whimper. His face was drawn up into a hideous, painful grin. Ice caked his beard.

"Bring them in!" I yelled, though his head was only inches from mine. His fingers felt like chunks of ice against my stomach.

"They're stiff!"

"Move them!" I reached for a better grip on the parachute. It slipped. I lunged. Pirate caught it as it whipped past him. He winced in pain.

"Aw, the hell with it!" Pirate sighed. As he let loose, the parachute twisted through the air. It snagged on a rock. I saw it starting to rip, then it was gone.

For the first time I noticed the sky. It was a blue wall, smashing into the mountain. Thin pieces of cloud shredding–everything grew blurred. My eyes were watering and stinging from squinting into the wind. Compared to anything I had ever experienced, this wind was like another element. It was as if gravity had shifted and, instead of holding us down, was pulling us across the landscape.

Pirate began digging his hands in under my parka. The top of my bag had fallen open to the wind. As I pulled it shut, I fell against Pirate. We grabbed each other.

"Hold onto me!"

"Art, let's get into one bag."

"How? There's no room. . . . Give me your hands." I felt his icy fingers grabbing the skin around my middle. My bag had opened again, and to keep the wind from getting to me Pirate pushed himself over the opening. I just leaned against him, trying to catch my breath. Shivering, teeth chattering, my whole body was shaking with cold.

"Pirate, it's no good!" Wind was coming into my bag. We were both losing our warmth. "Each in his own bag . . . it's better."

"I can't feel my fingers!"

"Put 'em between your legs!"

"I don't want to lose my hands!"

I remembered Dave. If it was less windy on the other side of the rocks, he would have come back to tell us. If it was just as windy, I thought he would have returned to be with us.

Something must have happened to him. But maybe he had found a sheltered corner.

"Pirate, let's try the other side!"

"Naw . . . the wind's everywhere!"

We huddled together, hunched upright in our sleeping bags, wedged tightly between two rocks. Whenever we relaxed the wind caught us, started us sliding along the ice which gradually sloped away, and forced us to push and fight our way back up into the rocks. Leaning against Pirate didn't make me any warmer, but it was comforting—I wasn't alone. We didn't talk. I could breathe more easily with my head inside my bag. I wondered what the others were doing down in the cave. Shiro's cough, Gregg's foot, John's swollen ear—it was too frightening to think about.

Beneath me I felt the ice sliding. Slipping onto my side, I brought an arm out in time to grab Pirate's knee. I pulled myself back against the rocks. My arms trembled from exhaustion. Pirate stared blankly out of his bag. His head turned slowly toward me with a groggy nodding motion. Was he slipping into a stupor? I wondered whether I looked as awful.

"It's no use here," I sighed.

I could barely keep myself up against the rocks. There was nothing I could do for Pirate. Maybe Dave had found a safe spot. I had to check the other side of the rocks, but that would be deserting Pirate. Yet there was no way I could help. How could I just leave him? I had to do something for myself!

"I'm going over." He didn't move. "Pirate," I yelled, "I'm going after Dave!"

His head shook from side to side as he half mumbled, half shouted, something I couldn't understand. I grabbed at the rock above me and pulled myself up the slope. Another rock; its sharp cold cut through the wool socks. Another pull. I reached the crest. To my tremendous relief I saw Dave crouched on the ice only about fifteen feet away. His back was toward me.

"Dave!" He couldn't hear me. I worked a little closer to him. The wind threatened to throw me off the crest. Beyond lay bare glacier where I'd never catch anything to hold onto if I was blown from the rocks.

"Dave!" This time he turned and saw me. I was out of breath and must have been gasping as much as yelling. "Is it better where you are?"

"What? . . . It's the same. Go back!"

I didn't want to go back, and waiting here on the crest was impossible because it was completely exposed to the wind. Before I'd decided which way to go, a crosscurrent gust caught me. I grabbed for rocks. One came loose. I caught another one nearer Dave. Somehow the sock on my left hand had blown off. I shoved the bare hand into my sleeping bag. The other hand held onto a rock. The wind flung and tossed my body as though it were weightless.

My right hand ached with cold from gripping the rock, and my forearm began cramping from the strain. I couldn't go back into the wind, but neither could my right hand cling to the rock much longer. The only other rock I could reach was three feet to my left, near Dave. My numb right hand had become so dead that I couldn't feel the rock it held onto. My shivering body seemed on the verge of going into convulsions.

I tried to think. If I lost my grip, I'd be blown across the ice. My mind was racing. I had to grab for the rock near Dave with my left hand: it was bare, no mitten or sock. It would be frozen. I had to. Suddenly, my bare hand shot out to grab the rock. Slicing cold.

I saw Dave's face, the end of his nose raw, frostbitten. His mouth, distorted into an agonized mixture of compassion and anger, swore at me to get a glove on. I looked at my hand. It was white, frozen absolutely white.

I pulled my body onto the rock. Dave was only five or six feet away on the ledge he had chopped in the slightly sloping ice.

"Christ, Art." His voice cracked. "You froze your hands!"

I pushed off from the rock, letting the wind throw me against Dave. He flung his arms around me. All I could do was lie across him, wheezing and shaking, trying to catch my breath.

"Man," he said, "we gotta dig in!"

17,200 Feet: Gregg, John, Shiro, George

GREGG'S JOURNAL

A frightening thing is developing. I roped in with Shiro to go up and see that the others were all right. When we reached the pass it was evident why they hadn't descended. The wind was howling like crazy. I tried to lead up to the pass but was turned back by the wind. Shiro went up and tried twice, but it was impossible. If we went one step too far it meant not getting back again.

Shiro said, "Three sleeping bags. They are in their sleeping bags." When we were just about back in camp he told me all he saw was one sleeping bag lying up against the rock and flapping in the wind. It's a bad situation . . . winds up to a hundred miles an hour, possibly more. It's a whiteout up there.

Those guys only had a bunch of lunch, one stove full of gas, a pot, their sleeping bags, and the parachute to cover themselves up. With their provisions and personal reserves they can probably last two more days at the longest. But practically speaking they have to make it down tonight or tomorrow morning at the latest.

On the bright side, they are the strongest of us. Dave and Art have plenty of experience. They're all tough as nails. Oh Lord, what anguish we are suffering for our friends' safety.

Later Shiro confided: "When I saw only one sleeping bag, I was certain they were dead."

Denali Pass: Art, Pirate, Dave

For more than an hour I clung to the ledge on the ice, feeling the frostbite blisters swell on my hands and watching help-lessly while Dave dug a cave in the ice. Just before he com-pleted it, Dave collapsed from exhaustion. By then Pirate had pulled himself together. Despite his hands and feet, which were beginning to swell with frostbite blisters, he had some-how made it over the crest and helped finish hollowing out the cave. Dave recovered enough strength to help me through the small hole in the ice which was the entrance to our new home.

"Dave," I said, "you know you saved us out there." My words sort of hung in the air. Dave bit at his lip self-consciously. I didn't say more, but my eyes followed Dave with admiration and a kind of love as he tucked Pirate into his bag and then reached for the stove.

Dave had quietly accepted the job of cooking because his were the only hands capable of working the stove. He had found some food to fix—four pound-and-a-half cans of ham, bacon, and peas which a previous expedition had cached among the rocks. Since our pot had blown away, he heated the ham in its own can, then used the can to melt water in.

Flattened against the wall, I realized how small our cave

was. At the wide end there was barely enough room for our shoulders. At the narrow end our feet in our sleeping bags were heaped on top of each other. Because of the rocks behind us, Dave and Pirate had been unable to make the cave long enough for us to stretch out completely. The ceiling was about a foot and a half above the floor. There was just enough height to turn or lie on our sides with one shoulder touching the ice on the floor and the other touching the ice on the ceiling. We were quickly learning that our every movement bumped the next person. This cave certainly wasn't pleasant or comfortable by ordinary standards, but it kept us safe from the wind, and that was all that mattered for the moment.

We had lost too much to the wind—the use of four hands and two feet, an incalculable amount of body warmth, two packs with half our food in them, the parachute, my wind parka, and—perhaps our greatest loss—the foam pads which would have insulated us from the ice and helped to keep our bags dry. Yet we felt secure. We had enough gas to make water for another day, maybe two more days if we stretched it. With four lunches left, and three remaining cans of food, we needn't worry about starving.

That night ham and hot water were a feast, not filling, but delicious nonetheless. It was our first warm food since leaving the cave down at 17,200 feet more than thirty hours before. My hands had become so inflexible that Dave had to place each bite of ham—there were five of them—in my mouth, then tip the can to my lips to let me drink. Eating made us giddy with pleasure and almost got us feeling warm.

We were actually exultant, not from any sense of conquering the wind, but rather from the simple companionship of huddling together in our little cave while outside in the darkness the storm raged through Denali Pass and on across the Alaska Range.

We figured the wind was funneling through the pass at 130 miles per hour or more. We remembered that a wind of such velocity, combined with the minus-thirty, minus-forty-five air temperature outside our cave, created an equivalent windchill temperature somewhere off the end of the chart. The last figure on the chart was minus one hundred and forty-eight.

"One hundred and forty-eight degrees below zero."

It was frightening to say, but the worst was over, we thought. In the morning the wind should slack off; we would descend, greet the others at 17,200 feet; tell them that we had made the summit. We would get off the mountain and go home. We wanted to believe the climb was over, that in a couple of days everything would be warm and easy again. Yet the wind, howling and pounding the slope overhead, reminded us that we couldn't move until it died down. We talked of the cave as our refuge, but the suspicion that we were being held captive in the ice must have entered each of our minds as we fell asleep listening to the wind.

March 2: "Light breaks where no sun shines."

17,200 Feet: Gregg, John, Shiro, George

GREGG'S JOURNAL, 9:30 A.M.

The nightmare goes on. They didn't show up last night. I can't believe this is happening. While they are still strong they must make a break for it, all three slowly. They must try. It is windy and white out this morning, very bad conditions. The irony of it: they are only one thousand feet above us, yet we can't help them.

Lord, I wish this nightmare would end. What a terrible ordeal they must be going through.

The waiting is hell. The wind stops, and you listen for

footsteps. I can't remember a more prolonged terror in my life. It is the damn quick changeable mountain weather that got us. When the wind dies down here, you can still hear it howling up above. . . . Nothing on the peak could hurt me once those guys come down.

Denali Pass: Art, Pirate, Dave

I slept restlessly, waking every time Dave's knees and shoulders pushed into me. Each time my mind started to clear, the thought that the wind might be down rushed up. But before I'd be fully awake the damnable roar would be running through my head. A shift of legs, or a roll to the other side—in any position the ice was too hard to be comfortable. Sleep made time pass, but the altitude caused a nervous wakefulness.

I looked forward to discussing a plan of action, then realized there was nothing to say. It was horribly simple. We would have to wait here until the wind stopped, at least until it died down. One sleepless hour after another we listened for the first lull.

During the morning the wind remained constant. The fluctuations in its monotonous tone were so slight that it reminded me of the perpetual roar inside a conch shell—only much, much louder. Later in the day, extraordinary blasts of wind hit the surface of the ice overhead with enough force to actually shake the roof of our cave, causing loose ice crystals to fall from the ceiling.

There was no joking, no idle conversation, hardly any talk at all. We retreated into ourselves, silent, waiting, staring at the ice on the ceiling, staring at the ice on the sides of the cave, staring into the darkness inside our sleeping bags.

I tried to think constructively, but it was useless. The altitude was heckling my mind—the same restless lightheadedness that was keeping me awake also prevented me from concentrating. Wandering thoughts always returned to the sound of the wind, and to the dreary question repeated continually—"When will it stop?"

The only event during the day that aroused any interest at all was our one meal. Dave, manning the stove again, thawed and melted more than he actually cooked. Patiently, he dropped chunks of snow and ice into the can, watched them melt, added more snow and ice, and finally—with what Pirate and I agreed was a stroke of genius—he dumped in a package of gorp. When the gorp became hot the chocolate bits melted into a fascinating brew, filled with cashews and raisins. Flavored partly with my considerable thirst, it was undoubtedly the best drink I had ever tasted. However, a curious, mildly unpleasant aftertaste remained.

About an hour after the hot drink, Dave served the rest of the ham. He heated it over the stove only long enough for it to thaw. Warming it would have meant wasting fuel, which we would need in case the wind held us here another day. Dave placed two pieces of ham, each about the size of an apricot, in my mouth, followed them with several slices of cheese and salami, and finished with three pieces of hard candy.

After another hour Dave melted enough snow and ice to fill the can with water. When it was warm he emptied a tiny can of chopped pork into the water to make a thin soup. Before I drank my portion I felt the need to relieve myself. Going outside was unthinkable.

"Dave," I asked, "isn't there a spare can we can use for a pee bottle?"

"Nope, Art," he answered. "All we've got is the cooking can."

"Then what did you use?"

"Well," Dave started uncertainly, "I thought you wouldn't eat or drink if I told you, but I used the cooking can."

Now I recognized the scent or flavor that had remained as an aftertaste—urine. It didn't matter. I thought it should, but it just didn't.

After Dave poured the last of the soup into me, I prepared to use the can myself—inside my sleeping bag. This would be the first thing I had attempted to accomplish with my swollen fingers; it was a task that even under more normal conditions required considerable technique. An accident would not only be unpleasant but disastrous as well. The extra liquid in my bag would consolidate the down, ruining its insulation.

I listened anxiously as the can began to fill. The liquid rapidly approached the rim, but in the nick of time I managed to maneuver out of my predicament and looked about for a place to empty the can. Not finding a suitable spot to my left and realizing Dave was guarding against my dumping it to my right, I raised the can precariously over my head and sloshed its contents against the ice behind me. Most of it melted in, but a little stream trickled under my bag. No matter, it would be frozen in seconds.

Dave calmly observed that my performance of holding the can was so skillful that I could damn well feed myself from now on.

Even though he lay only four feet from me, I could barely hear Pirate's voice above the wind. The altitude had cut off his exuberance and made him a shadow of his old self. When I asked Dave if Pirate was all right, he said that Pirate was worried about his feet, which had become worse than his hands. The swelling had leveled off, Dave told me, but most of his toes were insensitive to touch.

One particularly excruciating aspect of waiting was knowing that the longer we were held down the worse our frostbite would be. As our bodies began to dry up as a result of an inadequate liquid intake, they became more difficult to warm. Dave's toes were cold, but he didn't complain because he thought that was a good sign; better that they feel cold than numb. Only Dave and I had down booties, yet we had to frequently wiggle our toes to keep the circulation flowing through them. I considered lending my booties to Pirate, but the thought of my feet freezing while I slept held me back.

My main concern was my hands, which were swollen to nearly twice their normal size. To flex the tips of my fingers I had to painfully clench the muscles in my hand and forearm. I recalled the last time I had played my flute before leaving for McKinley. I had watched my fingers run over the keys. I had wanted to appreciate them in case I lost them. I had promised myself that this wouldn't happen. Now, I caught myself wondering if I would still be able to play my flute with the first and second joints of my fingers missing.

The others down below would be running short of food soon. Maybe they would have to retreat down the mountain. I asked Dave whether he thought the others had given up on us. He didn't answer; maybe he was asleep. Surely they'd come looking for us when the wind died down.

That night, long after it was dark, I found myself repeating the words of a Dylan Thomas poem: "Light breaks where no sun shines." Before I'd come on McKinley I had known the verses by heart; now I couldn't remember past "Where no sea runs the waters of the heart push in their tides." Further on there was something about the things of light filing through the flesh. That first line—"Light breaks where no sun shines"— ran over and over in my mind.

I lay a long time in the dark, unable to sleep. The wind, a persistent, audible ache in our heads, had been with us for so long that its incessant sounds were like a silence that had settled over our lives. That silent, paralytic quality in the wind recalled images of unalterable bleakness. I remembered seeing the wind run through the broken windows of an abandoned cabin, the wind in the dried grass of a beach in November after the birds had migrated, the wind over a frozen river.

I couldn't remember what it was like not to hear the wind, but the three of us knew that if we heard it in the morning, our situation would become critical. There appeared to be only enough gas to melt one more can of water.

Through more than thirty-six hours the wind had not even for a moment relinquished its hold on the mountain and on our lives. Surely, we reassured ourselves, the wind's force would be diminished by morning.

17,200 Feet: Gregg, John, Shiro, George

GREGG'S JOURNAL, 6 P.M.

It is nearly dark. Nasty weather all day—too bad for them to descend. If it is nice tomorrow, we will all go up to the pass. If not, John and I will try to make it to the radio at 7,600 feet. It would be a long day, especially in bad weather.

I hate splitting the party when there are only four of us here. Please, God, can't this weather end? What a hell this has been, and is. If the weather lasts for two more days, Shiro and George should come down too! There will be no hope for those above. Please God, don't let this happen. I surely must be dreaming. Can't the weather break, and the others show up, no matter how badly off they are, and then we can all go down together?

March 3: "Pieces are coming off my bad ear!"

Denali Pass: Art, Pirate, Dave

The infernal noise filled our heads.

The wind's vicious, I told myself. It's diabolical. Silently cursing it became a pastime. I tried to think of all the words that described its evil nature—fiendish, wicked, malicious. I called it a vampire sucking the life out of us.

But the wind didn't hear me, and I knew my words were irrelevant anyway. The wind wasn't malevolent; it wasn't out to get us; it had no evil intentions, nor any intentions at all. It was simply a chunk of sky moving about. It was a weather pattern, one pressure area moving into another.

Still, it was more satisfying, somehow more comforting, to personify the wind, make it something I could hate or respect, something I could shout at. I wished I were an old Eskimo shaman, seeing devils and demons in the storm and understanding the evil spirits that lived in the mountain. I thought that a good shaman would know how to chase away the wind. But I didn't know any magic. And I knew all my cursing was only an attempt to escape the simple facts. We had to descend. We couldn't descend in the wind. And the wind showed no sign of letting up.

We needed water most desperately. There was very little gas left in the stove; I wanted Dave to melt ice with it. I tried pleasant ways of reminding him that we needed to drink, but whatever I said he growled at. I knew he felt the strain of having to do all the chores for Pirate and me. I felt too thankful, too dependent, almost too much at the mercy of Dave to pester him about the water. He told me that "later" he would melt some ice and thaw the bacon or peas, but gradually the day slipped by without our eating or drinking. The altitude was cutting away our motivation. It was so much easier to say "later." Though we didn't really believe it, we always thought the wind might suddenly stop, letting us run down to the cave at 17,200 feet.

It was toward the middle of the afternoon when I heard Dave beginning to coax the stove back to life. He fiddled with it for several minutes without any luck, then decided to let it sit while he opened one of the large cans of bacon, ham, or peas.

It was the moment I had waited for all day.

"Which one do we want first?" he asked.

"Mix 'em all together," Pirate suggested.

Dave scraped the ice off the can of bacon with his knife, cleaning the top so he could open it. I could already taste the bacon.

"Damn!" Dave swore in disgust. "Holes in the can! We can't eat the bacon! It's rotten!"

He reached for a can of peas.

It couldn't happen again. Those holes had been an accident. Still Pirate and I listened intently as Dave cleared the ice from the can of peas.

When only about half the ice was off, he swore again. More holes! Then he tried the ham, our last can. It was the same!

We sank back into a numb depression. For two days we had anticipated the flavor of the bacon. We had let ourselves dream of the juice of the peas in our mouths. Suddenly the food we had counted on was gone. The gnawing cramps in our stomachs weren't going to be quieted.

Immediately, we were angry for being cheated. Only after several minutes did we realize how the spoiled food had transformed our hunger into a confrontation with starvation. We had almost nothing left to eat—three bags of gorp, a dozen slices of cheese, some hard candies, a little coffee, a three-ounce can of chopped pork, and maybe a dozen cookies. The combined calorie count of our remaining food was probably adequate for one person for one day. Solemnly, Dave divided a little less than half of the remaining food into three equal portions.

Dave battled with the stove long after his fingers were insensitive from handling the cold metal, but he failed to get it going. There was so little gas left that he couldn't build up enough pressure to vaporize it. At thirty below the gas was sluggish. He had to give up. Just like the punctured cans of food, our last drops of gas mocked us with their uselessness.

Our one hope was a gallon of gas Dave had cached on the far side of Denali Pass when he had climbed McKinley three years earlier. It might still be there; Dave had spotted the bottle of gas the first day we had tried for the summit. He thought we should take a look. But no one volunteered to go out. He said the gas was only about two hundred feet from where we lay. No one moved. Dave was the most fit to go out and the most certain of the place it was cached. But the horror of entering the wind overcame any inclination Dave might have had to go after it.

We tried to imagine what the others at 17,200 were doing. We hoped they wouldn't attempt anything rash for our sake— that the strain of their fear for us wouldn't break them. We thought of the gallon of gas. We imagined how delicious a cup of water would taste. We shifted our hips and shoulders to relieve the hard cold beneath us.

We talked very little. The grayness inside the cave faded into darkness.

17,200 Feet to 14,400 Feet: Gregg and John Descend

JOHN'S JOURNAL

We decided that Gregg and I should go down to 14,400 feet and then on to the radio to call for a helicopter overflight, or for Sheldon to fly over Denali Pass to drop fuel. George and Shiro will stay at 17,200 feet.

Set out about noon into heavy wind. Said thanks to Shiro and good-bye to George. Not a great deal of response from either—dozing.

Not too cold, much blowing sandy snow in eyes. Severe, buffeting winds down buttress made going very difficult. As usual, concern that the crampons would come loose, but they held.

Near the gendarme above sixteen thousand feet Gregg wrenched his ankle. We encountered terrible winds here and had to cling to the ridge rocks to save from being blown off our feet. Sometimes the wind blew up, sometimes down, unpredictable. Very difficult to maintain balance. On hands and knees to the fixed ropes in a screeching wind. I anchored Gregg, but this was not much use since I had Dave's ice axe, which had lost its point.

Gregg moved slowly on his bad ankle. The pace was just right. Both exhausted by the time we reached the igloos.

Pieces are coming off my bad ear.

March 4: Delusion

Denali Pass: Art, Dave, Pirate

I woke elated. The wind had stopped. I heard a helicopter.

Just outside the cave I heard the steady whir. Gregg must have gotten a rescue started. It sounded as if the copter had already landed. People must be searching the pass for us. I was afraid they wouldn't find our cave; it was such a small hole in the ice. Maybe they'd give up and leave.

"Dave!" I rolled toward him. "Dave, do you hear the helicopter? We'd better get outside right away."

"Go to sleep . . . it's the wind."

"No! It can't be. It's too steady, too constant. It's a copter. . . . Dave. . . ."

He didn't answer.

"It's a copter," I repeated to myself. "It's the steady whir of a copter." I listened to be certain; but I wasn't certain. Maybe it was the wind; it couldn't be. I almost asked Dave to listen; but I knew he was right; yet I strained my ears for a voice, any sound that would let me believe there were rescuers outside.

There was only the wind.

After a long silence Dave admitted that he had been susceptible to my delusion; he had convinced himself for several minutes that the sound of the wind really was a rescue helicopter.

"But you know," Dave said, looking toward me, "it makes you feel kind of humble to know a helicopter couldn't possibly get to us."

Dave went on to explain how he felt good to know that no device could reach us.

He said the three of us were alone and that our only security lay in ourselves, in our individual abilities to endure, and in our combined willpower and judgment.

I said, "Dave, it may sound funny, but I feel closer to you than ever before."

Dave beamed and said, "Yea, I know what you mean. If we can't fight our way out of this storm, at least we can stick together, and try to live in harmony with it."

I thought to myself how the storm itself was helping to protect us from its own fury.

For millions of years the wind had been packing the snow and ice of Denali Pass into contours of least resistance. We were sheltered inside ice that conformed to the pattern of the wind. We had nearly succumbed to the storm that first morning when we had fought it head on in the open. Now the force

of the wind pounded more stability into the roof of our cave
as it swept across the slope above us.

The altitude riddled our attention span into fragments of
thoughts. Discomfort was the only thing on which my mind
seemed able to concentrate. My lips were deeply cracked in
several places. Moving my tongue along the roof of my mouth
I felt clumps of dried-up mucus. I knew that if I didn't get
water soon, the rawest areas in my mouth would begin bleeding. The ligaments in my legs ached as they dried up. It was
especially painful to stretch or change positions; unfortunately, the hardness of the ice made my hips and back sore
whenever I remained still for more than a few minutes.

I complained very little, not because I was naturally stoic,
but because there was no one to complain to. Each of us experienced the same discomforts. Pain had become a natural condition of our life under the ice.

I was probably warmer than either Dave or Pirate because
their sleeping bags were icing up faster than mine. Every time
Dave cooked, steam from the warm liquid was absorbed into
his bag, where it froze. I didn't see how his bag could retain
any warmth. Pirate's wasn't much better. Against Dave's
advice and mine, he persisted in burying his head in his bag,
where his exhaled moisture had no escape and quickly froze.

All of us sorely missed the foam pads. Without them, we
were only able to place a spare wind parka or pair of wind
pants under our buttocks and shoulders, leaving the rest of
our sleeping bags on bare ice.

Pirate's hands were swollen, but he said he was worried
most about his feet. He asked about my down booties.
Though he didn't say it outright, I could tell he wanted to
wear them. I tried to ignore him, acting as if I hadn't heard.
My feet were cold inside the booties; without them they
would surely freeze. Of course, that was exactly what was

happening to Pirate's feet. He knew I didn't want to give them up and didn't ask again. As he kicked his feet inside his bag to relieve their numbness, I knew he must be thinking of the warmth of my booties. Pretending to be asleep, I tried to forget about Pirate's feet.

I couldn't remember how many days we had been in the cave. The day we had gone to the summit, then that first day of the wind, the day we ate ham, then a day without water—it must have been the fourth day, but I was uncertain.

Sometime during the middle of the day Dave rationed us each a fig bar and two hard candies. Sucking on the candies brought a few minutes of relief to the rawness in my mouth. I put the fig bar aside for later. After about an hour I couldn't wait any longer. I had looked forward to saliva coming back into my mouth but as I chewed the fig bar, the crumbs stuck to the gums and roof of my mouth. With some effort I swallowed the sticky wad, feeling it tumble into my stomach, where it set off a series of cramps. The pain constructed a morbidly amusing picture of four or five hands in my stomach grabbing for the fig bar, fighting each other for it, tearing and ripping at it.

Early in the afternoon it became obvious that we were going to spend another night in the cave. Even if the wind let up toward evening, we wouldn't have the time, nor perhaps the strength, to descend. Our dehydration was becoming critical. We hadn't drunk a cup of liquid for more than thirty-six hours. The lack of fluids was one reason we were all cold inside our bags even with our parkas and wind pants on. Occasionally, I could feel Dave's body tense and shake with shivers. We needed water, which meant we needed gas—which we didn't have.

The only possibility was the gas Dave had cached at Denali Pass three years before. If one of us went for the gallon of gas, he might not make it back through the wind to the cave. The gruesome reality of this possibility had kept us from retrieving the gas. But there was no longer an alternative. One of us had to go for the gas! Who? I couldn't go because of my hands, so I lay quietly in my bag, letting my silence ask someone else to go.

Dave resisted the thought of his going. He had dug the cave. He had cooked for us. He knew his efforts had kept Pirate and me alive. And we knew it.

It wasn't right that Dave go out to possibly disappear in the wind. Yet, knowing Dave, I sensed he was struggling with his weariness and fear to find it in himself to go out. Since he was the only one of us who knew for certain where the gas should be, it was logical that he go. Neither Pirate nor I could ask him. Semiconscious from the altitude and the numbing hypnotism of the wind, we still retained some sense of justice.

There was another reason we weren't anxious for Dave to go. He was our hands! We needed him to cook if we ever got some gas. We would need him to tie the rope around us and hold us on belay when we descended, whenever that might be.

Quietly—I don't remember hearing him say he would go— Pirate got out of his sleeping bag. When he started to pull on his boots, he found it difficult and painful to force his swollen feet into his boots. I offered him the use of my down booties. He took them and quickly had them tied on. Dave described the rocks where the gas had been cached. Pirate pulled down his face mask.

The wind had become more erratic. There were gusts and then short—ten- to thirty-second—lulls of comparative calm. Pirate lay on his stomach, facing the entrance, listening for the lull that sounded right to him. Suddenly, he gave a short and not too loud "Arahhaa!" and began squirming out the entrance, uphill, through loose snow. For a moment we heard Pirate placing the pack across the entrance again. Then the lull ended abruptly, and all we heard was the wind.

For the longest time Dave and I listened without saying a word. Ten, fifteen minutes passed. We knew Pirate should have returned, but we said nothing. He might call for help only ten feet from the cave and we'd never hear him. I couldn't help imagining what we'd have to do if he failed to return. Maybe Dave would make a try for the gas. Maybe the two of us would attempt to dash down from the pass. If Pirate didn't return within a few minutes there would be no reason to go looking for him.

We heard a movement at the entrance. Two immediate whoops of sheer joy expressed our relief. A flurry of snow, then a plastic jug shot into the cave, followed by an exhausted Pirate.

"Bad!" He was gasping. "I couldn't stand up, even in the lulls. Something's wrong with my balance." I had never before heard Pirate say anything was rough or dangerous. "I crawled all the way, clawing into the ice with two ice axes. I can't feel my feet now."

We had gas! We could drink water!

With a merriment we'd forgotten ever existed Dave melted chunks of ice and piles of snow. In the excitement of the moment we forgot why the first can of water tasted sweet.

Dave heated can after can of water till they became hot. We drank, and drank, and always waited for yet another canful. For the first time in five days we went to sleep with full stomachs. That we were only full of water mattered not at all—or so we thought.

My feet had become colder. I had to constantly wiggle my toes to keep them from becoming numb. Still, I was glad I had not asked Pirate to return my booties after his trip for the gas.

14,400 Feet: Gregg and John

GREGG'S JOURNAL

Damn, we are still here. . . . It is just too nasty out to move. . . . It is harder to sit than it is to move at this point. The waiting is terrible. But to move now might complete the destruction of the party. No, we must wait until we are reasonably sure we can make 10,200 feet at least.

I try hard to forget the situation that the three above are in, but it is a gnawing, sickening thought that won't go away.

March 5: "Hope gives out for the three above."

17,200 Feet: George and Shiro

GEORGE'S REPORT

The wind is still making a noise like Niagara Falls, just like a big body of water going over the rocks. All kinds of things enter our minds, one of which is: what could we do even if we did find the three above and they need help? Because of the altitude and the steep slope below Denali Pass we don't think we could carry them down on our backs. It is a very helpless feeling and a helpless situation.

The time has become more or less critical, and we just don't have the slightest hope. We don't discuss it. . . . Invariably this situation is a transition between life and death. It is so difficult to imagine somebody who was with you such a short time ago and is helpless up higher and we can't help them.

Invariably the picture of Farine comes to mind. The night we left him on the glacier he was still Farine—warm—and the next day he was just a frozen body, like a piece of ice. Things like this go through our minds.

Descending from 14,400 Feet to 8,000 Feet:
John and Gregg

JOHN'S JOURNAL

The first one awake went out of igloo to look at weather. To my surprise and relief, found clear sky, blowing snow. A quick breakfast, and away by 9:45. I fumbled with knots and had difficulty with frostbitten fingertips. Ear is raw. An overheavy pack—around sixty-five or seventy pounds.

Quiet around Windy Corner, to our great surprise and relief. Pleasant down to 12,500-foot cache of ill memory. Goldline rope snaking over snow, blue wind trouser, white boots, whip of rope marks on snow. Gregg's ankle giving some trouble. A bad time on steep pitch above Peters glacier. I came off. Gregg arrested, then I slid again. No control with too heavy pack and general malaise.

When we reached deep snow, we traveled very slowly. Both with headlamps, both fatigued, somewhat bewildered and uncertain, but anxious to get to 7,500 feet. Step by step, sometimes falling. Great effort to get up again. Some of the weight of the pack was due to a great deal of ice in the sleeping bag.

Finally decided to stop around 10 p.m.—not sure of our position. Are we above or beyond the 7,500-foot camp? I was extremely fatigued. Gregg was also extremely tired. I could barely carry the pack another step: Gregg dug out a cave in very soft snow.

Not at all certain of the prospects for the next day. Roaring still over Denali Pass and hope gives out for the three above.

Denali Pass: Art, Pirate, Dave

We woke to another cold, gray morning under the ice. The ragged end of the storm seemed to be blowing itself out. Had we been strong we might have tried to dash down from the pass immediately. We had become so weak that the wind would have to be completely gone before we could descend.

Yet, regardless of the wind this had to be our last day in the cave. By the next morning there would be no food at all. The three of us had only a handful of gorp, four slices of cheese, and three little hard candies. When this food ran out the cold would take over our bodies.

We lay silent and brooding in our bags. Cheerless as our situation was, I felt a curious sense of relief that it was so simple—without food, it was either descend or perish in this wretched cave.

Some loose, fine-grained crystals had sifted into Pirate's sleeping bag. The bag had so little warmth that the snow lay in it without melting. Pirate stared at the snow for ten or fifteen seconds, then mumbled hoarsely that he'd leave the snow in his bag because it might help insulate him. His reasoning sounded absurd. I thought of telling him to get the snow out of his bag as fast as he could. But it was easier to lie silent than begin talking. Then I began wondering whether Pirate might be right about the snow helping to insulate him. His bag and Dave's were now little more than matted down and chunks of ice held together by the nylon shell.

Because the entrance wasn't tightly closed off from the storm, a steady draft circulated the minus-thirty-five-degree air through our cave. With the chill factor increased, I began shivering again. This wasn't particularly painful, but it was unnerving to watch my body shaking uncontrollably. What happens after you lose control of your body? I thought of asking Dave, but said nothing.

My thoughts wandered back to my childhood. I recalled my parents saying that when I was first learning to walk I enjoyed toddling around in the snow naked. I remembered the times when I was eight or nine and we'd run out into the spring windstorms that sweep across the plains of eastern Colorado; with bales of straw we built shelters from the driving wind and dust, and considered ourselves pioneers.

In those days it had been great fun to run shouting from tree to tree in a thunderstorm or when the rain turned to hailstones the size of marbles and golf balls. How had those games in storms led to the desperate mess the three of us were in?

All I wanted now was to be free of the fear of freezing and being buried under the ice. I started imagining what we'd look like frozen solid. The feel of my mouth on Farine's cold lips came back. I saw his last expression frozen in his cheeks and eyelids. How much of a body could be frozen before the heart stopped? This wouldn't happen to us, not to me. Yet, there was the cold creeping into our bodies through our hands and feet.

To get these thoughts out of my mind, I asked Dave if the gusts were becoming less powerful. He said, "Don't think about it." But I couldn't help being attentive to every fluctuation of the wind, even though it was depressing to hear every lull end in a blast of wind.

Only food occupied our thoughts as much as the wind, especially the food in the punctured cans. Those cans haunted us. I felt the little holes staring at me whether the cans were in plain sight or hidden under a sleeping bag or out the entrance. After Dave had emptied the cans of their contents, he classified most of the food as definitely rotten, but there remained at least a pound of peas and a half pound of ham that he thought might be edible. He even thawed and heated some of the ham. It didn't smell or look bad. Still, it had come from a partly spoiled can.

"Aw, I'm going to eat it," Pirate insisted.

But we wouldn't let him. Weak as we were, food poisoning would do us in. As long as we could resist the canned food we had a chance. If we gave in and ate the tainted ham and peas we might eliminate that chance. Of course, the food might be

good, and it might provide the extra strength we would need
to get down.

As our stomachs tightened with cramps and the deafening
repetition of gusts and lulls whittled away our patience, each
of us changed our minds about eating the canned food. One
moment Pirate would declare he was going to eat the ham,
and the next he would be restraining Dave or me from trying
it. So far we had been able to check ourselves. But every
moment of hunger increased the temptation.

There was enough gas to make as much water as we could
drink. However, Dave had only enough energy to make a
minimal amount. As our dehydration continued, our frostbite
became more severe. The swelling in my fingers had started
to go down. I didn't know whether this was a sign of improvement or an indication that my body simply didn't have
enough liquid to keep the swelling up. Much as I worried over
the blisters, I realized they were my body's way of trying to
save the tissue that had been frozen.

Dave couldn't feel the large toe on his right foot, nor parts
of several other toes. There was so little he could do for his
feet—rub them, wiggle the toes. He said they were becoming
steadily colder. The scabby, frostbitten skin on the end of his
nose was sickening to look at, but not as frightening as the
freezing in his feet. The frostbite on his nose was isolated,
while the frostbite taking hold in his feet was a sign that the
cold was steadily creeping into his body. It was happening to
each of us.

At times I was surprised that I wanted Pirate to continue
wearing my down booties, which I had once guarded so self-
ishly. I knew I hadn't lost my desire to survive, but now Pirate
was sort of included in it. Since his feet had suffered on his
trip to get the gas, I had felt almost as protective toward his
feet as toward my own. Later in the day Pirate passed one

bootie back to me. Perhaps one bootie each would not be a practical way to halt the freezing in our feet, but it was still the most touching thing I had ever seen Pirate do.

During the first days of the wind, sleep had been an effective way of waiting. Now it had become a continual twisting of hips and shoulders away from the hardness of the ice, a twisting away from the cold that seeped into our bags from the ice beneath. None of us had even a momentary respite from hunger cramps and the cramps and aches in our dried-up ligaments and muscles. Nevertheless, wakefulness continued to be a worse kind of half consciousness. Pain is felt more acutely when you are awake. And we realized that we weren't dreaming, that we were not going to wake up to find everything friendly and warm.

At times I was unable to tell for certain whether I was awake or asleep. Dreams of Farine lying on the ice, of John calling from the bottom of that crevasse, of Shiro coughing, of our hands and feet turning black, filled my sleep and drifted over into the different levels of wakefulness that stretched through the day. Hours no longer existed. I once asked Dave how long we had been trapped under the ice; he said he didn't know.

Late in the afternoon, it seemed as though the wind was finally dying. The lulls had become much longer, maybe as long as five or six minutes. The gusts no longer hit with the force that had shaken our cave for so many days. I dozed fitfully, then woke in the dark to a strange sound. I was startled. To ears that had become unaccustomed to silence, the silence sounded nearly as deafening as the wind's roar that first morning.

"Dave, the wind's gone! We can descend!"

"Yea, man, I'm cooking us up a farewell dinner to this awful hole," Dave said.

In a moment his headlamp flicked on, and I heard the cheery purr of the stove. It was all over, we thought. We had made it through. Our farewell dinner was a farewell to the very last of our food, to the cave, and, we hoped, to the wind. Dave passed the hot water and divided up the four slices of cheese.

March 6: "We try to avoid the sentiments of death."

14,400 to 10,200 Feet: George, Shiro

GEORGE'S REPORT

We headed down: There was no trouble until we hit Windy Corner—then suddenly the wind was very severe again. We just barely made it down to the beginning of the basin below the corner. From there it was easier though it was late.

It was a condition of despair under which we climbed down. Looking at personal belongings of Art, Dave, and Pirate we just can't help discussing it again. There is a flicker of hope—as anyone would have hope—but logically we reject the possibility that any of the three could come down alive.

It just isn't real; it is very difficult to describe. Actually, the more we think about it the more agonizing it becomes. In conversation with one another we try to avoid the sentiments of death.

8,500 Feet: John, Gregg

GREGG'S JOURNAL:

What a fight! Woke up in partial whiteout and spent till noon finding the igloo. Then went back over the knee-deep snowshoe track to get our packs. It was about all I could do.

Dug out the igloo when we arrived, and at least had some

food. We didn't have a drink this morning, so we were really dehydrated. We only found four wands above the snow. The rest were buried. If it hadn't been for some long bamboo poles Ray picked up in Anchorage we would never have found this place. It was completely buried.

Bad weather is predicted for twenty-four to twenty-six hours. I hope it's a lie. Thank God we are here. I hope God is as kind to Shiro and George. I hope to the Lord the others are safe, but I can't imagine much hope for them after a week. . . .

Denali Pass: Art, Pirate, Dave

In the gray light and quietness we anxiously prepared to leave the cave, but it took us several hours to get ready. Dave melted ice. Pirate was a long time cramming his swollen feet into his boots. My feet and Dave's weren't as swollen, but during the night we had both lost feeling in several toes. With my hands still mostly useless, I relied on Dave to stuff my feet into my boots, then lace them up.

Keyed up by our departure, we felt more alert than we had at any time since the first day of the wind. I made a mental note to be damn careful if we had to make an important decision.

We weren't really worried. There was no wind. After sticking out the storm, we felt there was nothing we couldn't do. In a few hours we'd reach 17,300 feet. We might descend all the way to the 14,400-foot igloos before nightfall. It was going to be great to walk in on the others. They had probably given up on us by now. A new excitement quickened our movements. We were going down, going home! Dave was the first outside. With one word he cut short all our excitement.

"Whiteout!"

"Whiteout." The word hung in the air. We had never

considered the possibility of a whiteout after the wind. Dave could see only twenty to thirty feet. A mile of ice stretched between us and the 17,200-foot camp, if we took a direct course. The slope below us fell away through forty or fifty square miles of heavily crevassed glacier. Blinded by the whiteout, we might wander about the ice forever, or until we collapsed, or walked off an edge, or fell into a crevasse.

We hoped the whiteout was merely a small, passing cloud that would sift away in an hour or two. We dreaded to think of what would become of us if the whiteout proved to be the beginning of another storm.

I followed Pirate out of the cave only to see his hunched form stumble into Dave, who was also unable to straighten his back. For a moment I watched the two lean against each other like drunks trying to maintain their balance. A mist of ice crystals crept silently over the rocks behind them.

With short, painful jerks of his head, Pirate twisted his face up to look Dave in the eye: "Dave," he said in a hoarse whisper, "I think I'm too weak to go down."

For the first time since the night we had pulled Farine out of the crevasse, Dave's face went blank with shock. It wasn't Pirate's words that rattled him. In the half light of our cave we had been unable to see one another clearly. Now nothing was hidden. Pirate's appearance was appalling. It was as if he had emerged from the cave twenty years older. His voice was that of an old man. His face was furrowed with lines we had never seen before. His eyes were faded and glazed and sunk back into their sockets.

I felt shaky getting to my hands and knees and was unable to stand on my feet without Dave's help. I tumbled over with the first step I tried, hitting the ice with my shoulder to avoid falling onto my swollen hands.

None of us had a sense of balance. Our legs were dried up

and stiff from lying immobile for days. We practiced walking, but it took ten or fifteen minutes of stretching and limbering up before we regained enough coordination to walk in a relatively straight line.

To be able to walk again was an achievement, but hardly a consolation. Even if the whiteout cleared, we didn't have nearly enough balance to climb down the hundreds of yards of steep ice that separated us from 17,200 feet. Yet waiting in the cave would be suicide. One more day without food would certainly leave us without enough strength to descend.

Dave grew nervous. Pirate leaned against a rock and mumbled to himself. We began to voice wild plans for escaping the pass. We discussed the possibility of just Dave and I trying to make it out. Pirate said he'd wait by himself in the cave until we could get a rescue party to him. Assistance couldn't reach him for at least two days, and that would be too late.

Then I said I wanted to try it alone. I reasoned that if I made it down I could send help. If I didn't make it Dave and Pirate would still have a chance if the weather cleared.

How easy it might have been if I could have fully deceived myself. I knew my reasons for a solo descent were excuses to conceal my desire to save Art Davidson above all else. Fear was stripping away loyalty to the others. I didn't want Dave or Pirate to see my ruthless self-centeredness. But then, wasn't this need to save myself a sense of self-preservation? And wasn't this healthy, even necessary?

As I began to feel panicky, my eyes glanced swiftly over the ice and rocks and at the whiteness all around us. Dave looked at me. Pirate appeared lost in his thoughts. I didn't know what to say. Despite my desire to try it alone, that other sense of being unalterably bound to Dave and Pirate persisted. Maybe this inclination to stick it out with the others was only a reaction to loneliness, but perhaps it was some-thing deep and basic that I couldn't violate.

My fingers began to throb and my head felt light. I didn't seem to have control of my thoughts. I wanted to take off by myself, but I couldn't abandon Dave and Pirate. I had to save myself at any cost. But I wouldn't be alive now if it hadn't been for Dave and Pirate. What good was there in perishing together? If I had a better chance of making it alone, shouldn't I forget about Dave and Pirate and take off without them?

I felt I had to scream or run across the ice. To relieve my tension I looked at the different shades of grayness that walled us in.

Dave said we ought to hold off deciding what to do. The whiteout might clear. I nodded. Pirate looked at the hole in the ice that was our cave's entrance.

Clouds clung to the pass, filtering the sun's light into a bleak variety of flat grays and whites. An eerie quietness had settled over the mountain; soundless and still, it seemed impossible that this was the same pass the wind had stormed through. The sky that had been terrifyingly alive hung around us lifelessly. The entire range, that had seemed like some sort of living being trying to get at us, was now only a frozen waste of ice and rock.

Hiding under the ice from all the fury, I'd felt closed in. Now, standing outside in the stillness of the whiteout, I began to feel claustrophobic, as if I were being smothered along with the mountain and all the peaks around us. The whiteout had cut us off from the world. The sky was gone. We had only our little island of light in this immense grayness.

Pirate said we had to do something. We continued to stare into the cloud, hoping it would break open to let us descend. *Hoping*—we had come to understand it so well that it had lost much of its meaning; to hope was to ignore the reality of our situation in favor of a wishful belief that some stroke of luck would befall us. No one could come for us through this white-out. I berated myself for ever hoping. I warned myself never to hope again. Faith was what I needed. I needed faith that this whiteout, like any stretch of foul weather, would eventually end, and faith that we'd have the presence of mind and stamina to take advantage of that moment when it came.

I told Dave we'd be lost if we stopped believing in ourselves. He looked puzzled and said, "Huh?"

Several minutes later I realized I was once again staring at the clouds, hoping they'd part. Weary of waiting for the whiteout to clear we searched among the rocks for food—a cache someone else might have left behind or some of our own supplies that had been blown away—but found nothing. We stood at the edge of the pass, looking down toward the 17,200-foot camp. Through the grayness I tried to picture Gregg, Shiro, John, and George camped in the cave, waiting patiently for a chance to look for us. Then I remembered they would have run out of food by now. Yet surely they hadn't left us.

For many minutes no one spoke. All our mountaineering experience told us that we should not descend into the whiteout because we would almost certainly lose our way. Or weak and without a sense of balance, we would fall. At the same time, we were certain of what was in store for us if we waited in the cave.

Hours had slipped by since we had first crawled out of the cave. Although the lateness of the hour was beginning to force us to make up our minds, every alternative still appeared futile. It seemed absurd to choose.

Our situation demanded a degree of thoughtfulness that we probably didn't have. The most frustrating part of having our minds addled by the altitude was not knowing how badly we were affected. As our minds sunk into a dull stupor, the less we realized we were losing our ability to think clearly.

At length, it became apparent that our best chance was trying to make it down as soon as possible. We couldn't wait for the whiteout to clear. And crawling back into the cave would be crawling into our grave.

Dave said we'd better get our crampons on. Pirate said OK. I didn't say anything.

Dave and Pirate headed back to get our crampons. As they passed the scattered ruins of an old cache, I called to ask if they'd checked it for food. With food, just a bit of food, our decision would be easy. We'd go back to the cave, eat, and get a little strength back in our bodies.

Pirate said they had looked and hadn't found a thing to eat. He plowed through the rubble again—a shredded tarp, torn clothes, silverware, all sorts of things we couldn't eat. The cache might have been left by Washburn, but twenty years of storms and curious climbers had left it a trash heap half buried in the ice.

After a minute or two, Pirate stopped searching and looked at me without speaking. I asked if he'd found anything.

"No." Very slowly, he turned and went to get his crampons.

I stood in a daze, not wanting to do anything. Then, staring at the cache, I heard Shiro's voice as clearly as if he'd been standing next to me. "Art, when there is only one way to survive in the mountains, you must check every possibility to the very end in order to find the one that works."

Shiro had told me this before on a summer expedition. The cache was a possibility. Just possibly some food remained hidden at the bottom of the rubbish. I resisted Shiro's words. The cache was forty feet away. Forty feet uphill. I stood still with neither the will or strength to move.

Shiro's words kept repeating themselves in my mind. I could hear his gentle voice. "You can't give up halfway . . . you have to check every possibility to the very end."

I resisted. Checking the cache again was a waste of energy.

Then I was suddenly walking toward the cache. To get a grip on my ice axe I had to force my swollen hands around the shaft. I didn't care if the blisters broke—I was going to dig.

I attacked the ice where it held the canvas tarp. With the first strike, my hands revolted in pain and I dropped the axe. The tarp hadn't budged. I picked up the axe, and by the time I had swung a couple more times I was in a frenzy. I slashed and beat at the canvas frozen into the ice. I pried and yanked. Hitting with my axe as hard as I could, I must have struck a rock, because the axe's metal adze broke.

I became furious. I couldn't stop. I smashed at the pieces of wood, lashing out with my axe until I collapsed onto my knees. I was out of breath and dizzy, but as soon as my head began to clear I started swinging at the debris again. Still on my knees, I uncovered bits of rotten rope, pots, old socks, ladles, odd boots, and of all the absurd, useless luxuries there was even a colander.

I attacked the cache, driven by an obsession to reach the bottom of it. My hands throbbed with pain and my feet had become numb. But all that mattered was that I check every last inch of the trash. A rage drove me to see what was underneath. When I discovered another layer, I was careful not to destroy anything. I opened a box, but it was full of clothes.

I kicked some of the surface junk aside with my boots, then dug in again with my axe. Ice and splintered wood and strips of canvas were frozen around each other. I grabbed and yanked and kicked, and swung the axe. Eventually I reached another unopened box. I pried it open: more clothes on top, but underneath lay several cloth bags, small, white bags.

Excited and exhausted, I felt my heart beating wildly as I fumbled to see what was in one of the bags. The drawstring came loose, and as I looked into the bag I'm certain I would have cried, if my body had had enough fluid to spare for tears.

Dried potatoes!

Farther inside the crate sat a box of raisins packaged in a wrapper that had gone out of style at least fifteen years ago! I found two more bags of potatoes and even uncovered a can of ham without holes in it!

We ate!

Far into the night Dave brewed hot drinks and made quantities of raisin, ham, and potato stew. Life seemed easy again. Our cave felt more comfortable and we had the security of knowing there would be something to eat the next day. We settled in, determined to hold out another week if necessary but hoping, as we had hoped for the last six nights, that we could descend in the morning.

March 7: Green Feet

Denali Pass: Art, Pirate, Dave

I dreamed my feet were glowing a bright chartreuse green. They would swell to the size of basketballs and ache as if about to burst until someone cut them off. I was lying in a small, dark cellar and the shelves that lined the walls were filled with huge, luminous, green feet.

I woke with a sharp, pulsating ache that made both my feet feel as if they were about to explode. I had frozen the ends of my feet when I'd dug and clawed for the food. I wasn't sure if they had thawed or frozen some more during the night. The only way to relieve the pain was to shift the position of my

feet. In my dream, each shift was a slice of a knife that amputated my feet and brought a moment of relief.

The wind was gone and the whiteout had disappeared.
Soon we were all awake, eating, and drinking, and wondering
where we'd meet up with Gregg, Shiro, and the others.
Pirate's and my hands were too swollen to grip anything, so
Dave helped us pull on our boots. I screamed out loud as
Dave shoved and jammed my swollen feet into my boots.
When it was his turn, Dave could barely force his swollen feet
into his boots.

After crawling out of the cave, we bumped into one another
and sprawled onto the ice. We tried to control the blocks of
pain that were our feet, but each step sent a burning sensation
up our calves. Before setting foot on the steep ice below, we
had to learn to walk again. Unfortunately, going downhill was
the most painful because all our weight jarred onto the frozen
and half-frozen ends of our feet. With the only good hands
between us, Dave strapped on all of our crampons and then
took the important anchor position on the rope.

The ice wall fell away from Denali Pass at an angle of
thirty to forty degrees. On the ascent when our legs were
strong, we had climbed this section gingerly. Now, as we wobbled on spindly, dried-up remnants of legs, each step was near
the limit of our ability.

"Don't charge off," I called to Pirate, who was leading and
barely creeping down the ice. We tested each step before trusting our weight. Because the wind had taken our packs, we
had our sleeping bags draped around our shoulders. They
hung to our feet, sometimes snagging our crampons, but it
was the only way we could carry them.

"Slower, Pirate!"

The only thing certain about each step was the pain it sent
through our feet. Step after step, Pirate led us across and

down the ice. The rope tied us together with only a psychological protection. If one of us slipped, we would all peel off
the wall. A belay was impossible. If we did come off there
would be nothing we could do to arrest our fall until we
crashed into the basin six hundred feet below.

Pirate stopped.

"Oh, God," I whispered to myself. One of his crampons
had loosened. We were caught on the steepest section of ice.
Dave and I chopped out small ledges to relieve some of the
strain on our ankles. Pirate's fingers had been too stiff to tie
his crampon laces when we had started, but now they had to
bind his crampon to his boot.

Dave called anxiously at Pirate to hurry up. My ankles felt
on the verge of buckling. Pirate grappled with the stiff straps,
cursing at the cold cutting into his hands—he had to handle
the metal crampon with bare fingers. He knew everything
depended on him. Should he lose his balance while tugging at
the frozen bindings, all our efforts to hold out during the
storm would be for nothing.

Pirate straightened; he grabbed his ice axe. I sighed with
relief and turned to see Dave grinning behind me.

"All right, you guys. . . . We're goin' down!"

Tense with caution, we placed one foot in front of the
other. We didn't see Gregg, John, Shiro, and George climbing
up toward us. Their absence began to worry me because I
knew they'd be here to help us down the ice if they could possibly manage it.

"Slow down, Pirate!"

With the steepest ice behind us, Pirate quickened his pace.
Actually, he was taking a step only every two or three seconds, but that seemed dangerously fast to me.

"You're gettin' us down, Pirate."

Pirate paused to turn and holler, "Aaahaaaa. . . ."

The rough but level ice of the basin began passing beneath us.

"We did it, we did it," I repeated to myself.

Weary and growing apprehensive, we slowly approached the cave. Just before we peered into it, I was seized with a sudden fear that we might see bodies. They could have been trapped here and could have never made it down for more food. We looked in; to my relief the cave was deserted. In one corner a small pile of food was stacked against a stove. They must have descended thinking we'd never come down; yet on the slight chance that we would they had left us the most favored delicacies—sausage, coconut balls Gregg's wife had made, and some of the fruitcake my grandmother had baked for us.

While we ate, Sheldon's silver Cessna 180 appeared and flew low over the basin. We waved. He swung around and dropped a bag. I retrieved it. Bits of a smashed orange were scattered on the ice. I picked up a carefully wrapped kit but couldn't figure out what it was. I felt a bit foolish when Pirate immediately recognized it as a radio. The altitude was affecting me more than I wanted to admit. Either our minds were too fuzzy to operate the radio or else it had been damaged when dropped, because we couldn't get it to send or receive.

Filled with food and a little water, we continued the descent. With extreme caution we inched our way down among the rocks along the ridge. Reaching the fixed ropes, we lowered our bags in front of us to free our arms for handling the ropes.

Our feet suffered a cutting pain every time our boots hit the ice. It became almost unbearable for Pirate and me to grip the rope with our frostbitten hands. Once I slipped, and as I grabbed the rope to halt my fall I could feel the skin and blisters tearing across my fingers.

Near the end of the ropes we entered a cloud. Despite the whiteout, there could be no thought of waiting; we had to avoid bivouacking for another night. Since Dave had climbed this part of the route more often than Pirate or I, he took the lead.

We climbed down deeper into the cloud. The tops of the high ridges on either side disappeared. Somewhere ahead in the grayness were two igloos and our friends. Beyond the igloos lay enormous crevasses. Should we pass by the igloos, we would walk blindly over the edge of a crevasse. The grayness grew so thick that from my position in the middle of the rope I could see neither Dave nor Pirate.

Dave stopped, then started again. My knees and ankles seemed on the verge of collapsing. Slack rope on the snow in front of me indicated Dave had stopped again. We were lost.

Gray cloud and gray ice appeared the same. The glacier and the sky had become one wall of grayness. Since we couldn't see the slope where we set our feet, I began stumbling onto my hands with a crunching of stiff, swollen flesh.

I shouted into the grayness that I thought the igloos were to our right. The rope jerked me to a halt from behind; Pirate must have fallen. I heard him yell that we should head more to the left. Dave said nothing. I lay flat on the snow, waiting for Pirate to pick himself up.

After several minutes Dave called, "Let's go!" With considerable effort I got to my feet, and we started staggering on through the whiteout. As we passed through the endless grayness, I began to think we had already gone beyond the igloos. I tried to pull my befuddled mind together.

The rope disappeared in the grayness about ten feet in front of me. We might have passed within ten feet of the camp without spotting it.

The igloos would be buried. Dave plodded on. Blind, and uncertain that my legs could manage another step, I let the rope running to Dave pull me on.

"Waahoooo. . . ." A call in front of me—unable to see Dave, I wasn't sure it had been his voice.

"Igloos!" It was Dave's voice.

With luck or an astonishing instinct he had led us straight to the igloos.

Dave waited for Pirate and me to appear out of the white-out so the three of us could share that first moment of greeting the others. Nearly delirious with relief and joy we shoveled the entrance of the main igloo free of some drifted snow, then pulled back the tarp. We peered inside. Darkness! The igloo was empty. We found the other igloo also deserted and dark. There wasn't even a note.

Were we alone on the mountain? Where were they? None of us felt like voicing our disappointment that the others were gone. They must have given up on us. We attacked the food left in the largest igloo. Mashed potatoes, rice, Jell-O, gorp, freeze-dried meat.

Despite the excitement of our feast, we ate quietly because we were weary and apprehensive about the fate of the other four.

Coming Home

The next morning we crawled out of the dimness of the igloo to squint into a blazing sun that hung in the sky beyond Mount Foraker. It didn't seem to be a winter sun. Close and burning, its warm light felt so tangible that we playfully snatched at it to catch a handful.

The air temperature was minus sixteen, but the sun warmed our cheeks as we lingered near the igloos. After those cold and dark days without the sun, we absorbed the sunshine with a thirst almost as consuming as our need for food and water. I couldn't remember ever being so at peace with myself. I thought all I would ever ask of life would be to let me feel the sunshine.

Before the day was over, we flew off the mountain. Only now that we were leaving did we begin to realize fully how isolated we had been, and how closely the three of us had been bound together. It would never be that way again. I kept seeing our rope lying discarded on the ice.

In Talkeetna we had a joyous reunion with Gregg and John, who flew off the mountain the same day. Gregg threw his arm around my shoulder and we hugged for the longest time. John said that for the last few days he and Gregg had been so certain the three of us were dead that they had stopped talking about us and even avoided mentioning us in their journals.

Another week-long storm clamped down on Denali, and it would be nearly a week before George and Shiro could get off. Shiro's first words to a rescue climber were, "Did you find the bodies? Were you able to recover the bodies?" Then, as the climber recounted that, Nishimae's face at first went blank when he learned the others were safely off the mountain, then slowly changed to a look of sheer joy as he realized they were not dead.

Years later, Shiro visited Alaska and I asked if I had made any mistakes in writing *Minus 148°*. "Just one," he said, "when you wrote about the little pile of food you found in our snow cave at 17,200 feet. You see, in Japan we have a custom of sometimes leaving a small offering of food in the woods for the spirit of a loved one who has died. That food wasn't left for you to find and eat. You were dead. I left it there for your spirit."

George told me later, "Art, the really horrible part was knowing you, and Ray, and Dave were dying in the storm at Denali Pass. It was so hard to turn and start down, leaving you there." Neither Dave, Pirate, or I have ever felt the slightest bit of resentment for being left by the others. After a few days, there was no reason to think we were still alive. Yet our friends hung in there, under some of the most horrible conditions imaginable, hoping against hope that we'd somehow survive the storm and they could help us down.

George and John returned to their families and professional careers. When Shiro retired, he spent more time in Alaska. Our families built a cabin we share not far from Denali. Later still, we scattered Shiro's ashes over the Kahiltna glacier.

Our beloved Pirate went on to have a glorious career guiding on Denali, helping hundreds of people enjoy the mountain that came to define his indomitable spirit. At fifty he went to climb Everest, but got sick on the way in. Depleted physically, he reached the summit by sheer force of his will. On the descent another climber was too exhausted to continue, so Ray, also near his limits, bivouacked with her. They died in the night, a short way below the summit. His body rests there to this day.

Dave Johnston remained that loveable six-foot-seven manchild, bubbling over with enthusiasm and friendliness. He has a great view of Denali from his living room. One winter he started skiing from his cabin to make a solo winter ascent; but he was stopped short at about twelve thousand feet by the frostbite he suffered on our climb.

Gregg Blomberg waited nineteen years to read the book about our winter climb. He wrote me, "I had not read it for all these years because I simply did not wish to relive the experience. The climb was a low point for me. . . . Farine's death easily showed me that climbing was not important enough anymore to me to die for. For the rest of the climb I was ambivalent about being there."

What rare courage and loyalty Gregg showed by staying with us through all those miserably cold days, looking after us long after his heart was yearning to be in a warmer, safer place with his family. I'm forever blessed to have had Gregg, with his caring and courageous heart, in my life.

And Farine. We all think of him at times. His playfulness. His joy to be in the mountains. His life cut short.

I'm sometimes asked if we had any kind of spiritual experience up there; and I think to myself, it was all a spiritual experience, every bit of it . . . to be so close to the stars. To wander between life and death. To have a friend risk his life for you. To simply be alive. To breathe and walk about. To feel the sunshine on your face. . . .

Postscript: The horrendous storm brought winds of 130 miles an hour and temperatures dropping to 148 degrees below zero. The climbers' snow cave allowed them to escape those deadly forces and to save their lives, and survive they did.

At 13,025 feet, Switzerland's Eiger is not nearly as high as the world's highest peaks, but statistics alone can be deceptive. Its enticingly beautiful rock face is considered one of the most difficult climbs in the world. In 1938 an Austrian named Heinrich Harrer and three colleagues took on the challenge, which had previously claimed the lives of several accomplished climbers. This is the harrowing account of the first successful ascent of the north wall of the Eiger.

THE WHITE SPIDER
The Classic Account of the Ascent of the Eiger

HEINRICH HARRER

The First Ascent of the Face

The summer of 1938 began sadly enough, with the death of two young Italian climbers. Bartolo Sandri and Mario Menti, employees in a wool factory at Valdagno in the province of Vicenza, were both respected members of the Italian Alpine Club, though only twenty-three years old. Sandri, especially, was known to be an unusually fine rock climber, who had done a number of super-severe climbs ranking as Grade VI, among them some first ascents. True, they had hardly any experience ice climbing in the western Alps.

Like all true mountaineers, they came to Alpiglen and the Scheidegg quietly, without any fuss, indeed almost secretly. They studied the Face, tried themselves out by a reconnaissance of its lower structure, and came down again. They decided that the direct route, followed three years before by Sedlmayer and Mehringer, was easier than that discovered by Hinterstoisser. But it wasn't any easier. The fact is that the face was not yet fit for climbing at all.

Nonetheless, Bartolo and Mario started up it early on June 21. They reached a greater height than Sedlmayer and Mehringer had on their first day. Their courage and enthusiasm ran high, and they were driven on by a burning urge to succeed. They just couldn't wait. Nature, however, followed her own laws, heedless of courage, enthusiasm, or ambition. Late in the evening one of the Eiger's notorious thunderstorms set in. . . .

The very next day a search party of Grindelwald guides, led by Fritz Steuri Senior, found Sandri lying dead on a patch of snow at the foot of the Face. Menti's body was recovered only with some difficulty a few days later from a deep crevasse.

That was a bad-enough start to operations on the Eiger in the summer of 1938, but it could not hold up the developments that were due. The memory of the successful retreat of Rebitsch and Vörg, which had been the turning point in men's minds, was still vivid. So was the lesson that it was impossible to capture the Face by surprise. *Veni, vidi, vici* wouldn't work on the Eiger. Endless patience was required and long waiting . . . for days, even weeks.

Meanwhile, Fritz Kasparek was waiting impatiently for my arrival. That tremendous climber from Vienna, bursting with life, blessed with an optimism nothing could destroy, had already been in Grindelwald for some time, skiing around the

Bernese Oberland, keeping a constant watch on the Eiger's mighty Face. Though, so far, there hadn't been much to watch except continual avalanches, sufficient in themselves to nip in the bud even the thought of an attempt. All the same, Fritz would have liked by now to have had with him his partner on the big climb they had planned to do together; for one never knows what may happen to interrupt one's plans. Sepp Brunnhuber, too, with whom Fritz had done the first winter ascent of the North Face of the Grosse Zinne as long ago as February—to some extent as a training climb for the Eiger project—could still not get away. I had promised Fritz to arrive at Grindelwald by July 10; but at the bottom of his heart he had good grounds for mistrusting students' promises.

Actually I was no longer a student by the time I got to Grindelwald. My tutors at the University of Graz were greatly astonished at the speed with which I suddenly attacked my finals. I could hardly explain to them that I wanted my studies out of the way before I climbed the North Face of the Eiger. They would certainly have shaken their heads and—not without some justification—reminded me that it was quite in order to "come off" that climb without having graduated first. I told nobody of our plan, not a fellow student, not a mountaineering or sporting acquaintance. The only person I let into the secret was that wise, practical, and plucky woman, my future mother-in-law, Frau Else Wegener. In 1930 her husband, Professor Alfred Wegener, had given his life for his companions on Greenland's inscrutable inland ice, when he perished in a blizzard; so she might well have had strong grounds for being fiercely opposed to ventures involving a risk to life. She, however, uttered no warning word; on the contrary, she encouraged me, though well acquainted with the reputation of the Eiger's North Face.

My last paper was on the morning of July 9. At lunchtime I

mounted my heavily laden motor bicycle, and I arrived at Grindelwald punctually on July 10, as promised. Fritz Kasparek, burnt brown by the glacier sun, his fair mop almost bleached white, greeted me in unmistakable Viennese.

He was blessed with the gift of the gab. His was a positively original gift for inventing expletives when faced with apparently insurmountable difficulties of the kind he was never in the habit of giving in to—both in the mountains and in ordinary life. However, he never used to parade his feelings; nor did he waffle about companionship and friendship. But his nature was such that, at times of crisis, he would not only share his last crust of bread or crumb of chocolate with his companions, but would give the whole of it away to them. And then not as a pathetic gesture, but to the accompaniment of some good, nervous, Viennese expression or other.

With friends of that kind one could go horse rustling, invite the devil to a picnic, or—attempt the North Face of the Eiger.

Fraissl and Brankowski, those two old Eiger hands, were also in Grindelwald. We strolled up to a pasture above Alpiglen together and there set up house. It was our firm intention to avoid the errors which had proved fatal to previous parties. The most important thing was to get to know our mountain as a whole, before attempting its most interesting and difficult face. So we first of all climbed from the "Hoheneis" diagonally across the (northeast) flank to the Mittellegi ridge, then up it to the summit and down again by the normal route. In addition, we climbed the Mönch by the "Nollen."

Meanwhile, cows had been driven up onto our idyllic pasture. Fritz and I decided to move our abode, and pitched our little tent in a small meadow close under the Face. Fraissl and Brankowski stayed on the pasture. It was a fine day when

Fritz and I started up the lower part of the Face and after climbing about 2,300 feet, to the so-called bivouac cave above the "Shattered Pillar," parked a rucksack full of provisions and equipment there. We attached a label to it, which read, "The property of Kasparek and Harrer. Don't move."

This notice did not indicate any particular mistrust of other North Face climbers. It was simply that, thanks to the many attempts and frequent rescue and recovery operations, the Face was littered with pieces of equipment, ropes and pitons, which served as very welcome aids and additions to the equipment of subsequent parties. This made it absolutely necessary to mark clearly any rucksack intentionally parked on the Face like this one of ours.

We climbed down again to our tent. Conditions would not yet allow of an attempt with the slightest prospect of success. We had taken a firm stand not to let ourselves be pushed, driven, or goaded. Past tragedies and particularly the deaths of the two Italians earlier in the summer had taught us that unseemly haste can ruin every sober consideration and lead to the direst results. We could wait and we meant to wait.

Days of fine weather set in; and still we waited, watching how the snow which had fallen during storms and been whipped against the rocks altered in consistency, melted away, settled, and bound firmly with the old underlying layer. It now seemed reasonable to hope that conditions up on the higher, unknown sector of the Face too would be bearable.

By July 21 we decided that everything was in order. At about 2 a.m. on that day we started up the Face, crossing the edge crevasse in the dark, climbing independently, unroped, up toward the "Shattered Pillar." We moved in silence, each of us picking his own line, each of us thinking his own thoughts.

Those hours between night and day are always a keen

challenge to one's courage. One's body goes mechanically through the correct movements essential to gaining height; but the spirit is not yet awake nor full of the joy of climbing, the heart is shrouded in a cloak of doubt and diffidence. My friend Kurt Maix once described this diffidence as Fear's friendly sister, the right and necessary counterweight to that courage that urges men skyward, and protects them from self-destruction. It is certainly not fear that besets the climber; but doubts and questionings and "butterflies" are human failings. And climbers are after all only human beings.

They have to reconcile themselves with their own short-comings and with constraining feelings; they have to subject themselves to the willpower already geared to the enterprise in hand. And so the first hour, the hour of the grey, shapeless, colourless dusk before dawn, is an hour of silence.

Sheer thrustfulness is false, indeed fallacious, at times when a man is struggling to achieve a balance and is busy trying to reconcile subtle nuances of feeling with his willpower. And the glorious thing about mountains is that they will endure no lies. Among them, we must be true to ourselves, too.

Fritz and I climbed on up, in the darkness before dawn, to the right of the "Shattered Pillar." From time to time we heard voices behind us, could distinguish individual words. It was Fraissl and Brankowski, who like ourselves had waited for the fine weather, and had started up the Face behind us. We would get on well enough with them. Two parties on that great precipice are no hindrance to one another; indeed, they can help each other in a variety of ways.

The rocks looked grey, even the snow looked grey in the first livid light of dawn. And there was something else grey moving in front of us. Not rocks this time, but people, peeling out of their tent sacks in front of the bivouac cave.

In an instant all thought, doubts, and self-questionings that had risen up out of the secret depths of our ego had sunk back again. We did not talk about them, least of all in front of strange fellow climbers who were at one and the same time comrades and competitors.

Strangers? Climbers are never really strangers, least of all on this Face. We introduced ourselves to these two who had only just woken up from their night's sleep. Then they told us who they were: Andreas Heckmair and Ludwig Vörg. It was a unique place for such an introduction. The light of an unborn day was strong enough for each of us to be able to see the faces of our opposite numbers clearly, to sample their features, to assess their characteristics.

So this was the famous Andreas Heckmair. At thirty-two he was the oldest of us four. His face was limned by the hills themselves, spare, deeply lined, with a sharp, jutting nose. It was a stern, bold face, the face of a fighter, of a man who would demand much of his companions and the last ounce of himself.

The other man, Ludwig Vörg, seemed to be exactly the opposite type: a well-rounded, athletic type, not in the least sinewy or spare, nor were his features as prominent as Heckmair's. They radiated amiable relaxation; his whole being personified latent strength and an inner peace. His friends with whom he had been to the Caucasus two years before had nicknamed him the "Bivouac King." Even those nights in the open on the seven-thousand-foot ice face of Ushba, the "Terrible Mountain," had failed to rob him of his sleep. On a snap judgment one would attribute the dynamic force to Heckmair, the stamina to Vörg. In any case two such diverse and complementary characters couldn't help making up a rope of quite extraordinary climbing ability and strength.

We couldn't tell if the two men were disappointed at our all being on the Face at the same time. If they were, they certainly didn't show it. Heckmair said, "We knew you were trying the Face, too. We saw your rucksack and read the label." We couldn't quite grasp why we had been in the dark about the presence of these two men, who hadn't been living in a tent either at Alpiglen or Kleine Scheidegg, nor in the hay on any of the pastures. We found out only later that this time they had completely covered their traces. They had come to Grindelwald with luggage and taken a room in one of the hotels at Kleine Scheidegg. Who ever heard of a candidate for the North Face of the Eiger sleeping in a hotel bedroom? The ruse had worked perfectly.

Heckmair and Vörg had with them the best, most up-to-date equipment. They were in fact just as poor as we were, but had raised a sponsor for their climb in advance and had there-fore found themselves for the first time in their lives in a posi-tion to buy to their hearts' desire at Munich's best sports shop, and even to order gear which had to be specially manu-factured. Of course, they both had the twelve-pointer cram-pons that had just become fashionable. Fritz had ten-pointers, but I hadn't any at all. Admittedly this was a mistake, but it wasn't the result of carelessness, but rather of overcareful con-sideration. We had taken the view that the North Face was a rock wall with aprons of snow and ice embedded in it. A pair of crampons weighs a good deal, and we felt that if we did without it, we could take more equipment or provisions along. My boots were nailed with the well-known claw system popular in Graz, a layout providing an equally good grip on rock and ice. Our plan was for Fritz to lead on the ice pitches and me to take over on the rocks. We also hoped to avoid the irksome and time-wasting necessity of strapping crampons on and taking them off again all the time. We were quite wrong, and it was a mistake; but it did not prove disastrous, for all it did was to lose us time and provide me with extra exertion. But we hadn't yet discovered that as we stood talking to Heckmair and Vörg outside the bivouac cave.

Vörg, used to bivouacking in all sorts of conditions and places, was grousing about the night they had just spent. "It was cold and uncomfortable," he complained. "Falling stones wouldn't allow us to stay outside the cave, and the cave itself was narrow and wet. It dripped steadily on our tent sack all night long."

Heckmair studied his altimeter and shook his head dubiously. "It has risen about sixty meters," he announced, "which means the barometer has fallen about three points. I don't like the look of the weather."

Just at that moment Fraissl and Brankowski came up with us. Introductions and friendly greetings followed, but by now there was a note of real concern detectable in Heckmair's voice. Like a good trouper he concealed his disappointment. He just pointed to a fish-shaped cloud on the horizon and said, "I'm sure the weather's breaking. We're not climbing any further."

We ourselves felt certain that the weather would hold, and Fritz put forward that viewpoint in his optimistic way: "Oh, sure, the weather'll hold all right. And someone's got to climb the Face sometime, after all!"

Heckmair and Vörg were getting ready to go down, as we moved on up. I kept on thinking about the retreat of those two superb climbers and remembering the look of utter disappointment on Vörg's face. And what about Heckmair? I soon realised that his fishy cloud and the "rise in the altimeter" were only excuses. He knew that the presence of three ropes on the Face could mean serious delays, but he was too good a sport to stand on his rights of "first come, first served" and ask one of our parties to turn back. So he turned back himself:

instead of saying "you're in the wrong," he remarked that he
didn't like the look of the weather. It was a decision dictated
by a true sense of mountaineering responsibility.

Time and again climbers on the North Face had got into
difficulties, through allowing themselves to be hurried not only
by the state of the Face or by weather conditions, but by the
competition of others. Vörg, one of the finest climbers ever to
attempt the climb, was not going to let himself be hurried.

At the moment there was little time for psychological studies or similar problems. The Face itself was providing our
immediate problems, as we reached the "Difficult Crack."
Twilight had at last been forced to yield to the first full light of
morning. We roped up, and Fritz tackled the first severe pitch
with his own personal craftsmanship. The heavy Eiger pack
on his shoulders brought his first swift upward drive to a halt.
Down he had to come and leave his rucksack at my feet. Then
he began his second assault. It was a pleasure to watch him.
Higher and higher he went, stylishly, using every projecting
wrinkle, never breaking his rhythm, never struggling. And in
a staggeringly short time he had mastered this first great
defence work on the Face.

The job of roping Fritz's rucksack up after him was difficult and time wasting; it kept on jamming under overhangs.
However, the first one got up there in the end; the second,
weighing fifty-five pounds, followed, but on my shoulders.
We just hadn't time to indulge in another bout of roping up.
Fritz hauled on my rope; his assistance at least offset the
weight of my pack, and I, too, was soon at the top of the
crack. The pitch gave me a gentle foretaste of what the Face
had in store; but the fact that I hadn't lost my breath coming
up the crack strengthened my confidence that I was up to the
work in hand. There is, of course, a huge difference between
balancing upward like a gymnast totally unencumbered on

even the hardest Dolomite wall and climbing heavily laden up the Face of the Eiger. But then isn't the ability to hump heavy loads a requisite for every successful major climb?

Many climbers still to come will use rope slings on the "Difficult Crack." We preferred to climb it free. A rock climber of Kasparek's supreme skill only resorts to slings where they are absolutely unavoidable.

By now we were just below the Rote Fluh, that sheer wall, hundreds of feet high, which goes winging up to the sky in a sweep of incomparable smoothness. According to the book of the rules, based on man's experience, the mountain walls sleep quietly in the early morning, blanketed by the night frost. Even the stones are supposed to be frozen into inactivity. But the Eiger's Face doesn't go by any Queensberry rules; this was just another instance of the way it tips human experience overboard. Down came the stones. We could see them taking off over the top edge of the Rote Fluh and whizzing out through empty space in a wide arc. The Face was raking us with defensive fire. We hurried on upward, for the nearer we got to the foot of the Rote Fluh, the safer we should be.

We could hear another heavy block coming. It landed below us, splintering into a thousand pieces.

Then we heard Fraissl's voice. Not a call for help or an SOS, just a communication; one of them had been hit on the head and hurt.

"How bad is it? Do you need help?" we asked.

"No, but I'm pretty giddy. I think we've had it. We'll have to turn back."

"Can you manage it alone?"

"Yes, we can."

We were sorry that our two Viennese friends couldn't keep us company, but we didn't try to dissuade them. So Fraissl and Brankowski started to climb down again.

Now, before sunrise, we two were alone on the Face again. Only a little while ago there had been six of us; now Fritz and I had only each other to rely on. We didn't discuss it, but subconsciously it strengthened our feeling of mutual dependence and comradeship. We made rapid progress over easier ground; and then, suddenly, we were at the passage that Rebitsch and Vörg had christened the "Hinterstoisser Traverse" the year before.

The rocks across which we now had to traverse to the left were almost vertical, plunging away beneath into thin air. We were full of admiration for Hinterstoisser's brave achievement when he opened up this rope-assisted traverse across to the First Ice Field for the first time, feeling his perilous way from hold to hold. We were full of gratitude too to Vörg and Rebitsch for having left a traversing rope—shouting a welcome to us, it seemed—in place here. We tested it and found it firmly anchored and secure against any strain, although it had been exposed for twelve months to storms and showers, to the wet and the cold.

We knew from reports, descriptions, and photographs how to effect the traverse. Nobody, however, had described the pitch when heavily iced over. The rock was absolutely glazed, offering no hold whatever to a frictioning foot. Nonetheless, Fritz led off into the traverse with that tremendous skill of his, fighting for his balance on smooth, holdless film, winning his way, inch by inch, yard by yard, across that difficult and treacherous cliff. In places he had to knock away snow or a crust of ice from the rock with his ice hammer; the ice splinters swept down the slabs with a high whirring sound, to disappear into the abyss. But Fritz held on, pushing, feeling his way over to the left, climbing, hanging right away from the rock on the rope, from hold to hold, till he reached the far end of the traverse. Then I followed, shoving Fritz's rucksack along ahead of me on a snap link in the traversing rope, and soon joined him at the other end.

Soon after the traverse we came to the "Swallow's Nest," the bivouac place already made famous by Rebitsch and Vörg, and there we halted for a rest and some breakfast. The weather was holding, and a fine dawn had turned into a lovely day. The light was so good that it had already been possible to take pictures down on the traverse, a traverse that is certainly one of the most photogenic pitches in all the Alps. That one prosaic epithet tells the whole story—the extreme difficulty, the exposure, the daring of the traverse. And I should at once like to take the opportunity of correcting a misapprehension: the Hinterstoisser Traverse is one of the key pitches to the climb, not the only one. There are numerous critical places on this incredibly huge face, which—thanks to the safe return of Rebitsch and Vörg—had by now been reconnoitered as far as Sedlmayer and Mehringer's "Death Bivouac." As yet we didn't know what key pitches lurked up there on the final precipice. All we knew was that, wherever it might rise in the Alps, it would by itself have been an object of wonder to the beholder and a highly prized objective for the best rock climbers alive.

We were going splendidly, the weather was fine, and we had no doubt that we stood a good chance of success; but we also knew that the very best of climbers had had to beat a retreat. So we equipped the "Swallow's Nest" as a strong point in case of a withdrawal. The old rope left by the 1937 party on the traverse was not enough. We proposed to ensure the direct line of descent, which in 1936 had proved fatal to the party of four, a tragedy which only reached its appalling end with the ghastly death of Toni Kurz. At the "Swallow's Nest," we left behind us 330 feet of rope, pitons, snap links, rope slings, and provisions.

It was July 21, 1938. Exactly two years ago to a day Hinterstoisser had spent hour upon hour in desperate attempts to climb back along the traverse he himself had been the first to discover. All in vain. He, and with him Angerer and Rainer, died on that same day. We were tremendously impressed by that memory. If those four men had only left their traversing rope in place at the Traverse, if they had only had a long enough rope at the "Swallow's Nest," if only. . . . We had to thank the dead for our knowledge. The memory made us both proud and sad, but it did not scare us. Life has its laws, which we unconsciously obey. They pointed to the way up.

Fritz had strapped on his crampons; soon he was on his way up the First Ice Field. Here was no névé, but hard, brittle, somewhat watery ice. I assessed the angle at from fifty to fifty-five degrees, that is, somewhat steeper than the average slope of the Grossglockner's Pallavicini Couloir. After the first rope-length, Fritz cut a big stance and drove in an ice piton, to protect me on my ascent. We were already beginning to realise that our calculations had gone astray when we decided to leave my crampons behind. I now had to make up for lack of equipment by a considerable increase in muscular energy. Never mind, my training in several forms of sport would be a great asset. . . .

We were aiming for a vertical cliff, which leads from the First to the Second Ice Field. The only possible way seemed to be through an icy groove, later to be known as the "Ice Hose." This barrier between the two shields of ice is one of the many snares and delusions on this Face. Optically, a wall in the Dolomites is far more impressive than any single pitch on the Eiger's Face. When I recall the great Dolomite faces, there is much which seems more difficult, steeper, more inaccessible than it really is. But when you lay your hand on the Dolomite rock, you immediately delight in the rough surface, the horizontal stratification, the resulting proliferation of holds, and of the never-failing crannies and cracks into which pitons may safely be driven.

But here? The first illusion—the ice-covered rock barrier doesn't look particularly difficult. All you have to do is to hammer in a belaying piton below it . . . but it doesn't offer a belay. In fact there isn't a cranny anywhere for a reliable piton, and there aren't any natural holds. Moreover, the rock is scoured smooth by falling stones, bread-crumbed with snow, ice, and rubble. It isn't an invitation to cheerful climbing, it offers no spur to one's courage; it simply threatens hard work and danger. All the same, it is a part of the Eiger's North Face, which we are trying to climb. . . .

The "Ice Hose" does justice to its name. The rock was thickly plastered with the stuff; but even the hose part couldn't have been more accurate. Water was pouring down under the frozen layer, between the ice and the rock. The only way was up through it. The water poured into our sleeves, flowing right down our bodies, building up for a short time above the gaiters, which were supposed to separate our trousers from our boots, before finding its way out. There were practically no holds in this crack consisting of ice, rock, and water. It is severe, calls for the best climbing technique, and demands the most ingenious balancing maneuvers. Here, too, Fritz showed his supreme skill; but it took hours to reach the Second Ice Field. We were wet to the skin when we got there.

It was still early in the afternoon. High and wide above us loomed the Second Ice Field. Our way led diagonally up to the left towards the arête of the "Flatiron," in the direction of the last bivouac of Sedlmayer and Mehringer. The huge ice apron was greatly foreshortened from where we stood; but even allowing for the optical illusion and remembering that it had taken first-class ice exponents like Rebitsch and Vörg five hours—twenty rope-lengths—to reach its upper rim, we still had plenty of time to do it and probably even to reach the "Death Bivouac." For there would still be at least six hours of daylight.

In spite of all that, we decided to climb not to the left but to the right, to a little knob of rock sticking out of the snow above the upper edge of the Rote Fluh. The fine afternoon was letting the sun beat diagonally down on the upper part of the Face—up there where the "little icicles blow their noses." That was what started the avalanches; and stones, once released from the imprisoning ice up there, were in the habit of following the laws of gravity.

And farther over to the west—for one has to traverse diagonally across the Face for hundreds of feet on those ice shields— snowslides, stone falls, and cascades of water were coming down in their vertical, unhampered course from the "Spider."

Admittedly, every stone doesn't find a target. But we hadn't carefully built a strong point for a retreat down at the "Swallow's Nest" in order to be knocked out by stones or wiped off the Face by avalanches up here. Falling stones are numbered among the "objective" dangers of climbing, or in other words as circumstances over which man has no control; but to venture with one's eyes open into the line of fire of falling stones is no longer an objective but a subjective exposure to danger, the outcome of sheer carelessness or stupidity. This huge ice apron was a place to be climbed during the morning. Even then the danger from stones wouldn't be entirely eliminated, but it would be considerably less.

We reached our knob and were able to fix two belaying pitons; then we spent hours in digging a small seat out of the ice below it. It was still daylight when we began to make the final preparations for our bivouac. We tied ourselves and our

belongings to the pitons for security's sake, furnished our seat
with coils of rope, and started to cook our meal. The knob of
rock afforded us complete protection from stones; the view
from our perch was magnificent. All the conditions for a
happy bivouac were present, but we hadn't a dry stitch on us.
Yet, although we had warm clothing and a change of underwear in our rucksacks, we dared not risk getting it, too, damp
by putting it on under soaking clothes. We didn't know what
the weather might do, or how often, where, and under what
conditions we should have to bivouac. So we would have to
keep our spares dry against nights yet to come; but it needed
some strength of mind not to fetch them out of the packs and
put them on, even though we knew better.

The night was long, cold, and uncomfortable. The bivouac
was not a good one. We were only to know later on that it was
the worst on the whole Face, in spite of its comparatively good
sitting space. Our wet clothes made us doubly susceptible to
the cold; our minds and spirits were as busy as our bodies trying to cope with the discomfort. No training in the world is
proof against that.

Every night has to come to an end sometime. In the grey
light of dawn we got up with chattering teeth and prepared
the ropes for the day's climbing. The weather was still good
and the frost had anchored all the stones, as we started on the
diagonal climb across the Second Ice Field. It was only now
that we realised to the full what a mistake we had made in
leaving my crampons behind. Fritz counteracted the error by
a tremendous output of energy, as he built a positive ladder of
steps. It was amazing to see how expert with his ice axe was
this best of all Vienna's rock climbers. For hours on end he
swung it rhythmically to cut step upon step, resting only when
he stopped to safeguard me up them. And the steps were so
good that my claw nails gave me excellent holds in them.

From down below, the Ice Field looks like a smooth surface; but that is pure illusion. Huge waves in the ice constantly gave the impression that we were quite close to the safety of the rocks above; but we soon realised that we had reached only another bulge in the ice and that there was yet another ice valley to be crossed. It was the phenomenon the climber so often experiences in the western Alps, when he mistakes one of many subsidiary excrescences for the main summit.

The fully equipped modern mountaineer handles his ice axe like a guide of the classical Alpine era. Speed is the essence of modern climbing; steady, slow progress that of the classic past. We were naturally taking longer because we were using the technique of the past. Even Rebitsch and Vörg had taken five hours the year before to cross this huge patch of ice. We took exactly the same time.

Just before the rocks separating the Second from the Third Ice Field, I looked back, down our endless ladder of steps. Up it I saw the New Era coming at express speed; there were two men running—and I mean running, not climbing—up it. Admittedly, practised climbers can move quickly in good steps; but for these two to have reached this point quite early in the morning was positively amazing. They must have bivouacked last night on the lower part of the wall; it hardly seemed possible that they had only started up it today. But it was, in fact, the case.

These two were the best of all the "Eiger Candidates"— Heckmair and Vörg—wearing their twelve-pointer crampons. I felt quite outmoded in my old claws. We exchanged a brief greeting; then they went on up to Fritz. I knew my friend and his highly developed set of Alpine etiquette pretty well; I knew he preferred to find his own way, and that, though he wore the honourable badge of the Mountain Rescue Service, he himself didn't like assistance. Even Heckmair's obviously joking inquiry whether he wouldn't prefer to turn back only brought a good strong Viennese reply from Fritz.

But Anderl didn't mean to start a squabble. His is a character with no touch of malice in it; moreover, Kasparek and Heckmair had far too great a respect for one another, and so the result of the encounter was neither discord nor rivalry, but a teaming up such as has rarely been seen on this mighty Face. We naturally continued to climb as two separate ropes, with Heckmair and Vörg now taking over the lead. They told us later how they had seen Fraissl and Brankowski turn back; after that there had been no holding them. They had started up the Face early in the morning and now they had already caught us up. And now, too, we would be staying together. . . .

We moved on up the steep ridge toward the "Death Bivouac" at a uniform pace. During our extended midday rest at that point we felt completely united. Not a word was spoken indicative of any sense of disappointment. It was just as if we had always intended to climb together and now we were glad to have joined up at long last.

There could be no difference of opinion as to the continuation of the route. It led from our resting place diagonally downward across the Third Ice Field toward the foot of the "Ramp," the rock feature rising steeply toward the ridge up which lies the Lauper Route; then from the "Ramp" a right-hand traverse to the "Spider"; across the "Spider" and then up the adjacent exit cracks to the summit névé, crowning the final wall. It all sounds so easy. Yet each of the pitches named has its own big question mark. But when I looked at my companions, Fritz, Anderl, and Wiggerl, I felt quite certain that any pitch that offered the faintest possibility of a route up it would be climbed by our party of four.

It might perhaps have been possible to climb straight up the cliff from the "Death Bivouac" to the "Spider," but we could not see very far as we looked up the precipice. Mists were closing in on the mountain, and beginning to drift gently down to us. These were the mists that are known "out there" as the Eiger's "Wad of cotton wool" and hug every contour of its ice and rock. That didn't upset us very much. It is one of the Eiger's regular features to put on a skullcap for its after-lunch nap, much to the fury of the inquisitive people milling around the telescopes. We, of course, couldn't know the intensity of that fury, stemming from the fact that queue tickets were being issued and that their purchasers had to pay for three minutes' viewing, whether they saw anything or not. Meanwhile, unobserved by the great world outside, we were traversing across an ice slope, whose inclination exceeds sixty degrees, to the start of the "Ramp."

The "Ramp"—well, it fits that Face, on which everything is more difficult than it looks. You cannot run up it, for there are no rough slabs, no good footholds or handholds. Here too the rock-strata slope outward and downward and the crannies into which a piton can be driven can be counted on one hand. At all events, I had a good belaying piton at the foot of the "Ramp." I stood watching Fritz as he moved upward with even, rhythmic movements, to a point some eighty feet above me.

Suddenly he slipped. I couldn't tell whether a hold had come away in his hand or whether he had failed to find a foothold. Everything went so quickly—he was already out of sight. I took in as much slack as I could and stood there waiting for the shock. I knew the piton was firmly in and would hold. And the rope, cushioned by the belay around my shoulders, ought with any luck to take the strain. Anybody coming off unbelayed at this point would go winging straight down to the outcrops at the bottom of the Face. . . .

Luck was with us. The rope ran out over a little ridge of snow, cutting into the surface névé. This checked the velocity of Fritz's fall to such an extent that the shock I had to withstand was perfectly bearable. But was Fritz hurt?

My mind was soon at rest. Up from below came a couple of words intelligible only to one who knows Viennese slang inside out—a good aggressive oath. Then Fritz was climbing again. Soon he was at the top of the "Ramp," moving on above it, just as if nothing had happened, till presently I shouted up to him that there was no more rope. On my way up, I took a look at the place where he had come off. Fritz had fallen sixty feet through thin air straight down from the diagonal "Ramp" and had then calmly climbed back again by a difficult crack. We didn't mention the mishap again. Fritz carried it off as quietly as a player whom the dice condemn to go back to the start in Snakes and Ladders. We weren't in the least upset; we just laughed because we were enjoying life. No sentimental handshakes either. Back to the start—and then six forward up the next waterfall—that was the way we looked at it. It was quite natural for Fritz to have climbed straight up again after his fall, for he hadn't hurt himself. And it was quite natural for me to have held the rope because that was what I was there for. Fritz was just the right companion for this great Face. He treated irrelevancies as such, never burdening his friends with "if" and "suppose," nor with the thought "what might have happened," or the question "why did it happen?" What really mattered was that nothing *had* happened.

Late in the afternoon the four of us were all together again. Above us the "Ramp" had contracted to a narrow gulley with a crack blasted out of it. Water was running down the crack. None of us wanted to bivouac in wet clothes—our own had dried out during the morning, while we were traversing the Second Ice Field; moreover, we were beginning to find the day's labours sufficient. The crack would be a good prelude to the next day's work; so we prepared to bivouac.

That sounds easy enough. And we had thought it would be easy enough when we were looking at the "Ramp" in photographs or through a telescope. We even thought we could pick our seats. Actually there were no seats, in fact not a single seat. Indeed, good stances were a rarity.

We arranged our bivouac about eight feet below that of Heckmair and Vörg. We managed to drive a single piton into a tiny crevice in the rock. It was a thin, square-shafted piton. It held after only a centimeter, but it was just jammed. Obviously, once we hung our whole weight on it, it would very likely work loose with the leverage. So we bent it downward in a hoop, till the ring was touching the rock. In this way we did away with any question of leverage and knew we could rely on our little grey steely friend. First we hung all our belongings onto it and, after that, ourselves.

There was no room to sit down. The "Ramp" was very narrow and very steep at this point; but we managed to manufacture a sort of seat with the aid of rope slings, and hung out some more to prevent our legs from dangling over the gulf. Next to me there was a tiny level spot, just big enough for our cooker, so we were able to brew tea, coffee, and cocoa. We were all very much in need of liquids.

Heckmair and Vörg were no more comfortably lodged. The relaxed attitude of Vörg, the "Bivouac King," was quite remarkable; even in a place like this he had no intention of doing without every possible comfort. He even put on his soft fleece-lined bivouac slippers, and the expression on his face was that of a genuine connoisseur of such matters. It is absolutely no exaggeration to say that we all felt quite well and indeed comfortable. Experienced climbers will understand that statement, and laymen must simply believe it. A famous philosopher, when asked what true happiness was, replied, "If you have some broth, a place to sleep in, and no bodily pains, you are well on the way." We can improve on that definition. "Dry clothes, a reliable piton, and precious revivifying drinks—that is true happiness where the North Face of the Eiger is concerned."

Yes, we were quite happy. This huge mountain face had brought our lives down to the lowest common denominator. After cooking for hours we pulled the Zdarsky sack over us and tried to find as comfortable a position as possible, so that we could at least doze off occasionally. It was great to be able to look forward to a night in dry clothes. Our perch was about four thousand feet above the snowfields at the base of the precipice; if one of us fell off now, that was where he would certainly finish up. But who was thinking about falling off?

It was a good bivouac. Bodily aches and discomfort made no disturbing intrusion on the train of our thoughts. As I fell asleep, I saw a picture, a happy, sunny picture of something that happened when I was very young; no mirage of a sheltering roof over my head or a warm bed, but a memory of one of my first experiences in the mountains.

It happened when I was only fifteen. I had climbed all alone to the top of the Mangart, that proud summit in the Julian Alps, and was coming down, very impressed by my great experience. I reached a huge scree slope, of the kind one so often finds in the Julians, miles long. Down it I went, through the bleak hanging valley, taking long bounding strides. The sun was scorching and my tongue was sticking to my gums. There in the middle of the rubble, I saw two eagles tearing huge lumps of flesh from the carcass of a chamois. The birds of prey flew away only reluctantly as I came by. I was so fascinated by the sight that I momentarily forgot my thirst. Young as I was, the knowledge that the death of one thing can mean the life of another was borne in on me ineradicably. Was that an immutable law of Nature? I wondered. Was it true for people as well as for animals? Every fibre of my being protested against the notion.

I came down to the shore of the Weissenfelser See. There, by the lake, stood a shepherd's hut, next to a spring, from which fell a glittering column of water. I bent down and let the water run down over my wrists. Then I drank and drank and drank. . . .

Suddenly I felt a sharp box on my ears. A tall white-haired herdsman was standing there, his sharp-etched face burnt mahogany by the sun.

"Boy, why are you drinking water?" he asked. "There in my hut I have cool milk and sour cream. You can quench your thirst and drink your fill indoors."

I shall never forget that old man, who allowed his tongue to grow sharp in order to do me a good turn. I remained for days as his guest, eating and drinking everything the little farm produced, milk and cream and cream cheese. He was a proud, hospitable man and, what is more, educated and much travelled, who could speak eight languages fluently. For many years he had been a ship's cook over the face of the seven seas; and all his life's experiences added up to kindness toward his fellow men. I remembered the horrible picture of the eagles and the dead chamois. And instantly I realised, with the receptive idealism of early youth, that Nature's cruelty didn't hold among men. Men must be kindly. . . .

With that memory of the old man by the Weissenfelser See I nodded off, into a deep and dreamless sleep. I don't know how long I slept like that. Suddenly, dreaming now, I saw the old man there again in front of me. His face was no longer kind; he was angry as he tugged at my breast. I tried to shake him off, wanting to go on sleeping, but I could not, he was so strong. He tugged at me and shook me harder still.

I only half woke up, but could still feel the fierce pressure on my chest. It was the rope. I had slid off my perch as I slept, and was hanging on it with my full weight. I knew then that I was on the "Ramp," on the Eiger's North Face, and that I really ought to straighten myself out, raise myself, and resume a proper sitting posture; but I was too lethargic and only wanted to go on sleeping. Vaguely I recognised that one shouldn't for a moment longer than necessary weigh down a piton that is only a centimeter deep into the rock; but it was so pleasant to snatch just a few more minutes before straightening everything out. So I fell asleep again.

The moment I nodded off, there was the dream, back again. This time the old man shook me properly awake. I stood up in the slings, resumed my sedentary posture on that vertiginous little stance. Fritz mumbled something in his sleep.

Then I heard Andreas and Ludwig talking overhead. Vörg's voice sounded worried, so I asked what was the matter.

"Anderl feels sick," came the answer. "The sardines he ate last night have upset his tummy."

I was wide awake by now and fully restored. I could hardly feel the cold anymore. There, close by me, on its little level spot, stood the cooker.

"I'll brew you some tea, Anderl," I said. "It always helps."

Tea is surely the king of all drinks. It helps against cold, it helps against the heat, against discomfort and sickness, against weariness and weakness. And it helped on this occasion too. The sardines quieted down in Anderl's tummy. We dozed and slept till the stars began to pale and the light of a new day crept through the twilight before dawn. Night was over; it had not been a bad one.

Vörg began cooking at about four o'clock. Like everything else, he did it thoughtfully, unhurriedly, and thoroughly. He cooked porridge and coffee in large quantities. That cheered us up and drove away the cold. It was seven o'clock before we finally started to climb again. To have to cope with the crack in the gully as early-morning physical training was quite a big demand on bodies still stiff from a bivouac. It didn't look any easier this morning than it had yesterday evening, except that the waterfall had stopped. In its place there was a thin armoring of ice on the rocks. Even Anderl, leading up it, looked a little doubtful.

He seemed to think straight on up was the best way and took the gully direct, knocking in a piton wherever he could. One of them actually held safe. He worked his way higher and higher with supreme technical skill, trying to get off the ice by climbing into the overhanging cliffs on the Face. He was nearly up the overhang, trying out a hold from which to get a final pull-up; but it wasn't a hold, it was a loose block, and it broke away, bringing him down with it. A second or two later our friend was hanging safely from the good piton below the overhang. That wouldn't do at all for Andreas Heckmair: overhangs can't behave like that. He was very cross indeed. If it wouldn't go on the ice-free stuff, then it had better go right up the middle of the ice itself. So he put on his famous twelve-pointer crampons.

Then he treated us to an acrobatic tour de force, an exhibition exercise, such as we had rarely witnessed before. It was half superb rock technique, half a toe dance on the ice—a toe dance above a perpendicular drop. He got a hold on the rock, a hold on the ice, bent himself double, uncoiled himself, the front points of his crampons moving ever upward, boring into the ice. They got only a few millimeters' purchase, but that was enough. Heckmair defeated that difficult pitch, cut footholds, and banged pitons into the ice slope that began above it, then safeguarded Vörg up it after him.

We were still climbing as two separate ropes. It was now Kasparek's turn to tackle the crack in the gully. Not only had he no twelve-pointer crampons, he had a completely different conception of the pitch. He took it direct, avoiding entanglements with the icy and the ice-free containing walls alike. By a masterly piece of climbing he got up the crack as if climbing in the Gesäuse* at home rather than on the great Face of the Eiger.

I came up last. Then we were all four together again on the ice, looking up in incredulous astonishment at the menacing bulge of ice that here threatens finally to bar all progress up the "Ramp." Could anybody climb that?

The cliff was more than thirty feet high. I had never seen anything to match it; even the others at first seemed flabbergasted. Would it go on the left? No. On the right? No. Straight up seemed to be the best bet: but was this "best" a possible one? Heckmair had a go. He began by banging pitons into the ice below the bulge. One of them went in and held like a vice. Then he balanced his way delicately upward. There were icicles hanging from the bulge; to one of these he fastened a sling and pushed himself up a bit in it. It looked terrifying, but he didn't seem in the least impressed by the danger; inch by inch he moved upward, but as soon as he trusted his weight to the icicle, the pretty glittering thing broke away and off he came. . . .

The piton held.

Once again we saw the same reaction as before. A rebuff as thoroughgoing as a fall rouses Heckmair to a cold fury. He immediately tackled the bulge again. This time he didn't trust to the icicles with which the architect of our mighty prison

* The famous Austrian rock-climbing area in Upper Styria, with limestone faces of more than three thousand feet.–Translator's note.

had decorated it. Was it really a prison? Was this where we were going to have to give in and turn back?

No, our Andreas climbed up and out of our prison, having found an "ice handle." An icicle hanging down had coagulated with an ice stump pushing upward—a stalagmite and a stalactite, both of ice, had grown into one. And this object, carpentered by some freak of nature, proved to be the key to our prison door. Heckmair threaded another sling through the handle, leaned outward almost horizontally, banged some notches with his ice hammer in the ice above the bulge, felt around with one hand, took a firm hold.

I had never seen a pitch that looked so hazardous, dangerous, and utterly extraordinary. Fritz, who knows many of the famous key pitches in the Alps, thought that the famous overhanging roof on the Pillar of the Marmolata looked like child's play in comparison with this bulge. We were all pretty tense. Vörg had a tight hold on the rope, ready at any moment to hold Heckmair if he came off again.

But he didn't come off. We couldn't imagine how, but in some masterly fashion or other he had managed to drive an ice piton deep into the ice above the bulge and thread the rope through a snap link. Then he gave the order: "Pull!"

Vörg pulled him up on the rope, over the bulge, up to the piton.

Heckmair used his axe a few more times. Then "Let her go!" he said.

Vörg let the rope go loose, so that Heckmair could stand up; at the same time he was still keeping a careful watch in case of another fall. But Heckmair was soon in firm holds; he hurried a few feet up onto the ice slope above the bulge, cut a roomy stance in the ice, and drove a belaying piton deep into firm ice. Then as the curtain cue to an unusually dramatic scene we heard the welcome words "Up you come!"

Our prison gate was open. Vörg followed through it. The North Face of the Eiger is so vast, so difficult, and so serious that any display of human vanity would be out of place. No doubt Fritz and I could have climbed the bulge without any assistance from above, but it would have taken precious hours we would later have begrudged. So Fritz didn't hesitate a moment to take the rope Vörg let down to us. We who followed were robbed of the thrill and the adventure of this, the hardest pitch till now on the Face; we only tasted the toil it involves. And I, as last on the rope, had to knock out and retrieve all the pitons. I was decorated with them like a Christmas tree and the clank of the ironmongery drowned my gasps as I struggled up over the bulge.

The ice slope above was easy compared with what we had just done. We went straight up the ice for a short way only, then traversed out to the right at once.

It is of course easy enough for anyone who has made a successful first ascent to shake his head about the mistakes of those who follow. I do not propose to do it. But I am surprised that so many parties which climbed the Face after us went straight on up the ice slope toward the Mittellegi ridge and only tried to traverse across to the "Spider" much too high up. This was the cause of many delays and also brought about the disaster of 1957. It was perfectly clear to the four of us that the right-hand traverse must be attempted as soon as possible.

So we were traversing out to the right from the ice slope, all four roped together, along a brittle belt of rock below an overhanging cliff. It was midday by now, and we could hear the hissing of the avalanches and the tattoo of the stones, but we were protected from both by the overhang.

While we were traversing these broken rocks—Heckmair was about two hundred feet ahead of me at the time—we

suddenly heard a fearful humming and whining sound. It was
neither a stone fall nor an avalanche, but an airplane flying
past quite close to us. We could see the faces of its passengers
quite plainly. They waved and we waved back. Hans Steiner,
the Bernese photographer, managed to take some photographs of unique documentary value at that moment. His pictures showed three of us on the traverse while Heckmair had
already started up a crack beyond it.

That crack is the only possible line of ascent from where
the brittle belt peters out to a level on which the traverse to the
"Spider" can be completed. Heckmair thought he could climb
it by the usual methods; but every pitch on the Eiger's Face is
harder than it looks and tricky with ledges on which the snow
is only pressed against the rocks, with hand- and footholds that
let you down. So he had to leave his rucksack behind to have a
second go at the pitch, unencumbered. For this he kept his
crampons on, in view of the icing one continually meets on the
Face. It was an entirely new type of rock climbing, this ascent
of severe, often super-severe rock, overhanging in places—on
crampons. Heckmair frequently stood in imminent danger of a
fall, but somehow his fingers held him when he thought his
strength was used up. The scrape of his climbing irons on the
hard rock sounded like a furious gritting of teeth, which only
stopped when he disappeared from sight overhead.

We three followed without crampons.

It took ages before we had all got up that one-hundred-foot
vertical rock pitch. But surely not so long that it was dusk
already? It had suddenly grown very dark; but a glance at the
watch showed that, in spite of the darkness, it was still early
afternoon. Heavy clouds bulked up into the sky; and this time
the thundering roar caught up by the rocks and thrown back
in a hundred reverberations was not the sound of an airplane,
flying past dangerously near. This was genuine thunder.

By the time I reached Fritz's stance, the other two had gone ahead. They had untied from the communal rope again, so as to reach the "Spider" before the storm broke.

The thunderstorm provided a gloomy, menacing, but magnificent setting. A few minutes before, the sun had been shining, at least for the people down in Grindelwald. This sudden change was typical of the North Face; but we were already so familiar with its caprices that the oncoming storm caused us no alarm. Indeed, I was even sorry that there was no time to linger on the stance where Fritz had been waiting for me. That stance had all the elements of the miraculous; it was the first place, indeed the only one, in the whole six-thousand-foot Face where you could make yourself comfortable. It would have been grand to sit and rest there, looking down the great wall, into the valley, out over the surrounding hills. But the weather was hunting us on, and we followed the others.

The rock traverse to the "Spider" is no promenade. But at least the rocks at this point are horizontal and the stratification consequently favourable. And the patches of ice which link them were firm enough to allow us to bite deeply into them with our ice pitons. Not only is the traverse indescribably fine from the scenic angle, but it is so exciting and technically safe that we almost forgot the approaching storm. I cannot remember who first gave it the name of "the Traverse of the Gods," but it is comprehensively descriptive.

We reached the "Spider," the great sheet of ice set in the Face, quickly and without encountering any great difficulties. We hadn't time to examine the scene and the terrain more closely, and now even the possibility of so doing was withdrawn, for the sky had meanwhile taken on a blue-black tinge: then it disappeared altogether, as tattered mists chased across the Face, closing in on us, then lifting again to give a glimpse of things, then settling into a thick blanket of cloud.

As the storm set in it began to sleet, mixed with snow; lightning began to flash and thunder to grumble and roar.

We could still see Heckmair and Vörg, already on the way up the ice slope of the "Spider," about a rope's length and a half ahead of us; so we followed them up.

As I have already explained, the name "Spider" has been given to this steep patch of névé or ice high up in the almost vertical Face because of the white streaks spreading out from it in every direction like legs and clutching arms. These run more especially upward—in cracks and gullies up toward the summit snowcap—and down toward the "Death Bivouac." But nobody had discovered how apt the appellation was before we got there; nor had we, as yet, while we went up the first rope's length. We hadn't yet discovered that this "Spider" of snow, ice, and rock can become a fearful trap; that when hail or snow falls, ice particles and snow, coming sliding down from the steep summit névé, get canalised in the cracks and gullies, shoot out onto the "Spider" under pressure, there join up in a flood of annihilating fury and then sweep across the "Spider's" body, finally to fling themselves outward and downward, obliterating and taking with them everything that isn't part of the living rock. Nor is there any escape from the "Spider" for anyone caught on it by bad weather and avalanches.

We didn't know it then, but we very soon found out. Very soon. Immediately. . . .

I was already on the "Spider's" ice and had hacked out a reasonable stance in which I was able to stand quite well without crampons. I felt very safe on account of a deeply embedded ice piton. The rope ran through a snap link hung on the piton ring to Fritz, working his way up about sixty feet above me. I could see him vaguely through the mist and the driven snow.

Presently he disappeared from my sight, swallowed up

in the mist. The screaming of the storm, the rattle of the hail were alarming. I tried to penetrate the grey veils to catch a glimpse of him, but in vain. Only a greyness within a greyness. . . .

The howling of the wind increased, gathering a very strange note—a banging and swishing, a whistling hiss. This wasn't the voice of the storm anymore coming down out of a wild dance of ice particles and snowflakes, but something quite different. It was an avalanche, and as its harbingers, rocks and fragmented ice!

I snatched my rucksack up over my head, holding it firmly with one hand, while the other gripped the rope which ran up to my companion. I jammed myself against the ice cliff, just as the whole weight of the avalanche struck me. The rattle and hammering of stones on my pack was swallowed up by the clatter and roar of the avalanche. It snatched and clutched at me with fearful strength. Could I possibly survive such pressure? Hardly. . . . I was fighting for air, trying above all to prevent my rucksack from being torn away and also to stop the endless stream of rushing snow from building up between me and the ice slope and forcing me out of my footholds.

I hardly knew whether I was still standing, or was sliding down with it. Had the ice piton come adrift? No, I was still standing, and the peg was still firm; but the pressure was growing unbearable. And Fritz must be coming off any moment. Standing out there in the open he couldn't possibly withstand the fury of the avalanche . . . it must sweep him away. . . .

My thoughts were quite clear and logical, although I felt certain that this avalanche must hurl us all off the "Spider" and down to the bottom of the mighty wall. I was resisting only because one tries to resist so long as there is life in one. I was still gripping the rope with one hand, determined to do all I could to hold Fritz. At the same time I began to wonder whether we were already so high on the "Spider" that he wouldn't hit the rocks below, but would remain hanging on the ice slope if he came off, slid past me, and fetched up on the full run of the rope sixty feet below? And could I stand the shock if he hit me in passing?

All these thoughts were calm, without any sense of fear or desperation. I had no time for things like that. When would Fritz come off? I seemed to have been standing in this crushing, sliding Hell for endless ages. Had stones cut the rope and Fritz fallen alone, deprived of its protection? No, if that had happened the loose rope would have come sliding down to me. It was still stretching upward, so Fritz must somehow or other still be holding on. . . .

The pressure decreased, but I got no time to draw new breath or to shout before the next avalanche arrived. Its fury exceeded that of the first; it must bring the end for us. Even that realisation was almost objective. It was odd that no important thoughts moved me, such as one might expect on reaching the very frontier of existence itself. Nor did scenes from my whole life go chasing past in front of my eyes. My thoughts were almost banal, ridiculous, unimportant. I felt a little cross that the critics and wiseacres, and also the Grindelwald gravedigger, who had already numbered us, like all those who try the North Face, as belonging to his parish had been justified. Then I remembered my accident on the West Face of the Sturzhahn in the Totengebirge, years ago. I was trying to climb that difficult wall in the winter and fell 150 feet. On that occasion, too, I hadn't lived all my life over again, nor had I felt any great sense of despair, much as I loved life. Is everything different when one really crosses that border then?

And now, I was still alive; my rucksack was still protecting my head; the rope was still threaded through the snap link; and Fritz had still not fallen.

Then a new, unbelievable, and, this time, shattering realisation came over me. The pressure of the avalanche had ceased. The snow and the ice granules were tinkling away into the gulf. Even the raging of the storm seemed gentle to me, now that the crashing of the avalanche was stilled.

Then, tremulously, through the grey mists, came the first shouts, to be caught up by the cliffs framing the "Spider" and thrown back to the human beings, scarcely able to grasp the incredible truth. Names were being called, voices were answering: "Fritz! Heini! Anderl! Wiggerl!" I told myself that we were all alive. The others were all alive, and so was I. The greatest Eiger miracle had happened. The "White Spider" had not claimed a victim.

But was it really a miracle? Had the mountain been kind? Would it be true to say that the "Spider" had spared the lives of her victims?

Climbers are not only men of action, they are also matter-of-fact people. Such reflections are only to be explained by the first upsurge of joy at one's recaptured life; they won't stand up to sober judgment. The miracle and the mercy were none of nature's fashioning nor the mountain's, but were the result of man's will to do the right thing even in moments of direst peril. Who can say we were merely lucky?

A famous man once said, "In the long run only the efficient man has luck." I am not so presumptuous as to claim that we mountaineers are always efficient. It seems to me that one of Alfred Wegener's remarks fits our situation on the Eiger's "Spider" better. He said, "Luck is the output of one's last reserves."

We had put out our last reserves.

Kasparek was standing sixty feet above me on the ice

slope. When he heard the avalanche coming, he tried, with an instantaneous reaction, to drive in an ice piton. He had no time to be frightened even for a split second. The piton was only a few centimeters into the ice, and quite loose, when the first avalanche arrived. In spite of the danger, even while the avalanche was roaring down on him in all its fury, he thought of the loose piton. It would have to stay firm, it simply mustn't be torn out by the shock of the cascading masses of snow and ice, nor by a falling stone; so Kasparek kept one protecting arm over the piton. Stones hit him on the hand, tearing the skin away. He was in great pain, but his will to keep the piton firm was greater. And during the short respite between the first and second avalanche, he drove the piton into the ice up to its ring, hooked a snap link in, and attached himself to it. And that is why Fritz didn't come off. . . .*

It was only afterward, when the tension of the moment had passed, that I remembered having fastened myself by a rope sling to my own piton for greater protection during that same interval.

The avalanche took Heckmair and Vörg by surprise, on a projection about sixty feet below the rock rim above the "Spider." Owing to the configuration of the Face, it divided close above them into two separate streams; but the snow and ice granules pouring down over each of them were quite strong enough to sweep even men of their build away. Neither of them could obtain protection by driving in a piton, not only because there was no time, but because they hadn't one between them. I had the whole collection by then: owing to being last on the rope, I was carrying about twenty pounds of ironmongery that I had retrieved.

* Fritz Kasparek, "Vom Peilstein zur Eiger-Nordwand," *Das Bargland Buch* (Salzburg: 1951).

Heckmair had only his axe to hold him. The river of ice came up to his hips and threatened to whirl him away like a dead leaf; but he managed to resist the apparently irresistible pressure. At the same time he proved himself as an outstanding climbing partner as well as an outstanding leader of a climb. In spite of his own terrible distress, he had time to think of his number two, standing below him and still more exposed on the top of the knob. Holding his axe with one hand as an anchorage, he grabbed Vörg by the collar and held him tight. And so they both survived the assaults of the avalanches.

It was only now, when the danger was over, that Fritz felt the burning pain in his "scalped" hand. Only then did he shout up to Heckmair and Vörg, "Send a rope down, I'm hurt."

It took a long time to splice the ropes and send them down toward where Fritz was standing. And then they were still thirty feet short, so that Kasparek had to climb that distance unprotected.

How right Wegener is! Luck is certainly the output of one's last reserves.

This is how Heckmair described the end of the avalanche and his joy at finding that we were all still alive:

Slowly it grew lighter and the pressure eased. We knew then, but still could hardly believe, that we had come through safely. And how had the others fared? The mists were thinning now—and there—

"Wiggerl," I cried. "They're still on!"

It seemed impossible, an outright miracle. We started to shout, and there they were, actually answering. An indescribable joy swept over us. One only discovers how strong a thing team spirit can be when one sees the friends again whom one has counted for dead. . . .

We all joined up again at the upper rim of the "Spider."
Our feeling of delight at seeing the faces of our comrades
again was overwhelming. As the outward sign of our friendship we decided to tie up again in a single rope of four—all the
way to the top. And our leader should be Anderl. The "Spider's" avalanches hadn't been able to wipe us off the Face, but
they had succeeded in sweeping away with them the last petty
remnants of personal niggardliness and selfish ambition. The
only answer to this mighty wall was the enduring bond of
friendship, the will and the knowledge that each of us would
give of his very best. Each of us was responsible for the lives
of the others, and we refused to be separated anymore. We
were all filled with a great joy. From it stemmed the certainty
that we would climb out of the Face onto the summit and find
our way back to the valley where men live. It was in a mood
of almost cheerful relaxation that we resumed the climb.

— *Translated from the German by Hugh Merrick*

Postscript: Heinrich Harrer conquered the Eiger, and this
notable achievement led to his immediate recognition in the
mountaineering world as a first-rate climber. When Austria
was absorbed into Germany in 1939, he promptly joined the
expedition to climb one of the most daunting of Himalayan
peaks, Nanga Parbat.

In 1950 the Himalayas were a vast, unexplored range that justifiably provoked fear among climbers. In spite of this, the Frenchman Maurice Herzog led an expedition to the top of the 28,000-foot massif known as Annapurna. Perhaps more difficult than the ascent was the descent through unimaginable avalanches, crevasses, and bitter cold. His account became the most widely read mountaineering memoir of all time.

ANNAPURNA

First Conquest of an
8,000-meter Peak [26,493 Feet]

MAURICE HERZOG

The End of June

On the third of June 1950, the first light of dawn found us still clinging to the tent poles at Camp V. Gradually the wind abated, and with daylight, died away altogether. I made desperate attempts to push back the soft icy stuff which stifled me, but every movement became an act of heroism. My mental powers were numbed: thinking was an effort, and we did not exchange a single word.

What a repellent place it was! To everyone who reached it, Camp V became one of the worst memories of their lives. We had only one thought—to get away. We should have waited for the first rays of the sun, but at half past five we felt we couldn't stick it any longer.

"Let's go, Biscante," I muttered. "Can't stay here a minute longer."

"Yes, let's go," repeated Lachenal.

Which of us would have the energy to make tea? Although our minds worked slowly, we were quite able to envisage all the movements that would be necessary—and neither of us could face up to it. It couldn't be helped—we would just have to go without. It was quite hard enough work to get ourselves and our boots out of our sleeping bags—and the boots were frozen stiff so that we got them on only with the greatest difficulty. Every movement made us terribly breathless. We felt as if we were being stifled. Our gaiters were stiff as a board, and I succeeded in lacing mine up; Lachenal couldn't manage his.

"No need for the rope, eh, Biscante?"

"No need," replied Lachenal laconically.

That was two pounds saved. I pushed a tube of condensed milk, some nougat, and a pair of socks into my sack; one never knew, the socks might come in useful—they might even do as balaclavas. For the time being I stuffed them with first-aid equipment. The camera was loaded with a black-and-white film; I had a color film in reserve. I pulled the movie camera out from the bottom of my sleeping bag, wound it up and tried letting it run without film. There was a little click, then it stopped and jammed.

"Bad luck after bringing it so far," said Lachenal.

In spite of our photographer Ichac's precautions to lubricate it with special grease, the intense cold, even inside the sleeping bag, had frozen it. I left it at the camp rather sadly: I had looked forward to taking it to the top. I had used it up to 24,600 feet.

We went outside and put on our crampons, which we kept on all day. We wore as many clothes as possible; our sacks were very light. At six o'clock we started off. It was brilliantly fine, but also very cold. Our super-lightweight crampons bit deep into the steep slopes of ice and hard snow up which lay the first stage of our climb.

Later the slope became slightly less steep and more uniform. Sometimes the hard crust bore our weight, but at others we broke through and sank into soft powder snow which made progress exhausting. We took turns in making the track and often stopped without any word having passed between us. Each of us lived in a closed and private world of his own. I was suspicious of my mental processes; my mind was working very slowly and I was perfectly aware of the low state of my intelligence. It was easiest just to stick to one thought at a time—safest, too. The cold was penetrating; for all our special eiderdown clothing we felt as if we'd nothing on. Whenever we halted, we stamped our feet hard. Lachenal went as far as to take off one boot which was a bit tight; he was in terror of frostbite.

"I don't want to be like Lambert," he said. Raymond Lambert, a Geneva guide, had to have all his toes amputated after an eventful climb during which he got his feet frostbitten.* While Lachenal rubbed himself hard, I looked at the summits all around us; already we overtopped them all except the distant Dhaulagiri. The complicated structure of these mountains, with which our many laborious explorations had made us familiar, was now spread out plainly at our feet.

The going was incredibly exhausting, and every step was a struggle of mind over matter. We came out into the sunlight,

---

* In May 1952 Lambert, with the Sherpa Ang-Tsering, reached 28,215 feet on Mount Everest, possibly the highest point yet attained. –Translator's note

and by way of marking the occasion made yet another halt. Lachenal continued to complain of his feet. "I can't feel anything. I think I'm beginning to get frostbite." And once again he undid his boot.

I began to be seriously worried. I realized very well the risk we were running; I knew from experience how insidiously and quickly frostbite can set in if one is not extremely careful. Nor was Lachenal under any illusions. "We're in danger of having frozen feet. Do you think it's worth it?"

This was most disturbing. It was my responsibility as leader to think of the others. There was no doubt about frostbite being a very real danger. Did Annapurna justify such risks? That was the question I asked myself; it continued to worry me.

Lachenal had laced his boots up again, and once more we continued to force our way through the exhausting snow. The whole of the Sickle glacier was now in view, bathed in light. We still had a long way to go to cross it, and then there was that rock band—would we find a gap in it?

My feet, like Lachenal's, were very cold and I continued to wriggle my toes, even when we were moving. I could not feel them, but that was nothing new in the mountains, and if I kept on moving them it would keep the circulation going.

Lachenal appeared to me as a sort of specter—he was alone in his world, I in mine. But—and this was odd enough—any effort was slightly *less* exhausting than lower down. Perhaps it was hope lending us wings. Even through dark glasses the snow was blinding—the sun beating straight down on the ice. We looked down upon precipitous ridges which dropped away into space, and upon tiny glaciers far, far below. Familiar peaks soared arrow-like into the sky. Suddenly Lachenal grabbed me:

"If I go back, what will you do?"

A whole sequence of pictures flashed through my head: the days of marching in sweltering heat, the hard pitches we had overcome, the tremendous efforts we had all made to lay siege to the mountain, the daily heroism of all my friends in establishing the camps. Now we were nearing our goal. In an hour or two, perhaps, victory would be ours. Must we give up? Impossible! My whole being revolted against the idea. I had made up my mind, irrevocably. Today we were consecrating an ideal, and no sacrifice was too great. I heard my voice clearly:

"I should go on by myself."

I would go alone. If he wished to go down it was not for me to stop him. He must make his own choice freely.

"Then I'll follow you."

The die was cast. I was no longer anxious. Nothing could stop us now from getting to the top. The psychological atmosphere changed with these few words, and we went forward now as brothers.

I felt as though I were plunging into something new and quite abnormal. I had the strangest and most vivid impressions, such as I had never before known in the mountains. There was something unnatural in the way I saw Lachenal and everything around us. I smiled to myself at the paltriness of our efforts, for I could stand apart and watch myself making these efforts. But all sense of exertion was gone, as though there were no longer any gravity. This diaphanous landscape, this quintessence of purity—these were not the mountains I knew: they were the mountains of my dreams.

The snow, sprinkled over every rock and gleaming in the sun, was of a radiant beauty that touched me to the heart. I had never seen such complete transparency, and I was living in a world of crystal. Sounds were indistinct, the atmosphere like cotton wool.

An astonishing happiness welled up in me, but I could not define it. Everything was so new, so utterly unprecedented. It was not in the least like anything I had known in the Alps, where one feels buoyed up by the presence of others—by people of whom one is vaguely aware, or even by the dwellings one can see in the far distance.

This was quite different. An enormous gulf was between me and the world. This was a different universe—withered, desert, lifeless; a fantastic universe where the presence of man was not foreseen, perhaps not desired. We were braving an interdict, overstepping a boundary, and yet we had no fear as we continued upward. I thought of the famous ladder of Saint Theresa of Avila. Something clutched at my heart.

Did Lachenal share these feelings? The summit ridge drew nearer, and we reached the foot of the ultimate rock band. The slope was very steep and the snow interspersed with rocks.

"Couloir!"

A finger pointed. The whispered word from one to another indicated the key to the rocks—the last line of defense.

"What luck!"

The couloir up the rock, though steep, was feasible.

The sky was a deep sapphire blue. With a great effort we edged over to the right, avoiding the rocks; we preferred to keep to the snow on account of our crampons and it was not long before we set foot in the couloir. It was fairly steep, and we had a minute's hesitation. Should we have enough strength left to overcome this final obstacle?

Fortunately the snow was hard, and by kicking steps we were able to manage, thanks to our crampons. A false move would have been fatal. There was no need to make handholds—our axes, driven in as far as possible, served us for an anchor.

Lachenal went splendidly. What a wonderful contrast to

the early days! It was a hard struggle here, but he kept going. Lifting our eyes occasionally from the slope, we saw the couloir opening out on to . . . well, we didn't quite know, probably a ridge. But where was the top—left or right? Stopping at every step, leaning on our axes we tried to recover our breath and to calm down our racing hearts, which were thumping as though they would burst. We knew we were there now—that nothing could stop us. No need to exchange looks—each of us would have read the same determination in the other's eyes. A slight detour to the left, a few more steps—the summit ridge came gradually nearer—a few rocks to avoid. We dragged ourselves up. Could we possibly be there?

Yes!

A fierce and savage wind tore at us.

We were on top of Annapurna! 8,075 meters, 26,493 feet.

Our hearts overflowed with an unspeakable happiness.

"If only the others could know . . ."

If only everyone could know!

The summit was a corniced crest of ice, and the precipices on the far side which plunged vertically down beneath us, were terrifying, unfathomable. There could be few other mountains in the world like this. Clouds floated halfway down, concealing the gentle, fertile valley of Pokhara, twenty-three thousand feet below. Above us there was nothing!

Our mission was accomplished. But at the same time we had accomplished something infinitely greater. How wonderful life would now become! What an inconceivable experience it is to attain one's ideal and, at the very same moment, to fulfill oneself. I was stirred to the depths of my being. Never had I felt happiness like this—so intense and yet so pure. That brown rock, the highest of them all, that ridge of ice—were these the goals of a lifetime? Or were they, rather, the limits of man's pride?

"Well, what about going down?"

Lachenal shook me. What were his own feelings? Did he simply think he had finished another climb, as in the Alps? Did he think one could just go down again like that, with nothing more to it?

"One minute, I must take some photographs."

"Hurry up!"

I fumbled feverishly in my sack, pulled out the camera, took out the little French flag which was right at the bottom, and the pennants. Useless gestures, no doubt, but something more than symbols—eloquent tokens of affection and good-will. I tied the strips of material—stained by sweat and by the food in the sacks—to the shaft of my ice axe, the only flagstaff at hand. Then I focused my camera on Lachenal.

"Now, will you take me?"

"Hand it over—hurry up!" said Lachenal.

He took several pictures and then handed me back the camera. I loaded a color film and we repeated the process to be certain of bringing back records to be cherished in the future.

"Are you mad?" asked Lachenal. "We haven't a minute to lose: we must go down at once."

And in fact a glance round showed me that the weather was no longer gloriously fine as it had been in the morning. Lachenal was becoming impatient.

"We must go down!"

He was right. His was the reaction of the mountaineer who knows his own domain. But I just could not accustom myself to the idea that we had won our victory. It seemed inconceivable that we should have trodden those summit snows.

It was impossible to build a cairn; there were no stones; everything was frozen. Lachenal stamped his feet; he felt them freezing. I felt mine freezing too, but paid little attention.

The highest mountain to be climbed by man lay under our feet! The names of our predecessors on these heights raced through my mind: Mummery, Mallory and Irvine, Bauer, Welzenbach, Tilman, Shipton. How many of them were dead—how many had found on these mountains what, to them, was the finest end of all?

My joy was touched with humility. It was not just one party that had climbed Annapurna today, but a whole expedition. I thought of all the others in the camps perched on the slopes at our feet, and I knew it was because of their efforts and their sacrifices that we had succeeded. There are times when the most complicated actions are suddenly summed up, distilled, and strike you with illuminating clarity: so it was with this irresistible upward surge which had landed us two here.

Pictures passed through my mind—the Chamonix valley, where I had spent the most marvelous moments of my childhood; Mont Blanc, which so tremendously impressed me! I was a child when I first saw "the Mont Blanc people" coming home, and to me there was a queer look about them; a strange light shone in their eyes.

"Come on, straight down," called Lachenal.

He had already done up his sack and started going down. I took out my pocket aneroid: 8,500 meters. I smiled. I swallowed a little condensed milk and left the tube behind—the only trace of our passage. I did up my sack, put on my gloves and my glasses, seized my ice axe; one look around and I, too, hurried down the slope. Before disappearing into the couloir I gave one last look at the summit which would henceforth be all our joy and all our consolation.

Lachenal was already far below; he had reached the foot of the couloir. I hurried down in his tracks. I went as fast as I could, but it was dangerous going. At every step one had to take care that the snow did not break away beneath one's weight. Lachenal, going faster than I thought he was capable of, was now on the long traverse. It was my turn to cross the area of mixed rock and snow. At last I reached the foot of the rock band. I had hurried and I was out of breath. I undid my sack. What had I been going to do? I couldn't say.

"My gloves!"

Before I had time to bend over, I saw them slide and roll. They went further and further straight down the slope. I remained where I was, quite stunned. I watched them rolling down slowly, with no appearance of stopping. The movement of those gloves was engraved in my sight as something irredeemable, against which I was powerless. The consequences might be most serious. What was I to do?

"Quickly, down to Camp V."

Rébuffat and Terray would be there. My concern dissolved like magic. I now had a fixed objective again: to reach the camp. Never for a minute did it occur to me to use as gloves the socks which I always carry in reserve for just such a mishap as this.

On I went, trying to catch up with Lachenal. It had been two o'clock when we reached the summit; we had started out at six in the morning, but I had to admit that I had lost all sense of time. I felt as if I were running, whereas in actual fact I was walking normally, perhaps rather slowly, and I had to keep stopping to get my breath. The sky was now covered with clouds, everything had become gray and dirty looking. An icy wind sprang up, boding no good. We must push on! But where was Lachenal? I spotted him a couple of hundred yards away, looking as if he was never going to stop. And I had thought he was in indifferent form!

The clouds grew thicker and came right down over us; the wind blew stronger, but I did not suffer from the cold. Perhaps the descent had restored my circulation. Should I be able to find the tents in the mist? I watched the rib ending in the beak-like point which overlooked the camp. It was gradually swallowed up by the clouds, but I was able to make out the spearhead rib lower down. If the mist should thicken I would make straight for that rib and follow it down, and in this way I should be bound to come upon the tent.

Lachenal disappeared from time to time, and then the mist was so thick that I lost sight of him altogether. I kept going at the same speed, as fast as my breathing would allow.

The slope was now steeper; a few patches of bare ice followed the smooth stretches of snow. A good sign—I was nearing the camp. How difficult to find one's way in thick mist! I kept the course which I had set by the steepest angle of the slope. The ground was broken; with my crampons I went straight down walls of bare ice. There were some patches ahead—a few more steps. It was the camp all right, but there were *two tents*!

So Rébuffat and Terray had come up. What a mercy! I should be able to tell them that we had been successful, that we were returning from the top. How thrilled they would be!

I got there, dropping down from above. The platform had been extended, and the two tents were facing each other. I tripped over one of the guy-ropes of the first tent; there was movement inside, they had heard me. Rébuffat and Terray put their heads out.

"We've made it. We're back from Annapurna!"

The Crevasse

Rébuffat and Terray received the news with great excitement.

"But what about Biscante?" asked Terray anxiously.

"He won't be long. He was just in front of me! What a

day—started out at six this morning—didn't stop . . . got up at last."

Words failed me. I had so much to say. The sight of familiar faces dispelled the strange feeling that I had experienced since morning, and I became, once more, just a mountaineer.

Terray, who was speechless with delight, wrung my hands. Then the smile vanished from his face: "Maurice—your hands!" There was an uneasy silence. I had forgotten that I had lost my gloves: my fingers were violet and white and hard as wood. The other two stared at them in dismay—they realized the full seriousness of the injury. But, still blissfully floating on a sea of joy remote from reality, I leaned over toward Terray and said confidentially, "You're in such splendid form, and you've done so marvelously, it's absolutely tragic you didn't come up there with us!"

"What I did was for the Expedition, my dear Maurice, and anyway you've got up, and that's a victory for the whole lot of us."

I nearly burst with happiness. How could I tell him all that his answer meant to me? The rapture I had felt on the summit, which might have seemed a purely personal, egotistical emotion, had been transformed by his words into a complete and perfect joy with no shadow upon it. His answer proved that this victory was not just one man's achievement, a matter for personal pride; no—and Terray was the first to understand this—it was a victory for us all, a victory for mankind itself.

"Hi! Help! Help!"

"Biscante!" exclaimed the others.

Still half-intoxicated and remote from reality I had heard nothing. Terray felt a chill at his heart, and his thoughts flew to his partner on so many unforgettable climbs; together they had so often skirted death, and won so many splendid victories. Putting his head out, and seeing Lachenal clinging to the slope a hundred yards lower down, he dressed in frantic haste.

Out he went. But the slope was bare now; Lachenal had disappeared. Terray was horribly frightened, and he could only utter unintelligible cries. It was a ghastly moment for him. A violent wind sent the mist tearing by. Under the stress of emotion Terray had not realized how it falsified distances.

"Biscante! Biscante!"

He had spotted him, through a rift in the mist, lying on the slope much lower down than he had thought. Terray set his teeth, and glissaded down like a madman. How would he be able to brake without crampons on the wind-hardened snow? But Terray was a first-class skier, and with a jump turn he stopped beside Lachenal, who was suffering from concussion after his tremendous fall. In a state of collapse, with no ice axe, balaclava, or gloves, and only one crampon, he gazed vacantly around him.

"My feet are frostbitten. Take me down . . . take me down, so that Oudot can see to me."

"It can't be done," said Terray sorrowfully. "Can't you see we're in the middle of a storm . . . It'll be dark soon."

But Lachenal was obsessed by the fear of amputation. With a gesture of despair he tore the axe out of Terray's hands and tried to force his way down but soon saw the futility of his action and resolved to climb up to the camp. While Terray cut steps without stopping, Lachenal, ravaged and exhausted as he was, dragged himself along on all fours.

Meanwhile I had gone into Rébuffat's tent. He was appalled at the sight of my hands and, as rather incoherently I told him what we had done, he took a piece of rope and began flicking my fingers. Then he took off my boots with great difficulty for my feet were swollen, and beat my feet and rubbed me. We soon heard Terray giving Lachenal the same treatment in the other tent.

For our comrades it was a tragic moment: Annapurna was conquered, and the first eight-thousander had been climbed.

Every one of us had been ready to sacrifice everything for this. Yet, as they looked at our feet and hands, what can Terray and Rébuffat have felt?

Outside the storm howled and the snow was still falling. The mist grew thick and darkness came. As on the previous night, we had to cling to the poles to prevent the tents being carried away by the wind. The only two air mattresses were given to Lachenal and myself while Terray and Rébuffat both sat on ropes, rucksacks, and provisions to keep themselves off the snow. They rubbed, slapped, and beat us with a rope. Sometimes the blows fell on the living flesh, and howls arose from both tents. Rébuffat persevered; it was essential to continue, painful as it was. Gradually life returned to my feet as well as to my hands, and circulation started again. Lachenal, too, found that feeling was returning.

Now Terray summoned up the energy to prepare some hot drinks. He called to Rébuffat that he would pass him a mug, so two hands stretched out toward each other between the two tents and were instantly covered with snow. The liquid was boiling though scarcely more than sixty degrees centigrade (140° Fahrenheit). I swallowed it greedily and felt infinitely better.

The night was absolute hell. Frightful onslaughts of wind battered us incessantly, while the never-ceasing snow piled up on the tents.

Now and again I heard voices from next door—it was Terray massaging Lachenal with admirable perseverance, only stopping to ply him with hot drinks. In our tent Rébuffat was quite worn out, but satisfied that warmth was returning to my limbs.

Lying half-unconscious I was scarcely aware of the passage of time. There were moments when I was able to see our situation in its true dramatic light, but the rest of the time I was plunged in an inexplicable stupor with no thought for the consequences of our victory.

As the night wore on the snow lay heavier on the tent, and once again I had the frightful feeling of being slowly and silently asphyxiated. I tried, with all the strength of which I was capable, to push off with both forearms the mass that was crushing me. These fearful exertions left me gasping for breath and I fell back into the same exhausted state. It was much worse than the previous night.

"Rébuffat! Gaston! Gaston!"

I recognized Terray's voice.

"Time to be off!"

I heard the sounds without grasping their meaning. Was it light already? I was not in the least surprised that the other two had given up all thought of going to the top, and I did not at all grasp the measure of their sacrifice.

Outside, the storm redoubled in violence. The tent shook and the fabric flapped alarmingly. It had usually been fine in the mornings: did this mean the monsoon was upon us? We knew it was not far off—could this be its first onslaught?

"Gaston! Are you ready?" Terray called again.

"One minute," answered Rébuffat. He did not have an easy job: he had to put my boots on and do everything to get me ready. I let myself be handled like a baby. In the other tent Terray finished dressing Lachenal whose feet were still swollen and would not fit into his boots. So Terray gave him his own, which were bigger. To get Lachenal's onto his own feet he had to make slits in them. As a precaution he put a sleeping bag and some food into his sack and shouted to us to do the same. Were his words lost in the storm? Or were we too intent on leaving this hellish place to listen to his instructions?

Lachenal and Terray were already outside.

"We're going down!" they shouted.

Then Rébuffat tied me on the rope and we went out. There were only two ice axes for the four of us, so Rébuffat and Terray took them as a matter of course. For a moment as we left the two tents of Camp V, I felt childishly ashamed at leaving all this good equipment behind.

Already the first rope seemed a long way down below us. We were blinded by the squalls of snow and we could not hear each other a yard away. We had both put on our *cagoules*, for it was very cold. The snow was apt to slide and the rope often came in useful.

Ahead of us the other two were losing no time. Lachenal went first and, safeguarded by Terray, he forced the pace in his anxiety to get down. There were no tracks to show us the way, but it was engraved on all our minds—straight down the slope for 400 yards then traverse to the left for 150 to 200 yards to get to Camp IV. The snow was thinning and the wind less violent. Was it going to clear? We hardly dared to hope so. A wall of seracs brought us up short.

"It's to the left," I said, "I remember perfectly."

Somebody else thought it was to the right. We started going down again. The wind had dropped completely, but the snow fell in big flakes. The mist was thick, and, not to lose each other, we walked in line: I was third and I could barely see Lachenal who was first. It was impossible to recognize any of the pitches. We were all experienced enough mountaineers to know that even on familiar ground it is easy to make mistakes in such weather. Distances are deceptive, one cannot tell whether one is going up or down. We kept colliding with hummocks which we had taken for hollows. The mist, the falling snowflakes, the carpet of snow, all merged into the same whitish tone and confused our vision. The towering outlines of the seracs took on fantastic shapes and seemed to move slowly around us.

Our situation was not desperate, we were certainly not lost. We would have to go lower down; the traverse must begin further on—I remembered the serac which served as a milestone. The snow stuck to our *cagoules*, and turned us into white phantoms noiselessly flitting against a background equally white. We began to sink in dreadfully, and there is nothing worse for bodies already on the edge of exhaustion.

Were we too high or too low? No one could tell. Perhaps we had better try slanting over to the left! The snow was in a dangerous condition, but we did not seem to realize it. We were forced to admit that we were not on the right route, so we retraced our steps and climbed up above the serac which overhung us. No doubt, we decided, we should be on the right level now. With Rébuffat leading, we went back over the way which had cost us such an effort. I followed him jerkily, saying nothing, and determined to go on to the end. If Rébuffat had fallen I could never have held him.

We went doggedly on from one serac to another. Each time we thought we had recognized the right route, and each time there was a fresh disappointment. If only the mist would lift, if only the snow would stop for a second! On the slope it seemed to be growing deeper every minute. Only Terray and Rébuffat were capable of breaking the trail and they relieved each other at regular intervals, without a word and without a second's hesitation.

I admired this determination of Rébuffat's for which he is so justly famed. He did not intend to die! With the strength of desperation and at the price of superhuman effort he forged ahead. The slowness of his progress would have dismayed even the most obstinate climber, but he would not give up, and in the end the mountain yielded in face of his perseverance.

Terray, when his turn came, charged madly ahead. He was like a force of nature: at all costs he would break down these

prison walls that penned us in. His physical strength was
exceptional, his willpower no less remarkable. Lachenal gave
him considerable trouble. Perhaps he was not quite in his
right mind. He said it was no use going on; we must dig a hole
in the snow and wait for fine weather. He swore at Terray and
called him a madman. Nobody but Terray would have been
capable of dealing with him—he just tugged sharply on the
rope and Lachenal was forced to follow.

We were well and truly lost.

The weather did not seem likely to improve. A minute ago
we had still had ideas about which way to go—now we had
none. This way or that . . . We went on at random to allow for
the chance of a miracle which appeared increasingly unlikely.
The instinct of self-preservation in the two fit members of the
party alternated with a hopelessness which made them completely irresponsible. Each in turn did the maddest things:
Terray traversed the steep and avalanchy slopes with one
crampon badly adjusted. He and Rébuffat performed incredible feats of balance without the least slip.

Camp IV was certainly on the left, on the edge of the
Sickle. On that point we were all agreed. But it was very hard
to find. The wall of ice that gave it such magnificent protection was now ironical, for it hid the tents from us. In mist like
this we should have to be right on top of them before we spotted them.

Perhaps if we called someone would hear us? Lachenal
gave the signal, but snow absorbs sound and his shout
seemed to carry only a few yards. All four of us called out
together: "One . . . two . . . three . . . Help!"

We got the impression that our united shout carried a long
way, so we began again: "One . . . two . . . three . . . Help!"
Not a sound in reply!

Now and again Terray took off his boots and rubbed his

feet; the sight of our frostbitten limbs had made him aware of the danger and he had the strength of mind to do something about it. Like Lachenal, he was haunted by the idea of amputation. For me, it was too late: my feet and hands, already affected from yesterday, were beginning to freeze up again.

We had eaten nothing since the day before, and we had been on the go the whole time, but men's resources of energy in the face of death are inexhaustible. When the end seems imminent, there still remain reserves, though it needs tremendous willpower to call them up.

Time passed, but we had no idea how long. Night was approaching, and we were terrified, though none of us made any complaint. Rébuffat and I found a way that we thought we remembered, but were brought to a halt by the extreme steepness of the slope—the mist turned it into a vertical wall. We were to find next day that at that moment we had been only thirty yards from the camp, and that the wall was the very one that sheltered the tent which would have been our salvation.

"We must find a crevasse."

"We can't stay here all night!"

"A hole—it's the only thing."

"We'll all die in it."

Night had suddenly fallen and it was essential to come to a decision without wasting another minute; if we remained on the slope, we should be dead before morning. We would have to bivouac. What the conditions would be like, we could guess, for we all knew what it meant to bivouac above twenty-three thousand feet.

With his axe Terray began to dig a hole. Lachenal went over to a snow-filled crevasse a few yards further on, then suddenly let out a yell and disappeared before our eyes. We stood helpless: should we, or rather would Terray and Rébuffat,

have enough strength for all the maneuvers with the rope that
would be needed to get him out? The crevasse was completely blocked up save for the one little hole which Lachenal
had fallen through.

"Lachenal!" called Terray.

A voice, muffled by many thicknesses of ice and snow, came
up to us. It was impossible to make out what it was saying.

"Lachenal!"

Terray jerked the rope violently; this time we could hear.

"I'm here!"

"Anything broken?"

"No! It'll do for the night! Come along."

This shelter was heaven-sent. None of us would have had
the strength to dig a hole big enough to protect the lot of us
from the wind. Without hesitation Terray let himself drop
into the crevasse, and a loud "Come on!" told us he had
arrived safely. In my turn I let myself go: it was a regular
toboggan slide. I shot down a sort of twisting tunnel, very
steep, and about thirty feet long. I came out at great speed
into the opening beyond and was literally hurled to the bottom of the crevasse. We let Rébuffat know he could come by
giving a tug on the rope.

The intense cold of this minute grotto shriveled us up, the
enclosing walls of ice were damp and the floor a carpet of
fresh snow; by huddling together there was just room for the
four of us. Icicles hung from the ceiling and we broke some of
them off to make more headroom and kept little bits to suck—
it was a long time since we had had anything to drink.

That was our shelter for the night. At least we should be
protected from the wind, and the temperature would remain
fairly even, though the damp was extremely unpleasant. We
settled ourselves in the dark as best we could. As always in a
bivouac we took off our boots; without this precaution the

constriction would cause immediate frostbite. Terray unrolled the sleeping bag which he had had the foresight to bring, and settled himself in relative comfort. We put on everything warm that we had, and to avoid contact with the snow I sat on the movie camera. We huddled close up to each other, in our search for a hypothetical position in which the warmth of our bodies could be combined without loss, but we couldn't keep still for a second.

We did not open our mouths—signs were less of an effort than words. Every man withdrew into himself and took refuge in his own inner world. Terray massaged Lachenal's feet; Rébuffat felt his feet freezing too, but he had sufficient strength to rub them himself. I remained motionless, unseeing. My feet and hands went on freezing, but what could be done? I attempted to forget suffering by withdrawing into myself, trying to forget the passing of time, trying not to feel the devouring and numbing cold which insidiously gained upon us.

Terray shared his sleeping bag with Lachenal, putting his feet and hands inside the precious eiderdown. At the same time he went on rubbing.

Anyhow the frostbite won't spread further, he was thinking.

None of us could make any movement without upsetting the others, and the positions we had taken up with such care were continually being altered so that we had to start all over again. This kept us busy. Rébuffat persevered with his rubbing and complained of his feet; like Terray he was thinking: we mustn't look beyond tomorrow—afterward we'll see. But he was not blind to the fact that "afterward" was one big question mark.

Terray generously tried to give me part of his sleeping bag. He had understood the seriousness of my condition, and knew why it was that I said nothing and remained quite passive; he realized that I had abandoned all hope for myself. He massaged me for nearly two hours; his feet, too, might have frozen, but he didn't appear to give the matter a thought. I found new courage simply in contemplating his unselfishness; he was doing so much to help me that it would have been ungrateful of me not to go on struggling to live. Though my heart was like a lump of ice itself, I was astonished to feel no pain. Everything material about me seemed to have dropped away. I seemed to be quite clear in my thoughts and yet I floated in a kind of peaceful happiness. There was still a breath of life in me, but it dwindled steadily as the hours went by. Terray's massage no longer had any effect upon me. All was over, I thought. Wasn't this cavern the most beautiful grave I could hope for? Death caused me no grief, no regret—I smiled at the thought.

After hours of torpor a voice mumbled "Daylight!"

This made some impression on the others. I felt only surprised—I had not thought that daylight would penetrate so far down.

"Too early to start," said Rébuffat.

A ghastly light spread through our grotto and we could just vaguely make out the shapes of each other's heads. A queer noise from a long way off came down to us—a sort of prolonged hiss. The noise increased. Suddenly I was buried, blinded, smothered beneath an avalanche of new snow. The icy snow spread over the cavern, finding its way through every gap in our clothing. I ducked my head between my knees and covered myself with both arms. The snow flowed on and on. There was a terrible silence. We were not completely buried, but there was snow everywhere. We got up, taking care not to bang our heads against the ceiling of ice, and tried to shake ourselves. We were all in our stockinged feet in the snow. The first thing to do was to find our boots.

Rébuffat and Terray began to search, and realized at once that they were blind. Yesterday they had taken off their glasses to lead us down and now they were paying for it. Lachenal was the first to lay hands upon a pair of boots. He tried to put them on, but they were Rébuffat's. Rébuffat attempted to climb up the chute down which we had come yesterday, and which the avalanche had followed in its turn.

"Hi, Gaston! What's the weather like?" called up Terray.

"Can't see a thing. It's blowing hard."

We were still groping for our things. Terray found his boots and put them on awkwardly, unable to see what he was doing. Lachenal helped him, but he was all on edge and fearfully impatient, in striking contrast to my immobility. Terray then went up the icy channel, puffing and blowing, and at last reached the outer world. He was met by terrible gusts of wind that cut right through him and lashed his face.

Bad weather, he said to himself, this time it's the end. We're lost . . . we'll never come through.

At the bottom of the crevasse there were still two of us looking for our boots. Lachenal poked fiercely with an ice axe. I was calmer and tried to proceed more rationally. We extracted crampons and an axe in turn from the snow, but still no boots.

Well—so this cavern was to be our last resting place! There was very little room—we were bent double and got in each other's way. Lachenal decided to go out without his boots. He called frantically, hauled himself up on the rope, trying to get a hold or to wiggle his way up, digging his toes into the snow walls. Terray from outside pulled as hard as he could. I watched him go; he gathered speed and disappeared.

When he emerged from the opening he saw the sky was clear and blue, and he began to run like a madman, shrieking, "It's fine, it's fine!"

I set to work again to search the cave. The boots *had* to be found, or Lachenal and I were done for. On all fours, with nothing on my hands or feet I raked the snow, stirring it around this way and that, hoping every second to come upon something hard. I was no longer capable of thinking—I reacted like an animal fighting for its life.

I found one boot! The other was tied to it—a pair! Having ransacked the whole cave I at last found the other pair. But in spite of all my efforts I could not find the movie camera, and gave up in despair. There was no question of putting my boots on—my hands were like lumps of wood and I could hold nothing in my fingers; my feet were very swollen—I should never be able to get boots on them. I twisted the rope around the boots as well as I could and called up the chute:

"Lionel . . . Boots!"

There was no answer, but he must have heard for with a jerk the precious boots shot up. Soon after the rope came down again. My turn. I wound the rope around me. I could not pull it tight so I made a whole series of little knots. Their combined strength, I hoped, would be enough to hold me. I had no strength to shout again; I gave a great tug on the rope, and Terray understood.

At the first step I had to kick a notch in the hard snow for my toes. Further on I expected to be able to get up more easily by wedging myself across the runnel. I wriggled up a few yards like this and then I tried to dig my hands and my feet into the wall. My hands were stiff and hard right up to the wrists and my feet had no feeling up to the ankles, the joints were inflexible and this hampered me greatly.

Somehow or other I succeeded in working my way up, while Terray pulled so hard he nearly choked me. I began to see more distinctly and so knew that I must be nearing the opening. Often I fell back, but I clung on and wedged myself in again as best I could. My heart was bursting and I was forced to rest. A fresh wave of energy enabled me to crawl to the top. I pulled myself out by clutching Terray's legs; he was just about all in and I was in the last stages of exhaustion. Terray was close to me and I whispered:

"Lionel . . . I'm dying!"

He supported me and helped me away from the crevasse. Lachenal and Rébuffat were sitting in the snow a few yards away. The instant Lionel let go of me I sank down and dragged myself along on all fours.

The weather was perfect. Quantities of snow had fallen the day before and the mountains were resplendent. Never had I seen them look so beautiful—our last day would be magnificent.

Rébuffat and Terray were completely blind; as he came along with me Terray knocked into things and I had to direct him. Rébuffat, too, could not move a step without guidance. It was terrifying to be blind when there was danger all around. Lachenal's frozen feet affected his nervous system. His behavior was disquieting—he was possessed by the most fantastic ideas:

"I tell you we must go down . . . down there . . ."

"You've nothing on your feet!"

"Don't worry about that."

"You're off your head. The way's not there . . . it's to the left!"

He was already standing up; he wanted to go straight down to the bottom of the glacier. Terray held him back, made him sit down, and though he couldn't see, helped Lachenal put his boots on.

Behind them I was living in my own private dream. I knew the end was near, but it was the end that all mountaineers wish for—an end in keeping with their ruling passion. I was

consciously grateful to the mountains for being so beautiful
for me that day, and as awed by their silence as if I had been in
church. I was in no pain, and had no worry. My utter calmness was alarming. Terray came staggering toward me, and I
told him, "It's all over for me. Go on . . . you have a
chance . . . you must take it . . . over to the left . . . that's
the way."

I felt better after telling him that. But Terray would have
none of it: "We'll help you. If we get away, so will you."

At this moment Lachenal shouted, "Help! Help!"

Obviously he didn't know what he was doing . . . Or did
he? He was the only one of the four of us who could see
Camp II down below. Perhaps his calls would be heard. They
were shrieks of despair, reminding me tragically of some
climbers lost in the Mont Blanc massif whom I had endeavored to save. Now it was our turn. The impression was vivid:
we were lost.

I joined in with the others: "One . . . two . . . three . . .
Help! One . . . two . . . three . . . *Help!*" We tried to shout
together, but without much success; our voices could not have
carried more than ten feet. The noise I made was more of a
whisper than a shout. Terray insisted that I should put my
boots on, but my hands were dead. Neither Rébuffat nor Terray, who were unable to see, could help much, so I said to
Lachenal: "Come and help me to put my boots on."

"Don't be silly, we must go down!"

And off he went once again in the wrong direction, straight
down. I was not in the least angry with him; he had been
sorely tried by the altitude and by everything he had gone
through.

Terray resolutely got out his knife, and with fumbling
hands slit the uppers of my boots back and front. Split in two
like this I could get them on, but it was not easy and I had to

make several attempts. Soon I lost heart—what was the use of it all anyway since I was going to stay where I was? But Terray pulled violently and finally he succeeded. He laced up my now gigantic boots, missing half the hooks. I was ready now. But how was I going to walk with my stiff joints?

"To the left, Lionel!"

"You're crazy, Maurice," said Lachenal, "it's to the right, straight down."

Terray did not know what to think of these conflicting views. He had not given up like me, he was going to fight; but what, at the moment, could he do? The three of them discussed which way to go.

I remained sitting in the snow. Gradually my mind lost grip—why should I struggle? I would just let myself drift. I saw pictures of shady slopes, peaceful paths, there was a scent of resin. It was pleasant—I was going to die in my own mountains. My body had no feeling—everything was frozen.

"Aah . . . aah!"

Was it a groan or a call? I gathered my strength for one cry: "They're coming!" The others heard me and shouted for joy. What a miraculous apparition! "Schatz . . . it's Schatz!"

Barely two hundred yards away Marcel Schatz, waist deep in snow, was coming slowly toward us like a boat on the surface of the slope. I found this vision of a strong and invincible deliverer inexpressibly moving. I expected everything of him. The shock was violent, and quite shattered me. Death clutched at me and I gave myself up.

When I came to again the wish to live returned and I experienced a violent revulsion of feeling. All was not lost! As Schatz came nearer my eyes never left him for a second—twenty yards—ten yards—he came straight toward me. Why? Without a word he leaned over me, held me close, hugged me, and his warm breath revived me.

I could not make the slightest movement—I was like marble. My heart was overwhelmed by such tremendous feelings and yet my eyes remained dry.

"It is wonderful—what you have done!"

The Avalanche

I was clearheaded and delirious by turns, and had the queer feeling that my eyes were glazed. Schatz looked after me like a mother, and while the others were shouting with joy, he put his rope around me. The sky was blue—the deep blue of extreme altitude, so dark that one can almost see the stars—and we were bathed in the warm rays of the sun. Schatz spoke gently:

"We'll be moving now, Maurice, old man."

I could not help obeying him, and with his assistance succeeded in getting up and standing in balance. He moved on gradually, pulling me after him. I seemed to make contact with the snow by means of two strange stilt-like objects—my legs. I could no longer see the others; I did not dare to turn around for fear of losing my balance, and I was dazzled by the reflection of the sun's rays.

Having walked about a couple of hundred yards, and skirted around an ice wall, suddenly, and without any sort of warning we came upon a tent. We had bivouacked two hundred yards from the camp. Couzy got up as I appeared, and without speaking held me close and embraced me. Terray threw himself down in the tent and took off his boots. His feet, too, were frostbitten; he massaged them and beat them unmercifully.

The will to live stirred again in me. I tried to take in the situation: there was not much that we could do—but we would do whatever was possible. Our only hope lay in Dr. Oudot;

only he could save our feet and hands by the proper treatment. I heartily agreed to Schatz's suggestion that we should go down immediately to the lower Camp IV which the Sherpas had reestablished. Terray wanted to remain in the tent, and as he flailed his feet with the energy of despair he cried out:

"Come and fetch me tomorrow if necessary. I want to be whole, or dead!"

Rébuffat's feet were affected too, but he preferred to go down to Oudot immediately. He started the descent with Lachenal and Couzy, while Schatz continued to look after me—for which I was deeply grateful. He took the rope and propelled me gently along the track. The slope suddenly became very steep, and the thin layer of snow adhering to the surface of the ice gave no foothold; I slipped several times, but Schatz, holding me on a tight rope, was able to check me.

Below there was a broad track: no doubt the others had let themselves slide straight down toward the lower Camp IV, but they had started an avalanche which had swept the slope clear of snow, and this hardly made things easier for me. As soon as we drew in sight of the camp the Sherpas came up to meet us. In their eyes I read such kindliness and such pity that I began to realize my dreadful plight. They were busy clearing the tents which the avalanche had covered with snow. Lachenal was in a corner massaging his feet; from time to time Pansy comforted him, saying that the Doctor Sahib would cure him.

I hurried everyone—we must get down—that was our first objective. As for the equipment, well it could not be helped; we simply must get off the mountain before the next onslaught of the monsoon. For those of us with frostbitten limbs it was a matter of hours. I chose Aila and Sarki to escort Rébuffat, Lachenal, and myself. I tried to make the two Sherpas understand that they must watch me very closely and hold me on a short rope. For some unknown reason, neither Lachenal nor Rébuffat wished to rope.

While we started down, Schatz, with Ang-Tharkey and Pansy, went up to fetch Terray who had remained on the glacier above. Schatz was master of the situation—none of the others were capable of taking the slightest initiative. After a hard struggle he found Terray:

"You can get ready in a minute," he said.

"I'm beginning to feel my feet again," replied Terray, now more amenable to reason.

"I'm going to have a look in the crevasse. Maurice couldn't find the camera and it's got all the shots he took high up."

Terray made no reply; he had not really understood, and it was only several days later that we fully realized Schatz's heroism. He spent a long time searching the snow at the bottom of the cavern, while Terray began to get anxious. At last he returned triumphantly carrying the camera which contained the views taken from the summit. He also found my ice axe and various other things, but no movie camera. So our last film shots would stop at twenty-three thousand feet.

The descent began—Ang-Tharkey was magnificent, going first and cutting comfortable steps for Terray. Schatz, coming down last, carefully safeguarded the whole party.

Our first group was advancing slowly. The snow was soft and we sank in up to our knees. Lachenal grew worse: he frequently stopped and moaned about his feet. Rébuffat was a few yards behind me.

I was concerned at the abnormal heat, and feared that bad weather would put an end here and now to the epic of Annapurna. It is said that mountaineers have a sixth sense that warns them of danger—suddenly I became aware of danger through every pore of my body. There was a feeling in the atmosphere that could not be ignored. Yesterday it had snowed heavily, and the heat was now working on these great masses of snow which were on the point of sliding off. Nothing in Europe can give any idea of the force of these avalanches. They roll down over a distance of miles and are preceded by a blast that destroys everything in its path.

The glare was so terrific that without glasses it would have been impossible to keep one's eyes open. By good luck we were fairly well spaced out, so that the risk was diminished. The Sherpas no longer remembered the different pitches and oftentimes, with great difficulty, I had to take the lead and be let down on the end of the rope to find the right way. I had no crampons and I could not grasp an axe. We lost height far too slowly for my liking, and it worried me to see my Sherpas going so slowly and carefully and at the same time so insecurely. In actual fact they went very well, but I was so impatient I could no longer judge their performance fairly.

Lachenal was a long way behind us and every time I turned around he was sitting down in the track. He, too, was affected by snow blindness, though not so badly as Terray and Rébuffat, and he found difficulty in seeing his way. Rébuffat went ahead by guesswork, with agony in his face, but he kept on. We crossed the couloir without incident, and I congratulated myself that we had passed the danger zone.

The sun was at its height, the weather brilliant, and the colors magnificent. Never had the mountains appeared to me so majestic as in this moment of extreme danger.

All at once a crack appeared in the snow under the feet of the Sherpas, and grew longer and wider. A mad idea flashed into my head—to climb up the slope at speed and reach solid ground. Then I was lifted up by a superhuman force and, as the Sherpas disappeared before my eyes, I went head over heels. I could not see what was happening. My head hit the ice. In spite of my efforts I could no longer breathe, and a violent blow on my left thigh caused me acute pain. I turned round and round like a puppet. In a flash I saw the blinding light of the sun through the snow which was pouring past my eyes. The rope joining me to Sarki and Aila curled round my neck—the Sherpas shooting down the slope beneath would shortly strangle me, and the pain was unbearable. Again and again I crashed into solid ice as I went hurtling from one serac to another, and the snow crushed me down. The rope tightened around my neck and brought me to a stop. Before I had recovered my wits I began to pass water, violently and uncontrollably.

I opened my eyes to find myself hanging head downward with the rope around my neck and my left leg, in a sort of hatchway of blue ice. I put out my elbows toward the walls in an attempt to stop the unbearable pendulum motion which sent me from one side to the other, and I caught a glimpse of the last slopes of the couloir beneath me. My breathing steadied, and I blessed the rope which had stood the strain of the shock.

I simply *had* to try to get myself out. My feet and hands were numb, but I was able to make use of some little nicks in the wall. There was room for at least the edges of my boots. By frenzied, jerky movements I succeeded in freeing my left leg from the rope, and then managed to right myself and to climb up a yard or two. After every move I stopped, convinced that I had come to the end of my physical strength, and that in a second I should have to let go.

One more desperate effort, and I gained a few inches. I pulled on the rope and felt something give at the other end—no doubt the bodies of the Sherpas. I called, but hardly a whisper issued from my lips. There was a death-like silence. Where was Rébuffat?

Conscious of a shadow, as from a passing cloud, I looked up instinctively, and lo and behold! two scared black faces were framed against the circle of blue sky. Aila and Sarki!

They were safe and sound, and at once set to work to rescue me. I was incapable of giving them the slightest advice. Aila disappeared, leaving Sarki alone at the edge of the hole; they began to pull on the rope, slowly, so as not to hurt me, and I was hauled up with a power and steadiness that gave me fresh courage. At last I was out. I collapsed on the snow.

The rope had caught over a ridge of ice and we had been suspended on either side. By good luck the weight of the two Sherpas and my own had balanced. If we had not been checked like this we should have hurtled down for another 1,500 feet. There was chaos all around us. Where was Rébuffat? I was mortally anxious, for he was unroped. Looking up I caught sight of him less than a hundred yards away.

"Anything broken?" he called out to me.

I was greatly relieved, but I had no strength to reply. Lying flat, and semiconscious, I gazed at the wreckage about me with unseeing eyes. We had been carried down for about five hundred feet. It was not a healthy place to linger in—suppose another avalanche should fall! I instructed the Sherpas:

"Now—Doctor Sahib. Quick, very quick!"

By gestures, I tried to make them understand that they must hold me very firm. In doing this I found that my left arm was practically useless. I could not move it at all, the elbow had seized up—was it broken? We should see later. Now, we must push on to Oudot.

Rébuffat started down to join us, moving slowly; he had to place his feet by feel alone. Seeing him walk like this made my heart ache; he too had fallen and he must have hit something with his jaw, for blood was oozing from the corners of his mouth. Like me, he had lost his glasses and we were forced to shut our eyes. Aila had an old spare pair which did very well for me, and without a second's hesitation Sarki gave his own to Rébuffat.

We had to get down at once. The Sherpas helping me up, I advanced as best I could, reeling about in the most alarming fashion, but they realized now that they must hold me from behind. I skirted round the avalanche to our old track which started again a little further on.

We now came to the first wall. How on earth should we get down? Again, I asked the Sherpas to hold me firmly:

"Hold me well because . . ."

And I showed them my hands.

"Yes, sir," they replied together like good pupils. I came to the piton; the fixed rope attached to it hung down the wall and I had to hold on to it—there was no other way. It was terrible; my wooden feet kept slipping on the ice wall, and I could not grasp the thin line in my hands. Without letting go I endeavored to wind it around my hands, but they were swollen and the skin broke in several places. Great strips of it came away and stuck to the rope and the flesh was laid bare. Yet I had to go on down, I could not give up halfway.

"Aila! *Pay attention! . . . Pay attention!"*

To save my hands I now let the rope slide over my good forearm and lowered myself like this in jerks. On reaching the bottom I fell about three feet and the rope wrenched my forearm and my wrists. The jolt was severe and affected my feet. I heard a queer crack and supposed I must have broken something—no doubt it was the frostbite that prevented me from feeling any pain.

Rébuffat and the Sherpas came down and we went on but it all seemed to take an unconscionably long time, and the plateau of Camp II seemed a long way off. I was just about at the limit of my strength. Every minute I felt like giving up; and why, anyway, should I go on when for me everything was over? My conscience was quite easy: everyone was safe, and the others would all get down. Far away below I could see the tents. Just one more hour—I gave myself one more hour and then, wherever I was, I would lie down in the snow. I would let myself go, peacefully. I would be through with it all, and could sleep content.

Setting this limit somehow cheered me on. I kept slipping, and on the steep slope the Sherpas could hardly hold me—it was miraculous that they did. The track stopped above a drop—the second and bigger of the walls we had equipped with a fixed rope. I tried to make up my mind, but I could not begin to see how I was going to get down. I pulled off the glove I had on one hand, and the red silk scarf that hid the other, which was covered with blood. This time everything was at stake—and my fingers could just look after themselves. I placed Sarki and Aila on the stance from which I had been accustomed to belay them, and where the two of them would be able to take the strain of my rope by standing firmly braced against each other. I tried to take hold of the fixed rope; both my hands were bleeding, but I had no pity to spare for myself and I took the rope between my thumb and forefinger, and started off. At the first move I was faced at once with a painful decision: if I let go, we should all fall to the bottom: if I held on what would remain of my hands? I decided to hold on.

Every inch was a torture I was resolved to ignore. The sight of my hands made me feel sick; the flesh was laid bare and red, and the rope was covered with blood. I tried not to tear the strips right off: other accidents had taught me that one must preserve these bits to hasten the healing process later on. I tried to save my hands by braking with my stomach, my shoulders, and every other possible point of contact. When would this agony come to an end?

I came down to the nose of ice which I myself had cut away with my axe on the ascent. I felt about with my legs—it was all hard. There was no snow beneath. I was not yet down. In panic I called up to the Sherpas:

"Quick . . . Aila . . . Sarki . . . !"

They let my rope out more quickly and the friction on the fixed rope increased.

My hands were in a ghastly state. It felt as though all the flesh was being torn off. At last I was aware of something beneath my feet—the ledge. I had made it! I had to go along it now, always held by the rope; only three yards, but they were the trickiest of all. It was over. I collapsed, up to the waist in snow—no longer conscious of time.

When I half-opened my eyes Rébuffat and the Sherpas were beside me, and I could distinctly see black dots moving about near the tents of Camp II. Sarki spoke to me, and pointed out two Sherpas coming up to meet us. They were still a long way off, but all the same it cheered me up.

I had to rouse myself; things were getting worse and worse. The frostbite seemed to be gaining ground—up to my calves and my elbows. Sarki put my glasses on for me again, although the weather had turned gray. He put one glove on as best he could; but my left hand was in such a frightful state that it made him sick to look at it, and he tried to hide it in my red scarf.

The fantastic descent continued and I was sure that every step would be my last. Through the swirling mist I sometimes caught glimpses of the two Sherpas coming up. They had already reached the base of the avalanche cone, and when, from the little platform I had just reached, I saw them stop there, it sapped all my courage.

Snow began to fall, and we now had to make a long traverse over very unsafe ground where it was difficult to guard anyone; then, fifty yards further, we came to the avalanche cone. I recognized Foutharkey and Angawa mounting rapidly toward us. Evidently they expected bad news, and Angawa must have been thinking of his two brothers, Aila and Pansy. The former was with us all right—he could see him in the flesh—but what about Pansy? Even at this distance they started to ask questions, and by the time we reached them they knew everything. I heaved a deep sigh of relief. I felt now as if I had laid down a burden so heavy that I had nearly given way beneath it. Foutharkey was beside me, smiling affectionately. How can anyone call such people primitive, or say that the rigors of their existence take away all sense of pity? The Sherpas rushed toward me, put down their sacks, uncorked their flasks. Ah, just to drink a few mouthfuls! Nothing more. It had all been such a long time . . .

Foutharkey lowered his eyes to my hands and lifted them again, almost with embarrassment. With infinite sorrow, he whispered, "Poor Bara Sahib—Ah . . ."

These reinforcements gave me a fresh access of courage, and Camp II was near. Foutharkey supported me, and Angawa safeguarded us both. Foutharkey was small and I hung on around his neck and leaned on his shoulders, gripping him close. This contact comforted me and his warmth gave me strength. I staggered down with little jerky steps, leaning more and more on Foutharkey. Would I ever have the strength to make it even with his help? Rousing what seemed my very last ounce of energy, I begged Foutharkey to give me yet more help. He took my glasses off and I could see better then. Just a few more steps—the very last . . .

Postscript: Maurice Herzog's climb to the crest of Annapurna was the first successful completion of a peak over eight thousand meters. Herzog was a national hero in France, but with his great victory came considerable loss. He had to have his frostbitten toes and most of his fingers amputated in the field, and without the use of an anesthetic.

In 1963, Everest had been climbed by only eight individuals, and always by way of the North or South Col routes. That year Thomas Hornbein and Willi Unsoeld attempted to climb the mountain via the more daunting West Ridge. They left their camp early in the morning and reached the summit at six that evening, but unfortunately hours behind the schedule necessary to increase the odds of a safe return. A descent at night was not only extremely dangerous, but they had another serious problem: Unsoeld had run out of oxygen.

EVEREST
The West Ridge

THOMAS F. HORNBEIN

A Blusterous Day

May 13 was a day for celebration. Thirty long, frustrating days after our descent from the Reconnaissance, Camp 3W was finally stocked. I accompanied Willi and the last load of oxygen bottles up the slope late that afternoon as Al, not visible above, reigned supreme over the winch motor, nursing, begging, coercing. His virtuosity kept the motor running till this last load of eighteen bottles was hauled over the final edge. From a single tent the camp had grown to five four-man structures, housing a record population that night—fifteen Sherpas and three sahibs. I was weary after the long haul up from Advance Base, but my communication to my diary was expectant. "3W again, at last!"

We had enough carrying power to afford some attrition, but not much. The Sherpas were tired. Many had carried to the South Col twice and several had been to Camp 6. Whether they were physically drained or whether they figured that now the mountain was climbed it was foolish to ask for more trouble, I don't know. Phu Dorje and Dawa Tenzing, two of the strong men on the Col route, turned back from the carry that Willi took to 4W. Before their lack of enthusiasm could infect the others, I sent them on down to Advance Base. Illness and inertia ran rampant, but were cured in part by Jimmy Roberts's voice over the radio promising extra pay: each carry beyond 3W would count on the wage scale as one camp higher than on the Col route. Our progress held to schedule.

On the afternoon of May 15, Willi and I moved up to 4W. We were alone with the grandeur that had captivated us that magical afternoon a month before. Wanting to shout my elation to those below, I climbed on to the rock promontory, walkie-talkie in one hand and signal mirror in the other. I lay down on my belly at the edge of the precipice and tried to arouse someone at Advance Base, four thousand feet below. No one was outside. I waited a few minutes, then scooted gingerly back from the edge and returned to the tent. Its orange-yellow radiance in the afternoon sun was in garish contrast to the brown of barren hills rolling enigmatically onward beyond the North Col. Certainly there was no more fantastic place on the entire mountain, and it belonged to us!

But we were only guests, and the mountain proceeded to remind us of it, but with humour. It was 9 p.m. and diaries were finished. Tomorrow's water, two quarts of it, was melting on the stove as we prepared for an early start. Now, where did my plastic oxygen mask go? I groped through the innards of my sleeping bag; no mask. I emerged for my flashlight, then dove back in again. The glimmer of light penetrating the down bag caught Willi's attention.

"What are you doing in there?"

"Hunting for my mask. Had it in my hand a minute ago."

"Maybe it's under your bag."

Emerging, I turned on my knees and looked under the bag. No mask. Along the edge of the tent, under my air mattress—still no mask.

"Maybe it's in your bag, Willi. Take a look, will you?"

"How could it get in mine?"

"I don't know, but it's got to be somewhere." My exploratory gymnastics were becoming violent.

"Watch the water, Tom!"

I did—as my air mattress flipped the two quarts, won so hard, cleanly off the stove and sent them coursing down the groove between our air mattresses.

"What's that on your bag, Tom, behind you?"

There, innocently, lay my mask. I stared, chagrined. This was too much. I wasn't about to begin melting more water tonight. Worry about that tomorrow. Since we were well above the high tide of what had spilled, it could darn well wait till morning too. When it froze we could pick it up and throw it out. I put on my sleeping mask, turning the regulator to one litre per minute.

"Night, Tom. You seem to be cracking under the strain. Maybe you'd better go down tomorrow."

"Drop dead, Unsoeld. Good night."

The next day was windy, not the sort on which you'd want to wander far from home, especially without water.

Lethargically we melted more, and scraping up the frozen remainder of last night's catastrophe, tossed it out the door. By noon our reluctance to join the wind outside succumbed to boredom within. We decided to go as far as the Diagonal Ditch for a possible view across the North Face.

Unfortunately, from the top of the Ditch we couldn't see a thing.

"Let's go around one more corner," Willi said.

Curiosity and the deceptive foreshortening of distance on this vast face lured us on to unintentional fulfillment of our original plan. At 3:30 we sat down on the limestone slabs at the bottom of Hornbein's Couloir. Here, at the anticipated site of our next to last camp, the altimeter read 26,250 feet, a shade higher than the South Col. Above us the snow gully cut steeply up into the heart of the mountain, clear sailing for at least five hundred feet, then a slight bend obscured the view. Wind sent clouds of snow scurrying down the gully and momentarily blotted even the foreground from sight. Our traverse had been steep at times on rotten wind-slabbed snow. Crampons scraped across down-sloping shingles of limestone. I felt haunted by history and thoughts of Mallory. Might we be near the point where he had walked? Where is he now?

Suspense lightly seasoned the journey back. Snow carried by the rising wind had obliterated our tracks and now limited our visibility to scarcely a rope-length. On this slanting expanse it would be easy to become confused. But luck and an instinctive feeling for terrain acquired over many years of climbing homed us in on the rock castle that marked the top of the Diagonal Ditch. We reached 4W at 6 p.m., along with a lot more wind. During our absence the camp had grown. Behind our two-man tent were two four-man Drawtites, hooked together end-to-end. Inside, Barry, Al, and four Sherpas were eating.

"Hi, Barry, where's Emerson? Didn't he come up with you?"

"No. We started out from Advance Base together yesterday, but he was going so slow it was obvious that he'd never make it to 3W. He said something about trying again today."

At 7 p.m., Barry called Base.

> *Corbet (4W):* Willi and Tom have located Camp 5 at 26,300 feet. The route to Camp 5 is good, the route above Camp 5 looks good. The West Ridge is on schedule. No further traffic. Over.
>
> *Prather (Base):* Tremendous! Tremendous! Get some snow and soil samples for Will. Over.
>
> *Corbet (4W):* Roger, Roger. All we have to do is hold the bottles up in the air and let the wind do the rest. Over.
>
> *Prather (Base):* Norman and the whole gang down here say "Good deal on Camp 5W."
>
> *Bishop (Advance Base):* Those of us here at 2 are jumping up and down. Good show! Get some sleep tonight in that heavy wind up there. One last thing—you'd better not count on Emerson from the way things are going. He's moving real slow. We can look up now and see he's just about at the New Dump, about three or four hours out at his present pace, and he said something about a possible bivouac on the way.
>
> *Prather (Base):* Norman says here, and it's agreed, that Dick should not fiddle around any more up there. Dick should come down.
>
> *Bishop (Advance Base):* Well, we'll have to wait till he gets to 3W and hope there's a radio.

But Dick was nowhere near a radio, or 3W.

"If I was strong," he wrote later, "I could have made it in a day, but I knew I would either have to bivouac en route or arrive exhausted.

"Lute counselled me against exposing myself to frostbite in the bivouac. However, there was one bottle of oxygen and a convenient crevasse at what had been the New New Dump at a little over twenty-three thousand feet. I had been down in the crevasse before, retrieving a fouled winch cable, and knew it to be suitable. If I slept on oxygen there would be no frostbite. Next day I started up, carrying an air mattress, which I concluded would be more useful than a sleeping bag. With the crevasse as my objective, I took a slow and steady pace and arrived at dusk feeling very well. I debated continuing the last seven hundred vertical feet to 3W, but it would be totally dark, and I was confident about the bivouac. In fact, I think I wanted the bivouac, but I don't know exactly why.

"It must have taken me almost two hours to get myself prepared for the night. I found the bottle half buried, put it in my pack, anchored a piece of rope to a picket, and rappeled into the dark hole as light was failing. About thirty feet down, the crevasse closed to four feet wide, plugged with powder snow. I stamped it firm, then started to inflate the mattress. I stopped. (Stupid, you'd better get those crampons off or you'll puncture it for sure.) As I fiddled with things in the dark, I could hear the wind rising. (No worry—but it's dumping a lot of snow in here.) I removed my down gloves to work with the oxygen gear. (Careful! Put the right glove in the right pocket—now left in left. Don't misplace one. Don't let snow sift into them. Hold the hose in your teeth. Now, work fast with the metal attachments—hose to regulator, regulator to tank—keep the snow away and hope the threads seat well. Good, gloves. Now, down pants over the boots, wind shell, mask in place, regulator in reach. Flow? One litre. And now for sleep. Wait! Let's review: Where's my axe? Upright behind my head. Crampons? In the pack. Damn! I'll bet the flap's open. Goggles? Top left pocket.) This poor-man's countdown put my mind at ease and I drifted into sleep in perfect comfort, never suspecting the storm I was creating at Base Camp.

"Sometime during the night I was awakened by cold around my eyes, where powder snow was sifting in. I was thoroughly warm otherwise, but slowly realized that I was totally buried. I rose to my feet, cradling the oxygen bottle like a baby in one arm. I pulled the mattress to the surface, remade my bed, and listening to the wind roaring past my cavern, immediately fell back to sleep."

Just after midnight that same evening, Al unzipped the entrance to the yellow tent, stuck his head inside, and with effort roused Willi and me to report matter-of-factly, "A couple of tents just blew away."

Stupid with sleep, we mulled over his news, finally comprehending that the tents he, Barry, and the four Sherpas were in had got loose.

"We're about 150 feet down the hill," he said, "A real mess. I fixed them down as best I could, but you'd better check on them."

Fatigue imposed a strange detachment as Willi and I climbed into our boots and parkas. Leaving Al as ballast we stepped out into the staggering blast of the wind. Our headlights lit the swath planed by the sliding tents. Only then did we begin to appreciate the power of the storm, and imagine the horror of suddenly waking to find your tent sliding across the snow, accelerating in a headlong journey toward Tibet. By some miracle the tents had stopped in a shallow depression just below. Like surrealistic sculpture, their external frames were now a mass of contorted tubing from which the skin flapped noisily. The floor was uppermost. The end of Corbet's air mattress protruded from a hole in the side. There was a certain fatalistic humour in the voices within. Willi and I sank ice axes deep in the snow and proceeded to lash the wreckage to them with several lengths of climbing rope.

"All OK? Nawang? Everybody comfortable?" Willi called in.

"OK, sahib," came the reply.

"Lemunuk. Good job. Don't leave without us," he requested. Once the implications were understood, we were answered with good-humoured laughter.

"See you in the morning, Barry. Keep cool," Willi said.

Leaning into the breeze, we plodded up the hill, fighting for breath every five or six steps. Eventually we poured in on Al, who was holding down the fort, and soon the three of us were sound asleep.

The sun touched the top of Everest before seven on May 17. Four thousand feet below, on the crest of a ridge sat our yellow-orange tent. Beaten nearly to submission, it clung to the mountainside. Roar of wind against the mountain served as background for the staccato vibration of the tent walls. Inside two of us sat hunched at the windward corners, leaning into the gale, convinced our effort was all that held our perch to the mountainside. The third enjoyed brief respite from the battering ordeal that had grown in intensity with the dawn. Above, the sky was immaculately blue.

It was enough to give you a headache. I sat at the back corner, leaning into the pole, which obligingly had conformed to the curvature of my spine. My head was being riveted as if by a jackhammer. Al held the other corner, while Willi unfolded a grisly tale of another windstorm from his not-forgotten youth. Half the story was lost in the racket of the tent walls. For the moment I found myself not terribly captivated anyway. The power unleashed upon us was frightening. What was there to keep it from sweeping us off the mountain? We were powerless to alter the scheme of things. It was humbling.

I wondered briefly what I was doing here, what insanity had led me to become trapped in such a ridiculous endeavour. The thought was rapid, cathartic; anybody so stupid deserves to be in a place like this. Since you're here you might as well enjoy it, T., even Unsoeld's stories.

I looked at Al leaning silently against the other corner. His doubts were under control. And Willi's also. Or was he more talkative than usual? All three of us were certainly aware of our tenuous hold on the hillside, but what could we do besides make light of it?

At eight we called Base Camp on the radio. Corbet was already talking to Prather when we came on.

Corbet (4W-lower site): Let me fill you in. We've had a mishap during the night. Both Drawtite tents with the four Sherpas and Al and myself blew 150 feet down the slope and we're currently lying in a tangle of oxygen bottles. Al has gone up to join Willi and Tom, both of whom came down at midnight when it happened, and roped us to the slopes and I guess we're safe. We're currently waiting rescue by Willi and Tom and Al.

Unsoeld (4W-upper site): Can you read 4W now?

Prather (Base): I read you loud and clear, Willi. Did you get what Barry wanted?

Unsoeld (4W): I think I did. Yes, it's going to be a while yet, Bear, because we're just barely holding on to the Gerry tent. Here's a question, Bear; how's the wind down your way? Over.

Prather (Base): It's blowing a little bit down here, not very hard though—twenty or twenty-five miles per hour. Over.

Unsoeld (4W): I see. Well, we may not be able to hold out here much longer, Bear. Tent's taking a beating. Wind's blowing about a hundred pretty steady. Over.

Prather (Base): We can see a hell of a lot of wind coming

off Nuptse and it really sounds bad. There's a big roar we can hear, from down here even. Over.

Unsoeld (4W): I can believe it. Over.

Our growing concern over Dick's whereabouts was relieved when Dingman came on.

Dingman (Advance Base): Willi, did you hear about Emerson? Over.

Unsoeld (4W): No I didn't, Dave. What's the latest word? Over.

Dingman (Advance Base): We looked out of the tent a few minutes ago and lo and behold, we saw him between the New Dump and the crest, still going up. Over.

Unsoeld (4W): Did I get that right? You saw him between the New Dump and the crest and he was going up? Over.

Dingman (Advance Base): Roger.

Unsoeld (4W): And that was *this* morning? Over.

Prather (Base): Roger, that's this morning, just a few minutes ago. Over.

Unsoeld (4W): Holy cow! I can't believe it! Over.

Prather (Base): Roger. You're not the only one.

Unsoeld (4W): That's great news, Dave! Great news! Now if we can get out of this mess, we'll be fine. Over.

Well protected in his fastidiously prepared hole, Dick had hibernated peacefully through the night, oblivious of the storm above. He described what took place when he woke for the second time:

"Soft light filled the crevasse, but I couldn't see the opening above me for the swirling snow. My watch said seven o'clock, but the light suggested four o'clock. (Radio contact is at 8:15. Get on your way again by then so they can see you from Camp 2 and know all is well. But no rush now.) So I lay there marvelling at the comfort of such a formfitting bed, watching the snow sweep by above me with unbelievable velocity.

"Eventually I rose and started putting things in shape. (Will the weather block visibility from Camp 2?) I pulled the plug to let the mattress deflate and found it had frozen up when only half-deflated. I rolled it up under my pack flap and, using the front points of my crampons, started up the rappel rope to rejoin the elements.

"It was 8:45, the sky was blue, and I could see the tents at 2 far below, yet I couldn't see my own feet in the blowing snow. I started up the home stretch for 3W, wondering if I could be seen in the ground blizzard. My route went straight up the 35-degree slope, scoured hard by the crosswind. Once, standing erect to see over the turmoil of moving particles, I was hit like a hammer by a wind change and did a self-arrest moving horizontally across the slope. I continued steadily on front points and a pick. Soon, snow filtering through the air vents filled my goggles. Since there was no feasible way to clean them, nor any point in doing so, I put them away and continued, squinting out through the wolverine fur of my hood. All I had to do was go straight up. I didn't have to see. The wind tore the partly inflated mattress from my pack and I last saw it gaining altitude westward."

About nine, Barry crept up the slope to join us. The four Sherpas had headed down to 3W. We felt sure such tremendous power must soon spend itself, but nothing in the behaviour of the wind lent support to our wishful thinking. Momentary lulls left the tent walls hanging limp; the sudden staccatoless silence was filled by the roar of the wind across the ridge above. Was the storm subsiding? In seconds the answer came, unnecessarily malicious in its suddenness. The tent strained against its anchors in response to a blast that had gained strength in its momentary pause for breath. Then there was just more roar. We decided to retreat while there was still something to retreat from. Al headed out on his hands and knees in search of his rucksack. His concern for something so inconsequential seemed strange.

At Base Camp the crew sat comfortably about the breakfast table sipping tea, listening to the radio set in the corner of the tent.

Dingman (Advance Base): Have you got the weather forecast?

Prather (Base): Yes. Just a second here. Forecast is generally cloudy with strong winds and a few snow showers likely. The outlook, a low pressure area is now over Punjab, the one that was over Afghanistan, and may affect us in about forty-eight hours. Over.

Unsoeld (4W): Four to Base, Four to Base. Over.

Prather (Base): Roger, Willi. Reading you loud and clear. Go ahead.

Unsoeld (4W): OK. Here's the latest report, Bear. (Suddenly the tent began to slide.) O-o-v-e-e-r-r-r!

Prather (Base): You want the weather report? Over.

Unsoeld (4W): God damn! The tent's blowing away!

Prather (Base): Roger. The tent's blowing away. We'll stand by.

Unsoeld (4W): Stand by. We're headed over the brink!

Prather (Base): Roger.

Unsoeld (4W): Barry! Out! Out!

Nearest the door, I shucked my mitts and dove for the zippers, ripping them down. Happily they didn't jam. As we gained speed, I shot from the tent. A metal rappel picket was lying on the snow. I rammed it in, spreading my legs in the vestibule, and held tight. The tent stopped. Barry emerged. "What do we do now, Tom?" he asked, and as I thought, he piled oxygen bottles on the structure to complete what little remained of the final flattening process. I turned to see Willi, hunched low before the wind, still talking on the radio.

> *Unsoeld (4W):* Well, we're all out, the tent's gone, and we're headed for 3 as fast as possible. Over.

Leaning into the blast, the four of us staggered down to retrieve our axes which held the lower tents to the slope. Suddenly the wind caught the wreckage, whipping it about with a frenzy that threatened to sweep Barry off the mountain. We shouted at him to get away, but he couldn't possibly have heard. A box of food skidded over the snow bound for the depths of the Rongbuk. A sleeping bag shot from a rent in the fabric and, inflating like a giant green windsock, flew upward to disappear into the wall of blowing snow.

Unroped, we were blown stumbling and falling the remaining distance to the shelter of the ridge behind the crest. There we could stand erect, but now the wind came in gusts from every direction. Ground blizzard obscured the track. Snow stung my face like flying sand and filtered in to cake the inside of my goggles. I couldn't see a thing. Where'd Willi disappear to? A gust jarred me from the track and I dropped about six feet down a wall. From somewhere Willi appeared and looked down as if to ask, What are you doing there, Tom?

It seemed an eternity before we reached the border, crossed over, and started down the other side out of the wind. Only then was there time to think about what had happened. I sat in the snow a hundred feet above the tents to wait, not sure whether Willi was hanging back out of sheer fatigue or for a bit of aloneness. After a while, he trudged slowly into view and settled down beside me. He was tired. The wind-sculptured ice on his face was like the frost feathers in winter on timberline trees back in the Northwest. The frozen extension of his nose held a strange fascination, enough for me to overcome fatigue and bring out my camera.

As we sat there, the realization came that we were finished, demolished, literally blasted off the mountain. We hadn't even sunk our teeth solidly into the climb. I felt no gratitude that we had escaped with our lives, only awe at the power unleashed on us, and a dissatisfied feeling of finality to all our dreams. After a while we struggled to our feet and wobbled wearily down to the tents at 3W.

Severing the Cord

We were stacked irresolutely about the tent: Barry, Al, Willi, Ang Dorje, Dick, and I. Dick appeared none the worse for his night out. It was hard to regret that we were beaten, so enticing was the prospect of fresh meat and unlimited eggs awaiting us at Base Camp, and the prospect of our homeward journey. To be off this mountain once and for all was the only goal with any meaning. We would have continued down to Advance Base that same day, but we were too tired. We crawled into our bags that night with the feeling that it was all over. The prospect of escaping from this inhospitable lump that could out of sheer whimsy blot us neatly from the scheme of things was pure delight. The lure of home was stronger still, the welling-up of love and longing. And strongest of all was the prospect of finally being freed from the lure of the mountain. The invisible line that linked me to Everest was frayed.

But it hadn't broken. I wasn't yet free to make my own decision. We hadn't given it all we had. Descend now, and we must live the rest of our lives with that knowledge. So the bond still held fast. But it would be sheer fanaticism to suggest

going back up. Weary muscles voted against the taunting of
my mind; still I couldn't shake it off. Our tents were ruined, a
lot of food blown away. And oxygen? Four Sherpas had beat a
hasty retreat to Advance Base. Three days ago we had fifteen,
now only three remained, Ang Dorje, Passang Tendi, and
Tenzing Nindra. We could salvage two four-man tents from
here. Maybe we could get a small one from Advance Base.
And a couple more Sherpas. But time was running out. We
were scheduled to leave Base in a week.

Months before, in our early planning we had toyed with
the idea of having only five camps, instead of six as on the Col.
It would cut down the number of carries high on the mountain over terrain few of our Sherpas would be skilled enough
to climb. The idea was ridiculous. How could we hope to
travel farther in a day over steep, difficult terrain than on the
easier ground of the regular route? We discarded the idea as
naïve folly. We'd need at least six camps. Two two-man summit teams on successive days went without saying.

We had been hamstrung by the wind, and new questions
kept me awake: Can we possibly consider going up? Suppose
we eliminate a camp and try for a very long carry above 4W?
A long shot, but it's the only chance we have. Over two thousand vertical feet in a day? Maybe, if the climbing isn't too
tough and the loads are light. If we can get two more Sherpas,
that'll still be forty pounds apiece—for just one summit team.
There isn't time for a second one anyway. No time to send
our recon a day early to locate the high camp. They'll just
have to get up early and hope the going is not too hard.

So we have a chance. If the Sherpas will agree to one more
carry. It's worth a try. I was bursting to tell my plan to Willi.
With the dawn I could contain myself no longer. I kneed him
in the ribs.

"Excuse me. I didn't mean to wake you up. But since you
are, what do you think of this?"

Willi forced open a sleepy eye and listened, wondering whether what he heard was sheer genius or only my pathological fanatacism. Undoubtedly the latter, he must have thought, but still it was a chance.

"OK. Let's try it on Barry."

Barry bit. We crossed to the other tent and accosted Dick and Al. And so it was agreed. We called Base on the radio and Willi presented our plan.

Dyhrenfurth (Base): Willi, I'm delighted by your plan. This is exactly what we were going to suggest, that only two men make the attempt. And all I can say is, Willi, you've had a hell of a lot of tough luck. You've worked awfully hard. And we're all 200 percent with you. We wish you all the luck in the world and hope you make it. Over.

Unsoeld (3W): Thanks a lot, Norm. We appreciate that and I'm especially appreciative that we're thinking along the same lines. Really, this is probably a terrifically long shot. If we can carry through to twenty-seven thousand or so and then have to retreat we would all feel as if we had completed an adequate reconnaissance of the route. With 90 percent of the labour already done, getting the things up to 4W, it seems too bad to come down without one last all-out push, which, with a little bit of luck, we'll carry out. Thanks a lot, Norm. Over.

Dyhrenfurth (Base): Willi, we all thank God, of course, that you are all alive, that nobody got hurt, and whether you make it or not, in any case you have accomplished miracles. I think the mountaineering world, I'm sure, will recognize that this is an incredible accomplishment on a long and difficult and unknown route. Over.

Willi (3W): Thanks a lot. We share your joy in all being alive, all right. There were a few times when things were flying around wildly that we weren't sure but that some of the

objects were us. And, I don't know, if we just get one break in
the weather now, it's entirely possible to go all the way. The
Couloir really looks good. The section of it that Tom and I
were in looked like it was the steepest of all that we could see
and it was a maximum of thirty to thirty-five degrees. So it
didn't look like a difficult route as far as we could see. The
upper part of the mountain might give us something we can
really sink our teeth in. Over.

Dyhrenfurth (Base): Willi, it sounds very, very good. All the
luck in the world. As they say in German, *Hals und Beinbruch.*
Over.

Al took to the air to consult Prather about replacing gear
lost in the storm.

Auten (3W): We'll need a couple of packs. Mine and Barry's
took off and are somewhere in China by now. Also two pairs
of goggles, and two of down mitts. Hornbein says he needs
some Bouton goggles, too, and a balaclava. And Jimmy's two-
man Gerry tent at Advance Base if he can give it up.

Prather (Base): Mighty fine. Big Jim sends good word up to
you. He's sending his pack up to you, and he says that the
pack's been to the summit. It's a very expensive pack. And he
says if you lose his pack your soul had better go to heaven
because your ass will be his. Over.

We were completely on our own. For all the well-wishing
we knew the impatience of those below to be homeward
bound. They knew our chances were dim; it was kindness
that they still waited. I guess they also knew we wouldn't
come down until we were damned well through. We had kept
the ridge attempt alive against an opposition which we
thought was founded on doubt and lack of interest. Though

hardly burdened with manpower or supplies, we were finally in position.

We rested the next two days and waited for supplies. On the first morning Al wanted to go down. He had worked hard and well, but only a little of our enthusiasm for the route had rubbed off on him. Now he could see Dick assuming his original role in the foursome, with himself as excess baggage. I protested.

"We need all the man power we can get," I said. "Dick's strength is still a big question and any one of the rest of us could wake up sick tomorrow. Let's not cut it any thinner than it is already. We need you."

Al stayed.

The eighteenth and nineteenth were perfectly clear. Our colourful down clothes bloomed atop the tents. The summit of Everest stood a mile above, windless and inviting. The afternoon of the nineteenth, Ila Tsering and Tenzing Gyaltso arrived, all smiles, with our fresh supplies. Our discussion that afternoon went once more over the final plans. Till now we had not decided on the final route. Hornbein's Couloir lay far out on the Tibetan North Face, almost in a fall linc bclow the summit; Jake's was a large snowfield leading back up toward the West Ridge. We were drawn toward the latter, because it would return us to the Ridge we had meant to climb. But we no longer had the strength to move a camp up that kind of terrain. We had to get it above twenty-seven thousand feet in the easiest way possible. With time for but one long carry, Hornbein's Couloir appeared to offer us the only chance. Where the Couloir went, above the camp, we couldn't guess. We'd just have to take our chances on the final day.

Dick broached the last unaired issue.

"I'd think in all fairness we ought to discuss the choice of the summit team. I don't mind being outspoken since I'm not in shape for it anyway. There's no question that Barry, Tom, and Willi are in the best shape. I think this is the first consideration."

We weighed the various pairings.

"I think Willi and Tom should go," Barry said. "For one thing you've plugged harder on the route than any of the rest of us."

"All the more reason for you to have a turn, Barry," Willi replied.

In the six weeks we'd been on the mountain, Barry had not tasted a day of real climbing, of pushing a route over new terrain. He'd spent his time humping loads and toiling over the winch, or sitting restlessly at Advance Base. Though he said little, his frustration and disappointment were apparent. He had discovered that there wasn't much real climbing involved in climbing the highest peaks on earth. He was a superb mountaineer. He could have easily gone to the top.

"Another thing," Corbet continued, "you two have been climbing together; you know each other, and you'll make the strongest team. What's more, you're both just about over the hump. This is my first expedition. I'll be coming back again someday."

So, tentatively Willi and I were to be the summit team. The final decision would be made at our high camp two days later. If either of us fell out, Barry would plug the hole. We tackled the final problem in our tent that night. Barry would reconnoitre to find high camp. We had to decide who would accompany him. They'd have to start early and move fast to find and prepare a route for those following a few hours later. Dick had still not fully recovered from his illness. We doubted he could hold the pace. All things considered, it was decided that Al would go with Barry.

May 20 was the third perfect day in a row. How long could the weather hold? We struck the two tents that were to go to 4W. The snow had drifted level with their flat tops on the uphill side. Then the warmth from inside had caused a layer of ice to form. They were solidly imbedded. Much chopping finally extracted the tents with only a few additional holes for better ventilation. Willi and I sorted personal gear, some to stay at 4W, some to go up. A few pages were torn from the back of our diaries so that Emerson's study could continue uninterrupted without our having to carry the entire books over the summit. Shortly after noon we saddled up, set our oxygen at two litres per minute, and headed for the West Shoulder. The two days' rest had worked wonders.

Thinking of the possible traverse of Everest I said, "You know, Willi, if we're really lucky this may be the last time we see 3W." We both must have shared the next thought: Yes, and also if we're unlucky.

As we approached the Shoulder we could see the prayer flag Ang Dorje had planted there, flapping in the wind. Like a couple of proud children about to reveal their most treasured hideaway, we watched Dick come over the top for his first view of the other side. His silence as he looked was all we needed to make the moment perfect. We pointed out the landmarks of our route, so far as it went.

As Dick began to photograph the route, Willi remembered leaving his haze filter in my rucksack at 3W. Deciding that such picture-taking opportunities might not come his way again, he left his pack and headed back down. The others moved on up toward 4W to begin the salvage job while I waited on the crest of the ridge for Willi.

For almost the first time during the entire expedition I was completely alone. I sat atop the ridge with my mittens off, soaking up the windless warmth of the afternoon sun. I looked across brown hills, deep glacial valleys, snow peaks ranging westward into haze. My thoughts knew only the restriction imposed by the limits of my ability to feel and comprehend. A vertical mile above, at the far end of the West Ridge, was the highest point on earth. The day after tomorrow? The dream of childhood, not to be lost? My gaze climbed lightly up each detail of our route, to the base of the Couloir at twenty-six thousand feet. The rest was unknown, partly hidden, grossly foreshortened, but all there.

Like pain, a mountain can be a subjective sensation; for all its solidity and fixity of form, it is more than what one sees. It is awe, pleasure, respect, love, fear, and much, much more. It is an ever-changing, maturing feeling. Over the weeks since we had first stood on the Shoulder to see the black rock of the last four thousand feet, my feelings toward the climb had steadily ripened. That rock couldn't be divorced from the summit to which it led. Yet each time we looked, the slope seemed a few degrees gentler, the vertical distance not quite so unreasonable. After all, we had climbed steeper faces and longer distances, and on more rotten rock. But all together? And above twenty-seven thousand feet instead of half that high? However, you can't see altitude. Might as well ignore it. We chose not to dwell on problems like what happens if you run out of oxygen below the summit. And what it's like to climb on rotten rock at twenty-seven thousand feet, ballasted by a forty-pound pack.

Everest came down off Everest. It became, in a climbing sense, just another mountain to be approached and attempted within the context of our past experience in the Rockies, Tetons, or on Mount Rainier. Not quite, really. But much of the battle lay inside. That battle was nearly won.

I looked out beyond the Great Couloir to the step where Mallory and Irvine were last seen. So near the Everest of my boyhood, I felt uneasy, as if I were trespassing on hallowed ground. I looked on the same North Face at which they had looked forty years before; I felt what they must have felt. The past was part of the rightness of our route.

Beyond the remains of the Rongbuk Monastery were the barren hills of Tibet, a strange land of strange people, living beneath the highest mountain on earth—did they know it? What difference did it make to them? I thought of home. It would be night there, everyone asleep. Can Gene feel my thoughts coming home? I took my photo album from my shirt pocket, and looked at the portraits inside. Tears came. Sheer happy loneliness, the feeling of being nearly finished with the task I had set myself. It wouldn't be long now.

Completely alone. Range on range hazed westward. Beneath me clouds drifted over the Lho La, chasing their shadows across the flat of the Rongbuk Glacier. I remembered afternoons of my childhood when I watched the changing shapes of clouds against a deep blue sky, seeing elephants and horses and soft mountains. On this lonely ridge I was part of all I saw, a single, feeble heartbeat in the span of time and space about me.

Willi was back. He came steaming up the hill on full flow from a cylinder strapped to his back, his haze filter clutched in one hand. He checked his watch to confirm what undoubtedly must stand as a world's record for the run from 3W to the West Shoulder. Once he had caught his breath we took one last look at the sweep of mountain above us; henceforth we would be too much a part of it, able to locate ourselves only in the memory of this last soaring view. Squandering oxygen, we pressed the pace to join the others in rehabilitating the wreckage of 4W. Most of the oxygen bottles were still there, and enough butane if we used it carefully. But of twelve food boxes only three remained. One, fortunately, contained our high-camp ration. As Barry busily filmed us we began to pitch the tents. Four days before we had been forcibly made aware of the reason for our flat campsite, but there was no place else to put it. We oriented the two four-man tents with their broadsides less exposed to any recurrence of storm. The walls flapped disconcertingly in the westerly breeze. Al carefully enmeshed the cluster with climbing ropes.

The remnant of our original two-man tent was suspended from the frame of one of the larger tents; its own poles had been bent beyond repair. This sagging structure was to be Barry's and Dick's. Al would share one of the big tents with Ang Dorje and Tenzing Gyaltso. Feeling isolated, Al objected. Reluctantly, the Sherpas consented to inhabit the ruined tent. They straightaway crawled inside and refused to come out for supper.

"Not hungry, sahib," said Ang Dorje, "only need sleep. OK tomorrow."

But we wondered how much they were offended. Knowing the highs and lows of their temperament, we worried that they might remain in bed sick in the morning. I crawled into their tent to rig their sleeping oxygen and try to persuade them to have some tea. Later, Willi went over through the cold of the night to chat with Ang Dorje.

Our plans for May 21 seemed a little ridiculous. First, Barry and Al had to explore and prepare an unknown route to the site for our high camp, 5W. We would give them a two-and-a-half-hour head start. Next, five untried Sherpas must traverse the North Face, climbing more than two thousand vertical feet with loads, twice the distance ever carried before at that altitude.

In the bitter pre-sun cold, Al and Barry departed. They carried fixed rope, pitons, ice screws, and one oxygen cylinder each. They also carried all our hopes for the following day. After breakfast Dick, Willi, and I prepared the loads for the Sherpas. I checked the pressure in all the oxygen cylinders, setting aside the six fullest for the final push. By nine the sun was warming the tents, but there was still no sign of Ang Dorje and Tenzing Gyaltso. We began to consider seriously the consequences should they not show, when a smiling face appeared at their tent door.

"Good morning, sahibs. Ready go," Ang Dorje said.

Ila Tsering looked over at Ang Dorje, supposedly past his prime but somehow totally infected with the pleasure of our gamble, then at the three other young Sherpas, all on their first expedition.

"All good Sherpas Base Camp, sahib. Only bad Sherpas up here," he said.

Delighted laughter, theirs and ours, got us on our way. Each shouldered a load of about forty pounds, counting the oxygen he would use during the day. Ila hefted his load.

"Very heavy, sahib," he said. We took turns lifting it.

Sure enough, our food ration weighed about ten pounds more than the other loads. He grinned. "But this last day," he said. "I carry."

At 9:30 the five Sherpas were roped together. I checked their masks as they filed past and set their regulators at a flow of one and a half litres per minute. They followed Barry and Al's tracks toward the Diagonal Ditch. Twenty minutes later Willi, Dick, and I pulled out. Willi and I carried only a single bottle of oxygen, cameras, radio, flashlight, and our personal belongings.

The Sherpas stayed one jump ahead. The three of us were completely absorbed in the pleasure of climbing together for the first time since Masherbrum. Since our visit five days before, the slope had changed radically. Entire snow-fields had been blasted into oblivion, leaving us to scrape our crampons across an abundance of downsloping, fractured rubble. Far ahead we could see the figures of Barry and Al

silhouetted against the snow as they disappeared into Hornbein's Couloir.

For me the pleasure of the walk was tempered by anxiety.
Could Al and Barry get to 27,500?

It was early afternoon before we reached the base of the
Couloir, at 26,250 feet. Showers of ice cascading from above
drew our attention to the tiny figures etched against the snow
eight hundred feet higher. Barry was chopping away for all he
was worth, hewing a staircase for us. We joined the Sherpas
under a partly protected wall to await the end of the onslaught
and nibble a bit of lunch. The Sherpas seemed less enthusias-
tic as they huddled to avoid the constant bombardment of ice
spewing out the end of the gully and whirring past our heads
with a high-pitched whine. We dallied over our sardines,
pineapple, and chocolate, all frozen and tasteless. The prospect
of entering the gully was too much like becoming tenpins in a
high-angle bowling alley.

A little after 2 p.m. the ice fall abated. With Ang Dorje
paternally in the lead, the Sherpas started up, their flow
increased to three litres per minute. Dick had reached this
select eight-thousand-metre level with little difficulty. He
would have liked to go higher, but it seemed more sensible for
him to remain here, conserving his energy and oxygen to
assist the others on their late return to 4W. Our masks could
not hide tears when it came time to head on up.

"Must be the altitude," said Willi.

"Don't do anything foolish, you nuts," Dick said. Then, as
an afterthought, with a twinkle in his eye, "See you back at 2."

For a long time as we climbed we could look down on the
back of Dick's head as he sat on that lonely ledge, looking out
into Tibet.

The shadows were lengthening across the glaciers twelve
thousand feet below. It was nearly 4 p.m. when we looked up

to see Al and Barry, their two heads peering gnomelike from a snow ledge at the base of the Yellow Band. We shouted encouragement to the Sherpas, now below us, for they were beginning to suspect their sahibs of wanting to pitch the last camp on the summit itself. The slope of the staircase Barry had carved steepened to about forty degrees as we came up to them. He filmed our arrival.

"OK. Willi, come up around the end and turn toward me, and smile."

Willi smiled beneath his oxygen mask. My first breathless question as I reached the ledge was, "How high are we, Barry?"

"The altimeter says 27,200 and it's still rising."

"Wow! Tremendous. You guys did it!"

We'd have a long day tomorrow—but it was possible.

Willi had been hastily surveying their choice of a campsite. It was a wind-scooped depression running beneath the cliff for about ten feet. At the wide end it might have been twelve inches across.

"Where'd you find such spacious accommodations?" he asked.

"We knew you'd be satisfied with nothing but the best," Barry said, "but it's the only possibility we've seen all afternoon. Anyway you'll be able to keep warm digging a platform when we leave. Only please don't knock any ice down on us."

With the Sherpas clinging to the slope by their axes, we hacked out a hasty ledge, then gingerly passed the tent, food, and oxygen bottles up to it.

"Careful. If we lose a bottle of oxygen we're through."

It would be dark before they reached 4W. Again tears came as we thanked Ang Dorje, Ila, the two Tenzings, and Passang Tendi. "Good luck, sahib," each one said as we clasped hands. Then we said goodbye to Barry. And to Al.

Barry sank his axe into the snow to anchor the rope. Al led off, followed by the Sherpas. They slid quickly down the fixed line. Then Barry pulled his axe, descended carefully to them and repeated the process.

"Just like guiding Mount Owen, Willi," he shouted up.

There was only a brief moment to feel the grandeur of our impending isolation. We had to contrive some architectural plan for carving a tent platform from an excessively steep slope of snow.

"How about parallel to the cliff?" I asked.

"I think it'll take less digging if we diagonal it out into the gully."

For the next hour and a half we chopped, jumping on the pieces to pulverize them to a size less painful should they accidently be launched onto the party descending below. Every effort was breathtakingly slow.

"Think it's big enough?" Willi asked.

"Let's give it a try."

With the wind threatening to blow it away, we pitched the tent.

"Nope. Not quite big enough. It seems to hang over a bit on the outside," I said. The platform was a good foot too narrow.

"How much do you weigh, Tom, boy?"

"About one hundred and thirty, stripped. Why?"

"I have you by twenty-five pounds. Maybe you better sleep on the outside."

I climbed in to start supper while Willi secured the tent to the slope. One rock piton driven half an inch into the rotten rock of the Yellow Band anchored the uphill ties, our axes buried to the hilt in equally rotten snow pinned the outside corners.

Willi ceremoniously planted the prayer flag Ang Dorje had left. "I think we'd better count on this," he said.

It promised to be a classical high-camp night on Everest: wind batters the tent while its occupants cling to the poles inside, sipping a cold cup of meagre tea. We had the wind, the insecure platform—and the enticing prospect of a two-mile vertical ride into Tibet if our tent let go. But these modern tents had the poles on the outside; there was nothing to cling to. We turned to our meagre fare. This began with chicken-rice soup, followed by a main course of butter-fried, freeze-dried shrimp in a curried tomato sauce, crackers and blackberry jam, and a can of grapefruit segments for dessert. All this was interspersed with many cups of steaming bouillon. Our greatest sorrow was that we could do away with only two-thirds of the four-man luxury ration. We turned to a bit of oxygen as a chaser; once again we had overeaten.

Everything was readied for an early start. For this one night I succumbed to Unsoeld's slovenly habit of sleeping fully clothed, except for boots, which were the foundation under the outer half of my air mattress. While Willi stacked the oxygen bottles in the vestibule, I melted snow for tomorrow's water. This and the butane stoves would share the warmth of our sleeping bags to prevent their freezing during the night.

About nine, Willi awoke from his after-dinner nap, gripped by an overwhelming urge to relieve himself which had for some time been overwhelming me. I promptly encouraged his leaving the tent by offering him a belay.

"No thanks, Tom. A guide can handle these things himself."

He disappeared into the gusty blackness, his flashlight inscribing chaotic circles of light. What a horrible way to go, I thought. And he has the flashlight!

After a time he returned, triumphant. We finished the evening religiously filling out Emerson's diary. Once more violating the classical Everest tradition, we turned our sleeping oxygen to one litre each and settled into the humidity of our plastic sleeping masks. To the lullaby of the wind shaking our high and lonely dwelling, we fell into a deep sleep. But just before that I wrote a letter home, without oxygen:

May 21
Camp 5W, 27,200

Genie:

Just a brief note on our hopeful summit eve. 9 p.m. Willi and I perched in a hacked-out platform at the base of the Yellow Band in Hornbein's Couloir. The morrow greets us with two thousand feet to the top, the first of which looks like some good rock climbing. Very breathless without oxygen. Mainly, as wind rattles the tent and I hang slightly over the edge, would have you know I love you. Tomorrow shall spell the conclusion to our effort, one way or another.

Good night.

Love always,
Tom

Promises to Keep . . .

At four the oxygen ran out, a most effective alarm clock. Two well-incubated butane stoves were fished from inside our sleeping bags, and soon bouillon was brewing in the kitchen. Climbing into boots was a breathless challenge to balance in our close quarters. Then overboots, and crampons.

"Crampons, in the tent?"

"Sure," I replied. "It's a hell of a lot colder out there."

"But our air mattresses!"

"Just be careful. We may not be back here again, anyway. I hope."

We were clothed in multilayer warmth. The fishnet underwear next to our skin provided tiny air pockets to hold our body heat. It also kept the outer layers at a distance which, considering our weeks without a bath, was respectful. Next came Duofold underwear, a wool shirt, down underwear tops and bottoms, wool climbing pants, and a lightweight wind parka. In spite of the cold, our down parkas would be too bulky for difficult climbing, so we used them to insulate two quarts of hot lemonade, hoping they might remain unfrozen long enough to drink during the climb. Inside the felt inner liners of our reindeer-hair boots were innersoles and two pairs of heavy wool socks. Down shells covered a pair of wool mittens. Over our oxygen helmets we wore wool balaclavas and our parka hoods. The down parka lemonade-muff was stuffed into our packs as padding between the two oxygen bottles. With camera, radio, flashlight, and sundry mementos (including the pages from Emerson's diary), our loads came close to forty pounds. For all the prior evening's planning it was more than two hours before we emerged.

I snugged a bowline about my waist, feeling satisfaction at the ease with which the knot fell together beneath heavily mittened hands. This was part of the ritual, experienced innumerable times before. With it came a feeling of security, not from the protection provided by the rope joining Willi and me, but from my being able to relegate these cold, grey, brooding, forbidding walls, so high in such an unknown world, to common reality—to all those times I had ever tied into a rope before: with warm hands while I stood at the base of sun-baked granite walls in the Tetons, with cold hands on a winter night while I prepared to tackle my first steep ice on Longs Peak. This knot tied me to the past, to experiences known, to difficulties faced and overcome. To tie it here in this lonely morning on Everest brought my venture into context with the known, with that which man might do. To weave the knot so smoothly with clumsily mittened hands was to assert my confidence, to assert some competence in the face of the waiting rock, to accept the challenge.

Hooking our masks in place, we bade a slightly regretful goodbye to our tent, sleeping bags, and the extra supply of food we hadn't been able to eat. Willi was at the edge of the ledge looking up the narrow gully when I joined him.

"My oxygen's hissing, Tom, even with the regulator turned off."

For the next twenty minutes we screwed and unscrewed regulators, checked valves for ice, to no avail. The hiss continued. We guessed it must be in the valve, and thought of going back to the tent for the spare bottle, but the impatient feeling that time was more important kept us from retracing those forty feet.

"It doesn't sound too bad," I said. "Let's just keep an eye on the pressure. Besides, if you run out we can hook up the sleeping T and extra tubing and both climb on one bottle." Willi envisioned the two of us climbing Everest in lockstep, wed by six feet of rubber hose.

We turned to the climb. It was ten minutes to seven. Willi led off. Three years before in a tent high on Masherbrum he had expounded on the importance of knee-to-toe distance for step-kicking up steep snow. Now his anatomical advantage determined the order of things as he put his theory to the test. Right away we found it was going to be difficult. The Couloir, as it cut through the Yellow Band, narrowed to ten or fifteen feet and steepened to fifty degrees. The snow was hard, too hard to kick steps in, but not hard enough to hold crampons; they slid disconcertingly down through this wind-sheltered, granular stuff. There was nothing for it but to cut steps, zigzagging back and forth across the gully, occasionally finding a bit of rock along the side up which we could scramble. We were forced to climb one at a time with psychological belays from axes thrust a few inches into the snow. Our regulators were set to deliver two litres of oxygen per minute, half the optimal flow for this altitude. We turned them off when we were belaying to conserve the precious gas, though we knew that the belayer should always be at peak alertness in case of a fall.

We crept along. My God, I thought, we'll never get there at this rate. But that's as far as the thought ever got. Willi's leads were meticulous, painstakingly slow and steady. He plugged tirelessly on, deluging me with showers of ice as his axe carved each step. When he ran out the hundred feet of rope, he jammed his axe into the snow to belay me. I turned my oxygen on to 2 and moved up as fast as I could, hoping to save a few moments of critical time. By the time I joined him I was completely winded, gasping for air, and sorely puzzled about why. Only late in the afternoon, when my first oxygen bottle was still going strong, did I realize what a low flow of gas my regulator was actually delivering.

Up the tongue of snow we climbed, squeezing through a passage where the walls of the Yellow Band closed in, narrowing the Couloir to shoulder width.

In four hours we had climbed only four hundred feet. It was 11 a.m. A rotten bit of vertical wall forced us to the right onto the open face. To regain the couloir it would be necessary to climb this sixty-foot cliff, composed of two pitches split by a broken snow-covered step.

"You like to lead this one?" Willi asked.

With my oxygen off I failed to think before I replied, "Sure, I'll try it."

The rock sloped malevolently outward like shingles on a roof—rotten shingles. The covering of snow was no better than the rock. It would pretend to hold for a moment, then suddenly shatter and peel, cascading down on Willi. He sank a piton into the base of the step to anchor his belay.

I started up around the corner to the left, crampon points grating on rusty limestone. Then it became a snow-ploughing procedure as I searched for some sort of purchase beneath. The pick of my axe found a crack. Using the shaft for gentle leverage, I moved carefully onto the broken strata of the step. I went left again, loose debris rolling under my crampons, to the base of the final vertical rise, about eight feet high. For all its steepness, this bit was a singularly poor plastering job, nothing but wobbly rubble. I searched about for a crack, unclipped a big angle piton from my sling, and whomped it in with the hammer. It sank smoothly, as if penetrating soft butter. A gentle lift easily extracted it.

"Hmmm. Not too good," I mumbled through my mask. On the fourth try the piton gripped a bit more solidly. Deciding not to loosen it by testing, I turned to the final wall. Its steepness threw my weight out from the rock, and my pack became a downright hindrance. There was an unlimited selection of handholds, mostly portable. I shed my mittens. For a few seconds the rock felt comfortably reassuring but cold. Then not cold anymore. My eyes tried to direct sensationless fingers. Flakes peeled out beneath my crampons. I leaned out from the rock to move upward, panting like a steam engine. Damn it, it'll go; I know it will, T, I thought. But my grip was gone. I hadn't thought to turn my oxygen up.

"No soap," I called down. "Can't make it now. Too pooped."

"Come on down. There may be a way to the right."

I descended, half rappeling from the piton, which held. I had spent the better part of an hour up there. A hundred feet out we looked back. Clearly we had been on the right route, for above that last little step the gully opened out. A hundred feet higher the Yellow Band met the grey of the summit limestone. It had to get easier.

"You'd better take it, Willi. I've wasted enough time already."

"Hell, if you couldn't make it, I'm not going to be able to do any better."

"Yes you will. It's really not that hard. I was just worn out from putting that piton in. Turn your regulator clear open, though."

Willi headed up around the corner, moving well. In ten minutes his rope was snapped through the high piton. Discarding a few unsavoury holds, he gripped the rotten edge with his unmittened hands. He leaned out for the final move. His pack pulled. Crampons scraped, loosing a shower of rock from beneath his feet. He was over. He leaned against the rock, fighting for breath.

"Man, that's work. But it looks better above."

Belayed, I followed, retrieved the first piton, moved up, and went to work on the second. It wouldn't come. "Guess it's better than I thought," I shouted. "I'm going to leave it." I turned my oxygen to four litres, leaned out from the wall, and scrambled up. The extra oxygen helped, but it was surprising how breathless such a brief effort left me.

"Good lead," I panted. "That wasn't easy."

"Thanks. Let's roll."

Another rope-length and we stopped. After six hours of hiss Willi's first bottle was empty. There was still a long way to go, but at least he could travel ten pounds lighter without the extra cylinder. Our altimeter read 27,900. We called Base on the walkie-talkie.

Willi: West Ridge to Base. West Ridge to Base. Over.

Base (Jim Whittaker, excitedly): This is Base here, Willi. How are you? How are things going? What's the word up there? Over.

Willi: Man, this is a real bearcat! We are nearing the top of the Yellow Band and it's mighty tough. It's too damned tough to try to go back. It would be too dangerous.

Base (Jim): I'm sure you're considering all about your exits. Why don't you leave yourself an opening? If it's not going to pan out, you can always start working your way down. I think there is always a way to come back.

Willi: Roger, Jim. We're counting on a further consultation in about two or three hundred feet. It should ease up by then! Goddammit, if we can't start moving together, we'll have to move back down. But it should be easier once the Yellow Band is passed. Over.

Base (Jim): Don't work yourself up into a bottleneck, Willi. How about rappeling? Is that possible, or don't you have any *reepschnur* or anything? Over.

Willi: There are no rappel points, Jim, absolutely no rappel points. There's nothing to secure a rope to. So it's up and over for us today . . .

While the import of his words settled upon those listening ten thousand feet below, Willi went right on:

Willi (continuing): . . . and we'll probably be getting in pretty late, maybe as late as seven or eight o'clock tonight.

As Willi talked, I looked at the mountain above. The slopes looked reasonable, as far as I could see, which wasn't very far. We sat at the base of a big wide-open amphitheatre. It looked like summits all over the place. I looked down. Descent was totally unappetizing. The rotten rock, the softening snow, the absence of even tolerable piton cracks only added to our desire to go on. Too much labour, too many sleepless nights, and too many dreams had been invested to bring us this far. We couldn't come back for another try next weekend. To go down now, even if we could have, would be descending to a future marked by one huge question: what might have been? It would not be a matter of living with our fellow man, but simply living with ourselves, with the knowledge that we had had more to give.

I listened, only mildly absorbed in Willi's conversation with Base, and looked past him at the convexity of rock cutting off our view of the gully we had ascended. Above—a snowfield, grey walls, then blue-black sky. We were committed. An invisible barrier sliced through the mountain beneath our feet, cutting us off from the world below. Though we could see through, all we saw was infinitely remote. The ethereal link provided by our radio only intensified our separation. My wife and children seemed suddenly close. Yet home, life itself, lay only over the top of Everest and down the other side. Suppose we fail? The thought brought no remorse, no fear. Once entertained, it hardly seemed even interesting. What now mattered most was right here: Willi and I, tied together on a rope, and the mountain, its summit not inaccessibly far above. The reason we had come was within our grasp. We belonged to the mountain and it to us. There was anxiety, to be sure, but it was all but lost in a feeling of calm, of pleasure at the joy of climbing. That we couldn't go down only made easier that which we really wanted to do. That we might not get there was scarcely conceivable.

Willi was still talking.

Willi: Any news of Barry and Lute? Over.

Jim: I haven't heard a word from them. Over.

Willi: How about Dingman?

Jim: No word from Dingman. We've heard nothing, nothing at all.

Willi: Well listen, if you do get hold of Dingman, tell him to put a light in the window because we're headed for the summit, Jim. We can't possibly get back to our camp now. Over.

I stuffed the radio back in Willi's pack. It was 1 p.m. From here we could both climb at the same time, moving across the last of the yellow slabs. Another hundred feet and the Yellow Band was below us. A steep tongue of snow flared wide, penetrating the grey strata that capped the mountain. The snow was hard, almost ice-hard in places. We had only to bend our ankles, firmly plant all twelve crampon points, and walk uphill. At last, we were moving, though it would have appeared painfully slow to a distant bystander.

As we climbed out of the Couloir the pieces of the puzzle fell into place. That snow rib ahead on the left skyline should lead us to the Summit Snowfield, a patch of perpetual white clinging to the North Face at the base of Everest's final pyramid. By three we were on the Snowfield. We had been climbing for eight hours and knew we needed to take time to refuel. At a shaly outcrop of rock we stopped for lunch. There was a decision to be made. We could either cut straight to the Northeast Ridge and follow it west to the summit, or we could traverse the face and regain the West Ridge. From where we sat, the Ridge looked easier. Besides, it was the route we'd intended in the first place.

We split a quart of lemonade that was slushy with ice. In spite of its down parka wrapping, the other bottle was already frozen solid, as were the kippered snacks. They were almost tasteless but we downed them more with dutiful thoughts of calories than with pleasure.

To save time we moved together, diagonalling upward across down-sloping slabs of rotten shale. There were no possible stances from which to belay each other. Then snow again, and Willi kicked steps, fastidiously picking a route between the outcropping rocks. Though still carting my full load of oxygen bottles, I was beginning to feel quite strong. With this excess energy came impatience, and an unconscious anxiety over the high stakes for which we were playing and the lateness of the day. *Why the hell is Willi going so damned slow?* I thought. And a little later: *he should cut over to the Ridge now; it'll be a lot easier.*

I shouted into the wind, "Hold up, Willi!" He pretended not to hear me as he started up the rock. It seemed terribly important to tell him to go to the right. I tugged on the rope. "Damn it, wait up, Willi!" Stopped by a taut rope and an unyielding Hornbein, he turned, and with some irritation anchored his axe while I hastened to join him. He was perched, through no choice of his own, in rather cramped, precarious quarters. I sheepishly apologized.

We were on rock now. One rope-length, crampons scraping, brought us to the crest of the West Ridge for the first time since we'd left camp 4W yesterday morning. The South Face fell eight thousand feet to the tiny tents of Advance Base. Lhotse, straight across the Face, was below us now. And near at hand a hundred and fifty feet higher, the South Summit of Everest shone in the afternoon sun. We were within four hundred feet of the top! The wind whipped across the Ridge from the north at nearly sixty miles an hour. Far below, peak shadows reached long across the cloud-filled valleys. Above, the Ridge rose, a twisting, rocky spine.

We shed crampons and overboots to tackle this next rocky bit with the comforting grip of cleated rubber soles. Here I unloaded my first oxygen bottle though it was not quite empty. It had lasted ten hours, which obviously meant I was getting a lower flow than indicated by the regulator. Resisting Willi's suggestion to drop the cylinder off the South Face, I left it for some unknown posterity. When I resaddled ten pounds lighter, I felt I could float to the top.

The rock was firm, at least in comparison with our fare thus far. Climbing one at a time, we experienced the joy of delicate moves on tiny holds. The going was a wonderful pleasure, almost like a day in the Rockies. With the sheer drop to the Cwm beneath us, we measured off another four rope-lengths. Solid rock gave way to crud, then snow. A thin firm knife-edge of white pointed gently toward the sky. Buffeted by the wind, we laced our crampons on, racing each other with rapidly numbing fingers. It took nearly twenty minutes. Then we were off again, squandering oxygen at three litres per minute, since time seemed the shorter commodity at the moment. We moved together, Willi in front. It seemed almost as if we were cheating, using oxygen; we could nearly run this final bit.

Ahead, the North and South ridges converged to a point. Surely the summit wasn't that near? It must be off behind. Willi stopped. What's he waiting for, I wondered as I moved to join him. With a feeling of disbelief I looked up. Forty feet ahead, tattered and whipped by the wind, was the flag Jim had left three weeks before. It was 6:15. The sun's rays sheered horizontally across the summit. We hugged each other as tears welled up, ran down across our oxygen masks, and turned to ice.

. . . and Miles to Go . . .

Just rock, a dome of snow, the deep blue sky, and a hunk of orange-painted metal from which a shredded American flag cracked in the wind. Nothing more. Except two tiny figures walking together those last few feet to the top of the earth.

For twenty minutes we stayed there. The last brilliance of the day cast the shadow of our summit on the cloud plain a hundred miles to the east. Valleys were filled with the indistinct purple haze of evening, concealing the dwellings of man we knew were there. The chill roar of wind made speaking difficult, heightening our feeling of remoteness. The flag left there seemed a feeble gesture of man that had no purpose but to accentuate the isolation. The two of us who had dreamed months before of sharing this moment were linked by a thin line of rope, joined in the intensity of companionship to those inaccessibly far below, Al and Barry and Dick—and Jake.

From a pitch of intense emotional and physical drive it was only partly possible to become suddenly, completely the philosopher of a balmy afternoon. The head of steam was too great, and the demands on it still remained. We have a long way to go to get down, I thought. But the prospect of descent of an unknown side of the mountain in the dark caused me less anxiety than many other occasions had. I had a blind, fatalistic faith that, having succeeded in coming this far, we could not fail to get down. The moment became an end in itself.

There were many things savoured in this brief time. Even with our oxygen turned off we had no problem performing those summit obeisances, photographing the fading day (it's a wonderful place to be for sunset photographs), smiling behind our masks for the inevitable "I was there" picture. Willi wrapped the kata given him by Ang Dorje about the flagpole and planted Andy Bakewell's crucifix alongside it in the snow; Lhotse and Makalu, below us, were a contrast of sun-blazed snow etched against the darkness of evening shadow. We felt the lonely beauty of the evening, the immense roaring silence of the wind, the tenuousness of our tie to all below. There was a hint of fear, not for our lives, but of a vast unknown which pressed in upon us. A fleeting feeling of disappointment—that after all those dreams and questions this was only a mountaintop—gave way to the suspicion that maybe there was something more, something beyond the three-dimensional form of the moment. If only it could be perceived.

But it was late. The memories had to be stored, the meanings taken down. The question of why we had come was not now to be answered, yet something up here must yield an answer, something only dimly felt, comprehended by senses reaching farther yet than the point on which we stood; reaching for understanding, which hovered but a few steps higher. The answers lay not on the summit of Everest, nor in the sky above it, but in the world to which we belonged and must now return.

Footprints in the snow told that Lute and Barrel had been here. We'd have a path to follow as long as light remained.

"Want to go first?" Willi asked. He began to coil the rope.

Looking down the corniced edge, I thought of the added protection of a rope from above. "Doesn't matter, Willi. Either way."

"OK. Why don't I go first then?" he said, handing me the coil. Paying out the rope as he disappeared below me I wondered, Is Unsoeld tired? It was hard to believe. Still he'd worked hard; he had a right to be weary. Starting sluggishly, I'd felt stronger as we climbed. So now we would reverse roles. Going up had been pretty much Willi's show; going down would be mine. I dropped the last coil and started after him.

Fifty feet from the top we stopped at a patch of exposed rock. Only the summit of Everest, shining pink, remained above the shadow sea. Willi radioed to Maynard Miller at Advance Base that we were headed for the South Col. It was 6:35 p.m.

We almost ran along the crest, trusting Lute and Barrel's track to keep us a safe distance from the cornice edge. Have to reach the South Summit before dark, I thought, or we'll never find the way. The sun dropped below the jagged horizon. We didn't need goggles anymore. There was a loud hiss as I banged my oxygen bottle against the ice wall. Damn! Something's broken. I reached back and turned off the valve. Without oxygen, I tried to keep pace with the rope disappearing over the edge ahead. Vision dimmed, the ground began to move. I stopped till things cleared, waved my arms and shouted into the wind for Willi to hold up. The taut rope finally stopped him. I tightened the regulator, then turned the oxygen on. No hiss! To my relief it had only been jarred loose. On oxygen again, I could move rapidly. Up twenty feet, and we were on the South Summit. It was 7:15.

Thank God for the footprints. Without them, we'd have had a tough time deciding which way to go. We hurried on, facing outward, driving our heels into the steep snow. By 7:30 it was dark. We took out the flashlight and resumed the descent. The batteries, dregs of the expedition, had not been helped by our session with Emerson's diary the night before; they quickly faded. There was pitiful humour as Willi probed, holding the light a few inches off the snow to catch some sign of tracks. You could order your eyes to see, but nothing in the blackness complied.

We moved slowly now. Willi was only a voice and an occasional faint flicker of light to point the way. No fear, no worry, no strangeness, just complete absorption. The drive which had carried us to a nebulous goal was replaced by simple desire for survival. There was no time to dwell on the uniqueness of our situation. We climbed carefully, from years of habit. At a rock outcrop we paused. Which way? Willi groped to the right along a corniced edge. In my imagination, I filled in the void.

"No tracks over here," Willi called.

"Maybe we should dig in here for the night."

"I don't know. Dave and Girmi should be at 6."

We shouted into the night, and the wind engulfed our call.

A lull. Again we shouted. "Helloooo," the wind answered. Or was it the wind?

"Hellooo," we called once more.

"Hellooo," came back faintly. That wasn't the wind!

"To the left, Willi."

"OK, go ahead."

In the blackness I couldn't see my feet. Each foot groped cautiously, feeling its own way down, trusting to the pattern set by its predecessor. Slowly left, right, left, crampons biting into the snow, right, left, . . .

"*Willeeee!*" I yelled as I somersaulted into space. The rope came taut, and with a soft thud I landed.

"Seems to be a cornice there," I called from beneath the wall. "I'll belay you from here."

Willi sleepwalked down to the edge. The dim outline of his foot wavered until it met my guiding hand. His arrival lacked the flair of my descent. It was well that the one of lighter weight had gone first.

Gusts buffeted from all directions, threatening to dislodge us from the slope. Above a cliff we paused, untied, cut the rope in half, and tied in again. It didn't help; even five feet behind I couldn't see Willi. Sometimes the snow was good, sometimes it was soft, sometimes it lay shallow over rocks so we could only drive our axes in an inch or two. With these psychological belays, we wandered slowly down, closer to the answering shouts. The wind was dying, and so was the flashlight, now no more than an orange glow illuminating nothing. The stars, brilliant above, cast no light on the snow. Willi's oxygen ran out. He slowed, suddenly feeling much wearier.

The voices were close now. Were they coming from those two black shapes on the snow? Or were those rocks?

"Shine your light down here," a voice called.

"Where? Shine yours up here," I answered.

"Don't have one," came the reply.

Then we were with them—not Dave and Girmi, but Lute and Barrel. They were near exhaustion, shivering lumps curled on the snow. Barrel in particular was far gone. Anxious hungering for air through the previous night, and the near catastrophe when their tent caught fire in the morning, had left him tired before they even started. Determination got him to the top, but now he no longer cared. He only wanted to be left alone. Lute was also tired. Because of Barrel's condition he'd had to bear the brunt of the climbing labour. His eyes were painfully burned, perhaps by the fire, perhaps by the sun and wind. From sheer fatigue they had stopped thinking. Their oxygen was gone, except for a bit Lute had saved for Barrel; but they were too weak to make the change.

At 9:30 we were still a thousand feet above Camp 6. Willi sat down on the snow, and I walked over to get Lute's oxygen for Barrel. As I unscrewed Lute's regulator from the bottle, he explained why they were still there. Because of the stove fire that had sent them diving from the tent, they were an hour late in starting. It was 3:30 p.m. when they reached the summit. Seeing no sign of movement down the west side, they figured no one would be any later than they were. At 4:15 they started down. Fatigue slowed their descent. Just after dark they had stopped to rest and were preparing to move when they heard shouts. Dave and Girmi, they thought. No—the sounds seemed to be coming from above. Willi and Tom! So they waited, shivering.

I removed Barrel's regulator from his empty bottle and screwed it into Lute's. We were together now, sharing the support so vigorously debated a week before. Lute would know the way back to their camp, even in the dark. All we had to do was help them down. Fumbling with unfeeling fingers, I tried to attach Barrel's oxygen hose to the regulator. Damn! Can't make the connection. My fingers scraped uncoordinately against cold metal. Try again. There it goes. Then, quickly, numb fingers clumsy, back into mittens. Feeling slowly returned, and pain. Then, the pain went and the fingers were warm again.

Willi remembered the Dexedrine I had dropped into my shirt pocket the evening before. I fished out two pills—one for Barrel and one for Lute. Barrel was better with oxygen, but why I had balked at his communal use of Lute's regulator, I cannot say. Lack of oxygen? Fatigue? It was fifteen hours since we'd started our climb. Or was it that my thoughts were too busy with another problem? We had to keep moving or freeze.

I led off. Lute followed in my footsteps to point out the route. Lost in the darkness sixty feet back on our ropes, Willi and Barrel followed. The track was more sensed than seen, but it was easier now, not so steep. My eyes watered from searching for the black holes punched in the snow by Lute's and Barrel's axes during their ascent. We walked to the left of the crest, three feet down, ramming our axes into the narrow edge. Thirty feet, and the rope came taut as Barrel collapsed in the snow, bringing the entire caravan to a halt. Lute sat down behind me. Got to keep moving. We'll never get there.

We had almost no contact with the back of the line. When the rope came taut, we stopped, when it loosened we moved on. Somewhere my oxygen ran out, but we were going too slow for me to notice the difference. Ought to dump the empty bottle, I thought, but it was too much trouble to take off my pack.

Heat lightning flashed along the plains to the east, too distant to light our way. Rocks that showed in the snow below seemed to get no closer as the hours passed. Follow the axe holes. Where'd they go? Not sure. There's another.

"Now where, Lute?"

"Can't see, Tom," Lute said. "Can't see a damn thing. We've got to turn down a gully between some rocks."

"Which gully. There's two or three."

"Don't know, Tom."

"Think, Lute. Try to remember. We've got to get to 6."

"I don't know. I just can't see."

Again and again I questioned, badgering, trying to extract some hint. But half-blind and weary, Lute had no answer. We plodded on. The rocks came slowly closer.

Once the rope jerked tight, nearly pulling me off balance. Damn! What's going on? I turned and looked at Lute's dim form lying on the snow a few feet farther down the Kangshung Face. His fall had been effectively if uncomfortably arrested when his neck snagged the rope between Willi and me.

We turned off the crest, toward the rocks. Tongues of snow pierced the cliffs below. But which one? It was too dangerous to plunge on. After midnight we reached the rocks. It had taken nearly three hours to descend four hundred feet, maybe fifteen minutes' worth by daylight.

Tired. No hope of finding camp in the darkness. No choice but to wait for day. Packs off. Willi and I slipped into our down parkas. In the dark, numb fingers couldn't start the zippers. We settled to the ground, curled as small as possible atop our pack frames. Lute and Barry were somewhere behind, apart, each alone. Willi and I tried hugging each other to salvage warmth, but my uncontrollable shivering made it impossible.

The oxygen was gone, but the mask helped a little for warmth. Feet, cooling, began to hurt. I withdrew my hands from the warmth of my crotch and loosened crampon bindings and bootlaces, but my feet stayed cold. Willi offered to rub them. We removed boots and socks and planted both my feet against his stomach. No sensation returned.

Tired by the awkward position, and frustrated by the result, we gave it up. I slid my feet back into socks and boots, but couldn't tie them. I offered to warm Willi's feet. Thinking that his freedom from pain was due to a high tolerance of cold, he declined. We were too weary to realize the reason for his comfort.

The night was overpoweringly empty. Stars shed cold, unshimmering light. The heat lightning dancing along the plains spoke of a world of warmth and flatness. The black silhouette of Lhotse lurked half-sensed, half-seen, still below. Only the ridge on which we were rose higher, disappearing into the night, a last lonely outpost of the world.

Mostly there was nothing. We hung suspended in a timeless void. The wind died, and there was silence. Even without wind it was cold. I could reach back and touch Lute or Barrel lying head to toe above me. They seemed miles away.

Unsignalled, unembellished, the hours passed. Intense cold penetrated, carrying with it the realization that each of us was completely alone. Nothing Willi could do for me or I for him. No team now, just each of us, imprisoned with his own discomfort, his own thoughts, his own will to survive.

Yet for me, survival was hardly a conscious thought. Nothing to plan, nothing to push for, nothing to do but shiver and wait for the sun to rise. I floated in a dreamlike eternity, devoid of plans, fears, regrets. The heat lightning, Lhotse, my companions, discomfort, all were there—yet not there. Death had no meaning, nor, for that matter, did life. Survival was no concern, no issue. Only a dulled impatience for the sun to rise tied my formless thoughts to the future.

About four o'clock the sky began to lighten along the eastern rim, baring the bulk of Kangchenjunga. The sun was slow in following, interminably slow. Not till after five o'clock did it finally come, its light streaming through the South Col, blazing yellow across the Nuptse Wall, then on to the white wave-crest of peaks far below. We watched as if our own life was being born again. Then as the cold yellow light touched us, we rose. There were still miles to go.

Postscript: The four climbers started down the mountain again, where they were at last met by colleagues carrying additional oxygen for the trip to Base Camp. For the next thirty years, Hornbein continued climbing high peaks around the world, in addition to working as a professor of anesthesiology at the University of Washington.

On October 13, 1972, a small plane filled with a Uruguayan rugby team and a handful of friends and family crashed into a twelve-thousand-foot mountain in the Andes. After two months, a weak radio transmission informed those still surviving that the search party had been called off. Nando Parrado and two others were forced to leave the mountain and find help.

MIRACLE IN THE ANDES

*72 Days on the Mountain
and My Long Trek Home*

NANDO PARRADO

None *of us had much to say as we* followed the gentle incline of the glacier up to the mountain's lower slopes. We thought we knew what lay ahead, and how dangerous the mountain could be. We had learned that even the mildest storm could kill us if it trapped us in the open. We understood that the heavily corniced snow on the high ridges was unstable, and that the smallest avalanche would whisk us down the mountain like a broom sweeping crumbs. We knew that deep crevasses lay hidden beneath the thin crust of frozen snow, and that rocks the size of television sets often came crashing down from crumbling outcrops high on the mountain. But we knew nothing about the techniques and strategies of mountaineering, and what we didn't know was enough to kill us.

We didn't know, for example, that the Fairchild's altimeter was wrong; the crash site wasn't at seven thousand feet, as we thought, but close to twelve thousand. Nor did we know that the mountain we were about to challenge was one of the highest in the Andes, soaring to the height of nearly seventeen thousand feet, with slopes so steep and difficult they would test a team of expert climbers. Experienced mountaineers, in fact, would not have gone anywhere near this mountain without an arsenal of specialized gear, including steel pitons, ice screws, safety lines, and other critical gadgets designed to keep them safely anchored to the slopes. They would carry ice axes, weatherproof tents, and sturdy thermal boots fitted with crampons—metal spikes that provide traction on the steepest, iciest inclines. They would be in peak physical condition, of course, and they would climb at a time of their own choosing, and carefully plot the safest route to the top. The three of us were climbing in street clothes, with only the crude tools we could fashion out of materials salvaged from the plane. Our bodies were already ravaged from months of exhaustion, starvation, and exposure, and our backgrounds had done little to prepare us for the task. Uruguay was a warm and low-lying country. None of us had ever seen real mountains before. Prior to the crash, Roberto and Tintin had never even seen snow. If we had known anything about climbing, we'd have seen we were already doomed. Luckily, we knew nothing, and our ignorance provided our only chance.

Our first task was to choose a path up the slopes. Experienced climbers would have quickly spotted a ridge winding down from the summit to meet the glacier at a point less than a mile south of the crash site. If we had known enough to hike to that ridge and climb its long, narrow spine, we would have found better footing, gentler slopes, and a safer and swifter path to the top. We never even noticed the ridge. For days I had marked with my eye the spot where the sun set behind the ridges, and, thinking that the best path was the shortest path, we used that point to chart a beeline path due west. It was an amateurish mistake that would force us to weave our way up the mountain's steepest and most dangerous slopes.

Our beginning, though, was promising. The snow on the mountain's lower flank was firm and fairly level, and the cleats of my rugby boots bit well into the frozen crust. Driven by an intense adrenaline surge, I moved quickly up the slope, and in no time I had pulled fifty yards ahead of the others. But soon I was forced to slow my pace. The slope had grown much steeper, and it seemed to grow steeper yet with every step, like a treadmill that constantly increases its incline. The effort left me gasping in the thin air, and I had to rest, with my hands on my knees, after every few yards of progress.

Soon the sun was strong enough to warm us as we climbed, but it warmed the snow as well, and the firm surface beneath my feet began to weaken. Now, with every step, my foot was breaking through the thinning crust and I would sink up to my knees in the soft, deep drifts below. Each step required extreme effort. I would lift my knee almost to my chest to clear my boot from the snow. Then I would swing that foot forward, shift my weight onto it, and break through the ice again. In the thin air I had to rest, exhausted, after every step. When I looked behind me I saw the others struggling, too. I glanced at the sun above us, and realized that we had waited too long that morning to start the climb. Logic told us it would be wiser to climb in daylight, so we'd waited for the sun to rise. Experts, on the other hand, know that the best time for climbing is in the predawn hours, before the sun can turn the slopes to mush. The mountain was making us pay for another amateur mistake. I wondered what other blunders lay ahead, and how many of them we'd be able to survive.

Eventually all the crust melted away, and we were forced to wade uphill through heavy drifts that sometimes were as deep as my hips. "Let's try the snowshoes!" I shouted. The others nodded, and in moments we had slipped Fito's makeshift snowshoes off our backs and strapped them to our feet. They worked well at first, allowing us to climb without sinking into the snow. But the size and bulk of the cushions forced us to bow our legs as we walked, and to swing our feet in unnaturally wide circles to keep the fat cushions from colliding. To make things worse, the stuffing and upholstery quickly became soaked with melted snow. In my exhausted state, I felt as if I were climbing the mountain with manhole covers bolted to my shoes. My spirits were rapidly sinking. We were already on the verge of exhaustion, and the real climbing hadn't even begun.

The incline of the mountain grew steadily sharper, and soon we reached slopes that were too steep and windblown to hold deep drifts of snow. With relief, we removed the snowshoes, strapped them to our backs, and kept climbing. By midmorning we had worked our way to a dizzying altitude. The world around us now was more blue air and sunlight than rock and snow. We had literally climbed into the sky. The sheer altitude and the yawning openness of the vast slopes left me reeling with a sense of dreamlike disbelief. The mountain fell away so steeply behind me now that when I looked down on Tintin and Roberto, I saw only their heads and shoulders outlined against two thousand feet of empty sky. The angle of the slope was as steep as a roofer's ladder, but imagine a ladder you could climb to the moon! The height made my head swim and sent tingling spasms along my hamstrings and spine. Turning to look behind me was like pirouetting on the ledge of a skyscraper.

On steep, open slopes like these, where the incline seems intent on tipping you off the mountain and good handholds are hard to find, experts would use safety lines tethered to steel anchors driven into rock or ice, and they'd count on their crampons to give their footing a secure grip on the mountainside. We had none of those things, but only the fading strength of our arms, legs, fingertips, and freezing toes to keep us from sailing off into the blue void behind us. I was terrified, of course, but still I could not deny the wild beauty all around me—the flawless sky, the frosted mountains, the glowing landscape of deep virgin snow. It was all so vast, so perfect, so silent and still. But something troubling was hiding behind all that beauty, something ancient and hostile and profound. I looked down the mountain to the crash site. From this altitude it was just a ragged smudge on the pristine snow. I saw how crass and out of place it seemed, how fundamentally *wrong*. Everything about us was wrong here—the violence and racket of our arrival, our garish suffering, the noise and mess of our lurid struggle to survive. None of it fit here. *Life* did not fit here. It was all a violation of the perfect serenity that had reigned here for millions of years. I had sensed it the first time I gazed at this place: we had upset an ancient balance, and balance would have to be restored. It was all around me, in the silence, in the cold. Something wanted all that perfect silence back again; something in the mountain wanted us to be still.

By late morning we had climbed some two thousand feet from the crash site and were probably fourteen thousand feet or more above sea level. I was moving inch by inch now as a vicious headache tightened like an iron ring around my skull. My fingers felt thick and clumsy, and my limbs were heavy with fatigue. The slightest effort—lifting my head, turning to speak to Roberto—left me sucking for air as if I'd just run a mile, but no matter how forcefully I inhaled, I couldn't fill my lungs. I felt as if I were drawing breath through a piece of felt.

I would not have guessed it at the time, but I was suffering from the effects of high altitude. The physiological stress of climbing in oxygen-depleted air is one of the great dangers mountain climbers face. Altitude sickness, which generally strikes in the zone above eight thousand feet, can cause a range of debilitating symptoms, including headache, intense fatigue, and dizziness. Above twelve thousand feet, the condition can lead to cerebral and pulmonary edemas, both of which can cause permanent brain damage and rapid death. At high altitude, it's hard to escape the effects of mild and moderate altitude disease, but the condition is worsened by rapid climbing. Experts recommend that climbers ascend no more than one thousand feet per day, a rate that gives the body a chance to acclimate itself to the thinning air. We had climbed twice that far in a single morning, and were making matters worse by continuing to climb when our bodies desperately needed time to rest.

In response, my oxygen-starved body was struggling to cope with the thinning air. My heart rate soared and my blood thickened in my veins—the body's way of conserving oxygen in the bloodstream and sending it more rapidly to vital organs and tissues. My respiration rate rose to the brink of hyperventilation, and with all the moisture I lost as I exhaled, I was becoming more severely dehydrated with every breath. To supply themselves with the huge amounts of water needed to stay safely hydrated at high altitude, expert climbers use portable gas stoves to melt pots of snow, and they guzzle gallons of fluids each day. Our only source of fluids was the snow we gulped in handfuls, or melted in the glass bottle we had in one of the packs. It did little good. Dehydration was rapidly sapping our strength, and we climbed with a constant, searing thirst.

After five or six hours of hard climbing, we had probably ascended some 2,500 feet, but for all our striving, the summit seemed no closer. My spirits sagged as I gauged the vast distance to the top, and realized that each of my tortured steps brought me no more than fifteen inches closer. I saw with brutal clarity that we had taken on an inhuman task. Overwhelmed with fear and a sense of futility, I felt the urge to sink to my knees and stay there. Then I heard the calm voice in my head, the voice that had steadied me in so many moments of crisis. "You are drowning in distances," it said. "Cut the mountain down to size." I knew what I had to do. Ahead of me on the slope was a large rock. I decided I would forget about the summit and make that rock my only goal. I trudged for it, but like the summit it seemed to recede from me as I climbed. I knew then that I was being tricked by the mountain's huge scale of reference. With nothing on those vast empty slopes to give me perspective—no houses, no people, no trees—a rock that seemed ten feet wide and a hundred yards away might really be ten times larger and more than a mile distant. Still, I climbed toward the rock without resting, and when I finally got there I picked another landmark and started all over again.

I climbed that way for hours, focusing my attention completely on some target—a rock, a shadow, an unusual ruffle in the snow—until the distance to that target became all that mattered in the world. The only sounds were my own heavy breathing and the rhythmic crunch of my shoes in the snow. My pace soon became automatic, and I slipped into a trance.

Somewhere in my mind I still longed for my father, I still suffered from fatigue, I still worried that our mission was doomed, but now those thoughts seemed muted and secondary, like a voice on a radio playing in another room. *Step-push, step-push*. Nothing else mattered. Sometimes I promised myself I'd rest when the next goal was reached, but I never kept my promise. Time melted away, distances dwindled, the snow seemed to glide beneath my feet. I was a locomotive lumbering up the slope. I was lunacy in slow motion. I kept up that pace until I had pulled far ahead of Roberto and Tintin, who had to shout to make me stop. I waited for them at an outcrop that offered a level place to rest. We ate some meat and melted some snow to drink. None of us had much to say. We all knew the kind of trouble we were in.

"Do you still think we can make it by nightfall?" asked Roberto. He was looking at the summit.

I shrugged. "We should look for a place to camp."

I looked down to the crash site. I could still make out the tiny shapes of our friends watching us from seats they'd dragged outside the fuselage. I wondered how things looked from their perspective. Could they tell how desperately we were struggling? Were their hopes beginning to fade? If at some point we stopped moving, how long would they wait for us to start moving again? And what would they do if we didn't? These thoughts occurred to me only as passing observations. I was no longer in the same world as the boys down below. My world had narrowed, and the feelings of compassion or responsibility I had felt for the other survivors were now crowded out by my own terror and my own furious struggle to survive. I knew it was the same for Tintin and Roberto, and while I was certain we would fight side by side as long as possible, I understood that each of us, in his desperation and fear, was already alone. The mountain was teaching me a hard lesson: camaraderie is a noble thing, but in the end death is an opponent each of us would face in solitude.

I looked at Roberto and Tintin, resting sullenly on the ledge of rock. "What did we do to deserve this?" muttered Roberto. I looked up the mountain, searching for a cliff or a boulder that might give us shelter for the night. I saw nothing but a steep, endless blanket of snow.

As we worked our way up the mountain, that snow cover gave way to an even more difficult landscape. Now rocks were jutting from the snow, some of them huge and impossible to climb. Massive ridges and outcrops above us blocked my view of the slope ahead, and I was forced to choose my path by instinct. Often I chose wrong, and found myself trapped under an impassable ledge, or at the base of a vertical rock wall. Usually I could backtrack, or inch my way diagonally across the slope to find a new path. Sometimes I had no choice but to press on.

At one point in the early afternoon, I found my way blocked by an extremely steep, snow-covered incline. I could see a level rock shelf at the far upper edge. Unless we could climb the incline diagonally and scramble up onto that narrow shelf, we'd have to backtrack. That could cost us hours, and with sunset growing closer by the minute, I knew that was not an option. I looked back at Tintin and Roberto. They were watching to see what I would do. I studied the incline. The slope was sheer and smooth, there was nothing to grip with my hands. But the snow looked stable enough to support me. I'd have to dig my feet into the snow and keep my weight tilted forward as I climbed. It would all be a matter of balance.

I began to climb the frozen wall, carving the snow with the edges of my shoes and pressing my chest against the slope to keep from toppling backwards. The footing was stable, and with great caution I inched my way to the rock ledge and scrambled up onto level ground. I waved to Tintin and Roberto. "Follow my steps," I shouted. "Be careful, it is very steep."

I turned away from them and began to climb the slopes above me. Moments later I glanced back to see that Roberto had made it across the incline. Now it was Tintin's turn. I began climbing again, and had ascended thirty yards or so when a terrified shout echoed up the mountain.

"I'm stuck! I can't make it!"

I turned to see Tintin frozen in the middle of the incline.

"Come on, Tintin!" I shouted. "You can do it!"

He shook his head. "I can't move."

"It's the backpack!" said Roberto. "It's too heavy."

Roberto was right. The weight of Tintin's backpack, which he carried very high on his back, was pulling him off the face of the mountain. He was struggling to shift his balance forward, but there was nothing to offer him a handhold, and the look on his face told me he could not hold out for long. From my vantage point I could see the dizzying drop behind him, and I knew what would happen if Tintin fell. First he would swim away from us for a long time in thin air, then he would hit the slope, or an outcrop, and tumble down the mountain like a rag doll until some drift or crag eventually brought his broken body to a stop.

"Tintin, hold on!" I shouted. Roberto was at the lip of the rock shelf above the incline, stretching his arm down to Tintin. His reach was short by inches. "Take off your backpack!" he shouted. "Give it to me!" Tintin removed the backpack carefully, struggling to keep his balance as he slowly worked the straps off his arms and handed it up to Roberto. Without the weight of the backpack, Tintin was able to find his balance and climb safely up the incline. When he reached the ledge, he slumped to the snow. "I can't go any farther," he said. "I'm too tired. I can't lift my legs."

Tintin's voice betrayed his exhaustion and fear, but I knew we had to climb until we found a sheltered place to rest for the night, so I kept going, leaving the others no choice but to follow. As I climbed, I scanned the slopes in every direction, but the mountain was so rocky and steep there was no safe place to spread our sleeping bag. It was late afternoon now. The sun had drifted behind the western ridges, and shadows were already stretching down the slopes. The temperature began to fall. At the crash site below, I saw that our friends had retreated into the fuselage to escape the cold. A clot of panic was rising in my throat as I frantically searched the slopes for a safe, level place to spend the night.

At twilight I scaled a tall rock outcropping to get a better view. As I climbed, I wedged my right foot in a small crevice in the rock, then, with my left hand, reached up to grab a horn of boulder jutting from the snow. The boulder seemed solid, but when I pulled myself up, a rock the size of a cannonball broke free and plummeted past me.

"Watch out! Watch out below!" I shouted. I looked down to see Roberto beneath me. There was no time to react. His eyes widened as he waited for the impact of the rock, which missed his head by inches. After a moment of stunned silence, Roberto glared at me. "You son of a bitch! You son of a bitch!" he shouted. "Are you trying to kill me? Be careful! Watch what the fuck you are doing!" Then he fell silent and leaned forward, and his shoulders started to heave. I realized he was crying. Hearing his sobs, I felt a pang of hopelessness so sharp I could taste it on my tongue. Then I was overtaken by a sudden, inarticulate rage. "*Fuck* this! *Fuck* this!" I muttered. "I have had *enough*! I have had *enough*!" I just wanted it to be over. I wanted to rest. To sink into the snow. To lie still and quiet. I can't remember any other thoughts, so I don't know what led me to keep going, but once Roberto had gathered himself, we started climbing again in the fading light. Finally I found a shallow depression in the snow beneath a large boulder. The sun had warmed the boulder all day, then the heat radiating from the rock had melted out this compact hollow. It was cramped, and its floor tilted sharply down the slope, but it would shelter us from the nighttime cold and wind. We laid the seat cushions on the floor of the hollow to insulate us from the cold, then spread the sleeping bag over the cushions. Our lives depended upon the bag, and the body warmth it would conserve, but it was a fragile thing, sewn together crudely with strands of copper wire, so we handled it with great care. To keep from tearing the seams, we removed our shoes before sliding in.

"Did you pee?" asked Roberto, as I eased myself into the bag. "We can't be getting in and out of this bag all night."

It reassured me that Roberto was becoming his grumbling self again.

"I peed," I answered. "Did you pee? I don't want you peeing in this bag."

Roberto huffed at me. "If anyone pees in the bag it will be you. And be careful with those big feet."

When the three of us were all inside the sleeping bag, we tried to get comfortable, but the ground beneath us was very hard, and the floor of the hollow was so steep we were almost standing up, with our backs pressed to the mountain and our feet braced against the downhill rim of the hollow. That small rim of snow was all that kept us from sliding down the slope. We were all exhausted, but I was far too frightened and cold to relax.

"Roberto," I said, "you are the medical student. How does one die of exhaustion? Is it painful? Or do you just drift off?"

The question seemed to irk him. "What does it matter how you die?" he said. "You'll be dead and that's all that matters."

We were quiet for a long time. The sky was as black as ink now, and studded with a billion brilliant stars, each of them impossibly clear and blazing like a point of fire. At this altitude I felt I could reach out and touch them. In another time and place I would have been awestruck by all this beauty. But here, and now, it seemed a brutal show of force. The world was showing me how tiny I was, how weak and insignificant. And temporary. I listened to my own breathing, reminding myself that as long as I drew breath I was still alive. I promised myself I would not think of the future. I would live from moment to moment and from breath to breath, until I had used up all the life I had.

The temperature dropped so low that night that the water bottle we carried shattered from the cold. Huddled together in the sleeping bag, we kept ourselves from freezing, but still we suffered terribly. In the morning we placed our frozen shoes in the sun and rested in the bag until they thawed. Then, after eating and packing our things, we began to climb. The sun was bright. It was another perfect day.

We were climbing above fifteen thousand feet now, and with every hundred yards or so the incline of the mountain tilted closer to the vertical. The open slopes were becoming unclimbable, so we began to work our way up the rocky edges of the winding couloirs—the steep plunging ravines that gashed the side of the mountain. Experienced climbers know couloirs can be killing zones—their shape makes them efficient chutes for all the rocks that tumble down the mountain—but the packed snow inside them gave us good footing, and the tall rock walls at their rims gave us something firm to grip.

At times, one edge of a couloir would lead us to an impassable point. Then I would work my way across the snow-covered center of the couloir to the opposite edge. As we climbed the couloirs, I found myself worrying more and more about the lethal void behind me. Perhaps it was the dizzying altitude, perhaps it was fatigue or a trick of my oxygen-starved brain, but I felt that the emptiness at my back was no longer a passive danger. Now it had presence and intention, very bad intention, and I knew that if I didn't resist it with all my strength, it would lure me off the mountain and toss me down the slope. Death was tapping me on the shoulder, and the thought of it made me slow and tentative. I second-guessed every movement, and lost faith in my balance. I realized with searing clarity that there were no second chances here, there was no margin for error. One slip, one moment of inattention, one bit of bad judgment, would send me headlong down the slope. The tug of the void was constant. It wanted me, and the only thing that could keep me from it was the level of my own performance. My life had collapsed to a simple game—climb well and live, or falter and die—and my consciousness had narrowed until there was no room in my thoughts for anything but a close and careful study of the rock I was reaching for, or the ledge on which I was about to brace my foot. Never had I felt such a sense of concentrated presence. Never had my mind experienced such a pure, uncomplicated sense of purpose.

Put the left foot there. Yes, that edge will hold. Now, with the left hand, reach up for the crack in that boulder. Is it sturdy? Good. Lift yourself. Now, put the right foot on that ledge. Is it safe? Trust your balance. Watch the ice!

I forgot myself in the intensity of my concentration, forgot my fears and fatigue, and for a while I felt as if everything I had ever been had disappeared, and that I was now nothing more than the pure will to climb. It was a moment of pure animal exhilaration.

I had never felt so focused, so driven, so fiercely alive. For those astonishing moments, my suffering was over, my life had become pure flow. But those moments did not last. The fear and exhaustion soon returned, and climbing once again became an ordeal. We were very high on the mountain now, and altitude was making my motions heavy and my thinking slow. The slopes had become almost vertical and were harder than ever to climb, but I told myself that inclines this steep could only mean we were nearing the summit. To steady myself, I imagined the scene I'd see from the summit just as I'd imagined it so many times before—the rolling hills partitioned into green and brown parcels of farmland, the roads leading off to safety, and somewhere a hut or a farmhouse . . .

How we continued to climb, I cannot say. I was shivering uncontrollably from cold and fatigue. My body was on the verge of complete collapse. Only the simplest thoughts could take shape in my mind. Then, in the distance above me, I saw the outline of a sloping ridge in sharp relief against a background of clear blue sky, and no more mountain above it. The summit! "We made it!" I shouted, and with renewed energy I clawed my way to the ridge. But as I pulled myself over its edge, the ridge gave way to a level shelf several yards wide, and above the shelf the mountain rose again. It was the steep angle of the slope that had fooled me. This was only another trick of the mountain, a false summit. And it wasn't the last. We spent the afternoon struggling toward one false summit after another until, well before sunset, we found a sheltered spot and decided to pitch our camp.

Roberto was sullen that night as we lay in the sleeping bag. "We will die if we keep climbing," he said. "The mountain is too high."

"What can we do but climb?" I asked.

"Go back," he said. For a moment I was speechless.

"Go back and wait to die?" I asked.

He shook his head. "Do you see across there, that dark line on the mountain? I think it's a road." Roberto pointed across a wide valley to a mountain ridge miles away.

"I don't know," I said. "It looks like some sort of fault line in the rock."

"Nando, you can barely see," he snapped. "I tell you it's a road!"

"What are you thinking?" I asked.

"I think we should go back and follow that road. It must lead somewhere."

That was the last thing I wanted to hear. Since the moment we'd left the fuselage, I had secretly been tormented by doubts and misgivings. *Are we doing the right thing? What if rescuers come while we're in the mountains? What if the farmlands of Chile are not just over the ridge?* Roberto's plan seemed like lunacy, but it forced me to consider other options, and I did not have the heart for that now.

"That mountain must be twenty-five miles away," I said. "If we hike there and climb to that black line, and find that it is just a layer of shale, we won't have the strength to return."

"It's a road, Nando, I'm sure of it!"

"Perhaps it's a road, perhaps it's not," I replied. "The only thing we know for sure is that to the west is Chile."

Roberto scowled. "You've been saying that for months, but we'll break our necks before we get there."

Roberto and I argued about the road for hours, but as we settled down to sleep, I knew the matter had not been resolved. I woke the next morning to yet another clear sky.

"We've been lucky with the weather," said Roberto. He was still inside the sleeping bag.

"What have you decided?" I asked him. "Are you going back?"

"I'm not sure," he said. "I need to think."

"I'm going to climb," I said, "maybe we'll reach the summit soon."

Roberto nodded. "Leave your packs here," he said. "I'll wait until you return."

I nodded. The thought of going on without Roberto terrified me, but I had no intention of turning back now. I waited for Tintin to gather his pack, then we turned to the slope and began to climb. After hours of slow progress, we found ourselves trapped at the base of a cliff towering hundreds of feet above us. Its face was almost dead vertical and covered with hard-packed snow.

"How can we climb this?" asked Tintin.

I studied the wall. My mind was sluggish, but soon I remembered the aluminum walking stick strapped to my back.

"We need a stairway," I said. I drew the stick off my back, and with its sharp tip, I began to carve crude steps into the snow. Using the steps like the rungs of a ladder, we continued to climb. It was excruciating work, but I kept at it with the dull persistence of a farm animal, and we ascended one slow step at a time. Tintin followed behind me. He was frightened, I know, but he never complained. In any case, I was just dimly aware of his presence. My attention was focused on the task at hand: *Dig, climb, dig, climb.* I felt, at times, that we were climbing the sheer sides of a frozen skyscraper, and it was very difficult to keep my balance as I dug, but I no longer worried about the void at my back. I respected it, but I had learned to tolerate its presence. A human being, as I've said before, gets used to anything.

It was an agonizing process, inching up the mountain that

way, and the hours passed slowly. Sometime in late morning I spotted blue sky above a ridgeline and worked my way toward it. After so many false summits, I had learned to keep my hopes in check, but this time, as I climbed over the ridge's edge, the slope fell away flat and I found myself standing on a gloomy hump of rock and wind-scoured snow. It dawned on me slowly that there was no more mountain above me. I had reached the top.

I don't remember if I felt any joy or sense of achievement in that moment. If I did, it vanished as soon as I glanced around. The summit gave me an unobstructed 360-degree view of creation. From here I could see the horizon circling the world like the rim of a colossal bowl, and in every direction off into the fading blue distance, the bowl was crowded with legions of snow-covered mountains, each as steep and forbidding as the one I had just climbed. I understood immediately that the Fairchild's copilot had been badly mistaken. We had not passed Curicó. We were nowhere near the western limits of the Andes. Our plane had fallen somewhere in the middle of the vast Cordillera.

I don't know how long I stood there, staring. A minute. Maybe two. I stood motionless until I felt a burning pressure in my lungs, and realized I had forgotten to breathe. I sucked air. My legs went rubbery and I fell to the ground. I cursed God and raged at the mountains. The truth was before me: for all my striving, all my hopes, all my promises to myself and my father, it would end like this. We would all die in these mountains. We would sink beneath the snow, the ancient silence would fall over us, and our loved ones would never know how hard we had struggled to return to them.

In that moment all my dreams, assumptions, and expectations of life evaporated into the thin Andean air. I had always thought that *life* was the actual thing, the natural thing, and that death was simply the end of living. Now, in this lifeless place, I saw with a terrible clarity that *death* was the constant, death was the base, and life was only a short, fragile dream. I was dead already. I had been born dead, and what I thought was my life was just a game death let me play as it waited to take me. In my despair, I felt a sharp and sudden longing for the softness of my mother and my sister, and the warm, strong embrace of my father. My love for my father swelled in my heart, and I realized that, despite the hopelessness of my situation, the memory of him filled me with joy. It staggered me: The mountains, for all their power, were not stronger than my attachment to my father. They could not crush my ability to love. I felt a moment of calmness and clarity, and in that clarity of mind I discovered a simple, astounding secret: Death has an opposite, but the opposite is not mere living. It is not courage or faith or human will. The opposite of death is *love*. How had I missed that? How does anyone miss that? Love is our only weapon. Only love can turn mere life into a miracle, and draw precious meaning from suffering and fear. For a brief, magical moment, all my fears lifted, and I knew that I would not let death control me. I would walk through the godforsaken country that separated me from my home with love and hope in my heart. I would walk until I had walked all the life out of me, and when I fell I would die that much closer to my father. These thoughts strengthened me, and with renewed hope I began to search for pathways through the mountains. Soon I heard Tintin's voice calling to me from the slope below.

"Do you see any green, Nando?" he cried. "Do you see any green?"

"Everything will be fine," I called down to him. "Tell Roberto to come up and see for himself." While I waited for Roberto to climb, I pulled a plastic bag and the lipstick from my backpack. Using the lipstick as a crayon, I wrote the words MT. SELER on the bag and stuffed it under a rock. *This mountain was my enemy,* I thought, *and now I give it to my father. Whatever happens, at least I have this as my revenge.*

It took three hours for Roberto to climb the steps. He looked around for a few moments, shaking his head. "Well, we are finished," he said flatly.

"There must be a way through the mountains," I said. "Do you see there, in the distance, two smaller peaks with no snow on them? Maybe the mountains end there. I think we should head that way."

Roberto shook his head. "It must be fifty miles," he said. "And who knows how much farther after we reach them? In our condition, how can we make such a trek?"

"Look down," I said. "There is a valley at the base of this mountain. Do you see it?"

Roberto nodded. The valley wound through the mountains for miles, in the general direction of the two smaller peaks. As it neared the small mountains, it split into two forks. We lost sight of the forks as they wound behind larger mountains, but I was confident the valley would take us where we needed to go.

"One of those forks must lead toward the small mountains," I said. "Chile is there, it's just farther than we thought."

Roberto frowned. "It's too far," he said. "We'll never make it. We don't have enough food."

"We could send Tintin back," I said. "With his food and what's left of ours, we could easily last twenty days."

Roberto turned away and looked off to the east. I knew he was thinking about the road. I looked west again, and my heart sank at the thought of trekking through that wilderness alone.

We were back at camp by late that afternoon. As we ate

together, Roberto spoke to Tintin. "Tomorrow morning we are going to send you back," he said. "The trip will be longer than we thought, and we're going to need your food. Anyway, two can move faster than three." Tintin nodded in acceptance.

In the morning Roberto told me he had decided to stay with me. We embraced Tintin and sent him down the mountain.

"Remember," I said as he left us, "we will always be heading west. If rescuers come, send them to find us!"

We rested all that day in preparation for the trek that lay ahead. In the late afternoon we ate some meat and crawled into the sleeping bag. That evening, as the sun slipped behind the ridge above us, the Andes blazed with the most spectacular sunset I had ever seen. The sun turned the mountains to gleaming gold, and the sky above them was lit with swirls of scarlet and lavender. It occurred to me that Roberto and I were probably the first human beings to have such a vantage point on this majestic display. I felt an involuntary sense of privilege and gratitude, as humans often do when treated to one of nature's wonders, but it lasted only a moment. After my education on the mountain, I understood that all this beauty was not for me. The Andes had staged this spectacle for millions of years, long before humans even walked the earth, and it would continue to do so after all of us were gone. My life or death would not make a bit of difference. The sun would set, the snow would fall . . .

"Roberto," I said, "can you imagine how beautiful this would be if we were not dead men?" I felt his hand wrap around mine. He was the only person who understood the magnitude of what we had done and of what we still had to do. I knew he was as frightened as I was, but I drew strength from our closeness. We were bonded now like brothers. We made each other better men.

In the morning we climbed the steps to the summit. Roberto stood beside me. I saw the fear in his eyes, but I also saw the courage, and I instantly forgave him all the weeks of arrogance and bullheadedness. "We may be walking to our deaths," I said, "but I would rather walk to meet my death than wait for it to come to me."

Roberto nodded. "You and I are friends, Nando," he said. "We have been through so much. Now let's go die together."

We walked to the western lip of the summit, eased ourselves over the edge, and began to make our way down.

Postscript: After ten days of unspeakable agony walking through the bitterly cold mountains, Nando Parrado and his colleague spotted a peasant across a wide raging river. Their successful rescue had begun.

In 1988 Peter Potterfield chose to climb an impressive 7,680-foot spire in the North Cascades of Washington state called Chimney Rock. On the way up he fell 150 feet to a ledge, where he was trapped and badly injured, having suffered several compound fractures which protruded grotesquely from his body. Far from civilization and bleeding profusely, he feared the rescue team would not make it in time to save his life.

IN THE ZONE

*Epic Survival Stories
from the Mountaineering World*

PETER POTTERFIELD

Chimney

We had the stove going by 5 a.m. The dawn came steely gray, cold and still, the sun up but still below the ridgelines. The roar of glacier meltwater tearing down the mountain in midsummer torrents put a layer of white noise on the alpine quiet. The tent was pitched on a gently sloping heather bench, the fuel and cooking pots laid out on a big rock, the packs and the rest of the gear strewn about our camp at the edge of a big snowfield. We were smack in the middle of classic summer high pressure, the kind that brings spells of reliably good weather to the stormy Cascades. The sky was clear, the surrounding peaks big and black where they were silhouetted against the brightening sky. We prepared the usual breakfast of instant oatmeal (extra raisins for me) and coffee, and ate standing up around the hissing stove. I cradled the plastic bowl in my hands, warming them. There were just the two of us, as usual, and not much conversation. We had done this so many times before. We rinsed the dishes with the leftover hot water in the cooking pot. Into the packs went two racks of hardware and two ropes, little else: lunch, a few extra clothes, the maps, and other usual stuff. The plan was to start high, travel light, and move fast. From this camp at about five thousand feet we figured to be on top of 7,680-foot Chimney Rock by midmorning.

With breakfast done and the packs ready, I sat on a big rock at the edge of the snow and with chilled fingers strapped crampons—racks of steel spikes—to my boots. The air was bracing, aromatic with heather and high-country timber. There was the subtle, familiar tension, the pregame jitters, the not unpleasant mixture of anticipation and anxiety that comes before the climbing begins. Shouldering our packs, we stepped off the uneven vegetation and crunched across two hundred yards of frozen snow toward a gully in the rocky shoulder of the mountain. The snow-filled cleft led steeply upward out of our small basin. We quickly warmed as we moved up and out of the sparse, stunted timber. The cramponing and easy scrambling had us gaining altitude fast.

Our route up the mountain was slightly off the beaten path. Our camp on the pretty little heather bench was higher and farther to the east than the basin directly below Chimney Rock's South Peak, which is the usual starting point for the climb. But here on the road less taken the going was obvious, and pleasant. After about seven hundred feet of climbing, our crampons scraping on the rocks that protruded from the snow, our cleft opened onto a rounded dome of rock and scree from which we stepped onto the broad expanse of the upper Chimney Glacier. We stopped for a drink and a moment to take in the scene. The rising sun illuminated the reddish rock of the mountain above us. We were in the shallow cirque formed by the three summits of the mountain, our view of neighboring Summit Chief, to the east, blocked by the North Peak, the adjacent peaks of Chickamin and Lemah out of sight behind the South Peak. Below us, draining a multitude of small creeks from the surrounding glaciers and ridges, a big forested valley doglegged south, one lake out in the middle distance, a bigger one farther down where the valley turned east. The white ice of the lower Chimney Glacier spread away beneath us. Glaciated mountains punctured by rocky towers marched down the ridge to our right as we faced the valley. In the distance, Cascade ridgelines arced away to the horizon. There was not a cloud to be seen. It was going to be hot, even up this high.

Our slightly unorthodox route put us on the glacier hundreds of feet higher than the standard route, circumventing the icefall and broken ice farther below. In high summer the icefall can present crevasse problems that necessitate long detours.

We checked our maps against the upper mountain before us. Our position was directly under the North Peak, one of three prominent spires that make up the craggy bulk of Chimney Rock. Already above six thousand feet, we would have only to traverse a mile or so across the glacier to reach the start of the more technical rock climb. As we moved west on the ice we would pass, in turn, the three possible routes we might take to the summit of Chimney Rock: first we would reach the start of the East Pace Direct, a midfifth-class route going straight up the big face of the Main Peak; next would be the start of the East Face or so-called normal route, which follows a prominent gully between the South and Main peaks; and last, a circuitous route called the U Gap that begins on the south side of the South Peak and requires a long traverse on rocky ledges to join the East Face Route high on the face.

As we traveled across the upper glacier we could tell our choice of route was not going to be difficult. The size and condition of the *'schrund*—the moat where the glacier meets the rock of the upper mountain—made the first two routes impractical. We stood out on the expanse of ice gazing up at the long rock routes, discussing quietly what was clear just by looking. We adjusted our vector and began the long walk around the mountain to the steep snow chute that would take us up to the col known as the U Gap, hopeful it would prove feasible.

Traversing the glacier was pure pleasure. Doug and I followed in each other's footsteps by turn, sidehilling against the moderate ice slope, enjoying the scenery. We were still crunching along the glacier in cool shadow, but the sun was really working on the peaks, painting the rocky mass of the mountain above us a breathtaking Rembrandt gold. The sky behind was the acute blue of early morning in the mountains.

I was comfortable being here with Doug, the result of years of similar trips into the cursed and wonderful and wild mountains of the Northwest. Our party was small by design, two being the mutually preferred group size for our trips, though conventional wisdom urged bigger parties for the sake of safety. We were well matched in ability and temperament, confident we could deal with the weird and unpredictable turns that events can take in wilderness mountains, and which make traveling in them so interesting. Our specialty, when we had the time, was big mountains in remote areas. We could handle the long approaches and heavy packs, and we enjoyed the scarcity of other two-leggeds. In six years of climbing together we had taken minor falls, been lost in slide-alder-choked valleys and caught out in miserable weather, but we had not had so much as a close call, such was our combined skill, judgment, and dumb good luck.

Traveling together, we could move fast without the conversation or inertia that comes from larger groups. At times we had words over routes and camps and when to cook dinner, but we always seemed to reach a workable resolution without the dark animosity that can come between people when they travel for days in the backcountry. This business of climbing partners is complex, for it's merely prudent to take care in choosing those to whom you're willing to trust your life. But you want to have fun as well. Over the years, Doug and I had found we worked pretty well together, and we did a lot of laughing.

We shared a profession—journalism—as well as a penchant for a good story and a little high-proof whiskey by the fire. We had made our way up major and minor peaks in the Olympics and Cascades, camped in outrageous places, wandered remote little basins and spectacular ridges. Climbing like this in the Northwest is among the best things you can do, and we enjoyed ourselves. Our success rate was high. When climbing day came around we roused ourselves early, moved fast, and generally got where we were going.

That morning high on Chimney Rock was the fourth day of a fairly strenuous outing. From Seattle we had taken the hour-and-a-half drive on Interstate 90 over Snoqualmie Pass, turned off at the little town of Cle Elum, and meandered another hour or so through the national forest to the trailhead at Cooper Lake. Parking the car there, we set off on foot alongside the Cooper River as it flowed prettily through virgin fir and hemlock forest. About seven miles in, just within the boundary of the Alpine Lakes Wilderness Area, we reached Pete Lake. Across the lake we could see the spires of Chimney Rock and its near neighbor, Lemah Peak, rising abruptly from the trees. Both stand almost five thousand feet higher than the lake and from that vantage point are impressive despite being miles away. We dropped our heavy packs—nearly a week's worth of provisions, plus the ropes and hardware and ice axes, added up to real weight, maybe seventy pounds each—and had lunch while looking up at the rocky peaks.

First-day packs for extended climbing trips can take the highlight off anyone's wilderness experience. Doug was five years younger than my thirty-eight years, twenty pounds lighter than my 165 pounds, and a couple of inches shorter than my six-foot-one height. A marathoner, his youth and superb fitness enabled him to carry weight nearly half his own. We had done this pack-animal bit before, and did not particularly enjoy it, but it's the price you pay. We squirmed back into our loads and moved on up the valley a mile or so beyond Pete Lake. There we intersected the Pacific Crest Trail, a major thoroughfare of western backcountry that runs from Mexico to Canada along the spine of the Sierra and the Cascades. We turned right, north, in the direction of Dutch Miller Gap, though our destination was elsewhere.

This section of the Pacific Crest Trail along the north-central Cascade Crest is well maintained and generally easygoing, but in the July heat our steady uphill progress with our big loads took a toll. We cruised along the valley floor, then labored up the seemingly endless switchbacks on the big ridge separating the Pete Lake drainage from that of Waptus Lake. We were winded and our water bottles drunk dry when, about halfway up the ridge, we left the Crest Trail and set out over rocky, broken ground and sparse timberline vegetation toward tiny Vista Lakes (which don't appear on most maps).

There, at dusk, we pitched camp in splendid isolation, feasting and laughing, guzzling the beers Doug traditionally and unbelievably packs in for the first nights of our longer trips. We were giddy to be free of our loads, happy to be, once again, in the mountains.

The next day we explored the rugged country with luxuriously light packs and moved our camp into a little unnamed pass under the Summit Chief massif. We were touring an uncommonly wild corner of the Cascades and, though it was peak season, saw no one. Our intention was to travel off trail at timberline to Lake Ivanhoe, a body of water just south of Dutch Miller Gap, and from there climb a route on the vast west face of Bears Breast. From our new camp beneath Summit Chief, in fact, that massive mountain beckoned to us across miles of hard country. We discussed our options at length as we roamed about. In the end we had to concede that with only two climbing days left before we were due back in Seattle, Bears Breast was out of reach. Chimney Rock was the sensible alternative. We would return another day and do Bears Breast from the other side of the gap.

In the morning, then, back down the mountain we went, retracing our route to the Crest Trail down the boring, hated switchbacks. At the valley bottom I stashed some food, my trail boots, and other gear I wouldn't need, and we found the start of the climbers' track up toward Chimney Rock. Grunting and sweating our way up the steep, brushy, muddy, and unsavory way trail, we reached our high camp on Monday afternoon, July 25, 1988, and pitched the tent on the undulating bench of alpine heather. The next morning, our wristwatch alarms roused us in time for an early start on the mountain.

As we cramponed across the Chimney Glacier with the rhythmic, flat-footed gait such travel requires, each step punctuated with the bite of the ice ax ferrule, it was as if for all our hard work the Cascades rewarded us with their benign aspect. The high reaches of those mountains can be truly awful—gray, windy, wet, cold, colorless—and, in fact, usually are. That's why there are glaciers in the Cascades at the same altitudes at which highway passes are built in the Rockies. Spells of good weather do come in the summer and fall, however, and that morning the scenery and weather both were glorious. Like privileged guests we moved around up there in shorts and T-shirts over polypropylene long underwear, unburdened by sleeping bags, tents, and stoves. It was the kind of day that makes me revel in the tangible sense of freedom climbing sometimes brings—unlike the bad days on dangerous routes when I just feel stupid, the only rational thought coming as a recurring question: What am I doing here?

I think all climbers are ambivalent about what they do, but most keep doing it. The allure of mountaineering is something that persistently resists satisfactory explanation, probably because every climber has his own reasons. It nevertheless exerts a powerful attraction. For me it has something to do with being far away in a beautiful place, alone or nearly so, and traveling under one's own steam through rugged country completely unmarked by modern blight. Climbing is the best foil I've found for the onerous realities of the twentieth century. It keeps me in touch with the sun and moon and stars, with wind and terrain, with my body and my abilities, and, quite often, with the texture of my fear. I enjoy it immensely, when I don't hate it.

As we traversed under the summit towers of Chimney Rock—local relief was almost two thousand feet from glacier to summit—we saw that the mountain was made of slabby rotten rock—hard, contact-metamorphosed breccias with sedimentary interbeds. When Chimney Rock was first climbed in 1930 it was widely held to be the hardest rock climb then done in the

Cascades. It has since become a moderate route in the scheme
of things, interesting but not terribly technical. But its loose
rock is as threatening now as it was in the thirties. More
climbers get the chop from falling rock than from falling off; it's
a situation to regard with distaste.

With its three distinct summits, Chimney is a sprawling,
complicated mountain. Only from a distance does the main
summit stand out and give the peak its eponymous feature.
Our long traverse took us directly under all three towers.
After more than an hour crossing high on the glacier, we
passed under the 1,500-foot South Face of the South Peak and
began climbing a narrow snow-filled couloir up to the U Gap,
a notch between the South Peak and a high rocky prominence
called South Point. We were able to climb into the five-
hundred-foot snow chute without much trouble. It steepened
quickly, reaching maybe fifty-five degrees near the top. We
were still in shadow so our crampons bit well into the firm
snow, but the morning shadow line was chasing us up the
couloir as the sun rose in the sky, threatening to overheat us
and to soften the snow into sloppy stuff that would make
climbing more difficult.

About halfway up the chute Doug and I discussed the merits of exiting the couloir early to proceed on rock, but decided
that continuing up the snow chute to the top was our best
route. As we paused fifty feet apart on the steep slope,
anchored by the shafts of our ice axes, I heard Doug say, "Uh,
we've got a problem."

"What's that?" I said, curious, turning downhill to face him.

He was rifling energetically through his pack, and pointed
to a rock the size of a portable television set lying in the snow
a few feet from where he stood, downhill leg locked, on the
steep slope. "That thing almost hit me," he said. "I'm putting
my crack hat on." His helmet would have done him little good

had he been in the way of that rock, but I started digging for my helmet, too. I hoped the slabby slopes of Chimney would send us no more such greetings.

Climbers have a name for such random acts of fate as rockfall and avalanche: objective dangers. Short of staying home, there just isn't much to be done about them. By now a cautious old-timer, with recklessness burned out of me by years of climbing, I try to avoid objective dangers. There was nothing for it here, however. I strapped on my own blue helmet and cinched it up. Hard hats are hot, heavy, and uncomfortable. Like most climbers, Doug and I wore them only when we felt them necessary. But because they are most certainly indicated for wilderness climbs such as Chimney and Bears Breast, we had lugged the things with us for the past twenty miles. Retrieving my ax from the snow, I set out for the top of the gully, taking over from Doug the fatiguing chore of kicking steps in the steep hard snow. It was 8:30 a.m. We had been climbing three hours.

Finally reaching the top of the snow chute, we left the snow and climbed up to the crest of the small col, where we sat on a couple of big rocks. There we removed our crampons and strapped them—along with the ice axes—to our packs. From here on, we would climb on rock, not ice. Our route traversed the South Peak via a series of small ledges before joining the East Face route about five hundred feet directly under the summit. Unroped but helmeted, we set off on an obvious ledge system—the mountain here was made like a Mayan pyramid, stepping back as it went up, and we had merely to connect the wide ledges by easy scrambling.

We made reasonable time around to the south face of the South Peak. There the ledges began to get more problematic, less obvious, and generally a little more tenuous—smaller, downsloping, and covered with loose rock. I didn't like the look of it. Ahead of Doug, I called back to him that our route looked loose and unaesthetic and dangerous. When he joined me, he concurred but suggested we continue on to see what developed.

We stopped on the last comfortably sized ledge to pull out the hardware slings, don harnesses, and rope up for the harder ground ahead. From my hardware rack I selected a likely sized chock, a multisided piece of machined metal alloy with a short sling of nylon rope attached, and placed it into a handy crack. It wedged nicely. I clipped the sling into the back of my harness with a snap link called a carabiner—climbers just call them 'biners—to anchor myself to the mountain. Tied into one end of the 150-foot rope, I pulled out the slack until only a few feet remained between me and Doug, who was tied into the other end. Pushing a loop of rope through the slot on a thick metal disk called a Stitcht plate, I clipped the loop into my main harness 'biner. If Doug should fall now, even if I weren't conscious, the rope could not run through the Stitcht plate and, attached to my anchor, I could not be pulled off the mountain. Doug was on belay, protected from falling. As he climbed, I would pay out rope through the Stitcht plate.

Doug set off on the first lead. We dispensed with the usual signals, such as "ready to climb" and "on belay," because we had done this so often it would have been superfluous. Only when we were out of sight of each other were signals necessary between us. I settled in to belay him as he moved out of sight around a corner.

The morning was unbelievably fine, warm but not yet hot. While the rope paid out through my Stitcht plate as Doug climbed—or rather, moved horizontally around the mountain—I gazed out over the valley and our entire route for the past few days, from Cooper Lake up the big valley to Pete Lake, along the Crest Trail to the hot switchbacks of the big ridge, even part of Summit Chief itself. But as pleasant as it was to be up so high on that perfect Tuesday morning in the Cascades, I couldn't shake the feeling that something was wrong. I had become uneasy about the mountain and the route. It was an odd sensation, and for me an unfamiliar one. I called out to Doug. About a hundred feet of rope had paid out, but there had been no movement for some time. It seemed as if he was taking forever to set up his belay, and I was becoming irritated. My crankiness matched my uneasiness. Soon, though, he was shouting, "Belay on!" indicating that he was safely tied in and ready for me to follow.

I covered the one hundred feet or so to where Doug, anchored to the rock, was reeling me in. In that short distance, the misgivings I had expressed to Doug earlier had turned to grave premonition.

"I still don't like this, Doug," I said, and jokingly added, "I tell you, my love of life is stronger than my desire to climb Chimney Rock." I was now experiencing a powerful foreboding, but when I looked out over the benign landscape, I could not figure out why. The ledges were loose and unattractive, but we had negotiated worse. There was no rational basis for getting psyched out so, but there it was. Sitting down on the rubbly rock a few feet from Doug and his anchors, my doubts gnawed on me. I declared, "I think this might be my high point."

"Look, it'll probably get better around the corner," he said, as he sat in his belay stance, the rope piled at his feet, a few yards stretched between us. "We're almost around to the standard route by now. Let's check it out, anyway. OK?"

Clearly Doug wanted to press on, and given the perfect conditions I couldn't argue with him. To pansy out now would be bad form—I hated it when climbing partners did that to me. We were more than halfway up and moving well. We

were actually ahead of schedule, maybe an hour and a half
from the top. The weather was good and the morning young.
Reluctantly, I agreed to continue on.

There were two routes from Doug's belay stance that
looked feasible, though neither was particularly appealing.

"The one on the right?" Doug suggested, as he adjusted
the ropes and anchors to belay from a different direction as we
swapped the lead. On close inspection, the right-hand route
definitely looked more likely than the other to take us where
we wanted to go. I checked my gear, cinched up my pack, and
climbed past Doug onto new ground. He was ensconced in
his stance, back against the rock, the rope piled at his feet. His
new belay device, a Tuber, was unfamiliar to me, but he had
shown it to me on our last climb and seemed to like it.

My concentration was now on the rock. The ledge on
which I stood was covered with loose rocks, and a little farther
on narrowed and became increasingly downsloping, much
harder than our previous ground. From there I could go left
and up or down and right. My uneasiness did not abate. I
wondered if we were off route. Moving cautiously, I set out on
the lower of the two ledge systems, angling slightly downhill
from Doug's belay. As usual, so long as we remained in sight
of each other we dispensed with voice signals.

Leaning out around a corner near the end of the ledge, I
could see another ledge, big and grassy, about fifteen feet
away. The face in between was thin, but looked as if it would
go. I figured to make a descending traverse of the face on
small holds, and reach the big ledge. From there I could move
farther around the mountain toward the normal route.

Thirty feet or so from Doug, I hung a sling on a small horn
of rock protruding handily from the face and clipped the
climbing rope to it with a carabiner. Since I was actually below
Doug, my safety factor had improved. If I fell on the thin sec-

tion I would essentially be top roped—held from above—and if the sling held would face, at worst, a short fall. If the sling failed, I would pendulum across the face to a line directly under Doug, but with only thirty feet of rope between us, still not take a serious fall. I moved off around the gentle corner, leaving Doug behind and above as the rope paid out. Out of sight now of my partner, I moved down by strenuous moves on decent holds to the rock face between my protection—the sling—and the grassy ledge beyond. It was harder than it had looked.

Although there were good holds above my head, there wasn't much for my feet, and my boots scraped the rock before I saw some nubbins on which to place the tips of my Vibram soles. Another couple of moves over the thin face, not too bad, and I was halfway. And I knew I was in trouble, for I could see a blank stretch of rock offering no good holds. This climb isn't supposed to be this hard, I thought. We must be off route. By then I had one decent hold for my left hand and nothing but friction on a little bulge for my boots. I thought about trying to reverse my moves back to the narrow ledge, but knew I was kidding myself. I was in trouble and realized I was about to log some air time, a really awful thought. I have fallen only rarely, and then on bombproof-belayed practice crags. The idea of peeling for real scared my mule.

I hung on, looking everywhere for an idea, my left hand cramping up and beginning to slip. There was nothing but a small face hold I had seen before, marginal at best, barely out of reach of my right hand. Better holds just beyond it tempted me to try. I stretched out as far as I could and made a kind of controlled lunge. It wasn't enough. My fingers slid across it and down the rock. I was coming off, as my last maneuver had pulled me out of my previous hold. "Falling!" I yelled, and off I went.

———

It was a bad moment, but I had time to realize that it could be worse—I could have been way above Doug and have faced taking a long leader fall. As it was I expected a short fall before the rope, passing through the sling above, stopped my fall when Doug locked the rope in his belay device.

When I peeled, the attitude of my body was sideways—my head way out to my right side where I had reached for the hold, my left hand coming off the one hold above, my feet sticking out to the left. The face here was quite steep, and I just launched off, pretty clean, straight down. Below, the face steepened to overhanging, so I did not bounce or tumble. But the rope kept running through the 'biner above me as I sailed through space with only minor, scraping contact with the rock. I prepared for the jerk that would come when the rope caught me. But it didn't come, and I wondered why it was taking so long.

Then I smashed against the rock face. The blow knocked the breath from me and completely turned me around. I heard bones break. The violence of the impact was unbelievable, the pain spectacular. Another impact followed in rapid succession, worse than the first. I felt more bones break in my left shoulder, heard them crunch and felt my body give. It was nightmarish. So this is what it's like, I thought. After the second collision, I started tumbling down the steep face. My sensations were of cannon-loud explosions as my helmet crashed against the rock, and sledgehammer body blows as impact after impact jarred and tossed my body. I saw nothing after those last desperate moments looking for holds. I ultimately lost my sense of orientation as I hurtled downward, smashing against the south face as I fell.

I knew I was dying, and felt intense sorrow about that. My life did not flash before me, but I thought of Anne, the dark-eyed beauty who shares my life. I felt so sorry that I would

spend no more happy times with her and the eccentric fox ter-
rier that made up our family. I felt anger that my good life
would end this terrible way, being pummeled and broken by
the fall down the mountain.

The fall seemed to take a long time. A big surge of
fear swept through me, blocking thought, but as the fall
progressed the shock of dread replaced fear. I hated getting
beat up like that, dying like that. The thing was, it wouldn't
stop, and I knew no one could take that kind of abuse and
live. The impacts continued, they racked and tossed my body,
but strangely did not impair my lucidity or stop my stream of
consciousness. I kept thinking about Anne, kept coming back
to her, and how I wished this thing was not really happening
to me. Could this be a dream, a hallucination? No, but it took
time for me to admit that I was in the process of being killed
by falling off a mountain. Just another dead climber, I
thought, nobody's fault but mine. A paragraph in the *Seattle
Times*, I read them all the time.

I registered the pain and altered attitude of my body after
each collision. Some were worse than others, I could tell,
some breaking bones, some not. I began to feel somewhat separate from my body, but I was absolutely aware: it was as if
my body were being killed while I watched and listened.

There was a shape to it, starting with the slip and free fall,
and then the endless, terrifying, rag-doll impacts accompanied
by explosive blows to my helmet. Those were, by far, the
worst, then there was more painless free fall—pure air time—
and then *wham!* Suddenly my fall was arrested. I had arrived
at a tiny ledge just as the rope jerked me up short.

A shattering, unnerving quiet replaced the cacophonous
noise of my helmet banging against the rock face. It happened
fast. One nanosecond I was falling and dying, the next I was
suddenly looking out over the valley, suspended from the

climbing rope like a puppet, my feet barely touching the small ledge on the sheer rock face. I could hardly believe it. I felt overwhelmed, not ready to believe what had happened. Waves of pain rolled over me. I got a funny, shocky feeling. My field of vision began to shrink noticeably and rapidly. The world appeared unnaturally blurry and bright, but it was getting smaller. I felt ineffably strange, as if I were hardly there at all. Then, I noticed a change: the pain became extraneous, and my attention shifted to my diminishing consciousness and shrinking field of vision. I felt neutral, separate, and thought perhaps this might be death. I was not surprised. I hung there in a peaceful, sunlit silence. There was no hurry.

I don't remember how long I was in that state of suspended reality. I may have passed out. At some point, however, the scope of my world began to expand, slowly, definitely. A familiar feeling–that accustomed, essential sense of self–slowly reemerged. Squinting into the brightness, I realized that my prescription sunglasses had come off in the fall. But I was not dead. As if to reinforce that fact, the pain returned with a vengeance, shutting out thoughts of other matters. The pain was exacerbated by my awkward bouncing around at the end of the climbing rope.

I knew I must be badly hurt, but had no idea what the inventory of injuries might be. My left arm hung at a bizarre angle. My left leg was twisted outward and throbbing. My pelvis radiated a deep pain where it met my left hip. Each dangling movement registered in multiple points of pain on a scale I had never experienced. I was sufficiently loony that I was unable to truly grasp what had happened, barely able to take in the fact I was not dead. I kept thinking, Man, I am actually here on this little ledge, still breathing. *Unbelievable*.

Everything about my body was racked with pain and seemed oddly displaced or rearranged. I felt woozy and weird. Right then, more than anything else, I wanted to take a load off, to sit down on that little ledge. But there was too much tension on the taut rope, which ran like a steel cable from my harness up and out of sight beyond an overhang back to Doug. My line of sight above was restricted to about fifty feet of steep rock face, the blue rope running upward plumb-line straight. I could not unclip from my harness because there was too much tension on the rope, yet I wasn't quite standing on the ledge, either. Only by standing on my toes could I touch the ledge. Struggle as I might, I could not unclip. I hung there exactly like a doll on a string.

I tried to move my left arm to take weight off the rope so that with my right hand I could unclip the big harness carabiner from the knot in the rope. With that attempt, an explosion of pain ripped along my left arm. The limb literally flapped in the breeze. I reeled and moaned and I feared I would pass out. So this is what they mean by writhing in pain, I thought. I hung there limp, helpless, my full weight on the harness. Turning slowly at the end of the rope, first one way, then another, I stupidly looked out over the valley and felt a more lucid consciousness gradually return. My situation became clear: busted up and possibly dying after a bad mountaineering fall.

"Slack! Slack!" I cried in a plaintive voice, the loudest I could muster but not one I recognized as my own. "Slack, Doug! I'm hurt bad!" If Doug had me on belay, he could pay out a little rope through the belay device and lower me to the ledge. But no slack came. For a long time in the still of that summer morning, there was no reply. There was no noise at all. I hung there awkwardly. Then Doug's voice, small and disembodied, carried down to me:

"OK, but it might be kind of sudden."

I took that in and realized that I must be at the end of the rope—literally. Somehow the belay must have gone wrong. I must have fallen the full length of the rope, 150 feet. Only the anchors into which the other end of the rope was tied prevented me from plummeting entirely off the mountain, and pulling Doug off with me. Doug had no more rope at his end or he could have simply lowered me to the ledge. With my weight on the rope there was nothing he could do except cut it or untie from the anchors, or maybe rig some kind of Prusik arrangement. The prospect of Doug's unfastening the anchors and letting me drop suddenly—even a few feet—really got my attention. Such a move could send me careening beyond the ledge and off the mountain, or at least injure me more by dumping me in a heap on the ledge.

"No, no," I shouted back. "Don't do that!"

I was standing awkwardly on my tiptoes, trying to control the twisting and swaying. I was afraid I might pass out. I started to panic. Frantically, I dug for my pocketknife, thinking I might cut the rope above my harness. But I could not get my right hand into my left pocket. My shorts were pulled up and askew by the harness, which was loaded up with my weight. I was sweating profusely and feeling, by turns, faint and overcome by pain. A panicky thought took me over: if I don't do something real soon I'm going to die right here on the end of this rope.

I looked around. The ledge sloped slightly downward, and so was higher where it joined the mountain than it was at the outer edge. If I were able to back up enough I might gain five or six inches of elevation, enough to unload the rope and get sufficient slack to unclip. But as I began to maneuver on my toes, my weight came on my left leg. That same outrageous pain—I was beginning to know it now—blasted out of my hip and knee. I collapsed once again onto the rope, limp, wasted. I hung on the rope and closed my eyes. I tried to chase the

panic, which constantly nipped at the edge of my consciousness and threatened to screw up my thinking.

I either had to do something myself or yell for Doug to
chop the anchors and just take my chances. Hanging on the
taut rope, I mustered my concentration. Keeping some of my
weight on the rope I began to perform a sort of one-legged
soft shoe on the ledge, moving backward on my apparently
undamaged right leg and foot. Doing so gained me a few
inches in distance and altitude and took measurable pressure
off my harness. I was learning how to use my damaged body.
With two or three more spurts of grisly dancing I achieved
enough purchase on the ledge to heel-toe up the sloping rocky
shelf a foot or more, as far as the ledge allowed and just
enough to put a little slack in the rope. With my good right
hand, I reached around my body, opened the big Stubai lock-
ing carabiner on my harness, and pulled out the figure-eight
knot at the end of the rope. Free at last from the rope, I
crumpled slightly, but managed to keep my balance and hold
myself upright on my right leg.

Unroped now, I felt a new surge of fear—that I might fall
again. I was balanced on my one good foot on the downsloping rocky ramp of the small ledge, without any sort of safety
line. A fall here would send me over the lunch-tray-sized ledge
down to the glacier hundreds of feet below. To make matters
worse, my pack had slipped off my shoulders but was still
attached at the waist belt. It flopped around dangerously, my
ice ax with its three sharp ends still affixed to it. The ledge was
small. The pack might push me off. But it contained essential
items. I couldn't just kick it off the mountain.

Slowly, I reached across with my right hand and unfas-
tened the waist belt. The pack fell down behind my legs. I
kept it there, behind my body, so it wouldn't tumble off. Thus
encumbered, with my useless left leg flopping in front of me, I

began to lower myself with infinite care to a sitting position on
the ledge. The maneuver was horrendously painful, but the
ledge was big enough to accommodate me, back against the
rock face, heels hooked on an outstanding little lip that happened to lie exactly at the edge. I had been moaning softly,
making little sounds with my exhalations (they came naturally
and seemed to help) since my arrival on the ledge, but bending my left knee into the extreme sitting position required by
the ledge made me cry out loud for the first time. Panting, I
slid my pack from behind me to my left side, one shoulder
strap hooked over my left calf to keep it from falling off.
There barely was enough room for me, much less my pack. I
squirmed around on the uneven ledge. I thought: This will do.

But the perch was, in its own way, a screaming terror, a
tiny ledge hanging in space from the sheer expanse of rock.
The exposure was spectacular. The big south face of Chimney's South Peak rose vertically above and behind me, and
plummeted down six hundred or seven hundred feet below
me to the Chimney Glacier, easing in angle as it neared the ice.
Unlike the perfectly smooth granite walls of Yosemite, this
rock face was broken, faceted like a huge gemstone. In some
places overhanging, in others, slightly off vertical. To my right
the wall overhung dramatically, to my left a narrow, shallow
chute ran from about five feet above to end just at the left side
of the ledge. This small depression, perhaps two feet wide and
a foot or two deep at the top, was substantial enough to channel water but almost as steep as the rest of the face. I could see
no feature remotely level or flat save for my own tiny shelf.
Peering down to the glacier, I could see the line of footprints
Doug and I had made on our climb up this morning. It
seemed as if that pleasant morning climb had happened on
another planet.

Sitting there on the ledge was a big improvement over dan-

gling on the rope, a much less desperate situation. I was
amazed that I was still inside my body looking out at the
scene of forest, lakes, and mountains. My shattered arm fascinated me. It seemed to belong to someone else. My breathing
was rapid and shallow. I wondered if I were mortally
wounded in some way that I had not yet noticed.

I wondered what had gone wrong, why had I taken such a
long fall. But, I thought, it really doesn't matter now. I've got
to focus. I fought against the adrenaline and fear and disorien-
tation, and tried to concentrate. I looked again at my left arm
hanging in the dirt, smashed and crooked, my left leg swollen
to an alarming size, especially at the knee and hip. I heard
bones grinding when I shifted position. But my feet moved,
and inside my boots, I wiggled my toes vigorously: my spine
must have survived intact. I arched my back, reassured about
that. I sat back, feeling better about my chances. If I didn't
move or pass out, I thought that I might be able to stay put on
the ledge.

That's when I noticed big black blotches all over the rock
around me, on my pack and my clothes. Blood was everywhere. My blood. Big swashes, little pools, innocent-looking
stains.

I stared at this blood dumbly, then with rising alarm.
Where was it coming from? I looked over my body from my
sitting position, and saw that the left leg of my shorts was
soaked in blood. Feeling around my body, I found it pouring
from my left arm. I gingerly examined the smashed limb.
Splintered bones protruded from my elbow. Oh God, I
thought, I'm going to bleed to death.

"Doug! I'm hurt bad! I'm bleeding bad! Can you get down
to me?"

For a long time there was no reply. It occurred to me it had
been a while since the fall had happened. Or had it? What

time was it? What was going on at Doug's end? Then, his voice reached me, sounding very far away.

"No," he called back, "I can't get to you from here and get back. Can you get back up here?"

"No! No way!" I thought for a few seconds. "Doug! Go for help. I'm hurt bad, I'm bleeding bad. I might not make it. Go fast, Doug."

I was at the very edge of panic. This blood was bad business. My desire to live was overpowering, while my chances of doing so were diminishing. I sat on my south-facing ledge in the hot sun, and a clammy sweat coated me. I had to do something about the bleeding.

My bloody pack was precariously perched, poorly stashed into the little chute beside me, held in place by my immovable left leg. I thought about the first-aid kit I always carried, with its manual of emergency medicine. But what I saw with alarm was that the side pocket of the pack, which held my water bottle, was pointed downhill, threatening to dump the bottle down the mountain. I needed water to live. Gingerly, careful to keep from falling, I reached across my body and with my good right hand turned the pack around. The water bottle was secure.

"Wait!" I cried back to Doug. "Can you lower some water? Are you still there?"

Obviously he was, for his rope still hung beside me, the figure-eight knot from which I had unclipped dangling in space above my head. He called out to wait a second, and I watched the end of the rope rise up and out of sight. Minutes later I heard Doug shout, "Here it comes."

Into view came a water bottle and a blue fleece jacket clipped to the end of the rope with a 'biner. So steep was the face the bottle hung in midair, several feet away from the rock. By rocking the rope back and forth like a pendulum, Doug was able to swing the bottle and jacket to within my grasp, and I stashed them in my pack. He would be able to get more water on the way down—assuming he could manage the technical part of the descent alone. It wouldn't be easy.

"I'll send up the other rope," I shouted back, thinking that with both ropes he might be able to make long rappels and thereby get past the most difficult parts of his upcoming solitary descent. I pulled my red rope from my pack, clipped it to the 'biner and watched as he pulled it out of sight.

"Go fast, Doug," I urged. It felt strange to bid him good-bye. We had never before split up on a climb. Shortly thereafter my calls went unanswered. He was gone.

Alone and bleeding, I looked around. The ledge was unnervingly small. Save for the rock face I leaned against there was nothing but airy space in all directions. I sat vertiginously exposed in full sunlight at more than seven thousand feet on the south face of the mountain. The rock and air were heating up fast. My physical efforts of the past few minutes—stashing gear in the pack, shouting to Doug, squirming around on the sharp stones of the ledge—had left me light-headed and enervated. I gritted my teeth and concentrated on not passing out.

I was shattered by the fall and terrified of falling again. The pain from my leg, pelvis, and arm began to coalesce into a kind of bombardment, which may have helped me stay conscious but also kept me from thinking straight. I was determined to seize control. Blood was everywhere, still pouring from my left elbow and pooling around the little green succulents that grew in a shallow layer of dirt on my ledge. It looked like arterial bleeding to me. I stared incredulously at the smashed bone sticking out from the skin.

I didn't know what to do about the bleeding. But in my first-aid kit—a comfort kit really, with Band-Aids and aspirins

and moleskin and antacids and tweezers—was a little booklet
bound in survival orange I had been carrying around for a
decade. I dug around in my pack, unzipped the little case, and
pulled it out: *The Hip Pocket Emergency Handbook*. Sitting there
on the ledge with my knees bent, I opened the book on my
lap and began to read beneath the hot summer sun.

The table of contents was right on the cover. In the chap-
ter entitled "Bleeding," I immediately found what I was looking for: the top priority for injured people who are still
breathing is to stop bleeding. The little book put it this way:
"Work fast, be careful. Concentrate only on keeping blood
in the body!"

Nothing ambiguous there, and it even gave two suggestions on how this might be accomplished: pressure points and
compression. The appropriate pressure point for my elbow
was clearly illustrated as being in my armpit. I reached
around with my right hand and groped for my left armpit.
But my shoulder had been so smashed and dislocated, I actually could not recognize its architecture to find my armpit. Oh
no, I thought. Just how bad off am I? The possibility that
some as-yet-undiscovered injury might prove fatal still
haunted me. But I managed to shrug it off, say to hell with
that, do something else. Just keep yourself from bleeding to
death.

The next suggestion was compression, so from my pack I
pulled out a thin, foot-square, Ensolite-foam sit pad. This
item, a prized possession that comes along on every climbing
trip, affords a portable, comfortable place to sit on snow, rock,
or wet grass. I folded it in half like a piece of stationery and
slowly, ever so gradually, began to wrap my left arm from
midtriceps to wrist. I simply took my time and moved carefully. I could hear and feel the bones grinding together and
could feel them emerging from skin around my elbow. But the

pain was not greatly worse than before. My arm was most compliant, as if it had joints every few inches. I removed the rubber Japanese watch from my wrist and let it fall onto the ledge. Soon I had a sort of rude splint fashioned, which wrapped my arm like a hot dog in a bun. A stream of blood flowed out the back.

From the top of my pack, I pulled out the two nylon straps that held my crampons in place. With my one good arm, my teeth, and a lot of contorted wriggling, I managed to wrap both straps around my arm just fore and aft of the elbow. Because the booklet cautioned that a tourniquet could mean loss of the limb, I adjusted the tension just tightly enough to put some pressure against the open wound without cutting off the circulation. It looked to me a decent job: my smashed arm was well protected by the foam pad, and to some extent stabilized. The flow of blood even seemed to slow. The first-aid book also said to never take away compression bandages, just add more—"cloth of any kind." Rummaging around in my pack I found a pair of gloves, which I stuffed inside the makeshift splint. In, too, went some sling material that had been in my first-aid kit for years, finally put to good use, and a spare sock.

I let my head fall back against the rock, and realized my helmet had come off in the fall. It must have been toward the end, for I distinctly remembered my head bouncing off the face. The helmet had saved my life. Looking out over the landscape, focusing into the distance, I could make out hardly any detail. Was my vision damaged as well? Then I remembered my sunglasses had gone their separate way in the fall. What about my regular pair? Deep in the top pocket of my pack, in the black crushproof case, were my wire-rim glasses. Intact. Slipping them on was a genuine comfort. And what there was to see! My view was outrageous, and under normal circumstances the exposure would have been exhilarating. But instead I felt completely removed from normal sorts of responses. The sun was punishing. I couldn't believe what had happened to me. I was marooned, broken, exposed to the elements. I was scared.

I dug out my water bottle with my good right hand and carefully cradled it against my makeshift splint while I unscrewed the lid. Raising it to my lips I took a small sip, then another, then a big, long drink, then another. Drinking the water was restorative, calming, but I knew I'd have to ration carefully in this heat. Screwing back on the lid, I regarded the bottle's half-full state and carefully put it back in my pack.

My situation seemed unreal. The ledge was cramped, uncomfortable, and paved with sharp little rocky points, but it was a resting place. I pondered my luck at having landed on the only ledge in sight. Nobody lasts long at the end of a rope. My soft landing—arriving on the ledge exactly as the rope went taut—smacked of divine interference. A full-speed landing surely would have killed me.

I had no room to move, in fact could hardly shift my weight, but I had water and food and clothing. On the other hand, my injuries were probably serious, the bleeding might get worse, Doug might not make it off the mountain. Was I bleeding inside? Was I in shock? Can a person die of shock? Not much I could do about any of that. But I felt that if I kept myself screwed down pretty tight, I could hang on for—what? A day. A day for sure, maybe more.

How long would I have to hold out? I tried to think soundly. If Doug made it off the mountain, help surely would come within two days. If he didn't, no one would miss us for days, and it would take more days for a search effort to be organized. Too long. I had to believe in Doug's ability to get down safely and move fast. I fixed on that. I felt my resolve coming together. I was going to live if I could. I was going to try not to do anything stupid. I put a name to what I was doing: waiting to be rescued. I said it out loud.

Doug and I had discussed our progress shortly before the accident, so I knew the fall happened at about 9:30 a.m. In the dirt beneath my legs I found the Casio G-Shock watch. 11:20. Tuesday, July 26, 1988. It pleased me to be doing something normal, such as checking the time. But it was going to be many hours, even days, before my situation improved, and I had no stomach for the kind of clock watching I was prone to do. I let the watch fall back into the dirt and reached again for the water bottle.

With the midday summer sun cooking my south-facing ledge, the hot rock around me, like a reflector oven, magnified its effects. At more than seven thousand feet the sun baked my brains at solstice strength. But there was nowhere to go. I retrieved my yellow baseball hat, ripped and dirty, from the outside of my pack, and put it on. It helped immensely. My dress for the climb turned out to be most appropriate: the thin polypropylene material of my long underwear bottoms and long-sleeved top saved me from getting badly burnt. But I felt myself wilt under the combination of injury and exposure. I felt weak.

I took another drink. From that swallow, and all the others, I extracted maximum benefit: I held the water in my mouth, letting it soothe my parched throat, rolled it around, savored it. Only then did I swallow. I screwed the lid back on: down to a third of a bottle. If only I had more water. Maddeningly, far below me near the entrance to the steep couloir Doug and I had climbed to reach the U Gap, a stream of glacier meltwater picked up volume in the hot sun. I remembered climbing past that stream in the morning, thinking it would be a perfect place to tank up the water bottles after a long, hot morning on the rock. Now its trickle and splash, utterly out of reach, tormented me.

In those midday hours, the torment of heat and thirst incited me to plot insane schemes to escape my predicament. Maybe, I thought, there's a way I could get down. On the glacier I would be able to recline, wait for help more comfortably, drink water till I burst. Hell, I thought, I'll just rappel down—with one good arm and one good leg, I might make it. Then I remembered I had given Doug my rope. Then I remembered that even if I had the rope it was almost a thousand feet of rock face down to the glacier below. Then I remembered the intense pain from merely shifting around to look over the edge. I remembered I'd fall off if I so much as tried to stand, that I was apt to pass out from pain or shock or loss of blood at any exertion. I kept remembering. I was stuck.

The tumbling fall had put holes in my polypropylene, and I stared in disbelief as the skin under the bigger holes burned so badly that quarter-sized water blisters began to form. Jesus, I thought, that's bad. My whole body was overheating under the dark blue material, exacerbating the wooziness I already felt. I began to fear the sun might kill me. I consciously kept my head turned so that my face was in the shade of my hat bill. But it wasn't enough. I had to find some shelter.

My pack was by now securely stowed by my left side; it wasn't exactly within easy reach because only my right arm worked, but its mere presence was a comfort to me. Its contents already had saved me. The precious water bottles were in the side pockets, my first-aid kit with its medical manual in a top pocket, and a light fleece jacket, windbreaker, and wool hat in the main compartment. My lunch—the remnants of a salami, some Fig Newtons, a small piece of cheese, and some cracker crumbs—was in the lower compartment. Strapped to the outside was my red SMC ice ax, apparently no worse for wear after the fast ride down the mountain.

I thought about the ax, and gingerly began the tedious task of undoing its strap with my good hand. It took a long time. Finally freeing the ax, I placed it across my lap and pulled out my ugly orange Early Winters fleece jacket. These simple efforts so taxed me that I allowed myself a medium-sized slug from the water bottle and a long rest before moving again. Then, holding the head of my ax, I began to probe above me with the sharp end of the shaft. I couldn't see properly, but I did make out a small cleft in the rock right above my head. Into that crack I tried to stick the shaft of the ice ax, but it wouldn't stay put; the crack was too wide and shallow. I tried again and again in different parts of the cleft, without success. Finally, I lucked into finding a place where there was enough purchase on the shaft in the shallow crack to wedge it, leaving the adze and pick protruding two feet or so from the rock face immediately above my head. Perfect. I rested for a while. Then I reached up and draped the orange jacket over the head of the ax. It hung down sloppily, but created a small awning under which I could get my head and shoulders. I had shade.

It remained unpleasantly hot inside my makeshift parasol, but to be out of the direct rays of the sun was a tremendous relief. To celebrate my improved surroundings, I pulled out the water bottle for a victory slug and was alarmed to see it nearly empty. I rationalized before the onslaught of growing thirst: this heat might weaken me to the point of fainting and send me tumbling off. Better to drink it now and be parched during the cool of the night. But not wanting for some superstitious reason to empty the one bottle, I pulled out the nice heavy full bottle Doug had lowered. In the shade of my ridiculous shelter, I carefully unscrewed the bottle and drank deeply. Hallelujah! Lemonade! Doug often added fruit-juice mixes to his water, and, thanks to him, I was sitting in the shade drinking lemonade. It tasted great. I think it might have exacerbated my thirst in the long run, but I reveled in the pleasure of those first sips, my head stuck up under my jacket with nothing to see but the labels and the stains, thinking I might just make it.

Without the makeshift shelter, the long hot afternoon would have taken much more out of me than it did. Even with it, from midday on the sun and heat tortured me. I could feel my strength ebbing. I huddled under the jacket, my head and shoulders out of the sun, and drank all the water I had. Each sip was exquisite pleasure, a sweet surrender. I took no interest in the food in my pack. I put the blue jacket Doug had lowered to me under my butt, to ease the discomfort of the sharp stones on the ledge. Every now and then, lulled by heat and pain into numbness, I stuck my head out from under my shelter and watched the afternoon shadow line creep along the rock face, moving slowly yet steadily toward me. Because the face above me was overhanging, shade would come fairly early, by late afternoon. I hungrily awaited that moment, anticipating the rich relief it would bring.

It was a rare, fine day in the mountains, hot, still, perfectly clear, washed out with the blue haze of high-altitude ultraviolet light common in summer. From my perch I peered out at the panorama. Having climbed above the peaks that earlier had blocked our view, I could now see the jagged summits of Chickamin and Lemah just south of my ledge, to the right. The big valley below was completely revealed: Pete Lake down in the middle of the thickly forested valley, larger Cooper Lake off in the distance where the valley turned east, walled in by a low timbered ridge. The Cascades stretched on to the horizon to the east and south. That landscape is forever engraved on my memory. But the view held no real interest for me, and conversely, my precarious perch no more terror. I waited impatiently, but resignedly, for the relief of shade. I worried about my condition, particularly the unknown perils of shock. The idea that I might suddenly expire through no fault of my own seemed unfair. I resisted the temptation to root around for my watch to check the time again. Severely overheated, actually sick, the moisture sucked from me, I stuck my head back under the hanging jacket. I took another sip. If only it were a cloudy day.

Some blood was still seeping into the cloth I had stuffed inside the rude splint, but it did not seem a fatal flow. I went through my first-aid kit to see what else might be of use. I found a few of those alcohol wipe pads in foil, and took some pleasure in washing my face. The smell of the disinfectant was pungent. I thought of using some of them on my wounds, but decided it would do no good. The left side of my torso and leg were covered with big bloody scrapes and open wounds, the material from my long underwear tattered and dirty and stuck to the exposed bloody tissue. A protrusion pushed against the skin of my upper thigh, and I feared another bone might show itself. The smashed bones in my shoulder and arm caused me the most discomfort, grinding together ominously with every slight movement. The pain did not relent.

With some surprise I noticed I was still wearing the hardware sling, a half-dozen pieces hanging from it, and carrying slings of nylon webbing over my neck and shoulders. I removed two of the climbing slings and used one to support my left arm from my neck, like a conventional broken-arm sling, and the other to tie my upper arm close to my upper body. There was less movement and less pain that way.

I looked over the hardware rack, and thought maybe I could anchor myself in after all. I had small wired stoppers, medium hexcentrics, and some bigger stuff. I used my right

arm to feel around the rock above my ledge for a crack into
which I could wedge one of the hexes or stoppers. It's usually
possible to get something in somewhere, but I could not. The
crack into which I had wedged the shaft of the ice ax was too
ill-defined to accept any of the hardware I carried with me.
But I had plenty of time, and with my head still up under the
jacket I groped around all over the rock with the fingers of my
right hand. Finally, I was able to get my two smallest wired
stoppers to stay put in sloppy, shallow grooves to my right.
Thinking it was better than nothing, I clipped my harness
carabiner into the anchors with my last sling, and then clipped
my pack to me with another 'biner. But the more I thought
about the marginal anchors, I started to worry that if my pack
came dislodged it might fall and pull me off the ledge as well.
The poor anchors probably wouldn't hold. So I unclipped
from my pack. If it went, it went. I was going to stay on the
ledge. No dumb mistakes.

When my perch finally came into shadow, I could muster
no jubilation, only relief. I took down my parasol apparatus.
Stashing the ice ax and jacket, I watched the light over the valley soften into afternoon. There was a swallow or so left in my
original water bottle, nothing left of Doug's lemonade. I held
off finishing the last bit, knowing the night was going to be a
thirsty one. I didn't feel guilty about drinking it all because I
didn't think I could have survived the heat without it. I just
wished I had more, much more.

As the bright hot day moved toward muted warm afternoon, I spoke out loud, to hear the sound of my voice. I
looked down at Pete Lake, where Doug and I likely would
have jumped in for a cooling swim on our way out to the car.
By now, if things had gone as planned, we would have been
near the trailhead, an hour or so from a beer and a hamburger
somewhere. Instead I was smashed up and possibly done for

way up on the face. I thought about my life in Seattle with Anne, my friends, my brother in California—and felt morbid. I saw this kind of thinking as alarming. On the other side of that invasive sadness was a crushing sorrow, regret, and despair that would surely undo me. I tried willfully to avoid it. Pushing those thoughts out of my head, I torqued myself back: endure and do not make mistakes. I sat there.

For diversion, I tried to follow the route of the trail through the trees. I could see the major landmarks, and knew roughly where the trail lay, but could not discern its actual presence beneath the canopy. Across the big doglegged valley, the bright green of the trees turned black where the lowering sun cast shadows off the big mountains all around me. A raptor rode the thermals, hunting above the higher ground. During the heat of the day, coolness seemed an unattainable relief. Now, out of the direct sun, the temperature was comfortable and I wondered how cold the night might be. I remembered the cold of our dawn start, and I was now two thousand feet higher than our camp. I wondered if Doug had made it off the mountain. A few hours after his departure, the sound of a huge rock slide somewhere nearby had reached me. I wondered if he had set that off, perhaps been part of it. I felt remorseful about berating him for taking too much time to set up his belay. Those anchors had saved us both. I was angry at myself for my bad judgment earlier on the climb, angry that the belay had gone wrong. I marveled at the power of my premonitions, and wondered if I should have heeded them in the face of logic. I worked the fingers of my smashed left arm. I felt around my pelvis for signs of fractures. I washed my face with another sanitary wipe. I looked out at the softening light.

There was no way to be comfortable on the ledge. Sharp stones made sitting painful, and the ledge was too small and movement too painful to permit changing positions for comfort. Over and over I ran through my small repertoire of options: keep both knees bent, heels hooked over the ledge lip; then straighten good right leg (big relief), hanging right foot out in space; bring foot back on ledge, lock on small lip, and arch back, lifting butt off the ledge, getting a good stretch and brief respite from sharp stones on ledge. Occasionally I'd try to straighten my injured left leg, but the pain made anything more than slight movement intolerable. My arm I kept cinched close to my body, cradled in its protective foam pad. I was grateful to be out of the blasting sun.

As afternoon rolled into dusk, I took out the water bottle. I did so with a sense of fatalism—there would be nothing for it now but to gut it out. I figured I could endure a waterless vigil until the sun started baking my perch the next day. It would happen early. I was already dehydrated from the long day in the sun. I took the last swig of water and immediately felt my thirst begin to build.

A slight evening breeze began to stir, but the temperature remained comfortable, incredibly mild for so high an altitude. Yet I knew the day's heat would dissipate and the coldness of night would soon move in. I checked my clothing: I had a thick wool hat, probably most important, as well as the lightweight jacket I used for my parasol, wind pants, and a light Windbreaker. My gloves were currently stuffed into the makeshift splint to stanch the bleeding, so I would have to do without those. I put my hat on.

The day, this amazing, bad day, was drawing to a close. Warm greens and yellows replaced harsh whites and blues. The mountains fell into the stark contrast of warmly lit surfaces and black shadows. I sat alone in my aerie looking out, the beauty of this, my favorite time of day, not completely lost on me despite my troubles. At this latitude in July the night would be short. I figured I'd lose light at around ten o'clock, and get it back by five in the morning. I wondered how it would be, alone on the tiny platform in the huge face in the dark. I felt prepared for what was coming: for the past ten hours I had learned how to sit still on the tiny patch of rock. I worried that sleep or fainting would send me off the ledge, and resolved to remain awake. As there was nothing else for me to do, I leaned back and watched the trees on the east side of the valley go from green to black as the sun set lower. And then I heard it.

The faint and distant rumble of jets overhead had been with me all day, but this was a new noise—smaller, closer. I looked out into the valley and saw something flit quickly across my vision from left to right. I lost it, and the noise faded. Then I heard it again, and saw it: a small helicopter was moving back and forth across the valley between me and Pete Lake. It was five or six miles away, and appeared to have no definite direction. I became excited. Did this have something to do with me, or was this just some sort of random activity in the mountains in summer? It continued to fly back and forth but seemed to be moving closer. As I watched, I realized there could be no mistake. The helicopter was moving inexorably if indirectly toward my ledge. The constant zigzagging up and down the valley appeared to be a means of gaining altitude, not a search pattern.

I watched incredulously as the chopper flew higher and closer, always in my general direction, until it was perhaps a mile away and slightly higher than my ledge. It came closer still, and slower now, looking over the face above me. No doubt about it, the helicopter was looking for me, or at least somebody or something on the South Peak of Chimney Rock. Small and light, like the old whirlybirds, there wasn't much to this machine: just a big plastic bubble and exposed fuselage structure.

I got the orange jacket I had made shade with, and began to wave it in long, slow arcs above my head with my right arm. Between the red pack that was stashed beside me and the bright orange of the Early Winters pile jacket, I figured my position must stand out nicely against the drab red rock, even in this light. They'd have to see me. The chopper came closer, descending at a regular rate, scanning the big south face until it was just above me, maybe two hundred feet away. I was waving the jacket like crazy when abruptly the helicopter pointed right at me. It hovered in that spot. I flapped the jacket furiously. I could clearly see the two people inside; why couldn't they see me? Then the passenger leaned far outside the plastic canopy and waved. He was a big blond guy wearing a bright red shirt, and he repeatedly gave me sweeping, friendly, whole-arm waves. I thought I could make out an encouraging smile on his face as he hung out in the breeze. In the other seat I could see the pilot wearing headphones and watching the mountain. As I watched and waved, the chopper ascended a couple of hundred feet, and the guys inside looked over the face for perhaps a minute. It returned to hover directly in front of me. I felt the wind from the rotors.

I was stunned as I sat there on my ledge and the realization of what was happening came home. Doug had done it. He had somehow managed his solo descent. And he had reached civilization in good time. Without doubt that was why these guys had come and why they had known exactly where to find me. Now I could be sure that my predicament was known to the outside world. This was a great thing—I was still trapped on my ledge, but no longer lost.

I sat there stupidly gazing at the helicopter. It hovered in midair a few hundred feet from my ledge, carrying, I saw, two basket-style litters, one fixed to each skid. I watched the two people inside look intently over the south face above and below me. Then the guy in the red shirt leaned out into the breeze and gave another big wave. He looked right at me. The chopper was so close I could see his eyes. We both knew there was nothing they could do for me.

With that parting gesture, Red Shirt pulled himself back inside and the helicopter banked steeply and descended, heading back down the valley. I watched it go, silhouetted in the red sky of sunset, then lost it in the dark trees as it flew away. It left behind a great quiet in the fading dusk. To my surprise I felt tears welling up. If only, sometime during the day, I had been able to make it the six or seven hundred feet down to the glacier. These guys could have landed and picked me up, easy as pie. I could be on that bird right now, tied to the skids, on my way to a hospital. I was filled with frustration at my own helplessness. The helicopter's departure made me realize that I was truly marooned, so smashed up I could do nothing to save myself. There was nothing the guys in the helicopter could do either, except pinpoint my location, maybe look over the difficulties in getting me off the mountain.

Once again I had to get a grip on my emotions. The first human contact I'd had since Doug left had come and gone quickly, and I was left feeling small and lonely and disappointed. For all this long day I had wavered some, but pretty much kept my emotions at a distance. Now I felt abandoned. I so wanted to be carried away by the helicopter. After it left, I had to tell myself to just hang in and gut it out. The right mental state was essential to my survival. The rescue had begun—but it wouldn't be quick or easy.

Any attempt to get me off the face was going to be technical and difficult. I seriously wondered if it were even possible. There absolutely would not be any easy way of plucking me off the ledge with a helicopter. But at least I knew that Doug had not only gotten off the mountain by himself, he had

covered the miles back to the trailhead quickly and found
help. I wondered what that trip out was like for him, what he
had been thinking. It must have been interesting. I pictured
him banging through the door of a ranger station in Cle
Elum, exclaiming, "My buddy's hung up at seven thousand
five hundred feet on Chimney Rock and he's hurt bad." I
learned later that Doug had lucked out and had run into a forest service trail crew down in the valley. The supervisor had
had a radio, and rescue council pagers had gone off in Seattle
as early as 4 p.m. Serial reconnaissance was the first step in a rescue, I knew, and somewhere people were organizing, making
preparations, launching an effort in my behalf. I was a little
embarrassed thinking about that, but I took comfort in it, too.

Darkness was coming on fast. I felt around on the ledge
and found the watch: 9:35. The night shift was beginning; it
was time to hunker down. I struggled into the orange jacket
that had been my flag and my parasol. With my left arm
strapped to my body, this was a painful process. I managed to
get the right arm through the appropriate sleeve, the other
side wrapped around my smashed shoulder and arm. The
fabric was stretchy enough that I could pull it closed and zip it
up. The wind shirt was another matter. An anorak design, it
was tailored more narrowly and would not fit over my battered, trussed-up body. I cut the seam on one side with a pocketknife, which made it possible to get the thing over my head,
right arm through the sleeve, and the rest of it draped over my
upper body. The hard part of my preparations for night was
getting into my wind pants. I debated whether or not to
attempt it, but knew if a cold breeze kicked up I could get seriously hypothermic without some kind of protection. It was
the kind of mistake I was determined not to make. Fortunately, the Gore-Tex trousers zipped up the outside seams;
still, it took twenty or thirty minutes of struggle on the tiny

ledge to get the things on my damaged body. I feared the mere effort might cause me to fall off, but it was the prudent thing to do. I pulled the wool hat down over my ears. That was it. I was ready.

I marveled at my intense and growing thirst. I had never before experienced such elemental need and been so helpless to satisfy it. I tried hard to ignore it. The first stars appeared, and the gibbous moon emerged from behind the ridges to the east, but I found that night made little difference to my experience. By now I knew my world pretty well, felt confident I could stay put in it if nothing unexpected transpired. Darkness found me cramped and sore from sitting, throbbing and hurting from my broken bones, stinging from scrapes and abrasions. I was dirty and tired, covered with dried blood and painfully thirsty.

The fingers of my left hand felt cold and tingling, and moved clumsily. I wondered how badly the arm was damaged. The fact that my hand was cold made me concerned about circulation, because otherwise I was not feeling the chill. My gloves were lost to the cause of the makeshift splint, but I improvised by pulling a small nylon stuff sack with a wool sock inside over my bare left hand. I really coddled that arm and hand, keeping it as protected and immobile as possible. Even so, the bones ground away with every slight movement. My shoulder had swollen alarmingly, almost up to my ear.

I thought about eating, but thirst had ruined my appetite. My chief fear was falling asleep, for if I were to lean one way or the other in slumber, I'd tumble right off the ledge. My present lucidity was encouraging, but I doubted I could remain alert through the wee hours.

I was intensely paranoid that the weather might turn at any moment. From wishing for clouds earlier in the day, I had since reversed my thinking. The weather had to hold, or my chances would take a decided turn for the worse. I lived in fear of a mass of low clouds moving in from Puget Sound, grounding rescue aircraft. It happens all the time, so it was no idle worry.

From my high perch, I stared out at the clear star-filled sky and bright moon. With the valley in darkness, the night sky was the most interesting part of my expansive view. I thought about Anne and our home, the house on Queen Anne Hill with the flowers out front. We were planning to take a few days off on my return to town, to go up to Vancouver to spend a couple of days together. Throughout the hectic summer at work I'd been looking forward to this week off—a few days climbing in the heart of the Cascades, then a civilized and luxurious weekend with Annie at a good hotel in Vancouver. I certainly had screwed up this vacation. But someone must have contacted Anne by now. She must know. Even though it would be hard on her, I hoped she knew because she'd be rooting for me, and knowing that made me feel less alone.

The time passed slowly, measured by the movements of heavenly bodies from east to west. My south-facing ledge gave me the perfect observatory. In another couple of weeks I could have witnessed the Perseid meteor shower, a phenomenon I had often seen as it came in early August, the high point of the Northwest climbing season. But that night I had only the moon and stars, and the occasional lights of a passenger jet climbing east over the Cascades out of Sea-Tac. I passed the hours looking into the sky, doing my ledge calisthenics, and free-associating through the patterns of daily life, fixing on the glorious, mundane rhythms of home and the people I cared about. I was nagged by the idea that not surviving the ledge would be like disappearing, checking out without any sort of farewell. I never prayed. It seemed bad form to start now, when I had chosen to climb and had gotten myself into this fix with no help from God.

As the temperature gradually cooled, my thirst worsened, becoming a tormenting, painful presence. Each time I swallowed, the parched tissues of my mouth and throat rasped. I sometimes gagged. I continued pulling out the empty water bottles to drain the last remaining drops, even though there was absolutely nothing left in them.

I picked a handful of the small succulent plants growing around the ledge and examined them by moonlight, debating the merits of trying to extract from them some moisture. I worried they might poison me somehow, but in the end my thirst won out. Placing a small handful in my mouth, I crushed them with my teeth and sucked the moisture. There wasn't much in the way of wetness, but they seemed to provide some relief to the parched and gluey tissues in my mouth and throat. When I spit them out, they left an unpleasant and bitter taste. The slight relief was short-lived, but I thought I was ready to try them again if they didn't make me sick.

I reviewed again the inventory of edible items I carried. Five days into the trip there was nothing left offering much moisture. All the fruit and other goodies got consumed in the first day or two. I rummaged around in my pack, looking over the larder, and decided to try a Fig Newton. Might not be so bad, might give me some extra strength and energy for the rest of the long night. I took a small bite, tried to swallow, and the cookie turned to dust in my mouth. The gagging went on for so long I feared I might choke. I was too parched to swallow anything. In desperation I tried another small handful of succulent plants, but this time there was no improvement at all.

Above all, this was the night of thirst. It dominated my

consciousness even more than the pain from my injuries. For the first time I knew what thirst really was, and it was a deranging agony. Imagining all the sorts of beverages I might be having at home—cranberry juice mixed with club soda, or large glasses of ice water with a slice of lime or lemon—I conjured up in detail how they would look and taste. Tormented, I longed for a cool drink, and I fought the longing. I tried desperately not to swallow, and swallowed—or tried to—anyway. Despite my determination to remain lucid, my state of mind deteriorated. I reached for the watch: 12:20. Five more hours to daylight. I pinned my hopes on what the morning would bring; by first light, rescue teams surely would be in evidence. With luck, by midmorning I could be on my way. I felt weaker, and worried more now about falling asleep. My vigil, I feared, was on the verge of stupor. I wished I were able to eat something. I needed strength.

In the course of the night I was startled by a small, furious movement on top of me. One or two small rodents scurried across my body. I suddenly jerked upright. That scared me, as a sudden reflex move like that could throw me off my perch. The audacious animals skittered away, but they had given me an idea, or what seemed like an idea. Reaching for my knife, I opened the blade with my teeth, and laid it down beside me. If the creatures came again, I thought, I'll try to catch one, kill it if I can, and drink its blood. I was ready to do it, but I never got the chance. The rock rodents, as Doug and I called them, did not come again.

Late that night, I was surprised by a familiar discomfort: the need to urinate. Surely, the state of extreme dehydration I was in would preclude taking a leak, or so I thought. But it was a fact. I considered for a moment how this might be accomplished in my permanent sitting position. No problem. I simply got one of the empty water bottles, struggled with the fly of my wind pants and layers of shorts and long underwear, and slowly produced about an inch or two of bloody urine. In the moonlight it was as dark as wine.

What occurred to me next is perhaps obvious. There, suddenly, was liquid, right in the water bottle. I knew you could not drink seawater without becoming sick, but, I wondered, what about urine? Didn't that politician, Desai, do it in India? Had I heard stories about people stranded in the desert surviving by drinking urine? Or was it radiator water? Well, I was a guy already chewing on plants and quite prepared to drink the blood of small mammals, so I seriously considered it. I held the bottle to my lips. It was nauseating. I let a little liquid touch my lips. It stung. The thirst I felt was overwhelming, but I could not bring myself to swallow the evil-smelling, highly concentrated, bloody urine. I gagged and gagged. I put the lid back on. Maybe later.

Impatiently, I awaited the graying of the sky, the fading of stars that would come before dawn. But the moon still shone brightly down and the wooded valley remained a dark void. The glacier below, by contrast, was so brightly lit by moonlight that I could have seen people walking on it even at that distance. There was nothing. After peering all day and all night into the void of sky and valley, this scene, I thought, will remain permanently burned into my cortex, like words on a computer screen left on too long.

But now as I looked beyond the glacier into the void of that valley, where the trees were impenetrably black even under the moon, I saw movement. And light.

Actually rubbing my eyes with disbelief, I focused on a small point of light moving slowly deep within the forest of the valley bottom. Could it be rescuers approaching on foot, using headlamps like coal miners? No, it was too far. As I watched, I realized the light was part of a pair. It was a car or truck. And there were others behind it. The vehicles were a long way off, maybe ten miles. I put them somewhere just north of Cooper Lake. But they were real. I watched the slow movement of the lights without euphoria, but with the relief of the certainty that my rescue effort was truly under way.

I thought I knew precisely what was going on. No motorized vehicles could negotiate the trails Doug and I had come in on, but just to the east of that trail from Cooper Lake, and paralleling it for several miles, was a logging road that had formerly been open to hikers and climbers. The Forest Service had closed that road several years back, adding two or three miles to the hike into Pete Lake and the backcountry around it. Loggers don't work at three o'clock in the morning, so it seemed logical that the road had been opened to provide access for the rescue operation. Even from my distance I could make out the bouncing of the headlights as they moved slowly along the rough road. Incredible. From my perch high on the mountain, I could see hundreds of square miles. I was heartened to see the lights move slowly through the trees. I knew, though, that my position was still at least eight to twelve hours of hard hiking and climbing from where that road ended. If these guys were just getting to the road end, it would be afternoon before climbers could get up to me. That was disheartening. I wasn't sure I could last another six or seven hours under the sun. I was so thirsty. I looked everywhere in that big dark valley, trying to pick out other lights, perhaps those of people on foot, closer to me. But I saw nothing except the lights on the logging road. They moved slowly.

The night grew colder, my hands and feet became chilled and clammy. I tried to warm them by rubbing the extremities with my right hand. I was glad for the wool hat to ward off hypothermia. Bare heads lose more heat than any other part of the body. Warmth—and dawn—was not far off now. But that would also bring the relentless sun, and I was no longer so sure of what else it might bring. In fact, I felt a new and escalating anxiety about the morning.

I was getting weaker. I was weary of darkness, thirst, and pain. I longed for a drink, for the light of day. Scanning the horizon, I noticed a faint but definite orange glow. Could that be sunrise at last? But wait—it was not yet four o'clock. And that was the wrong direction. I stared at the bright patch of color against the black sky—too far south of east to be sunrise this time of year. What was that? I had no way of knowing that the orange glow marked the site of a major forest fire burning out of control near Snoqualmie Pass. At the time it mystified me, made me doubt my ability to reason.

I began to shiver against the cold. It wasn't the exhausting, killing shiver of being wet in winter, but it worried me. I knew the dangers of hypothermia, I knew I couldn't take too much of this. I was suffering from exposure. I tried to make myself small, to keep as much heat in my body as possible. My legs, hands, and feet became very cold, particularly my left arm and hand. If only I could move around, get some blood flowing. There was no clothing left to put on, nothing else I could do. The mysterious warm glow low in the southern sky continued to perplex me as, teeth chattering, I sat on the ledge. Now I feared my weakened condition might make me careless. I tried to be ever more vigilant.

I had been watching for this event for hours, yet oddly, when it finally came, it seemed to be well along before I recognized it. The black of night had faded to gray. I welcomed the first colorless light, then the band of orange to the east. Ah, and there was the familiar scene of forest, lakes, and mountains. The valley revealed, a tinge of blue appeared in the eastern sky. The rising sun was blocked by the mountain behind me, but I was relieved that it appeared on time and in the right place. The glow to the south was gone. In the valley, the trees were suddenly green. Morning had come, swiftly. As I gazed out over my world, not a soul stirred on the glacier below, nor could I see any activity farther down below. What was taking so long? I said it out loud. "Come on." The helicopter at sunset, the headlights in the night had not been hallucinations. "So where *is* everybody?"

My apprehensions turned to black despair. Thirst raged. My thinking seemed clouded and slow. I felt physically weaker. I tried to calm myself, to muster patience, to wait without anxiety, but I was overcome. I reached down for the watch—the time was near 6 a.m. As high as I was, day had fully arrived. Another perfect summer morning was getting on—good flying weather. But soon the sun would emerge from behind the main peak of Chimney and once again roast me. I couldn't believe I was going to have to deal with it again. I felt the sick, overpowering rise of panic. I could not withstand another day under that sun without water. Cold and shivering, I was terrified by the rising sun. *Where is everybody?*

I had no way of knowing that I wasn't the only impatient person on the mountain that morning. At the dusty end of the logging road a man named Bob McBride, sheriff of Kittitas County, was organizing a large and technically difficult rescue involving twenty-five climbers and rescue professionals from four cities, ham radio operators, the Red Cross, the U.S. Forest Service, and two military bases. Six people had been climbing toward my position since half past ten the previous night, many more were waiting to be airlifted to the mountain, others were standing by at various locations. The problem was a lack of air support. The county helicopter—the one I had seen last night—was out of commission. The military would eventually come through, but in the meantime

McBride and the growing collection of rescuers were becoming alarmed at the passing hours.

When the sun finally did reach me, its first warming rays brought relief from the cold. This early in the day, the warming was gentle. I felt myself regain body heat. The shivering stopped. But I could feel the sun begin to burn the skin on my face, which had taken a blasting the day before. My lips were cracked and split. I swapped my wool hat for my baseball hat. I wasn't sure I had the strength to rig my shade again. I was disconsolate. I had managed to hang onto my tiny ledge for a full day and night, I had survived the fall and kept myself going, and yet help had not arrived. After mere minutes in the sun, I overheated to the point where I had to struggle out of my Windbreaker, and open the zipper on my fleece jacket. I did not have sufficient strength to get out of my wind pants.

I took one last look at the watch—eight thirty. It seemed remarkable that it had survived on the ledge all day and night. Since it had, I felt I ought to take better care of it, so I put it in my pack. I gagged almost constantly. The raw, parched tissues in my throat tormented me.

With the first puny light of dawn, I had become intently watchful. Leaning out over the edge of my ledge, I constantly scanned the glacier below for activity. I searched the sky each time I heard a distant jet, but saw one only infrequently. I tried to pick out the spot where the lights had stopped last night, but could see only trees. I could discern no detail in the forest at that distance.

I leaned back against the face in despair. I could hear the meltwater stream below begin to gurgle audibly as the sun came upon it. The sun was building back up to its ferocity of the day before, yet I couldn't muster the effort to replace the ice ax in the rock above me to rig a sun shelter. Instead, I simply draped the jacket over my head. Soon I was stifled by the heat but was, at least, protected from the direct rays. My thirst was impossible. Hearing another aircraft, I looked out from under the jacket. I saw nothing in the sky. But something caught my eye down on the far edge of the glacier, perhaps 1,500 feet below me and a mile or two away. I stared more intently. There was movement. There were people.

Two tiny figures appeared at the edge of the glacier, so far away I had to squint to make sure it wasn't glacial debris. They moved. Definitely, then, people. Then a third figure, lagging behind, came into view. They looked like climbers—helmeted, small packs, ice axes. They moved incredibly slowly. I could relate. Chugging up that slope was a grunt. I could only hope they were part of a rescue effort. I would not admit the possibility that here were three guys out to do Chimney midweek. But even if they were part of a rescue, it would be afternoon before they could reach me.

I watched them trudge up the ice slope. God, it was going to take forever. I calculated: three hours to the top of the snow chute, then another couple of hours up to Doug's and my previous high point, then somehow down to me, if only a water bottle on the end of a rope. That meant a drink no earlier than 2 p.m., almost twenty-four hours since my last drink, and four or five more hours without water in this wilting heat. I put the jacket back over my head.

But immediately I jerked it away. Suddenly there was that sound, the sound I had been listening for since sunrise: the heavy, percussive beat of a big helicopter. I looked around but couldn't see it. There was a huge red dust cloud, however, building in a clearing way down in the valley, maybe eight or ten miles away. I realized that must be somewhere near the terminus of the logging road. It was a spectacularly big cloud of dust, spreading and rising, easily visible from my perch. Out of it emerged a big green helicopter. It hovered, rotated, and then headed my way. The whop and slap of its rotors grew rapidly to a deafening racket as it flew toward me with impressive speed. With none of the maneuvering of last night's light helicopter, this one fairly screamed up out of the valley toward my position. I recognized it immediately as a Huey, the classic Vietnam-era army helicopter. It was big and loud and to me, in my demoralized state, a beautiful sight.

Postscript: Peter Potterfield's rescue involved more than a hundred people in a complicated operation that took thirty-six hours. The helicopter pilot braved serious downdrafts in closing daylight to get close enough to the rock wall to save Potterfield, who may not have survived another day. Potterfield went on to a complete recovery and continues to climb today.

Four Harvard students, one of whom was David Roberts, left for Alaska in the summer of 1965 to climb Mount Huntington, which lies only a few miles south of the higher Mount McKinley, but whose striking and steep pyramid shape is considered even more difficult to climb. Huntington had been climbed only once, and Roberts and his colleagues planned to scale the mountain via the more challenging west face. The tragedy that ensued is unforgettable.

THE MOUNTAIN OF MY FEAR

DAVID ROBERTS

The Summit

July 29 dawned clear. Our fifth perfect day in a row, it was almost more than we could believe. Don and Ed got moving by 7:30 a.m. Quickly over the Nose, from there on, they faced unclimbed rock and ice. Ed started to lead the first new pitch. Suddenly he remembered he'd forgotten his ice ax in the rush to get started. It was down by the tent.

"What a dumb thing to do," he said to Don. "You think we should go back for it?"

"No. It would take too much time. We can make do with an icelite."

So Don and Ed took turns leading with Don's ax, while the second man used one of our aluminum daggers for balance and purchase. Although it was awkward, it seemed to work.

To make things more unsettling, they had only five or six fixed ropes and about a dozen pitons. Matt and I had not yet been able to bring up supplies to them; they could expect us to reach the tent sometime today with more of everything, but the beautiful weather couldn't be wasted. They would go as high as they reasonably could.

Ed led the next pitch, a traverse on steep crunchy snow, quickly and well, needing only a piton at the top to belay from. Don managed the same economy on the next, our thirty-seventh pitch, though the snow was becoming ice in which he had to chop steps. At the top of the fifty-five-degree pitch he found a protruding block of granite, but there didn't seem to be any good cracks in it. At last he hammered a short, stubby piton in about three-quarters of an inch, tied a loop around its blade to minimize the torque if a pull should come on it, and belayed Ed up. The pitch above required another steep traverse, again on the shallow snow-ice that lay uncomfortably close to the rock beneath. Ed led it carefully. Don could see him silhouetted against the sky all the way. The sun was beginning to hit the face, and they welcomed it after their first pitches in cold shadow. To be sure, sooner or later the sun might loosen the snow, but it would be very hard to climb difficult rock without its warmth. And it looked as if they would have to climb a steep cliff very soon.

They left fixed ropes on the first three pitches, then decided to save their few remaining ones, placing them only on the worst pitches, where they would be most helpful on the descent. Don led another pitch, their easiest yet. With excitement he realized at the top of it that he was standing beside

the large smooth pillar we had noticed in the Washburn pictures, and which he knew marked the beginning of the last
rock barrier. Ed led into a steep couloir, now hard blue ice in
which he laboriously and precariously had to chop steps. But
he reached rock on the opposite side where he could get in a
good anchor. So far they had used only five pitons in five
pitches—the absolute minimum, certainly fewer than they
would have used had they had plenty to spare. But they had
climbed fast. The snow was still solid, but the rock was warming up. It looked as if they might be able to climb the
seventy-degree cliff above them barehanded. They certainly
couldn't climb all of it with mittens on.

Don began the cliff. At least it had a few fine sharp-edged
holds. Trying to save the pitons, he went forty feet before he
put one in. It rang solidly as he pounded it—thank God for the
fine rock on this route! Thirty feet above that he was faced by
a blank section, unclimbable, free. He hammered in a poor
piton, one that wouldn't go all the way in, but vibrated noisily
as he hit it. But at last it would hold his weight, and with a stirrup he surmounted the blank stretch. Difficult as it was, the
climbing exhilarated him, especially knowing, as both Ed and
he did, that above the cliff lay only the long steep summit ice
field. Don climbed into a wide chimney, moved up fifteen feet,
and found the top blocked by a little ceiling. There was a way
out to the left if there was even one handhold at the top of his
reach. Except for a thin crack, though, there was nothing.
Choosing his smallest piton, he was able to hammer it in
about half an inch. He tested it cautiously, putting a carabiner
through the piton's eye to hold on to. It felt insecure, but
didn't budge; it would probably hold. He was forty feet above
the bad piton, seventy feet above his good one. Moving delicately, putting as little weight on the piton as possible, he
swung himself up and around the corner. Ed, watching

tensely, saw Don step onto the snow above the highest rock. The cliff was climbed. Don quickly brought Ed up. Ed led a short pitch of crusty snow above, which seemed to lie just below the edge of something. Topping the rim, he looked ahead in amazement. The smooth expanse of the summit ice field lay above him, swooping upward at an unbroken fifty-degree angle to the summit. After a month of climbing among jagged towers, inside chimneys, up enclosed couloirs, the summit ice field looked nightmarishly bare. It was like hacking one's way out of a jungle suddenly to stand on the edge of an empty desert.

It meant that they might have a chance for the summit that very day. Ed finished the pitch and brought Don up. Together they planned their attack. It was early afternoon, and going for the summit would undoubtedly require a bivouac. Four hundred feet above them stood the only bit of rock in the whole expanse, an outcrop about ten feet high. They decided to aim for it.

Four quick pitches on the unnervingly open slope brought them to it. The last fifty feet before the rock were steeper, and the sun had started to undermine the ice. They reached the rock with a feeling of relief, and agreed that the snow conditions would get worse for the next few hours. Choosing the one small ledge the rock offered, they chopped a little platform on it and pitched the tiny two-man bivouac tent Don had made. It was crowded inside, but consequently warm. Holding a stove on their laps, they could melt ice chips to make water. It was about five in the afternoon. They decided to wait for night, then go all out for the summit. It was still a long way, perhaps five more hours if things went well. But it was within reach. There was still not a cloud in the sky, no wind to disturb even a grain of snow. The afternoon sun gleamed on the mountains around them as they sat, drunk with the excitement of height, looking over the wilderness below them. For the first time they could see all of the Tokositna Glacier, even the dirty tongue sprawled on the tundra in the hazy distance, whose last ice Belmore Browne had crossed sixty years before . . .

Matt and I had started at 11:15 a.m. from the Alley Camp. On a hunch, I had suggested that we take our down jackets and an extra lunch, as well as the ropes and pitons we were relaying up to Don and Ed. We made very good time, reaching their tent beneath the Nose in only three and a half hours. It was still early; it seemed pointless to go down at once. We decided to climb above the Nose; at least we could put in extra rope and pitons to safeguard the route behind the leaders for their descent. We were encouraged by the fact that we couldn't hear their shouts; they must be far above.

As we were preparing to climb the Nose, Matt noticed Ed's ax beside the tent. That was very strange; why hadn't he taken it? Unable to think of a more ominous reason, we assumed he had simply forgotten it as he climbed the difficult ceiling and, once above, had decided it wasn't worth going back for. Matt put the ax in his pack so that we could give it to Ed if we caught them, or at least leave it hanging from a piton where they couldn't help finding it on their way down.

At the top of the Nose we saw the newly placed fixed rope stretching around the corner. Without much trouble we followed their steps. Matt led the first pitch, I the second. It was about 3:30 p.m.; the snow was just beginning to deteriorate in the sun. The steps they had chopped in the ice, therefore, occasionally seemed uncomfortably small; we enlarged a few of them. At the top of the thirty-seventh pitch I saw that the anchor piton was a poor one and looked around for a place to put a new one. About five minutes later I gave up and tied in to the eye of the piton. Since I wasn't sure how long the piton's blade was, I had no way of judging how far into the crack it had been hammered. But there was a fixed rope leading above to the next piton, so it seemed reasonably safe.

Matt started to lead, holding the fixed rope wrapped around his left arm. Only four feet above me he stopped on a steep ice-step to tighten his right crampon, which seemed to be coming off. As he pulled on the strap his foot slipped and he fell on top of me. Not alarmed, I put up a hand to ward off his crampon, holding him on belay with the other. As his weight hit me, I felt the snow platform I had stomped for my feet collapse. But I was tied in with only a foot or two of slack, and I knew that the anchor would catch me immediately, and I would have no trouble catching Matt a foot or two below me. Yet we were sliding suddenly, unchecked. I realized the piton must have pulled out, but wondered in a blur why the fixed rope wasn't holding me; had it come loose, too? We were falling together, gaining speed rapidly. Matt was on top of me. We began to bounce, and each time we hit I had the feeling, without any pain, that I was being hurt terribly. Everything was out of control. I was still probably holding the rope in a belay, but I could do nothing to stop us. The mountain was flashing by beneath us, and with detachment I thought, This is what it's like . . .

Suddenly we stopped. Matt was sitting on top of me. For an instant we didn't dare breathe. Then we carefully tried to stand on the steep ice.

"Don't move yet!" I said. "We could start going again!"

Now the fear, which we hadn't had time to feel as we fell, swept over us.

"Are you all right?" Matt asked urgently.

I couldn't believe those bounces hadn't broken any bones. I could move all right and I didn't seem to be bleeding. "I think so. Are you ?"

"I guess. I lost my ice ax, though."

Then I realized my glasses were missing. As I looked around I saw them balanced on the tip of my boot. I grabbed them and put them on.

"We've got to get a piton in immediately," I said.

I managed to hammer in several poor ones. We could relax a little now, but trying to relax only made us more frightened. Matt had lost the crampon he was adjusting and both mittens. I had lost the dark clip-ons to my glasses. My right crampon had been knocked off, but it hung from my ankle by the strap. We were bruised but otherwise unhurt. The fall seemed to have been selectively violent.

What had stopped us? Matt still had his hand wrapped around the fixed rope, yet we had been falling without any apparent retardation. I looked up. The fixed rope, no longer attached to the anchor I had been belaying from, still stretched in one long chain to the anchor on the next pitch beyond. We saw Matt's ax, too, planted in the ice where his fall had started. Then we saw that the climbing rope had snagged above us on a little nubbin of rock. That was apparently what had stopped us.

It was safer, at least at first, to go up than to go down. I led, soon getting a very good piton in. I traversed back into our steps. As I passed the nubbin that had caught the rope, I looked at it. It was rounded, no bigger than the knuckle of one of my fingers.

Finally I got to a safe anchor above the bad one. As Matt came up, I tried to figure out what had happened. Just after we stopped falling, I had noticed the piton dangling at my feet, still tied to me, but unconnected to the fixed rope. I realized that I had attached myself to the piton's eye, while the fixed ropes had been tied around its blade. When the piton came out, we were no longer connected to the fixed ropes, except by the grasp of Matt's left hand.

We were extremely shaken. We discussed whether to go back or go on. I wanted to go on. The accident, though it had scared us badly, shouldn't affect our general resolve, I said. I had the feeling, too, that if we went back now we might develop an overwhelming, irrational fear and never want to go above the Nose. Matt reluctantly agreed. Fortunately, I had an extra pair of mittens for him. I could get along without the dark glasses, since it was growing late; but the loss of Matt's crampon was more serious. If I led the rest of the pitches, though, enlarging the right-foot steps for him, we thought it would work.

We continued, still shaky and nervous. Now we deliberately overpitoned the route, making it as safe as was humanly possible. As we climbed, we regained confidence. Soon we no longer had Ed's and Don's fixed ropes to follow, but their steps were clear. Wondering where they had climbed the cliff, I caught sight of a fixed rope dangling. The sight was more than exciting; it was reassuring as well.

I led the cliff, marveling at the difficulties Ed and Don had overcome with only three pitons. I put in about five more. As the sun passed over Foraker, low to the west, I emerged on the summit ice field. There was still no sign of Don and Ed, but as I belayed Matt up, I heard Ed shout to us from somewhere above.

"Where are you?" I yelled back.

"In the rock outcrop!"

We couldn't see them, but hearing their voices again was thrilling. Matt and I hurried up the steep ice to join them. The conditions were at their worst now, even though it was 8 p.m. Twice I had to hammer rock pitons into the ice for anchors, never a dependable technique.

At last we were reunited. It was wonderful to see them. Ed said at once, "You didn't happen to bring my ice ax up, did— you did? What a couple of buddies!" Then, trying not to overstate it, we described our near accident. Ed, especially, seemed disturbed, but the safety of numbers and the realization that now we could go to the summit together, as a rope of four, made up for all our misgivings. We ate a few candy bars as the sun set behind McKinley and the mountains faded into the dusky pallor of early night. Around 10 p.m. we started.

Since we had only two ropes, we had to tie in at ninety-foot intervals instead of the usual 140. Don went first, I second, Matt third, while Ed brought up the rear. In order to save time, I belayed Don above me with one rope and one hand and Matt below me with the other simultaneously. It was growing dark rapidly. Soon I could see Don only as a faint silhouette in the sky, seeming to walk toward Cassiopeia. We were getting tired; the darkness made our effort seem more private, more detached from the mountain beneath us. After five pitches, at half-past midnight, we reached the summit ridge. We could scarcely tell we were there, except by the gradual leveling of the steep slope. We knew the far side was festooned with cornices overhanging the Ruth Glacier, so we didn't go all the way up to the ridge's level crest.

Now all that remained was the quarter mile across to the summit, a narrow, airy walkway with a 5,000-foot drop on the left and a 6,000-foot drop on the right. This was the first and only part of our climb that coincided with the French route. Although it was such a short distance to the top, we knew we couldn't afford to underestimate it, for it had taken the French four and a half hours to reach the summit from here a year and a month before. For six hundred feet we moved continuously, a ghostly walk in the sky. The night seemed to muffle all sound, and I had the illusion for an instant that we were the only people alive in the world. Soon we faced two flutings, short walls of vertical snow carved and crusted by the incessant wind, which spared the ridge only a few days each year.

Perhaps we had been lucky enough to hit one of them. Here it was imperative that the four of us spread as far apart as possible. Don started up toward the first fluting as I belayed from a not very solid ice ax. Traversing high, he stuck his foot through the cornice and quickly pulled it back. Through the hole he could see the dull blueness of the Ruth Glacier below. He returned to my belay spot near exhaustion from the tension and exertion of a whole day of leading. We traded places and I started for the fluting, approaching it lower. The light was returning; an orange wall of flame lit the tundra north of McKinley. I could see the contours of the nearby snow now, glimmering palely. As I neared the bottom of the first wall, I thought I saw something sticking out of the snow. I climbed over to it. Stretched tight in the air, a single frail foot of thin rope emerged from the ice. I pulled on it, but it was stuck solid. The sight was strangely moving. It testified, in a way, both to the transience and to the persistence of man. That bit of French fixed rope was the only human thing not our own that we had found during the whole expedition. It even seemed to offer a little security. I clipped in to it although I knew it was probably weather rotten.

It seemed best to attack the fluting high, probably even on top of the cornice. If it broke off, at least there would be the weight of the other three on the opposite side of the ridge to hold me. The snow was terrible, made more out of air than anything else. I used one of our longest aluminum daggers in my left hand, my ax in the right, trying to plant something in the snow I could hold on to. At last, by hollowing a kind of trough out of the fluting, I could half-climb, half-chimney up. Just beyond its top the second fluting began. Don came up to belay me for the new obstacle. It was a little harder, but with a last spurt of energy I got over it. Though things seemed to be happening quickly to me, I took a long time on each fluting,

and Matt and Ed grew cold waiting at the other end of the
rope. Eventually all four of us were up, however. Then there
were only three pitches left, easy ones, and suddenly I stood
on top, belaying the others up. The summit itself was a cornice, so we had to remain a few feet below it, but our heads
stood higher.

It was 3:30 a.m. We'd been going for sixteen hours without rest. Now we were too tired even to exult. The sun had
just risen in the northeast; 130 miles away we could see Debo-
rah, only a shadow in the sky. As Don looked at it I said,
"This makes up for a lot." He nodded.

There was no one to tell about it. There was, perhaps,
nothing to tell. All the world we could see lay motionless in
the muted splendor of sunrise. Nothing stirred, only we lived;
even the wind had forgotten us. Had we been able to hear a
bird calling from some pine tree, or sheep bleating in some
valley, the summit stillness would have been familiar; now it
was different, perfect. It was as if the world had held its breath
for us. Yet we were so tired . . . the summit meant first of all a
place to rest. We sat down just beneath the top, ate a little of
our lunch, and had a few sips of water. Ed had brought a
couple of firecrackers all the way up; now he wanted to set
one off, but we were afraid it would knock the cornices loose.
There was so little to do, nothing we really had the energy for,
no gesture appropriate to what we felt we had accomplished:
only a numb happiness, almost a languor. We photographed
each other and the views, trying even as we took the pictures
to impress the sight on our memories more indelibly than the
cameras could on the film. If only this moment could last, I
thought, if no longer than we do. But I knew even then that
we would forget, that someday all I should remember would
be the memories themselves, rehearsed like an archaic dance;
that I should stare at the pictures and try to get back inside

them, reaching out for something that had slipped out of my hands and spilled in the darkness of the past. And that someday I might be so old that all that might pierce my senility would be the vague heartpang of something lost and inexplicably sacred, maybe not even the name Huntington meaning anything to me, nor the names of three friends, but only the precious sweetness leaving its faint taste mingled with the bitter one of dying. And that there were only four of us (four is not many), and that surely within eighty years and maybe within five (for climbing is dangerous) we would all be dead, the last of our deaths closing a legacy not even the mountain itself could forever attest to.

We sat near the summit, already beginning to feel the cold. I got up and walked a little bit beyond, still roped, down the top of the east ridge, which someday men would also climb. From there I could see the underside of the summit cornice and tell that we had judged right not to step exactly on top. We had touched it with our ice axes, reaching out, but it might not have borne our weight.

Ed, who was normally a heavy smoker, had sworn off for the whole expedition. Now, out of his inexhaustible pockets, he pulled three cigarettes. He had no trouble lighting them; after smoking two, though, he felt so light-headed he had to save the third. One of the things he must have looked forward to, I realized, was that ritual smoke on the summit, partly because of the surprise he knew it would cause. But that was only one of Ed's reasons for being there, a minor one. I thought then, much as I had when Matt and I sat on the glacier just after flying in, that I wanted to know how the others felt and couldn't. Trying to talk about it now would have seemed profane; if there was anything we shared, it was the sudden sense of quiet and rest. For each of us, the high place we had finally reached culminated ambitions and secret

desires we could scarcely have articulated had we wanted to.
And the chances are our various dreams were different. If we
had been able to know each other's, perhaps we could not
have worked so well together. Perhaps we would have recognized, even in our partnership, the vague threats of ambition,
like boats through a fog: the unrealizable desires that drove us
beyond anything we could achieve, that drove us in the face of
danger; our unanswerable complaints against the universe—
that we die, that we have so little power, that we are locked
apart, that we do not know. So perhaps the best things that
happened on the summit were what we could see happening,
not anything beneath. Perhaps it was important for Don to
watch me walk across the top of the east ridge; for Matt to see
Ed stand with a cigarette in his mouth, staring at the sun;
for me to notice how Matt sat, eating only half his candy bar; for
Ed to hear Don insist on changing to black-and-white film. No
one else could see these things; no one else could even ask
whether or not they were important. Perhaps they were all
that happened.

It was getting a little warmer. We knew we had to get down
before the sun weakened the snow, especially on the summit
ice field. Each of us as we left took a last glance back at the
summit, which looked no different than when we had come,
but for the faint footprints we had left near it.

We put fixed ropes in on all the difficult pitches, refusing to
let up or get careless now that we were so tired. For the same
reason we didn't take Dexedrine tablets, though we carried
them. When we reached the bivouac tent, we split into pairs
to continue down. Ed and I went first, while Don and Matt
packed up the little camp before following us. The sun, high
in a still-perfect sky, had taken the magic out of the mountain's shapes. Only the soft early light and the tension of
our expectancy could have left it as beautiful as it had been.
At last, after twenty-five straight hours of technical climbing,

we rappelled off the Nose and piled, all four together, into the tent.

Now we could relax at last, but the tent was far too crowded. We felt giddy, and laughed and shouted as the edge of our alertness wore off. We had brought up our pint of victory brandy—blackberry flavored—and now indulged in a few sips, toasting everything from Washburn to Kalispell. Each of us managed to doze off at some time or other, with someone else's foot or elbow in his face. In the afternoon it grew unbearably hot and stuffy inside, and the Nose began to drip (appropriately enough), pouring water through the roof of the tent. We cooked all our favorite delicacies, robbing the two food boxes rapaciously. By 6 p.m. it had started to cool again, and we saw that, finally, the weather might be turning bad, after six consecutive perfect days, a spell almost unheard of in Alaska. It was as if the storms had politely waited for us to finish our climb. We slept a little more, but still couldn't get comfortable. Around 9 p.m. Ed suggested that he and I go down in the night to the Alley Camp. We were still tired, but it wouldn't be a difficult descent. Once he and I got to the Camp, moreover, all four of us could rest in luxurious comfort, a sleeping bag each, room to stretch out full length, and plenty of food to wait out any storm. We dressed and were ready to go by 9:40 p.m.

The Accident

The snow was in poorer condition than we liked; it hadn't refrozen yet, and might not that night since a warm wind was coming in. I knew the pitches below better than Ed, having been over them five times to his one, so I tried to shout instructions to him when the route was obscure. It got to be too dark to see a full rope-length. I went down the twenty-ninth pitch, our ice-filled chimney, feeling rather than seeing the holds. But the fixed ropes helped immensely, and since I came last on the two hard pitches (twenty-ninth and twenty-seventh), Ed didn't have to worry so much about not knowing the moves. Despite the conditions, we were moving efficiently.

At the top of the twenty-sixth pitch, the vertical inside corner Don had led so well in crampons, we stopped to rappel. We stood, side by side, attached to the bottom of the fixed rope we had just used on the pitch above. In the dark, we could discern only the outlines of each other's faces. Under our feet, we felt our crampons bite the ice. Just below the little ledge we stood on, the rock shrank vertically away, and empty space lurked over the chasm below. It was too dark to see very far down. Above us, the steepest part of the face, which we had just descended, loomed vaguely in the night. Up there, on another ledge, Don and Matt were probably sleeping. Beside us, in the mild darkness, icicles dripped trickles of water that splashed on the rocks. The fixed rope was wet; here and there, ice, from the splashing, had begun to freeze on it.

We didn't have an extra rope, so we untied and attached ourselves to the fixed line, setting up a rappel with the climbing rope. Ed attached a carabiner to the anchor, through which he clipped the climbing rope, so that we could pull it down from the bottom. He wrapped the rope around his body and got ready to rappel. We were tired, but were getting down with reasonable speed. It was ten minutes before midnight.

"Just this tough one," I said. "Then it's practically walking to camp."

"Yeah," Ed answered.

He leaned back. Standing about five feet from him, I heard a sharp scraping sound. Suddenly Ed was flying backward through the air. I could see him fall, wordless, fifty feet free, then strike the steep ice below.

"Grab something, Ed!" But even as I shouted, he was sliding and bouncing down the steep ice, tangled in the rappel rope. He passed out of sight, but I heard his body bouncing below. From the route photos I knew where he had fallen; there wasn't a chance of his stopping for four thousand feet.

Perhaps five seconds had passed. No warning, no sign of death—but Ed was gone. I could not understand. I became aware of the acute silence. All I could hear was the sound of water dripping near me. "Ed! Ed! Ed!" I shouted, without any hope of an answer. I looked at the anchor—what could have happened? The piton was still intact, but the carabiner and rope were gone with Ed. It made no sense.

I tried to shout for help to Matt and Don. But they were nearly one thousand feet above, hidden by cliffs that deflected and snow that absorbed my voice. I realized they couldn't hear me. Even the echo of my shouts in the dark seemed tiny. I couldn't just stand there; either I must go up or I must go down. It was about an equal distance either way, but the pitches above were more difficult. I had no rope. There was no point going up, because there was nothing we could do for Ed. His body lay now, as far as anyone could ever know, on the lower Tokositna, inaccessible. An attempt even by the three of us to descend the four thousand feet to look for him would be suicidally dangerous, especially since we would have only one rope for all of us. If I went up, I should eventually have to go down again. All it could do was add to the danger. I realized these things at the time. Yet the instinct, in my isolation, to try to join Matt and Don was so compelling that for a while I didn't even consider the other possibility. But it became obvious I had to go down.

At least the fixed ropes were still in. I used two carabiners to attach myself to them, then began to climb down the steep pitch we had started to rappel. I moved jerkily, making violent efforts, telling myself to go more slowly. But I had to use the adrenaline that was racing through me now; it was the only thing that could keep the crippling fear and grief temporarily from me.

I managed to get down the hard pitch. The snow on the Upper Park was in poor condition. I broke steps out beneath me, but held my balance with the fixed rope. I realized that I was going far too fast for safety, but slowing down was almost impossible. As I traversed to the Alley, I was sure the weak snow would break under my feet, but it held. At last I arrived at the tent. The seven pitches had taken eighteen minutes, dangerously fast. But I was there; now there was nothing to do but wait alone.

I crawled into the tent. It was full of water. Matt and I had left the back door open! In the dark I sponged it out, too tired to cry, in something like a state of shock. I took two sleeping pills and fell asleep.

In the morning I gradually woke out of a gray stupor. It seemed to be snowing lightly. I felt no sudden pang about the accident; even in sleep I must have remained aware of it. I forced myself to cook and eat a breakfast, for the sake of establishing a routine, of occupying myself. I kept thinking, *What could have happened?* The carabiner and rope were gone; nothing else had been disturbed. Perhaps the carabiner had flipped open and come loose; perhaps it had broken; perhaps Ed had clipped in, in such a way that he wasn't really clipped in at all. Nothing seemed likely. It didn't matter, really. All that mattered was that our perfect expedition, in one momentary mechanical whim, had turned into a trial of fear and sorrow for me, as it would for Matt and Don when they learned, and into sudden blankness for Ed. His death had come even before he could rest well enough to enjoy our triumph.

The time passed with terrible slowness. I knew Matt and Don would be taking their time now that it was snowing. I grew anxious for their arrival, afraid of being alone. I tried to relax, but I caught myself holding my breath, listening. Occasionally a ball of snow would roll up against the tent wall. I was sure each time that it was one of them kicking snow down from above. I would stick my head out the tent door, looking into the empty whiteness for a sign of them. My mind magnified even the sound of snowflakes hitting the tent into their distant footsteps.

I made myself eat, write in my diary, keep the tent dry, keep a supply of ice near the door. But I began to worry about Matt and Don, too. I knew there was no reason to expect them yet, but what if they had had an accident, too?

There were some firecrackers in the tent. We had tentatively arranged on the way up to shoot them off in an emergency. I might have done that now, but there was no emergency. It would be more dangerous to communicate with them than not to, because in their alarm they might abandon caution to get down fast.

I began to wonder what I would do if they didn't come. What if I heard them calling for help? I would have to go up, yet what could I do alone? I calculated that they had at most five days' food at the Nose Camp. I had enough for twenty days at the Alley Camp. I would wait five or six days, and if there was no sign of them, I would try to finish the descent alone. At the cave I could stamp a message for Sheldon; if he flew over, he would see it. If he didn't, I would eventually start to hike out, seventy miles down an unknown glacier, across rivers, through the tundra . . .

But these were desperate thoughts, the logical extremes of possible action I might have to take; I forced myself to consider them so that no potential course of events could lurk unrealized among my fears.

Already I had begun to miss Ed in a way separate from the shock and loneliness. I longed for his cheeriness, that fund of

warmth that Matt, Don, and I lacked. I had wanted so much
to relax in the tent, talking and joking with him, reliving the
long summit day. I hadn't climbed with him since July 11.
Now it was the last day of the month, and he was gone.

I went outside the tent only to urinate. Each time, I tied a
loop around my waist and clipped in to a piton outside, not
only because I was afraid but because I couldn't be sure that
the sleeping pills and the shock (if it was actually shock) were
not impairing my judgment or balance. I felt always tense,
aware that I was waiting, minute by minute. I could think of
very little but the accident; I couldn't get the sight of Ed
falling, sudden and soundless, out of my head.

The snow continued to fall lightly, but the tent got warmer
as the hidden sun warmed the air. In the afternoon I began to
hear a high faint whining sound. It was like nothing human,
but I couldn't place it. Could it be some kind of distress signal
from Matt or Don? Impossible . . . Could it be the wind blowing through a carabiner somewhere above? But there was
almost no wind. Was it even real? I listened, holding my
breath, straining with the effort to define the sound. I couldn't
even tell if it was above the camp or below. I sang a note of the
same pitch to convince myself the sound was real. It seemed
to stop momentarily, but I couldn't be sure I hadn't merely
begun to ignore it. Finally I noticed that when I went outside
the tent, I couldn't hear it. Therefore the sound had to come
from inside. At last I found it–vaporized gas, heated by the
warmth of the day, was escaping from the stove's safety valve!
I felt silly but measurably relieved.

I tried to relive every moment Ed and I had had together
the last day, as if doing so could somehow salvage something
from the tragedy. My recollections had stuck on a remark he
had made in the Nose Camp as we rested after the summit. I
had told him that it had been the best day I'd ever had climb-

ing. Ed had said, "Mine too, but I don't know if I'd do the whole thing again."

I thought he was still upset about Matt's and my near accident, and suggested so. Ed thought a moment, then said, "No. It's not only that."

We hadn't pursued it, but his attitude had seemed strange to me. For me, there was no question but that it would have been worth doing all over again. Nor for Don. And I thought Matt would have said so, too. But Ed had climbed less than we had; perhaps he wasn't so sure that climbing was the most important thing in his life, as we would have said it was in ours.

Now his remark haunted me. The accident, ultimately inexplicable beyond its mechanical cause, which itself we would never be sure of, seemed that much more unfair in view of what Ed had said. It would have been better, fairer, perhaps, had it happened to me. Yet not even in the depth of anguish could I wish that I had died instead. And that irreducible selfishness seemed to prove to me that beyond our feeling of "commitment" there lay the barriers of our disparate self-love. We were willing to place our lives in each other's hands, but I wouldn't have died for Ed. What a joke we played on ourselves—the whole affair of mountaineering seemed a farce then. But the numbness returned; I told myself to wait, to judge it all in better perspective months, years, from now.

By that night there had still been no sign of Matt or Don. I took another sleeping pill and finally dozed off. Sometime in the night, on the edge of sleeping and waking, I had a vision of Ed stumbling, bloody, broken, up to the tent, yelling out in the night, "Why didn't you come to look for me?" I woke with a jolt, then waited in the dark for the dream to dissolve. I hadn't considered, after the first moments, trying to look for Ed's body. For me alone, without a rope, to try to descend the four thousand feet would certainly have been suicide. Yet because there was nothing to do, and because I hadn't seen Ed's dead body, a whisper of guilt had lodged in my subconscious, a whisper that grew to Ed's shout in my nightmare.

I took a sip of water and fell asleep again. In the morning I discovered my watch had stopped. An unimportant event, it hit me with stunning force. It was as if one more proof of reality were gone, one more contact with the others, Matt and Don first of all, everyone else alive in the world eventually. I set the watch arbitrarily and shook it to get it started.

That day, August 1, dragged by as the last one had. I was no more relaxed than I had been before. The weather was good for a few minutes in the morning, then clouded up again; but at least it had stopped snowing. I felt surer now that Matt and Don would get to me, but I began to dread their arrival, for it would open the wounds of shock in them, and I would have to be the strong one, at first.

I thought of how rarely an expedition is both successful and tragic, especially a small expedition. Something like 95 percent of the dangers in a climb such as ours lay in the ascent. But we had worked for thirty-one days, many of them dangerous, on the route without a serious injury before finally getting to the summit. Going down should have taken only two or three days, and it is usually routine to descend pitches on which fixed ropes have been left. I was reminded of the first ascent of the Matterhorn, when only hours after its conquest the climbing rope broke, sending four of Edward Whymper's seven-man party to their deaths. Then I realized that the Matterhorn had been climbed one hundred years, almost to the day, before our ascent. I thought, also, of the ascent of Cerro Torre in Patagonia in 1959, still regarded by many as the hardest climb ever done. On its descent Toni Egger, one of the best mountaineers in the world, had fallen off a cold rappel to his death, leaving only Cesare Maestri to tell of their victory. But thinking of those climbs explained ours no better. I knew that Whymper, after the Matterhorn, had been persecuted by the public, some of whom even suggested he had cut the rope. I knew that, even in an age that understands mountaineering a little better than the Victorians did, vague suspicions still shrouded the Cerro Torre expedition. But even if we could explain Ed's death to mountaineers, how could we ever explain it to those who cared more about him than about any mountain?

Around 4 p.m. I heard the sound of a plane, probably Sheldon's, flying near the mountain. I couldn't see anything through the mist, but perhaps his very presence meant that it was clear up above, possibly that he could see our steps leading to the summit.

Around 10 p.m. I thought I heard a shout. I looked out of the tent, but saw nothing, and was starting to attribute the sound to a random noise of the mountain, ice breaking loose somewhere or a rock falling, when suddenly Matt came in sight at the top of the Alley. He let out a cheery yell when he saw me. I couldn't answer, but simply stared at him. Pretty soon Don came in sight and yelled, "How are things down there?" I pretended I couldn't hear him. Matt said later that they had seen our tracks from high on the mountain and therefore known that Ed and I hadn't completed the descent to the cave. This had disturbed them a little, and their mood had acquired gloominess during the treacherous last descent, on steps covered by new snow, using ice-coated fixed ropes, once belaying in a waterfall that had frozen their parkas stiff. But as they approached, Matt had seen my head poking out of the tent and for an instant had thrown off his worries. Yet my silence made him uneasy again; then, before he got to the tent, he saw that there was only one pack beside it. Then I said, "Matt, I'm alone."

He belayed Don all the way down before either of us said anything to him. When Matt told him, Don stood there frozen momentarily, looking only at the snow. Then, in a way I cannot forget, he seemed to draw a breath and swallow the impact of the shock. He said, "All right. Let's get inside the tent." His voice, calm as ever, was heavy with a sudden fatigue. But once they knew, once I saw that they were taking it without panic, being strong, I felt an overwhelming gratitude toward them: out of my fear, an impulse like love.

Remnants

We spent a crowded, uncomfortable night. The tent platform had begun to slope downhill, and it was too small for all of us. We had planned to finish the descent when the weather became good. But the next day it was storming, probably the worst day we had had. We began to worry about the pitches below getting unclimbably dangerous; perhaps even the fixed ropes might be buried. Although it was only August 2, winter was arriving: the days were growing not only shorter but noticeably colder.

We spent most of the day waiting for a letup, but our crowded situation was too unpleasant. As long as we had the rest of the descent before us we could not relax. We decided to go in the late afternoon despite the storm. We got dressed and moved outside the tent. A bitter wind whistled across the ridge, chilling us at once. We had a difficult time taking down the tent, because we got in each other's way trying to maneuver around the platform while staying tied in to our pitons. Moreover, the tent's back corner had frozen into the ice. At last we half-chopped, half-ripped it out. Our hands lost their feeling almost immediately when we had to take our mittens off; our toes grew numb after the first few minutes.

We were ready to leave by 7:30 p.m. We thought it should take about two hours to get down to the cave. In good weather we had done it in little more than one hour. Now we faced the problem of descending, three on a rope, pitches that were made for only two. Since Matt had just one crampon, he had to go in the middle. Don started off, while I waited to descend last.

The snow conditions were terrible, by far the worst we had yet run into. A full foot of loose powdery snow overlay our steps; often the steps themselves had melted out, leaving only the slick surface of the ice beneath. We went continuously at first, but at a pace slower than a snail's. Don had to rechop steps under the snow, reaching awkwardly down with his ax. The fixed ropes were coated with ice, sometimes in a solid sheath a quarter-inch thick. Moreover, since we were only seventy feet apart, two of us were often relying on the same section of fixed rope at the same time, threatening to pull each other off. Matt, despite his missing crampon, had to use the ropes as little and as gently as possible, because I, coming last, could not afford to fall, and Don wouldn't have been able to replace the steps without holding on to something.

But we seemed to move all right on the comparatively easy, rock-free pitches of the Lower Park. At least, once we got going we were all three in motion most of the time, and our feet and hands began to warm up a little.

On the thirteenth pitch, the one which joined the Stegosaur to the Lower Park, Don suddenly shouted, "Falling!" Matt and I braced ourselves, but the pull never came. Don had managed to hold himself with the fixed rope. The pitch was in terrible shape. We had to traverse awkwardly on steep ice that was coated with a rime-frost that looked solid until stepped on. Matt fell at the same spot Don had, but caught himself the same way. Gamely, he went back to rechop the steps so that I might get down safely. When I reached the spot, I found the fixed rope was of no use for balance, but I had to hold on to it in case of a slip. Even with the improved steps, I came as near falling as I ever have without coming off. Matt and Don had stopped to belay me. There were only three and a half more pitches above the rappel, but we realized we had to belay each one of them carefully. The rock added a factor of difficulty that made it too dangerous to travel continuously. First we tried tying Matt in only five feet above Don, while I belayed both of them from a solid stance. They crept down the twelfth pitch. I got very cold again, and begged the rope to pay out faster, since that was all I could see of their progress. Finally one of them yelled, "On belay!" and I could descend. The pitch was far more difficult than it ever had been on the way up. I was afraid that the fixed rope might have weathered enough to be dangerously weak, but I had to rely on it anyway. When I reached them, Don and Matt said the system was no good. They had kept getting in each other's way, pulling each other off; it was an impossible effort to coordinate their movements.

We moved Matt back to the middle of the rope. I went first, while Don, already quite cold, had to stand in the same spot for a much longer time to belay us ahead. It was starting to get really dark; it must have been near midnight. The darkness intensified my nervousness. Even for one in the best psychological state, that kind of climbing would make one very uneasy. Now, under the pall of fear Ed's death had imposed, the descent became, for me at least, a nightmarish episode. In addition, the cold and the biting wind increased our clumsiness and tended to isolate us further, because it was hard to hear our shouts against the wind and unpleasant to hold one's face into it in order to watch. Within a few minutes, it was too dark to see each other very far apart anyway.

I was glad at first to lead, to be rid of the responsibility of coming last. But I began to appreciate what a job it was to replace the steps. We couldn't take off our mittens, but I needed to scrape and chop the snow off holds whose location I only dimly recalled. Finally I would get to a piton, and Matt could start moving. It was still a while before Don could begin, though. When he shouted, his voice shook with the cold.

It grew almost pitch dark. The lower we got on the mountain, the darker it got, and the enclosed recesses between the towers of the Stegosaur shut out the faint light from the north, if not the wind.

At last we were getting down. We decided to go continuously again, for we were so cold we couldn't stand the immobility of belaying, and the rope now passed over fingers of rock between us that would catch a fall as well as would any belay we might make. At one point Don and I stood on top of two towers while Matt climbed in the gap between. The rope stuck; I yelled at Matt, but there was no answer. Don and I could hear each other's shouts perfectly, but Matt seemed oblivious. I started to go back for him, but at last Matt heard Don and answered. His voice sounded as far away as if he were on a different mountain.

I finally got within a few feet of the top of the rappel, but I couldn't reach it. Matt was stuck in an incredible tangle at the last piton. I heard him swearing at the ropes, then suddenly a frightened cry from Don as he fell. Again, the fixed rope caught him, but he couldn't find any of the steps. I felt annoyed because we were climbing so poorly. But it was so cold, and I felt the tiredness seeping even into the edge of nervousness I had known for three days. We were almost down; then there would be no more hard climbing. For eighteen days we had hung every minute over that abyss, never less than three thousand feet above its hidden floor: the place where Ed's body now lay.

At last Matt got the tangle straightened out. I reached the piton and belayed them down. We were together again. It almost seemed too great an effort to tie the two ropes together so that we could pull them down after we had rappelled. The rope we had left there had frozen in at the bottom so that we could scarcely pull up enough slack to pass around our bodies. But finally we managed to set the thing up. I stepped over the side of the ridge with a conscious sense of relief and quickly rappelled down, knocking the ice off the rope we had left. Matt and Don followed. Then we pulled the ropes down, cutting ourselves off for good from our route, from the far-frozen summit. We staggered back to the cave, arriving at 3:30 a.m. It had taken us eight hours to descend what we had expected to complete in two. It was the day of climbing I should least ever want to repeat.

We found the cave shrunk in size, but otherwise unchanged. The storm continued for three days. We went outside around noon on the third to stamp a sign, Fly Out, in the snow. Sheldon would see this if he flew over, we were pretty sure. There was no emergency now, no reason to call for help. If Sheldon didn't see our sign within ten days or so, we would begin to hike out.

We saw no point in searching for Ed's body. Any search we could make, even plane assisted, would be dangerous. We would have to scour the bottom of a six-thousand-foot avalanche chute, down which constantly spilled rocks and ice. After the five days of storm, his body was likely to be covered by new snow, and the chances were good that that snow wouldn't melt before winter. The body, for all we knew, had been crushed and torn in the fall. We did not want to offend its dignity by salvaging a mutilated, unrecognizable corpse. All that was mortal of Ed would freeze into an unknown glacier. Within a year there would be no part of him near its surface. Gradually the remnants of his being would sink within the Tokositna, locked in unfathomable ice. None of our words would ever stir the air above his tomb; never would anyone in that place lie about why he had died. No one would ever say there that it was right. If the unconcerned glacier should someday spill Ed's body out on the gravel bar at its mouth, rocks would still cover it; no one would ever know. Mysteries lie with Ed; but the most important of them, perhaps, could not be solved. Ed kept a diary. He had written more than a hundred pages in it in red ink, but it fell with him. That diary might have offered some clue to him, some clue to the urge that he, who made things come so easily, who understood people so well and cared about them, could have felt for an unwitnessable challenge in an inhuman place. But he had never been at rest within himself; he struggled to believe, to explain his fears and joys. The diary wouldn't have answered for those who loved him the pained question, Why did he have to go there?

But for Matt, Don, and me there was all of life to antici-pate. We wanted to get back, but we dreaded it, too. I could picture, even then, the reception we had to expect from those who had last seen us, exuberant and eager, going off (for all some of them knew) on a pleasant summer outing. I knew even then the taste of transmitted grief that would be our duty. Already I heard the stunned, empty silence over the phone from Pennsylvania, saw the bloodshot eyes drained of hope, felt the friend's stifled wince. A remark Ed's father had made when we had stopped at their house in early June stuck in my mind now. He had said, "It's hard for you boys to understand how parents can worry about this kind of thing." I had simply agreed—it *was* hard for us to understand. Now it was tragically easier.

In the snow cave we could relax, in a sense. We no longer had to hold on to something when we went outside the tent; we no longer felt the threat of empty space beneath us. But in the absence of the tension that had bound us together, a dull feeling of loss set in. We had been robbed not only of Ed, but of all but a few hours of exultation, and would never again recall our triumph with pleasure unmitigated by pain. Now there was only another wait. To make things worse, we began to feel some of the antagonisms which our common dependence had, for the last two weeks, obliterated. We couldn't agree on a few things. I wanted to hike out in eight days or so; Don preferred to wait as long as we could. Don wanted to climb the little peak west of Huntington to get pictures of the route. I had no enthusiasm for the idea and would have felt fear on the ridge again. Matt was indifferent, but agreed to accompany Don if there was time and good weather. Don wanted to arrange, if possible, to have more food dropped in to continue climbing in our basin. I wanted to get out to face notifying Ed's parents, and Matt had to get out for a job commitment. We had talked the accident dry. All our conversation could do now was attempt to recover the sense of joy we had begun to feel as we rested at the Nose Camp after the summit. We were able, in our few days in the cave, to regain a sense of pride. I felt a strong passion, a loyalty, toward our accomplishment, but I knew it wasn't joy. We wasted time methodically, waiting for Sheldon.

On August 6 the weather cleared. We spent most of the day outside in the sun. We hoped for Sheldon, but knew the chances were good he wouldn't fly by. After all, he had been over only once since July 20, even during the long spell of good weather we had had. The new snow had plastered our route, making it look cold and splendid. In the early evening the sun lit high, ribbed clouds above McKinley, and cast a brown warmth on the rock of the face, reflected in ghostly radiance on the shadowed floor of the glacier. Never had the mountain seemed more beautiful, not even in its first untouched magic. Sheldon didn't come, however. As it got dark, we lit the few candles we had brought and set them up in the snow cave to read and write by. When I went outside, I could see the warm glow diffused through the snow of the cave's roof, and I felt an old, childish fear of the dark. The cave seemed the only island of safety in a limitless sea of night.

After we extinguished the candles, I lay awake thinking. I was trying to imagine how I could tell Ed's parents. I thought of the things that, sooner or later, people would say about Ed's death, as attempts at consolation. There were three things, especially, that would be said, things that had been said before, by me as well as others, about men who had been killed mountaineering; but now, none of them seemed to offer real consolation. It would be said that Ed died doing what he enjoyed most, that his last conscious moments were happy ones. But he did not want to die; every part of him that was aware he was falling did not want that to be, but was powerless. There was never enough happiness to last as long as we would have it. It would be said that the way he died was somehow "right." But he did not have to die; to die young is never right. It would be said that, at least, he never had time to feel pain or even fear. But, though I could not have wanted Ed to die suffering, dying without pain or fear seems to me the equivalent of living without joy. Let us be aware of our end, because life is all we have. Yet, though I could not find consolation in these thoughts, and knew they would be little consolation to his parents, I could not rid my mind of some image of beauty connected with Ed's death, as if his fall without a sound had owned, for an instant, a freedom no one ever knew in life.

At 4 a.m. I woke, hearing the faint hum of an airplane. I put my boots on and ran out of the cave. It was Sheldon. Don

and Matt, awake now also, joined me as we tried to point at
our sign in the snow. Sheldon seemed to see it, acknowledged
us by circling, then dropped a note. It landed in the crevasse
below camp, but we roped up and went to get it. He
instructed us to proceed to the floor of the glacier. We packed
rapidly, then left the cave, looking back as we descended the
icefall for the last time. A few hours later Sheldon returned,
landing easily on the hard glacier. Matt and I got in the plane
first. In a second load he could pick up Don and the rest of
our equipment. Sheldon had seen our tracks to the summit
five days before, and Matt and Don in the Nose Camp, but he
had no idea that anything had gone wrong. He couldn't quite
believe Ed's death. We made several passes near the bottom
of the avalanche chute, but could see no sign of anything
human. Then we headed out over the tundra.

Sheldon kept saying, "Boy, that's rough. What happened?"
All I could do was explain the facts of the accident. I couldn't
explain beyond that; I couldn't tell him the urgency of our
happiness before. Huntington faded behind us; I couldn't
explain. We had spent forty days alone there, only to come
back one man less, it seemed. We had found no answers to
life: perhaps only the room in which to look for them.

In Talkeetna the grass smelled damp and sweet. Flies
swarmed, buzzing around us as we put down our packs, and
the air blazed with fireweed.

Postscript: David Roberts had made it to safety. He then went
on to become one of the most erudite and prolific writers of
mountaineering literature of his generation.

Nanda Devi is the third-highest mountain in the Himalayas. Of the 1976 expedition to climb her 25,645 feet, only John Roskelley, Lou Reichert, and Jim States made it to the top. One of the other climbers, the venerable Willi Unsoeld, had first seen the mountain in 1949. He was so impressed by its beauty that he vowed that one day he would name his daughter after it. As fate would have it, Willi's twenty-one-year-old daughter was part of the 1976 expedition and during it she would perish on her namesake.

NANDA DEVI

The Tragic Expedition

JOHN ROSKELLEY

I *didn't want to leave the tent on* the morning of the twenty-seventh. Lou was rustling about, dressing, and I was procrastinating, hoping the weather was too fierce to climb. Jim and I eventually dressed, made breakfast, and crawled from our tents. Neither of us wanted to admit we didn't want to go; we reluctantly loaded more ropes into our packs and set off along the Ridge at 8:30 a.m.

I didn't feel strong enough to break trail, but managed for half the distance before turning the miserable job over to Jim. We said little as we plugged along, punching through the windblown crust. Every so often we would stop to rest and I would search Jim's face for any hint to return to camp. His mirrored sunglasses hid any feelings he had. We reached the fixed lines not really thinking we would go up, but without stopping I got out my jumars and Étrier, fastened them to the line and jumared into the howling wind and blowing snow. I knew Jim would follow.

The second fixed rope scared me. Fifty feet above, the rope ran over a knife-sharp edge of rock. As I began jumaring, the rope stretched and the rock seemed to saw right through it. I couldn't move the rope to either side. Easing my weight up, I tried not to bounce as I ascended. In my thoughts the rope severed in half a thousand times before I passed the frayed section. Once finished, I moved the rope to the side to protect Jim.

The rest of the jumar to the end of our first day's climb was just as scary. I made the traverse of the previous day to the jam crack and waited in my harness for Jim so I could yell instructions to him. When I reached the snowfield above I flung the rope over to the pedestal. This erased the difficult traverse and made the ascent easier and safer. I busied myself at our high point arranging the hardware and ropes. Jim arrived exhausted, warm from the exertion. Spindrift blew into our eyes, noses, and clothing. We couldn't tell if it was snowing or the wind was just blowing old snow around us. After a while it didn't matter.

All the preparation of setting up a workable belay was in vain as I hooked up my belay line incorrectly, tangled the ropes, and had to step over Jim to get free. I began the pitch by descending and moving to my right over seventy-degree rock slabs covered with sugar snow. I feared the entire slab would break loose each time I moved. Thirty feet up I reached the bottom of the band and traversed left to a break through the overhanging wall. A bulging, off-width chimney looked like the only way.

I fiddled with bongs (two- to four-inch aluminum pitons), then blades (thin steel pitons), sunk back into the back of the chimney, but nothing seemed to work. Climbing into the chimney itself, I reached a large block with a thin crack and drove in a knife-blade piton the thickness of a razor. I was finally protected.

My Étriers caught on my crampons as I pulled them to the pin. I struggled desperately to hold on and free them, meanwhile catching my ice axe, which was hanging from my belt, under my foot. Once free of the hang-ups, I got into the Étrier and stood up. The bulge, compounded by the heavy load in my pack, was pushing me out. I slammed in a good angle piton and repeated my performance, complete with my ice axe tying up my legs and holding me until I was exhausted.

One more piton and I was able to mantle to the top of the chimney. I grabbed a two-foot-square boulder for support but was startled when it came with me. I froze, then put the rock back in place; the block would have flattened Jim, who was standing fifty feet directly below. He was already having to eat more than his share of the garbage that I was kicking down on him.

Jim's position often seemed more frightening to me than leading a difficult stretch of ground. His stance, often small and uncomfortable, was usually directly underneath me. He had full view of the twenty-four sharp points on my crampons as I climbed above him. These, and the needle-sharp points of my ice tools, would be lethal weapons if I were to fall. Although I tried not to kick snow and rocks down on him, there was a constant barrage of debris that I couldn't help but dislodge along with the snow that I had to deliberately clear away before each move. He must have been frozen during

several long belays, but did not complain. I couldn't have
wished for a better partner to second me.

From the top of the mantle I flailed away at the icy crust
that covered a sloping one-foot ledge I needed to traverse. If
someone had watched this desperate action, he would have
thought I was trying to kill Jim with ice and rock. But it was
our only choice.

Tiptoeing left for twenty feet positioned me in a small gully
where the garbage I was kicking down fell away from Jim's
position. Meanwhile, I was caught in a major spindrift avalanche zone that emptied a snowfield one hundred feet above.
Every thirty seconds I was hit by a mass of snow. The wall
above was broken, but vertical. How was I going to climb it
while being bombarded by constant avalanches? The rope
drag was terrible at this point as well. I hammered in two
good pins, tied off, and yelled for Jim to come up.

While waiting, I managed to kick out a place for my right
foot and put the left on a small rock for my stance. Forty-five
minutes later Jim appeared over the overhang, barely visible
through the spindrift and blowing snow. I argued with myself
on what to do next.

Could we continue under such adverse conditions? I was
freezing from inaction and Jim was faring no better. He followed the rope along the traverse, leaving in one pin in case
someone should slip off and not be able to get back on. As he
approached, a horrendous avalanche dropped upon us: Jim
drifted in and out of sight although he was only fifteen feet
away. The situation was so severe it was funny. Jim came out
of it laughing. When he reached me, we laughed for some
time as each avalanche hit us and sloughed off.

"What do you think, John? Do we rap off?"

"Let's give it five minutes. It's only two o'clock. If the avalanches quit, I'll give the next pitch a try."

Jim leaned over toward me as I lifted another coil of rope from his pack and we began to unravel the three-hundred-foot mess. He reached my water bottle and we each took our first swig of the day. We were hungry, but too cold to look for food, unwrap it, and eat.

As if the Goddess Nanda Devi heard us, the avalanches stopped. The sun's rays filtered through the billowing clouds, brightening our precarious little stance. I started one more pitch.

The rope was still like tangled spaghetti, but we unraveled enough for me to start. Jim pulled back his hood so he could watch carefully, ready for a fall. I inched up a slabby corner to a small overhang. Difficult chimneying took me to a tiny stance. Avalanches started again but I decided not to stop.

A thin crack led back right over Jim, and I worked my way up on pitons to several upside-down blocks. Several more loose pins and I had gained another thin, awkward stance. For climbing, gloves were useless but I did put them on at each stance to rewarm my frozen fingers. Avalanches streamed down the route, burying Jim and me for minutes at a time, threatening to sweep me off.

I had no choice but to free-climb the remainder of the wall. It was the most difficult mixed climbing I had ever encountered; pins were useless for protection in the loose blocks that were frozen in place, and my weight cracked them loose with each move. A tiny flake for one of my crampon points and a fingerhold kept me attached while I chopped away the layer of crusty snow. I found a cold hand-jam and hung on long enough to slam in a horizontal piton, sling it, and ready myself for the next move.

There seemed to be no handholds ahead, so I stepped up carefully while pulling down on the sling. Twenty pounds of rock moved with it. Luckily, I hadn't pulled straight out. I was out of carabiners. There were no more holds. I stuck the shaft of my axe in some spindrift crust at arm's length, tested slightly, and pulled down on it enough to muscle up on my left leg. I stepped cautiously onto sixty-degree sugar snow on smooth slab. There was no place to stand. Without putting my 145 pounds at any one place all at once, I maneuvered to a pedestal forty feet up. I was stuck again. The snowfield we had been hoping to reach was only six feet away but there were no holds or cracks.

I mantled, pulling up with my arms with every ounce of energy I had left until my crampons were level with my hands. There were no holds, only bottomless sugar snow. I balanced for several seconds, then placed my weight onto one foot. It stayed long enough for me to wade upward several feet and away from the lip of the wall. After swimming through sixty feet of waist-deep avalanche snow, I finally smacked in a bombproof angle piton.

It was late and again I couldn't hear Jim. I had taken more than an hour on the long pitch, so I secured the line to several pins, attached my rappel system and, cleaning the pins as I went, descended in the blinding snowstorm. Jim was waiting patiently, stamping his feet and slapping his hands for warmth, hiding beneath a small overhang and his pack.

A rainbow appeared through the thick clouds and, for a split second, the snow-covered peaks stood out boldly in the distance. The rappels in the storm were frightening but dramatically beautiful. But we desperately needed eleven-millimeter rope to replace the already fraying nine-millimeter; the ropes ran over countless edges of rock resembling broken glass. We hoped the sahibs below had carried drops to the cache for Lou to bring to Camp III.

On the pedestal, two rappels from the Ridge, I attached my rappel system to the rope and waited for Jim. He appeared directly above and lowered beside me.

"I'll see you at the bottom," I said.

"Say, use my camera and take a picture of me, will you?"

"Sure."

I began to wrap the rappel rope around my leg so I could free my hands. Only there was no rope, just twenty feet of tail. I had clipped onto the wrong rope. I was attached to a short section of leftover rope that hung over the Northwest Face.

I felt nauseous at the thought of what could have happened—plummeting thousands of vertical feet down the Northwest Face to eventually hit the glacier and sweep past Advanced Base for the Rishi ten thousand feet below. Dumbfounded, neither of us spoke but looked at each other with equally shocked expressions. How had I made that mistake? Exhaustion? One thing was certain: we would have to be extra careful from now on.

We reached the Ridge without further incident. I was still shaking from my close call. Rappeling has always been considered the most dangerous part of mountaineering. I had known climbers who rappeled off the end of their rappel line, but I had never been that close before.

As dusk turned the mountain into shadow, Lou was on the radio when we struggled into camp. His conversation was heated. Again, no one had carried from Camp II and Lou was disgusted. Even worse, we were running short of rope for the Buttress and needed several lengths of eleven-millimeter to make the climbing safer.

"I've got some bad news for you, Lou," Willi reported. "Peter has decided to descend and quit the mountain. Nirmal is on the verge of the same thing. Your insistence on keeping John and Jim on the Buttress is creating real problems down here."

Nirmal, disgusted with Himalayan climbing and the continual problems, decided this was his last expedition and descended to Camp I. Annoyed that I had told him to leave the mountain, Peter also descended to Camp I. He intended to leave. Andy moved from Camp I up to Camp II to take Peter's place. Only the porters at Advanced Base had carried, and only to Camp I.

"Well, they can't continue on the Buttress with no rope and I didn't see anyone carrying up to the dump again today," Lou snapped. "We need rope, Willi. At least have someone bring it up."

"My hands are tied. You've made it hard for me just to keep people here on the mountain. What are you going to do when John and Jim reach Camp IV, pull them off? We took a vote down here and decided the first team to the summit should be you and Devi."

Lou replied with caution. "I'm very honored, but I would never pull Jim and John off after doing such a great job. I'd always planned to join them . . . perhaps Devi could join us also? I see nothing wrong with a foursome."

The conversation had been a touchy one, but Lou had handled it with great tact, even though he was irritated with the decisions being made below.

Jim and I had to laugh at the other climbers' sudden change of commitment—from trying the mythical route to the left to the now-surer success up the fixed lines of the Buttress. Lou had told Willi in his first reports how we were nearing the gully two-thirds of the way and that it looked easier from that point on. This changed the situation completely for the others. What alarmed us was their desire to place Devi so high on the mountain without having her acclimatize by carrying and living higher.

Lou told us what to expect. "Devi, Kiran, or Nirmal will move up tomorrow, according to Willi. I requested a minimum of two ropes to Camp III and two more at Roskelley

Dump. I also asked for four tents, two for Camp IV and two for here. Willi promised they would be there."

At Camp III, Jim, Lou, and I tried to discuss only the Buttress and the route, but our conversation kept returning to the problems of the team. We needed teamwork if we were to summit, yet the two factions were getting farther apart physically and ideologically. Nothing was certain. We still had to surmount the Buttress, place a camp up high, and make a summit bid. Those were problems enough without this split in the team.

Jim and I rested on August 28. Exhausted mentally and physically, we needed to regain our strength after our desperate climbing for the past two days between twenty-three thousand and twenty-four thousand feet. Lou decided to descend to Roskelley Dump for a load and left early, hoping to get back to camp before the sun came up.

Most of the team was moving to one camp or another that morning and we were expecting Devi, Andy, Nirmal, and Kiran at Camp III. Lou had argued against anyone moving up until more loads had been carried to Camp III, but his explanations had fallen on deaf ears. Camp III was going to be a bottleneck of climbers with no food, tents, or equipment.

As Jim and I finished a late breakfast, Peter staggered into camp carrying a light load from Camp I. Heading straight for me, he was obviously there for a specific purpose.

"I want to talk with you, John," Peter said. I was immediately on the defense.

"I'm really pissed that you think you have the right to tell me to go home. I've been trying to do my job as well as any of you and what you've done on this climb doesn't give you the right to order me or anyone around. Lou told me you didn't want me on the Buttress. Why?"

I was surprised Peter had come all the way from Camp I to confront me with this. When I realized he hadn't even carried a load to supply us, I was angry.

"I don't care for your ways, Peter. Do you know why? Because you won't carry loads except when you want. Because you insist on following through on ideas when you've been asked not to. Because you want to move to higher camps without carrying or acclimatizing. Then, when you don't get your way, you descend and cause a rift in the team!"

We argued back and forth for some time. Jim kept out of the discussion.

"You told us you didn't want to work on the Buttress," I continued. "Jim and I are moving at a good clip and we should have it done in one more day. The ropes are fraying terribly and the fewer people on them the safer they'll be— that's why Lou hasn't been going up. The most important thing now is to get the equipment to us so we can continue working on it. No one except Lou has carried for several days. What kind of teamwork is that? You wanted to go left around the Buttress because you didn't think everyone could get up it even when it got fixed with rope."

Lou arrived as our argument ended. He was Peter's next target. "Lou, there's been an empty space in one of the tents up here and I want to know why you haven't given it to me," he demanded. "I feel good and I'll be a judge of my own health."

"Lou was voted by everyone as the climbing leader, Peter," I said, jumping to Lou's defense. "Whatever his reasons, he is trying to be fair. There are several climbers below who have carried much more than you and deserve to come up first, but the camp isn't ready logistically. There's not even enough food, gas, or tents here yet."

Peter acknowledged the problem Lou had been facing as

climbing leader: trying to keep the route progressing while keeping the sahibs below carrying gear up the mountain to supply those above. And from our camp now, Peter could see the top of our ropes on the Buttress. This alone was enough to make him realize our chances of success were good—for the expedition, for everyone. The route to the left was put aside, and Peter left Camp III with a better understanding. I was later glad that Peter had taken the initiative to confront us with his feelings. It was a relief to have had the issues discussed in the open. As the argument had progressed, I could see the cause of the team's problems: no communication.

Soon after Lou arrived, Devi and Andy came into camp. There were no extra tents, so they moved in with Jim. He wasn't pleased with the crowded conditions, especially when this was one of the reasons no one should have moved up. Nirmal and Kiran were the next to arrive, bringing with them another two-man tent. While Devi and Andy cooked dinner for seven, the rest of us helped dig a platform and pitch the tent for the Indians.

We crammed five into one tent to eat and passed food to Kiran and Nirmal several feet away. Everyone was uncomfortable, but it proved easier than passing food from tent to tent. The effort of trying to eat crammed into a small corner with my legs tucked under me was too much and I finally crawled back to my own tent for the night.

Blasts of wind against the tent woke me at 5 a.m. Hoarfrost, shaken off the tent ceiling, had soaked the tops of our bags and frozen into stiff white sheets.

"Hey, Jim!" I yelled. "What do you think we ought to do?"

"It's awfully windy, but we could at least go to the base," he replied. Lou agreed. He would go with us to help double some of the badly frayed fixed lines.

Out of the tent and into the cold wind was just the beginning to a long day. I took the lead up the Ridge, slowly breaking trail, stumbling in the deep, wind-packed crust. Pausing
after each step, we moved along like three spacemen. The
wind cut through our face openings and found the weak-
nesses in our clothing. No one spoke, only nodded or
pointed. That morning we all wondered why we were moving
instead of hiding from the storm.

Lou relieved me at the halfway point and continued breaking to the base of the Buttress. The bottoms of my feet ached
from a deep, numbing cold as though I had frostbite again.
Each time I sat down, I held them out of the snow and beat
them together to restore my poor circulation. The weather
was bad.

At the Buttress I began the long and dangerous jumar to
Sugar Delight Snowfield, the name I had given the high point
I reached two days before. Each rope stretched like a rubber
band before it pulled taut, took my weight, and let me inch
upward. The rope had frayed severely in spots from even the
few times Jim and I had jumared and rappeled. The sight of
the white core of the rope exposed through the frayed sheath
stretching over knife-edged rocks gave me a queasy feeling.
We definitely needed to double the lines.

Jim started immediately after me, but soon fell far behind.
I reached Sugar Delight Snowfield and the top of the ropes at
eleven o'clock, sat down, and waited. Around noon Jim
poked his head over the edge, then threw his body and load
onto the snowfield. He was exhausted.

"Where's Lou?"

"He's doubling two ropes down below," Jim replied. "I
don't know whether he's going to come up all the way with us
or not."

"I hope so—we've got only two ropes and we're going to
need a third today."

We opened a can of chicken spread for lunch, then I disappeared down several feet and traversed right through waist-deep snow onto a steep hundred-foot hidden chimney to our right. My ice axe proved to be the only hold and it was shaky at best. I climbed to the top of the chimney, which left me straddling a ten-foot crest that dropped off hundreds of feet on either side and butted up against a blank wall.

The gully we hoped to reach was forty feet to my right and definitely difficult to get to. By its looks, the gully would be easy for some four hundred feet. Lou yelled from below and I turned to see his cap appear at the edge of Sugar Delight. We would have the rope.

I noticed a foot-wide ledge running the length of the wall that blocked my way to the gully. Bashing in a knife-blade piton for protection, I lowered myself, hanging from my hands on the ledge. I moved hand over hand the thirty feet of ledge to just above an easy drop to the gully, placed another pin, and lowered myself to the ice below.

The fury of the storm increased and the spindrift avalanches at Sugar Delight seemed small compared to the steady, knee-deep avalanche that was running down the gully. It was clear this was how the gully had formed.

I was completely out of earshot of Jim; the rope, wrapped over and around the corner I had climbed, had me pulling like a draft horse. I had to reach a decent belay. The gully was deep, the left wall was 175 feet high and the right rose hundreds of feet to the top of the Buttress. Both were vertical. I had no choice but to ascend the gully to its top, some four hundred feet up. A difficult ice-and-rock section took me fifteen minutes to surmount on my way to what appeared to be a protected belay fifty feet from my landing point. The rope drag almost stopped me.

When I stopped, I was three hundred feet out from Jim and slightly above the avalanches in the gully. The little stance was perfect and had several cracks in which to place bombproof pins. I finally tied off the rope and yelled for Jim to follow. It was useless. In the storm, it was like a bullhorn trying to attract the attention of a deaf mute and neither one understanding the other. But, as if he could read my mind, Jim came anyway.

Jim had taken off his crampons and managed the chimney and traverse only with great difficulty. The drop into the gully took him valuable minutes, but he finally arrived fifty feet below me. He totally exhausted himself climbing up the steep icy section to my belay. "Lou's coming just behind me. He's bringing another rope."

"I'll lead this gully because I'm rested. As soon as you see me wave at the top, start up. You'll be tied off."

I grabbed the three hundred feet of rope from Jim's pack, uncoiled it, tied it to me, and started climbing. It caught below, but Jim managed to free it as I punched my way through the deep snow on the right side of the gully. It was slow, exhausting work. Sometimes I waded waist-deep and was completely stopped until I could grab a hold alongside the rock wall and pull myself forward a few feet to easier ground. The snow was bottomless. An overhanging chockstone was the last obstacle and I was able to chimney and jam its left corner to surmount it. Thirty feet more and I straddled a knife-bladed crest and the end of the gully.

I searched fruitlessly for a decent crack to tie the rope to, but finally settled on a thin blade driven in horizontally. I waved down to Jim.

Lou had reached Jim's side and now they both clipped to the rope and came together. They were having a difficult time without crampons. Slowly they waded to their waists, then slipped back. I was glad they didn't know how poor the anchor was.

They reached the overhanging chockstone and I watched

as Lou's head appeared over the edge, then disappeared back down. Again he appeared, struggling to get his jumar over the lip, but failed and fell back to Jim below. He straightened out the problem with Jim, who had been pulling on the rope and not giving him any slack, and he finally came over the top. He dropped into the snow, exhausted. After recovering, Lou climbed to my small stance, followed closely by Jim.

Jim's conversation and speech were difficult to understand. His attention seemed far away. I worried about his control.

Lou didn't speak, but took the rope and gazed at me dully, then at the wall above us. I moved back along the crest to get a better look at the problem. There was not much to go on, but I thought a traverse left should be tried first.

I felt confident and strong, even though I was cold and it was 4:45 p.m. The pitch would have to be done quickly. I traversed left across seventy-five-degree ice slope to ice-covered rock. Mantle after mantle for forty feet brought me to a stance and I stopped. There were no cracks with which to protect myself, but the rock was ledgy and I didn't feel that any one move as yet had been dangerous. I inched back to beneath several overhangs that looked difficult to bypass and paused to place a shaky pin in a rotten crack. This gave me the courage to move up on loose blocks covered with crusty snow. There weren't any good holds for another fifty feet, but I worked with finesse and leg muscles, chimneying and mantling. I hacked small holds in the ice with my hammer when nothing else was there. With a bombproof knife-blade piton, I chimney-stemmed across to a one-foot-square platform on a snow rib coming from the crest above, but it was a dead end. With extreme difficulty, I climbed up and left into a vertical snow chimney and managed to place another pin in a block alongside me. There were only seventy feet to go.

Digging and clawing away the snow, I inched forward by finding holds buried deep beneath the snow chimney. I stemmed out of this after twenty feet and was on another seventy-five-degree slope, but it was loose, unconsolidated snow. After each swimming motion with my hands, I thrust the shaft of my ice axe as deep as possible and pulled until I could get solid footing below. After fifty feet of swimming I pulled myself onto the relatively flat slope of the top of the Buttress. We were there!

I hammered several good pitons into a large rock outcrop twenty feet from the crest. Leaving the rest of the hardware attached to the anchor, I fastened my rappel system to the rope and descended, cleaning the pitons as I went. It was 5:30 p.m. and too late to waste a moment of time.

The two-hundred-foot rappel went quickly and soon I was beside Lou. He immediately descended into the darkening gully. My sweat began to freeze while I waited for him to finish the rappel so I could descend. It seemed like hours.

At each rappel station, I caught Lou and had to wait. He was being cautious, but I was freezing for it. The last two rappels were doubled ropes, giving us much-needed security to the bottom.

At the base, Jim congratulated me with a big hug. He then descended slowly, fearful he would make a mistake.

We were all excited, but near total exhaustion. After removing our climbing gear while watching a crimson sunset, we trudged wearily back to camp in the dark.

Weakened by the altitude, no one had moved from Camp III all day. Their move to Camp III the day before had only wasted food and had not produced any loads. Peter had moved up from Camp II as well, but we remained short on gas, tents, and food. Willi, John Evans, and several porters were still below carrying loads to Roskelley Dump, but no one from Camp III was descending to pick them up. The situation was becoming critical.

That night, Lou announced his decision that he, Jim, and I

would make the first summit attempt after a rest day. The others said little about the decision. Exhausted, we ate a good meal and turned in.

We slept late the next morning. Again, no one planned to descend. Devi, Andy, and Peter stayed in their tent, ate, and slept. Around 10 a.m. Nirmal and Kiran dressed and decided to descend for loads. Lou gave them a list of needed supplies supposedly at the cache.

Nirmal started down, leaving Kiran, who had a headache, to decide whether to attempt to carry. Jim finally convinced him not to bother. Lou questioned Peter, Devi, and Andy about their decision not to carry, but decided not to push the sensitive issue. Jim and I told them they should feel guilty watching Nirmal carry and not expecting to themselves. There was no love lost between our two tents.

It seemed like a day for petty grievances. The small inconsequential problems were growing with the stress and altitude. The next issue was sugar. Peter wanted some in his tea that night, while the rest of us wanted it for cereal in the morning. There wasn't enough for both. I longed to get away from Camp III.

Jim, Lou, and I loaded our packs that afternoon with more than seventy-five pounds of gear each. We wanted to carry only once up the frayed and dangerous ropes to Camp IV, at the top of the Buttress. The loads would be heavy but it beat climbing the ropes twice. We went to bed knowing the next few days would determine the outcome of the expedition. We had come too far, through too much, not to give it everything.

On the Ridge crest, gusts of wind continued to bury the already entrenched tents with snow. Jim soon had a boiling pan of

Jell-O prepared while I mixed the hot cereal for breakfast. We needed to get an early start to reach the top of the Buttress. The other climbers in camp had volunteered to break trail for us to its base. Peter left first, punching through the wind-pack to his knees. Andy and Devi followed closely. The day had fine possibilities despite the wind.

My muscles seemed unusually fatigued under the heavy load, but once I warmed up I kept a steady pace and soon overtook Andy and Devi. I followed Peter to the base of the Buttress.

Jim was tense and preoccupied with the thought of what we expected of him during the next few days. Lou and I had experienced this pressure on other trips and were, perhaps, slightly less anxious. Lou was having difficulties of another sort. Kiran insisted on carrying Lou's pack for him in an attempt to help, but the Indian's pace was much too slow. Lou diplomatically rescued his pack from Kiran partway along the Ridge to keep from falling far behind us.

I began the awesome job of jumaring to the top of the Buttress. The second lead, a slightly vertical overhanging section, proved extremely difficult to surmount with a load. I hooked the pack strap to the top jumar and slowly worked my way upward. Peter followed a short distance behind to fix the stronger eleven-millimeter ropes on the route's worst sections.

I noticed the rope had worn to the core beneath the overhanging red rock, and glared white against the dark blue sheath even from fifty feet away. My eyes never left that white core. The sharp overhang cut it even more as I jumared, and it seemed like hours before I was up and over the exposed core. Once past it, I tied an overhand knot to take the tension off the cut and to protect the others as they ascended. The next length was easier and I arrived at the top of Sugar Delight Snowfield at 12:40 p.m. I decided to wait there for Jim and Lou in case they were too slow to go farther that day.

Peter arrived at my small stance an hour later. We were quiet at first, then Peter broke the silence. "John, I'm totally with the route now . . . I want you to know that."

"That's sort of a switch, isn't it? I've always had the impression you didn't care for the route."

Peter paused. "This was supposed to be a relaxed trip, John," he replied thoughtfully. "I came to be with Marty, to enjoy the mountains. That's not the way it's been. I have to admit I've been dragging my feet all the way up the mountain. That's because I felt that you, Lou, and Jim pushed the climb into something not everyone can enjoy."

"Then why was this route chosen in the first place if you all wanted a mellow trip? No one except you said a word earlier about another route."

"Lou said that you didn't want me along on the first ascent team. Why not?"

"That wasn't my decision, Peter. All I know is you've hardly carried any loads and you're not acclimatized. You just got through telling me you've been dragging your feet all the way up and now you ask me why you're not going with us?"

"I'd like to be going, John, but . . . well, good luck anyway."

"Thanks, Peter. We're hoping to make the top of the Buttress today. That way the gear will at least be there so someone— probably you—will have an easier time of it."

Jim appeared at three o'clock, in white from head to toe because of spindrift avalanches. The weather had deteriorated since morning. "Lou said to wait here," he yelled. "He's coming behind me slowly, but he thinks we won't make it today at this rate. I think he wants to go down and try again tomorrow."

Lou had expressed this doubt to Jim at the base of the Buttress that morning. He said then we were too late to start. Jim had continued up after me anyway.

"Shall we go, Lou?" I yelled.

"Yeah . . . Why not?" he yelled back.

"Follow as fast as you can," I said to Jim. "We'll never make it before dark unless we hustle."

I jumared into the snowstorm. Peter waited patiently while Jim and Lou followed to Sugar Delight Ledge. I was long gone up the ropes when Peter turned to go back to Camp III.

I felt pressured to move fast and within an hour I was at the top of the gully, below the last pitch. I began to jumar for the crest, but exhaustion and the difficult terrain slowed me to a crawl. My hands became numb from gripping the cold metal jumars so tightly; I couldn't feel my toes. Toward the top, my pack got stuck in a snow chimney and it took me time and effort to free it. Several yards below the top, the rope had cut deeply into the cornice and, no matter how I tried, I couldn't get my jumars to slide up any farther. Fighting for every inch, digging deeper into the crest with each struggle, I finally released my jumars, throwing my body over the lip and onto the flat slope above.

It was almost dark. Looking back along the route, I couldn't see Jim or Lou. The storm had quieted; there was less wind but now night was almost upon us.

I dropped my load and walked up the Ridge a hundred yards in search of a campsite but found nothing large enough for a tent. Ten yards below, where I crested onto the Ridge, seemed to be the only place. The site, sloping at twenty degrees, was only one yard away from the Northwest Face. It was the only place I could see that was wide enough to accept a tent. I started excavating a tent platform, first with my hands, then by sitting and pushing the snow away with my feet.

Once the platform was leveled, I pitched the large two-man Eddie Bauer tent. Jim had not come over the lip yet, but as I finished in the dark he struggled into view, having had the same problem with the upper five feet I had. He was totally exhausted and lay still in the snow.

"Have you seen Lou?"

"He's at the bottom of this rope," Jim gasped.

"Lou! Hey, Lou! Start up!"

I heard a faint but affirmative reply. Jim yelled to Lou to tie into the extra rope he had hauled. Jim belayed Lou up the difficult jumar.

I entered the tent and took off my boots while talking with Jim about his trouble on the way up. His description would have scared the others into leaving the mountain. Lou finally appeared out of the dark and both he and Jim set their packs near the tent and crawled inside. We all lay quietly for several minutes.

"That's the heaviest load I've ever carried on a mountain," Lou mumbled.

The tent became a mess as clothing, sleeping bags, and cooking gear were pulled from our packs. I started melting snow as soon as everyone had settled down, but Lou accidentally kicked the pot over just as all the snow had melted. There was a sudden mad scramble to keep sleeping bags and clothing dry. Jim found a sponge in the tent kit and soon things were back to normal. Over dinner we agreed to start for the summit the next day. We didn't want to stay any longer than necessary.

Lou radioed to Camp III at 7 p.m.

"We read you, Lou," Willi responded. "How did everything go?"

Lou recounted the difficulties of the jumar and our late arrival to Camp IV. Willi seemed pleased with our progress. We made arrangements to talk again early the next morning. Jim took over the melting of snow after dinner and continued to keep all three of us supplied with hot liquids for several hours. At eleven o'clock the stove was turned off and we sacked out in the cramped but cozy tent.

It was the morning of September 1. "Camp III," I called.

"Read you, John," Willi answered. "How are things up there this morning?"

"Fine, Willi, but we've decided to relax and hydrate today. We won't be moving."

Lou moved to the forward vestibule to cook breakfast while Jim and I relaxed, munching cornnuts and candy.

"Certainly looks nice out there this morning," Lou observed, squinting into the sun. "No wind at all."

I leaned out the back of the tent. The skies were crystal clear and I noticed an unusual stillness in the air. "You know . . . maybe we better go for it with a day this calm."

"Do we have time?" Jim asked. "It's almost eight o'clock."

"Let's give it a try," Lou replied.

The tent became a madhouse. The stove was snuffed out with a flick of the wrist. We gulped down a warm milk-and-sugar drink Jim insisted we take before leaving, then scrambled for boots and clothes and were moving by eight thirty.

I broke trail through the knee-deep sugar snow to a saddle several hundred yards above camp. Then Lou took over. He had been slow so far and had voiced his irritation at being tugged on several times. Lou continued slowly through the deep snow and up the corniced Ridge to where it suddenly steepened. He surmounted a small rock problem and struggled above in waist-deep, baseless sugar snow. The terrain was terrible, sloping at fifty degrees and threatening to avalanche any moment. Lou slowed to a stop halfway up the slope. The altitude and deep snow were relentless antagonists.

I struggled to within a few feet of Lou, then took over the lead, moving steadily toward the top of the slope two hundred feet away. Soon I was pulling on Lou again; I didn't want to stay on that slope any longer than necessary.

"Goddamn it!" Lou burst out. "Stop pulling or I'm untying."

"Don't do that, Lou. I'll try not to pull on you from here."

He retied his knot and continued following in a swimming motion. Soon the three of us were together on a small hump on the ridge. "Your turn, Jim."

Jim moved on silently through the same waist-deep sugar along a knife crest. He stopped abruptly. "There's a small rock problem for John," he called over his shoulder.

"What do you mean?" I asked.

"You'll see." He turned and continued.

He surmounted the twenty-foot fluted gendarme and disappeared on the other side while Lou began to follow. I came last. After several of the gendarmes I was beside Jim and could see what he was referring to. Directly above him was a thirty-foot black horizontal rock band that mushroomed from the bottom up. Only to the right side, which dropped steeply over the Northwest Face, did there seem a climbable route. We had no rock hardware for use as protection.

"Get a better belay, Jim," I said tensely. He was too far from the difficult section and his belay looked poor. I needed to attack the pitch quickly to eliminate any second thoughts, so I examined the pitch carefully while he prepared. Lou sat down twenty feet away and waited.

"Belay on?" I asked. Jim sensed my determination.

I chimneyed and jammed a short section before moving onto the face to overcome a short but difficult rock overhang. I followed another ice-and-rock gully, chimneying when possible, to above the band.

"I need more slack!"

Jim untied, giving me all I needed to wade and front point

to the ridge crest above the rock band and place an acceptable belay.

"I'm up! Belay off!"

"Wait. Lou's decided not to go!" Jim shouted from below.

Lou was convinced by his altimeter that we had fifteen hundred feet still to go to the summit. If we went for the top, we would surely have to bivouac. He was not willing to take the chance of spending the night out without proper equipment. Lou also told Jim that he felt he had been forced against his will to ascend the Buttress the previous day; he was determined not to go against his better judgment this time.

"What do you think, Jim?" I yelled.

"I don't know. What do you think?" he yelled back.

"I'm going!" I shouted.

"I'm going too!" came Jim's reply.

Lou unroped and walked back along the Ridge until he could see me. "We're not high enough! We've only gone five hundred vertical feet in four hours. I'm going back."

"By the shadow of Nanda Devi in the valley we're halfway!" I argued. "Your altimeter is wrong!"

"Good luck. I'll wait up for you in camp."

"OK—will you leave your parka with Jim?"

"No!"

"How about coming out to meet us with sleeping bags on our way down?"

"No! I'm not that altruistic," he replied.

I couldn't believe my ears. "OK, Lou," I yelled, "Be careful on the way down. We're going on!"

Lou looked indecisive and angry. Jim and I got ready to continue. "All right, dammit, I'll come!"

"Good!" Jim replied with no hint of irritation.

They both made quick work of the rock band with tension from above. The next section appeared to be hard crampon snow but we were mistaken. Jim waded past and started breaking through the snow along a broad crest between two forty-five degree slopes. What looked firm from below was in reality a heavy wind crust over bottomless powder. He floundered badly. The snow had no support and it required intense effort to move upward against the falling tide of heavy powder snow.

I broke for a stretch, then Lou did. No one had an easy time. The slopes on either side were heavy with fresh powder. Each move required throwing a knee up and over the crust to break it down, then falling forward with a swimming motion to gain a foot of distance.

I seemed to be able to move more efficiently and felt strong even while breaking, so I took the lead again. The avalanche conditions were extreme. Each time I put my hands in the snow in front of me, cracks raced across the slopes on either side. A loud hissing from the slope on my left drew my attention. I stopped wading and watched a two-foot-deep slab avalanche slide away, breaking from our tracks. Lou and Jim froze, silently watching the snow plummet into space over the Northeast Face several hundred feet below. I didn't think of the danger—strangely enough—but only of how unusual the scene was. It was as if I were watching the episode on TV. Lou's horrified look brought me back to reality. We had to get off this slope quickly.

I moved onto the crest's right side, which hadn't received any sun as yet, and dug furiously at the snow, making significant progress in height. The snow became belly deep, but I managed to plow through fast enough to start pulling on Lou and Jim struggling behind me. Again Lou became angry at being forced to move too fast and began to untie. I slowed down.

The snow conditions improved slightly to give us a base to

move on. We topped out one by one onto a large open snow-field fifteen minutes after the avalanche. We moved together on a low-angled slope, Jim breaking trail in ankle-deep snow. The climbing was much easier. I led a stretch of steeper snow to a false summit and another expanse of lower-angled snow. After a brief discussion, we decided to have lunch on the slope. What we could see above might not be the summit.

Lou broke for a short distance after lunch, then Jim took the lead.

"That sure looks like a summit cornice," he said, approaching the overturned snow.

"Don't get your hopes up. It could be another false summit like the one below."

Jim stepped up and peered over the cornice.

"Do you see anything?" I asked excitedly.

"No!" he screamed, disappearing over the top. I followed closely and landed in a heap with Jim on the summit's other side. "This is it! We're here!" It was only 2 p.m.

Lou came over the crest. We grabbed one another, shaking hands and slapping shoulders.

The temperature was high enough for us to be comfortable. There was no wind. The weather had socked in below us and hid the surrounding peaks, including Nanda Devi East. We were able to remove our gloves and hats. Digging to the bottom of my pack, I brought out the American bicentennial flag and the Indian flag that we had been asked to take to the summit; Jim and Lou held them and beamed while I took pictures. Placing a flag inside an empty water bottle, I buried it deep in the summit snow. I couldn't have asked for better companions or a more magnificent ascent.

We sat comfortably, chatting about the expedition and the problems we had overcome to be there. Lou said he thought this was the best American climb since the West Ridge of Everest. I wondered if that team had faced similar problems, not knowing then that they had. After the months of preparation, difficulties within the team, and severity of route, it was hard to believe we were there.

Shortly after three o'clock we finished taking pictures, looked around us one last time, and descended single file into the clouds, through the deep trough of our ascent. Lou, the slowest, was first, then Jim, then me. I thought of our survival, my home, my family, our personal accomplishment. We were silent, each caught up in his own feelings. Although connected by one rope, we were in three different worlds.

We belayed the dangerous avalanche slopes and the rock band, then moved together down the steep bottomless snow to the rock step. Plunging forward, sometimes uncontrollably, we reached Camp IV by four.

————————————

Liquids were the first priority at Camp IV. We boiled pot after pot of water and drank deeply to rehydrate. Shadows deepened in the valleys while we savored a dinner of beef and vegetables. Lou reached Camp III on the radio at five thirty. "Devi! We took a rest day and climbed the nearest peak!"

"You went to the summit?"

"Yep, we were on top at two o'clock."

"Fantastic!" she cheered. "Congratulations on a wonderful job!" The rest of the team was returning from jumaring practice on the Buttress, so we agreed to talk with Willi at seven o'clock.

"Congratulations on your ascent," Willi's voice boomed over the radio. "We'll be sending a team up tomorrow to take your place—probably Devi, Peter, and Andy. Leave your sleeping bags at Camp IV and you can use theirs down here."

"John wants to know, what if they don't make it this far?" Lou asked. I didn't like the idea of being separated from my sleeping bag, but Lou later shamed me into agreement.

Andy's voice broke in: "Don't worry. We'll get there."

Hoping to get a good night's rest, Jim, Lou, and I slipped into our bags early. The altitude and crowded conditions, however, prevented us from sleeping very well. It was a long cold night after the summit.

We were awake at 6 a.m. It was too cold and too early to descend. Jim leaned forward, still in his bag, and lit the stove. After a small breakfast with several cups of steaming tea, we dressed and left the tent to pack. Jim and I were gloveless; our Dachsteins (preshrunk woolen mittens made in Austria) were frozen solid, having become wet the day before. We held them against our bodies, straightened our gear, and waited for the sun to warm our tiny perch. The weather was beautiful.

I was too cold to wait very long, so I hooked my rappel system to the first rope, snapped a few pictures, and descended. Jim followed as soon as the rope went slack. I made it a point to wait at the end of each rope to take pictures of Jim rappeling and to make sure he was all right. Lou descended close behind. At Sugar Delight, I waited for half an hour for Jim to appear. He was coming down slowly, carefully. I stuffed an extra three-hundred-foot nine-millimeter rope and a rack of hardware I found at the anchor into my pack to take to Camp III, then, after seeing Jim round the corner, descended the rest of the Buttress.

Jim and I were at the base of the Buttress two hours after leaving Camp IV. "We're down!" We clasped each other's arms. "I couldn't feel my feet or hands on the first rappels—I thought I was going to lose them," he said. We relaxed in the snow and warm air and waited for Lou.

"I wonder where Devi, Andy, and Peter are?" Jim asked.

I was puzzled too. "On Dhaulagiri, someone would have broken trail out here to meet us. Usually someone's there . . ."

"They asked us to leave our gear at IV because they said they would be going up. And no one's gotten even this far. I can't understand why someone didn't meet us here at least—they know we're tired."

Lou descended the last rope to where we were sitting and removed his crampons. He, too, was disappointed not to see the second team. He was the one who had argued for us to leave our gear when the others insisted, and now he felt responsible. There was a single track fifty yards from Camp III where someone had ventured out that morning, but then decided against it and returned to camp. Jim had tears in his eyes. We stopped just behind a rise outside of camp to collect ourselves.

Kiran and Nirmal ran out of their tent to greet us warmly. John Evans and Peter came over and congratulated us. The others were more reserved, however. Although the proper words were spoken, it was a very cool welcome. By contrast, the air was quite warm; everyone gathered outside in the sun to discuss the route and the next few days. Devi passed around a pot of pink lemonade.

"Why didn't anyone go up today?" I asked after sitting down with the others.

"It looked like the weather would turn bad," Andy said.

"But it's been perfect all morning!"

"It looked bad earlier this morning. A large black cloud hung over Nanda Devi," he insisted. Andy later confided to Lou that Devi had not been feeling well, further influencing their decision not to go. Willi and the others began talking about going to Camp IV the next day.

"Who's on the second team, Willi?" I asked, hoping the team had been changed.

"Devi, Andy, and Peter."

I had great misgivings. "Willi, I'm going to say my piece."

"Yes John, I thought you would," he said, laughing gently.

"I don't think Devi should go up, or Andy either, if he's still got that cough. Devi," I faced her, "you've got a hernia, which could give you problems, a bad cough you haven't shaken off since the expedition began, and you've been ill every other day from some stomach ailment. I think there are stronger people to go up—like Nirmal, or Evans. Willi could go with Peter. But neither you nor Andy have acclimatized."

They all looked right through me as if I were a phantom and not a man.

"That's it. I've said all I'm going to."

I expected to hear Jim or Lou back me up, but neither said a word. I was alone in voicing what I thought was a serious problem.

Devi showed her anger with calculated subtlety. Since Base Camp, Jim had asked everyone—for health reasons—to use a clean utensil or cracker to scoop out the peanut butter. Devi thought this was a ridiculous rule, but obliged. Now she asked for the pail of peanut butter and opened it. Jabbing her fingers deep into the pail, she scooped out a glob of peanut butter and waved it in the air toward me. "This is the way we do it at Camp III," she snapped, and ate from her fingers.

Several minutes later, Willi came over and we talked alone. "I just don't think she should go up, Willi."

"Well, John, what can a father do?"

"I don't know."

"What would you do if she were your daughter?"

"I don't know, Willi . . . she's not." Our conversation ended.

I finished unpacking while Willi went over to his tent to fix a jumar system for himself so that he could help on the Buttress the next day. The others had all disappeared into their tents. I was annoyed with Lou and Jim for not speaking up when I knew they believed in what I was saying, and I wanted to know why. Lou was in John Evans's tent. I went in and lay down beside him.

"Why didn't you back me up?"

"I guess I should have," Lou answered, but he had no explanation.

I found Jim in his tent, stretched out on a mat. As yet no one had offered us any sleeping bags for the night.

"Jim, why didn't you say something? You know Devi's got some health problems. They're not going to pay any attention to me."

"I don't think the hernia is that big a problem," he shrugged. "I haven't checked her out yet but I'll do that later this afternoon. Right now I don't have anything to go on."

Jim grew irritated with my questions, so I dropped the issue. No one wanted to argue with Willi. Dibrugheta and Marty's evacuation had been bad enough.

Meanwhile, Peter appeared outside our tent and peeked in. "Say, you guys want my sleeping bag? I'll be glad to let you have it."

We just about cried at Peter's offer. He had certainly changed in my eyes. "No, Peter, you need the rest if you expect to make it tomorrow. We'll do all right in down pants and coats," Jim said. "Could you loan us those?"

"Sure, I'll bring 'em right over." He turned to go.

"Say, Peter," I called impulsively. "Here's a bicentennial flag for you . . . Make sure you get it to the summit, OK?"

"Thanks, John," he smiled. "It'll get there."

That afternoon Jim did a short examination of Devi's hernia with Willi in attendance. "If she goes up, there's a chance of a problem," Jim concluded. "If the hernia strangulates and she develops pain in her abdomen, it will take about two hours to kill the bowel and up to two days to kill the patient." Devi and Willi accepted this.

With neither his own authority nor backing from Willi, the expedition leader, Jim could only warn them. "I didn't feel it was necessary to yell and scream," Jim told me later. "I knew Willi wouldn't take my advice, even though I told him I felt Devi shouldn't go up. He refused to take my advice at Dibrugheta on Marty's problem, even on a clear-cut medical issue. Devi's hernia was not clear-cut; it was only problematic."

We spent the rest of the afternoon drinking and eating dinner that Devi prepared. That night, Jim and I dressed heavily in down coats and pants. Lou, having spilled his urine bottle inside his bag during our last night at Camp IV, had brought his sleeping bag down to dry out. It felt good not to have to trust those ropes again, and we dozed off.

September 3 was warmer than usual, and the weather looked promising. The powder snow squeaked under their boots as Andy and Devi left for the Buttress and Camp IV. Having left earlier, Peter was only a dot on the Ridge. Willi, Kiran, Nirmal, Evans, and Jatendra followed to practice jumaring behind the second summit team. Willi and the Indians were new to the technique; John Evans, who was already experienced with jumars, would give them some pointers.

Only Lou, Jim, and I stayed behind, asleep in our tent, relaxing for the first time in days. We didn't have to ascend the Buttress again. I was concerned, though, for the others, knowing the difficulties they faced and the poor state of the fixed lines. Even the idea of practicing on the lower ropes made me nervous. The Buttress and upper slopes of Nanda Devi were socked in by drifting clouds, but we could monitor the second team's progress by listening to them calling to one another. The two parties seemed to spend a lot of time communicating. Jim, Lou, and I spent a leisurely day eating, relaxing, and listening to the climbers.

Jatendra, the only IMF trainee to reach Camp III, returned to camp first, exhausted by the hike from the Buttress. Willi, Kiran, Nirmal, and Evans returned several hours later, cold and tired. Practice on the ropes had not gone well. Willi and John had taught them what they could, but both Kiran and Nirmal had been too slow to reach Sugar Delight Snowfield. Jim cooked hot drinks for the returning climbers while Lou and I started dinner.

"Where did you last see the second team, Willi?" Lou asked.

"Andy was just below Devi and they were about to the snowfield," Willi guessed. "They were moving slowly."

There was no radio contact at 6 p.m., our scheduled time. We tried again at seven without success. Speculation as to what had happened spread among the tents. No one mentioned the possibility of the ropes breaking, but we all thought of it.

At eight-thirty Peter came in over the radio from Camp IV. He sounded weak and was probably hypothermic.

"OK, Peter," Willi asked, "have you seen Devi or Andy?'"

"I haven't seen them since four thirty on Sugar Delight Snowfield. They were still coming, but slowly. Since then I've been working to get to here. It was a bitch."

"We want half-hour radio contacts until they both arrive, understand?" Willi ordered. "Hold on—Jim wants to speak with you."

"Heat up some milk and sugar, Peter," Jim instructed. "We left some in the pan in the front vestibule."

Peter came on again at nine. No one else had shown up yet, but his stronger voice indicated a definite improvement in his condition.

Willi was worried. He left the tent to yodel to Devi, their

private mode of communication. Bell-like, his voice rang through the cold air, to be met only with silence. Then we heard Devi's faint, high-pitched reply. Her voice had cracked slightly; she was still alive.

Frozen and covered with snow, Andy arrived at Camp IV at 11 p.m. and piled into the tent with Peter. He had stayed behind Devi until Sugar Delight—where he had suggested turning back—but Devi had not taken the idea seriously. Andy continued staying just in front of Devi to keep an eye on her. She had a slow but even pace. He left her just below the ridge at the top of the gully and had managed to reach the crest. Devi should have been close behind.

Just before midnight, Lou thought he heard someone yell from the Buttress. It sounded like "Camp III, Camp III!" but he wasn't sure. Jim stepped outside in the clear starlit night and shone his headlamp at the Buttress, but there was no answer.

"Camp III, Devi's here!" Peter finally reported.

Devi got the rope and jumars stuck fifteen feet below the crest, the place we all had had trouble. Unable to move up or down in her exhausted condition, she had yelled for help. We had heard her, but Peter and Andy, only thirty feet away and over the crest, hadn't heard a word. Worried about her taking so long, Andy returned to the crest, heard her calling, and helped her up. The three of them were finally together and safe. It was 2 a.m. when they turned in to sleep. "There were many ominous signs . . . a very desultory start, poor weather, and Devi's hernia popped out," Lou wrote of their ascent in his diary. They had been lucky to get so far.

The next day, September 4, I was to descend to Base Camp and send a porter out to Lata to summon the rest of the porters we would need to leave the mountain. One of us had to go and I was the logical choice. As the only doctor, Jim would stay with the main group until everyone was down. Lou was torn between staying to help the summit team and leaving for the United States to be with his wife for the birth of their next child. We felt that all the climbers would summit in the next three or four days if everything worked out well. Already the second team was in position and the Indians needed only to perfect their jumar technique to follow a day or two later.

"We're not moving today," Andy told us at the morning radio call. "All of us need a day's rest. We're pretty tired."

"How's Devi?" Willi asked.

"Exhausted, but fine. Her hat fell off during her ascent yesterday, but we'll work something out."

I cooked rice pudding for breakfast, filled my water bottle, and packed to leave. Willi gave me last-minute instructions on how many porters to send for and where the money was hidden at Camp I. It was one of the finest days of the expedition and already, at eight thirty, the air temperature was warm. Evans and I floundered through deep snow down the Ridge a short distance from camp to photograph the Buttress and upper slopes of Nanda Devi. At one point on the Ridge we could see Nanda Devi East. After saying my goodbyes, I started down alone for Base Camp. The ropes were buried deep under a heavy crust of snow. Each step down was a difficult tug-of-war with the rope as I tried to free it from the mountain's icy grip. The load I was carrying, heavy with personal gear and ice hardware, kept throwing me off balance. My progress was almost as slow as it had been when I came up.

Camp II was a shambles after only three days. One of the tents was crushed from snowfall, the other in an equally bad condition. I searched through several opened food bags to

find only cornnuts and crackers. The sun was now viciously
hot, pounding the snowfield and me along with it. I stripped
some clothing along with my crampons, which were balling
up with snow, and continued down to Camp I, weaving and
jerking from side to side on each rappel. The arm pulling the
rope from the crust was drained of strength and almost useless, so I let my body weight pull the rope free.

Camp I was deserted, silent. Tent doors flapped in
the slight breeze; food bags were torn open and scattered. No
one had been there for some time. I found Jim's film but not
the expedition's money bag. I continued descending through
the same snow conditions. At the end of the fixed lines I slid
and punched my way through avalanche debris until I was
just above Advanced Base. None of the debris had been there
three weeks ago and I was amazed at the accumulation.

Dropping over a small cliff above Advanced Base, I
rounded the hillside, expecting to see a lively camp with several of the high-altitude porters, but I was wrong. Before me
were the ghostly skeletons of three tents. Only the poles were
standing; wisely, the nylon tents had been dropped in case of
avalanche blasts while the camp was empty. Like a victim of
war, I scavenged the dead camp for food and the rest of the
belongings I had left there a month before. Everything was
wet and filthy. Ravens were digging at the garbage and food
sacks, pecking apart the eight-man day units.

The mountain was silent, the camp ghostly. I never felt so
insignificant. Rummaging through an open box, I found
a two-month-old *Newsweek* and read it through. Later I
searched my duffel for personal gear and the exposed film I
had left, dumping the climbing hardware from my pack to
make room. It was almost as good as Christmas, finding gear
I had forgotten was there.

It was 2 p.m., but I decided to continue down and across

the glacier for Base because Advanced Base was too depressing. My pack made me sink in the snow at the side of the glacier, which I dreaded crossing. As I reached the side, I hesitated, then followed some several-day-old tracks until they disappeared under tons of avalanche debris. I didn't hurry. It was now or never and I didn't want to breathe hard or suck air. After ten minutes I was across. I hoped I would never have to cross that area again.

I passed through Ridge Camp quickly. Only a few torn boxes remained to indicate we had been there weeks before. I stayed to the side of another avalanche debris slope, then crossed where the stream had once been, now a trough of avalanche snow. An hour later I crossed the Rishi on an immense snow bridge. There was no more danger. I was down.

Dharamsingh, Kesharsingh, and Balbirsingh met me at the stream near camp. They were smiling and eager to help me across. Tears welled in my eyes when I saw them.

"Up, sahib?" Dharamsingh asked excitedly.

"Yes, yes, all the way up!" I answered, gesturing. They shook my hand and insisted on taking the pack from my weary shoulders. I knew in my heart they shared our success. It was good to be with them again. That night in their company was one of the most pleasant I spent in India.

Jim and Lou had enjoyed an easy day at Camp III. Willi, Evans, Kiran, and Nirmal also spent the day in camp resting because they planned to attempt Camp IV the next day. Willi was still unsure whether the Indians could jumar the ropes and decided to get an early start the next morning.

Lou continued to worry about his wife, Kathy, so Jim persuaded him to leave for home the following day. There was no reason for Lou to stay; Jim would take his responsibilities.

No one had moved from Camp IV that day either. During

the afternoon radio call Jim asked Devi about her hernia and about any symptoms of illness she may have had. Both Lou and Jim doubted she should go higher and Jim warned her about his concern.

"Willi, I only advised her to come down," Jim said. "I didn't order her."

"I'm glad you left it that way," Willi replied.

Before dawn on the fifth, Peter, Devi, and Andy at Camp IV were up and dressing. The weather was partly cloudy and a breeze was beginning to pick up. Devi was still lethargic and had some diarrhea. She decided to wait another day or until Willi could be with her to go for the summit. Andy complained of being tired and elected to stay with Devi. Peter wanted to go partway at least. He needed to make the attempt even if alone. His would be the expedition's last attempt for the summit.

Peter pushed hard, surmounting the major difficulties of the upper section, but turned back just below the rock band. The weather had worsened considerably as he climbed and snow began falling. He became exhausted in the deep snow and high altitude and, while descending, slipped and fell toward the abyss of the Northwest Face. Miraculously, he stopped after thirty feet, even though he had dropped his ice axe. After retrieving the axe, Peter descended more carefully and reached Camp IV in the afternoon. He retreated to the safety of the tent, where he, Devi, and Andy spent their third night at twenty-four thousand feet.

At Camp III, Willi, Kiran, Nirmal, and Evans had gone through a similar day of hardship on the Buttress. The third summit team was awake at six o'clock and viewed the same storm clouds in the south, but decided to attempt the ascent of the Buttress anyway. After Jim fed them a hot breakfast, the four headed for the ropes and Camp IV. Jim and Lou descended: Jim for a food bag for Camp III, Lou for home. Jim returned to camp slowly, reaching the Ridge in a snowstorm. He relaxed the rest of the day, boiling liquids and listening to the climbers on the Buttress arguing whether to go up or down.

The four climbers straggled into camp at nine o'clock that night. Nirmal and Kiran had again been too slow; it was wiser to descend rather than try for Camp IV. John Evans, usually placid and introverted, was furious. "Willi purposely overextended the whole team," he told Jim. "We were in real danger."

The climbers were hypothermic, particularly Evans, and Jim forced foods and fluids into them. According to Evans, they were lucky to have made it back to camp alive.

For me, it was a peaceful September 5. I sent all the porters to Advanced Base except Dharamsingh, who was to run to Lata for more porters, and Tesh, a porter who was ill. I bathed early, long before the sun's warmth arrived in the deep valley, then walked through the meadows. The sounds and smells of the valley pleased my senses. It was another world.

Fall had come to the upper Sanctuary. Frost covered the vegetation along the spring that flowed through camp. The bright plants and flowers, predominant in August, had faded and withered. I thought about the expedition as I walked along a sheep trail above camp. The team had never been together in spirit in the United States or on the mountain. We had been divided by philosophy and opinion since the beginning. Success under such circumstances seemed even sweeter. Yet I was worried deeply about those still trying to summit. Kiran scared me because he was irrational when it came to saving face. I knew he was not technically proficient and his tenacity could cause himself and others trouble on the Buttress.

Now that she had overcome the difficulties of the Buttress, Devi worried me less. But her illness and hernia made me think that she would only reach Camp IV. Willi had said that she was used to an unusual amount of stomach trouble and carried her own antacid. Perhaps she could mask her discomfort long enough to summit.

The day passed quickly for me at Base. I felt sure that someone had reached the top that afternoon because of the good weather, although it looked windy near the summit. I was hoping they would get up and down quickly so we could leave for home.

Early the next morning, on the sixth, I walked up the hill above Base to photograph Nanda Devi. Clouds sped past the summit and the winds looked fierce. Lou was at Base when I returned at noon. We briefly wished each other success and he continued to Pathal Khan, loaded with all the Gumperts drink mix and chapatis Tesh and I could give him. He hadn't heard anything from the others at Camp IV, but assumed they must have made the summit. I was entertained the rest of the day by two Japanese who were in the Sanctuary scouting a route on the northeast side that would eventually reach the North Ridge and ascend our Buttress. It would be a difficult, magnificent route if they could do it. Unfortunately, they didn't succeed.

Both Camp III and IV were awake and busy at six-thirty. Devi made the scheduled radio contact with Willi and Jim.

"I'm going alone to Camp IV," Willi announced. "Yesterday Kiran and Nirmal were too slow on the ropes. Kiran even ended up upside down trying to jumar." Kiran and Nirmal couldn't decide what they would do. Kiran thought of soloing to Camp IV like Willi, but Nirmal wanted to go down. Later, under pressure from Kiran, Nirmal changed his mind.

Evans was ambivalent. He was feeling very lethargic and had been sleeping constantly for the past twenty-four hours. Jim thought this was due to exhaustion and hypothermia from the previous day. He couldn't know Evans was coming down with hepatitis. Evans later decided to descend because he didn't want to guide Kiran and Nirmal up the Buttress and to the top. Willi left for Camp IV shortly after breakfast.

That day the three climbers at Camp IV again remained in camp. Peter was exhausted from his solo attempt and needed the rest. Andy's desire to summit now depended solely on Devi; he'd do whatever she decided.

In the weeks on the upper slopes of Nanda Devi, Andy had asked for Devi's hand in marriage, and Willi had given his blessing. They would set a date when they returned home. The rest of us didn't know of their intended marriage. They didn't know what our reaction would be and, frankly, didn't care. The engagement was their secret and comfort during a very difficult time on the mountain.

In the meantime, the mountain had taken second place for Andy. His affection for Devi preempted his previous goals. Before he and Devi had gone up the Buttress, Andy had told her that no mountain was worth the risk, that instead he wanted to "wrap her in cotton wool." They both laughed at this and agreed that wasn't what Devi wanted or needed. She promised to tell him if she had the slightest inkling of trouble.

Andy retrieved the rope below Camp IV that morning. Devi felt lethargic, as she had since her arrival, so they performed a little test to see how strong she was. She climbed about thirty feet out of camp, stopped, rested, then returned. Devi was simply exhausted for no apparent reason. Although she still had diarrhea that morning, she seemed fine as long as she wasn't moving.

At the two o'clock radio call, Jim informed Camp IV that Willi was on his way up and that they should dig another tent platform. Jim knew Devi was a stoic about illness and pleaded with her, "Devi, what aren't you telling me?"

"I'm telling you everything," she answered. "I have no pain." Later in the day Andy, Peter, and Devi decided she should descend. According to Andy, "Nothing suggested urgency, just her lassitude and diarrhea." Andy and Peter dug another tent site, but the wind prevented them from pitching a tent. Because Willi was on his way, they decided not to escort Devi down that afternoon.

Willi arrived around 7 p.m. He had never used a jumar in his life, yet had accomplished one of the most difficult jumar ascents a climber would ever encounter. Willi, Peter, and Andy decided to climb to the summit early the next morning. They would take Devi down upon their return. That night, Devi had terrible sulfur burps and complained of being cold and clammy.

High winds and snow pinned those at Camp IV down on September 7. The four had no choice but to sit out the storm. They made the best of a poor situation, cooking meals and boiling water to stay healthy. Devi's abdomen was tender and slightly distended, but the hernia appeared to be in place. She continued taking plenty of liquids and food. Toward evening, she again had severe sulfur burps and diarrhea. The others watched her carefully, although nothing suggested urgency to them.

"She ought to come down," Jim told Willi that evening. "Sounds to me as though she's getting some bowel obstruction."

"No, she has heartburn," Willi said. "Someone should bring up an antacid tomorrow."

Meanwhile, the climbers at Camp III sat out the bad day as well. Nirmal had complained of leg pains, acute chest pain, and shortness of breath, and Jim began to suspect a possible pulmonary embolism. His main concern now was Evans, who was revealing some real problems that Jim wasn't sure of. Jim evacuated both men with the help of Kiran and Jatendra the next morning.

Bad weather continued on September 8. The night at Camp IV had been difficult. The four occupants of the two-man tent had been cramped. Devi's condition was markedly worse.

Her sulfur burps were more frequent; she had to be helped into a sitting position, the only position she was able to assume with any degree of comfort. Andy had felt Devi's abdomen and it had become severely distended. The hernia was in place but she was in pain. They discussed the situation and decided, in spite of the bad weather, to help her down that morning.

Devi's burps became constant and her cheeks were puffy. Her face and lips took on a blue hue. At 10 a.m., according to Peter, she looked bad and everyone was concerned. Her face became puffier and puffier. The vicious storm, worse than any since we had arrived in the Sanctuary, delayed their departure until noon.

Willi went outside, leaving the others to put on their clothes and ready themselves to descend. Devi was sitting up in the back of the tent trying to drink some cocoa. Her stomach hurt terribly.

Devi suddenly became a ghostly white. "Take my pulse, Peter," she said. Then, calmly, "I'm going to die." Her eyes rolled as she pitched forward and vomited.

Andy grabbed her and started mouth-to-mouth resuscitation. Peter called Willi back into the tent. Willi immediately took over the mouth-to-mouth while all three tried cardiopulmonary resuscitation.

Willi would recall he knew they had lost her within fifteen minutes as he felt her lips grow cold against his. Despite this, they continued their efforts to revive her for another half hour without success. The three men were anguished. Devi was dead.

They clasped each other for comfort as their quiet moans

filled the tent. What could they do with Devi's body? Leave her in the tent? Bury her?

"No," Willi decided. "We will commit her to the mountain. As if a burial at sea."

Stricken, Willi, Peter, and Andy finished dressing. Hugs and touches consumed their last moments with Devi. The sleeping bag was zipped shut and the drawstring closed around her face. Then into the raging storm they crawled.

They dragged her body up the ridge a short distance. It was to the uphill side of the fixed lines so that her remains would find their way into the most remote icy grave on Nanda Devi—the Northeast Face. They fell to their knees in the storm and linked their hands in a circle around her corpse. Each sobbed a broken farewell to the comrade who had filled such a vivid place in their lives. Willi said last rites:

"Thank you for the world we live in. Thank you for such beauty juxtaposed against such risk . . . Thank you."

The three men dragged Devi to the edge of the face. With a horrible shove, her corpse disappeared into the bowels of the storm, into the mountain of the Goddess Nanda Devi.

"We laid the body to rest in its icy tomb, at rest on the breast of the bliss-giving Goddess Nanda," Willi later pronounced.

Now cold and exhausted, their judgment distorted by grief, the climbers knew one thing: they had to leave Camp IV immediately.

Postscript: Ten years after the expedition, John Roskelley would write his account of the tragic and ill-fated journey to Nanda Devi. As contentious as it was, the account would cause irreconcilable rifts among the members of the expedition.

Joe Simpson and his climbing partner Simon Yates were nearing the summit of a peak in the Peruvian Andes when unbelievable tragedy struck. Joe had fallen, completely shattering
his right leg. The two climbers did their best to struggle down
the mountain when Joe fell again. This time, he dangled in
midair over a deep crevasse, unable to reach the ice wall
with his axe. Joe's weight then began to pull Simon after him,
presenting Simon with the most difficult decision a climber
ever has to make. He winced—and cut the rope.

TOUCHING THE VOID

JOE SIMPSON

Storm at the Summit

Getting organised in the morning
was a much easier business than it had been previously. We
had the advantage of standing room when it came to rolling
up karrimats, packing sleeping bags, and sorting out the
climbing gear that had been dropped in a tangled mess on our
arrival the night before.

It was my turn to lead. Simon remained inside the snow
cave, belayed to a rock piton, while I gingerly stepped out of
the small entrance on to the sloped ice of the gully we had

ascended in the dark. The ground was unfamiliar to me. I was standing on good ice which funnelled down into a narrowing curved cone below me before disappearing into the top of the tube which I had struggled so hard to get out of last night. The huge ice field we had climbed yesterday was no longer visible. I looked over to my right. A short distance above me the top of the gully reared up in a vertical cascade of ice, but over on its far side I could see that the angle eased and there was a way up and past the cascade into another gully above.

I tiptoed to the right, stopping to drive in a screw before launching up the side of the cascade. It was excellent water ice and I enjoyed the aggressive, warming work. I glanced back at the entrance of the snow cave and saw Simon peeping out, feeding the rope as I climbed. The structure of the natural cave looked even more impressive than it had last night and I couldn't help wondering at our good fortune to have found it, for a night spent in the open at the top of the gully would have been, to say the least, uncomfortable.

Above the cascade I ran out the rest of the rope, following a snowy gully. Simon quickly joined me.

"Just as we thought," I said. "We should reach the hanging ramp on the next pitch."

He set off to the right before disappearing from the minor gully, where I stood resting, into the key ramp line we had seen so long ago on Seria Norte. I reckoned that the main difficulties were now behind us and it would be only a matter of running it out to the top of the ramp, and then up the summit slopes.

When I joined Simon in the ramp I realised that our problems were not over. At the top of the ramp we could see that there was a formidable barrier of tooth-shaped seracs with no apparent way through them. The vertical rock walls on each side of the ramp would be impossibly hard to ascend, and the seracs stretched from wall to wall without a break.

"Damn!"

"Yeah, it's bad news. I wasn't expecting those."

"There may be an exit," I said. "If not, we're stuck."

"Bloody hope not! It's a long way back."

I looked at the nearby peaks, trying to gauge our height on the mountain.

"We bivied at five eight hundred metres last night. That's what? Nineteen thousand feet . . . right, that means we have about fifteen hundred to go," I said.

"Two thousand, more like."

"Okay, two, but we did at least two and a half thousand on harder ground yesterday so we should top out today."

"I wouldn't be so sure. Depends on how hard that exit is, and remember the last bit is all flutings."

I set off up the fifty-five-degree ramp and made fast progress. We alternated leads, rarely talking to each other, concentrating on forcing the pace. Yesterday we had used ice screws to protect each rope length, and the steep ice had slowed us down. Today we could feel the thin air taking its toll where the easier ground enabled us to climb an almost continuous double pitch, kicking steps up to the leader for 150 feet, and then up past him for the same again.

I was breathing heavily as I dug through the soft surface snow to find the firm ice below. I drove in two ice screws and planted both axes above my stance before tying into them and shouting for Simon to come up. We were close to the serac barrier, having climbed one thousand feet up the ramp. I checked my watch: one o'clock. We had overslept and made a late start but, after ten pitches in four and a half hours, we had made up for it. I felt confident and at ease. We were a match for this route and I now knew that we would finish it. I felt a thrill at the knowledge that I was, at last, on the verge of achieving a first ascent, and a hard one at that.

As Simon panted up, the sun crept over the seracs at the top of the ramp and spilled bright white light down the sweep of snow below us. Simon was grinning broadly. I needed no explanation for his good humour. It was one of those moments when everything came together, and there were no struggles or doubts, and nothing more to do but enjoy the sensation.

"May as well get past the seracs and then rest."

"Sure," Simon agreed, as he studied the barrier above. "See those icicles? That's the way past."

I looked at the cascade of ice and, at first, I dismissed it as too difficult. It was clearly overhanging at the bottom. A leaning wall of smooth blue ice with a huge fringe of icicles dripping from its head provided the only solid surface across the otherwise powdery seracs. Yet, this cascade was the only weakness that I could spot in the barrier. If we were to attempt it, we would have to climb the initial ice wall for some twenty-five feet and then break a way through the icicles and continue up the more reasonably angled cascade ice above.

"It looks hard."

"Yes. I'd prefer to attempt the rock first."

"It's loose as hell."

"I know, but it might go. I'll give it a try anyway."

He moved some pitons, a few wires, and a couple of "friends" round to the front of his harness before edging left to the start of the rock wall. I was anchored firmly, just below and to the right of the cascade. The rock, yellow and crumbly, bordered the vertical powdery snow between the cascade and the rocky side of the ramp.

I watched Simon carefully, for I knew that if he fell it would be with the sudden violence of hand or footholds breaking away and not the gradual surrender to waning strength. He placed the camming device in a crack as high up the wall as he could. It expanded evenly into the crack with each of its four cams pressed hard against the rock. I guessed that it would be the rock which would break away, and not the "friend" if Simon fell.

He stepped up cautiously, testing his footholds with light kicks, and hitting the holds above his head to check their looseness. He hesitated a moment, stretched against the wall, gripping the rock above him at full reach, and then began to pull himself up slowly. I tensed, holding the ropes locked in the sticht plate, so that I could hold his fall immediately.

Suddenly, the holds tore loose from the wall, and for a second Simon held his poise, his hands still outstretched but now gripping two lumps of loose rock. Then he was off, falling backward into the gully below. I braced myself, expecting the "friend" to rip out as well, but it held firm, and I stopped his short tumble with ease.

"Brilliant!" I said, laughing at the surprise on his face.

"Shit! . . . I was sure those were solid."

When he had got back to me he looked at the cascade again.

"I don't fancy doing it directly, but if I can get past the right side I should be able to crack it."

"The ice looks mushy there."

"We'll see."

He launched himself up the right side of the cascade, avoiding the steep wall but attempting to make a slight traverse to the right before climbing back left above the icicles. Unfortunately the ice gave way to honeycombed snow and sugary ice crystals. He managed to reach a point parallel with the top of the icicles before the conditions became impossible and he could go no higher. He was twenty feet above me, and for a while it seemed as if he was stuck: reversing what he had just climbed would be to invite a nasty fall. Eventually he succeeded in fixing a sling around a thick icicle which had rejoined the cascade to form a loop, and he abseiled off this down to my stance.

"I'm knackered. You have a go."

"Okay, but I'd move further to the side if I were you. I'll have to knock most of those icicles away."

Many of them were as thick as a man's arm and nearly five feet long. Some even bigger. I started up the ice wall, which pushed me back off balance, and at once I felt the strain on my arms. The sack on my back pulled me away from the ice. I bunny-hopped my crampons quickly up the wall, smashing my axes hard into the brittle ice above, pulling up, hopping again—all the time trying to save my strength by climbing fast. As I neared the icicles I realised that I would be unable to hold on for very much longer; already I was too tired to break away the icicles while holding on to the wall with one axe. I swung as hard as I could until my axe bit in deeply, and was firm enough to hold me. I then clipped my harness into the wrist-loop on the axe and hung wearily from it. I kept a wary eye on the axe tip embedded in the ice, and only when I was sure it was holding my full weight safely did I extract my hammer axe from the wall and, reaching above me, hammer an ice screw into the wall.

I clipped the rope through the screw and breathed a sigh of relief. At least there was no longer a danger of falling more than five or six feet. The icicles were within easy reach. Without thinking I swung my hammer through the fringe of ice and, even more stupidly, looked up at what I was doing. The best part of a hundredweight of icicles smashed down on to my head and shoulders and clattered away down on to Simon. We both started swearing. I cursed myself and the sharp pain of a split lip and cracked tooth, and Simon cursed me.

"Sorry . . . didn't think."

"Yeah. I noticed."

When I looked up again I saw that although it was painful the hammer had done the trick and there was now a way clear through to the easier-angled ice above. It didn't take long to swarm up the top of the wall and run the remainder of the rope to a belay in the wide shallow gully above.

Simon came up covered in ice particles and frosted white by the powder snow which had swept down the cascade. He carried on past me to a slight ridge which marked the end of the ramp and the start of the summit slopes. He had lit the gas stove and cleared a place to sit in comfort by the time I joined him.

"Your mouth is bleeding," he said flatly.

"It's nothing. It was my fault anyway."

It was noticeably colder now that we were away from the shelter of the ice gullies and exposed to a steady breeze. For the first time we could see the summit, formed from a huge overhanging cornice which bulged out over the slopes eight hundred feet above us. The ridge sweeping off to the left would be our line of descent, but we couldn't see it very well in the swirling clouds which were steadily spilling over from the east. It looked as if bad weather was on the way.

Simon passed me a hot drink and then huddled deeper into his jacket with his back to the bitter wind. He was looking at the summit slopes, searching for the best line of ascent. It was the state of the snow on this last part of the route that worried us more than the angle or the technical difficulties. The whole slope was corrugated by powder flutings which had gradually built up as fresh snow had sloughed down the face. We had heard all about Peruvian flutings and hadn't liked the stories; it was best not to attempt them. The weather patterns in Europe never produced such horrors. South American mountains were renowned for these spectacular snow and ice creations, where powder snow seemed to defy gravity and form seventy-, even eighty-degree slopes, and ridges developed into tortured unstable cornices of huge size, built up one on top of the other. On any other mountains the powder would have swept on down and formed only on much easier-angled slopes.

Above us a rock band cut across the whole slope. It was not steep, but was powdered with a treacherous coating of snow. After one hundred feet it merged back into the snow slope, which grew steeper as it climbed up. The flutings started shortly above the rock band and continued without break to the summit. Once we had established ourselves in the gully formed between two flutings we would have to force a way to the top, for it would be impossible to traverse out by crossing a fluting and getting into the neighbouring gully. It would be vitally important to choose the right gully, and we could see that many of them closed down into dead ends as two flutings merged together. If I looked carefully I could make out a few gullies which did not close down, but as soon as I tried to look at the whole slope these became lost in the maze of gullies and flutings streaming down the face.

"Christ! It looks desperate!" Simon said. "I can't work out a way up at all."

"I can't see us getting to the top today."

"Not if those clouds unload, that's for sure. What time is it?"

"Four o'clock. Two hours' light left. Better get moving."

I wasted valuable time trying to cross the rock band. It was tilted like a steep roof, but unlike the rock in the ramp it was black and compact with only a few small holds mostly hidden beneath the snow. I knew it wasn't difficult, but I was standing on an open face with a drop of nearly four thousand feet below me and felt very unnerved by the exposure. There was also a long gap of unprotected rope between me and Simon who was belaying me from our resting place. His only anchor was his axes buried in the snow, and I knew all too well how useless these would be if I made a mistake.

My left foot slipped and the crampon points skittered on the rock. I hated this sort of delicate balance climbing, but I was committed to it now; no going back. As I balanced on two small edges of rock, front points teetering on the verge of slipping, my legs began to tremble and I shouted a warning to Simon. I could hear the fear in my voice and cursed myself for letting Simon know it. I tried moving up again, but my nerve failed me and I couldn't complete the move. I knew it would take just a couple of moves to reach easier ground, and tried convincing myself that if this wasn't so terrifyingly exposed I would walk up it, hands in pockets, but I couldn't shake off the fear. I was gripped.

Gradually, I calmed down and carefully thought out the few moves I needed to make. When I tried again I was surprised at how easy it seemed. I was above the difficulty and climbing quickly up easy ground before I realised it. The belay was little better than Simon's and I warned him of this before he started after me. The sudden fright still had me breathing hard and it annoyed me to see Simon climb easily over the difficulties and know that I had lost control and let fear get the better of me.

"God! I was gripped stupid on that," I said.

"I noticed."

"Which gully should we go for?" I had looked for a likely one but found it impossible to see, when close up to them, whether they closed off or not.

"I don't know. That one is the widest. I'll have a look at that."

Simon entered the gully and immediately began floundering in deep powder. The sides of the flutings rose up fifteen feet on either side of him. There was no chance of changing line. Spindrift avalanches poured down on to his struggling figure so that sometimes he disappeared from sight. The light was going rapidly, and I noticed that it had begun to snow, the spindrift getting heavier. I was directly beneath Simon and, after sitting still for two hours, I was chilled to the bone. Simon was excavating huge quantities of snow down on to me and I could do nothing to avoid it.

I switched my head-torch on and was surprised to see that it was eight o'clock. Four hours to climb three hundred feet. I seriously doubted whether we would be able to get up these flutings. At last, a distant muffled shout from the snow-filled clouds told me to follow on. I was dangerously cold, despite having put on my polar jacket and windproof. We would have to bivouac somewhere on these horrendous slopes because sitting still for such a long time while belaying was out of the question. I couldn't believe what Simon had done to climb that rope-length up the gully. He had dug a trench four feet deep by four wide all the way up it; his exhausting search for more solid snow yielding a weak layer of crusted ice which barely held his weight. Most of this had been broken away as he had climbed, so that I had great difficulty following his lead. It had taken him three hours to climb, and when I reached him I could see that it had tired him out. I felt very tired, too, and cold, and it was important we bivouacked soon.

"I can't believe this snow!"

"Bloody terrifying. I thought I was falling off all the way up."

"We have to bivi. I was freezing down there."

"Yeah, but not here. The fluting has got too small."

"Okay. You may as well lead up again."

I knew it would be easier and avoid rope tangles, but I regretted not being able to keep moving. Two freezing and interminable hours later I joined Simon one hundred feet higher up. He was belayed in a large hole he had dug into the base of the gully.

"I've found some ice."

"Good enough for an ice screw?"

"Well it's better than nothing. If you get in here we can enlarge this sideways."

I squeezed in beside him, fully expecting the floor of the cave to collapse down the gully at any moment. We began digging into the sides of the flutings, slowly enlarging the cave into a long rectangular snow hole set across the gully, with the entrance partially filled up by our excavations.

By eleven o'clock we had settled into our sleeping bags, eaten the last freeze-dried meal, and were savouring a last hot drink of the day.

"Three hundred feet to go. I just hope it isn't worse than what we've just done."

"At least the storm has stopped. But it's damned cold. I think my little finger is frostbitten. It's white down to the hand."

It must have been close to minus twenty when we had been exposed to the spindrift in the gullies, and the wind had brought the windchill temperature down nearer to minus forty. We were lucky to have found a place for a snow hole.

I hoped we would have clear sunny weather tomorrow.

The base of the gas canister was coated in a thick layer of ice. I knocked it against my helmet and managed to remove most of it, then I stuffed it deep into my sleeping bag, feeling the icy metal against my thighs. Five minutes later I was snuggled in again with only my nose sticking out of the bag, and one eye keeping a sleepy watch on the stove. It roared busily, but it was dangerously close to my bag. Blue light shone through the cave walls. It had been a long and bitterly cold night at twenty thousand feet, perhaps nearer twenty-one thousand.

When the water was boiling I sat up and hurriedly donned my polar jacket, windproof, and gloves. I fumbled in the snow wall of the cave looking for the sachet of fruit juice and the chocolate.

"Brew's ready."

"God's teeth! I'm bloody freezing."

Simon uncurled from his cramped foetal position, took the steaming mug and disappeared back into his bag. I drank slowly, hugging the hot cup to my chest, watching the second lot of snow melt down in the pan. The gas flame was not so strong.

"How much gas have we got left?" I asked.

"One tin. Is that one empty?"

"Not quite. We may as well drink as much as it will produce and save the other for the descent."

"Yeah. We haven't got much fruit juice left either. Just one packet."

"We'll have judged it right, then. Enough for one more bivi, that's all we need."

It was a long cold business gearing up, but that was the least of my worries. The flutings lay ahead and it was my turn to lead. To make things more difficult I had to exit the cave and somehow climb over the roof, which stretched the full width of the gully. I succeeded, but not without destroying most of the cave and burying Simon, who had belayed me from inside. Once on to the slope of the gully I looked back down to where we had climbed the previous night. All traces of the trench dug by Simon had disappeared. It had been swept clean and refilled by the incessant waves of spindrift which had poured down the gully during the snowstorm. I was disappointed to see that the gully ended about one hundred feet above me. The flutings on each side joined together to form a single razor-sharp ribbon of powder. I would have to try to cross over into another fluting after all.

The sky was clear and there was no wind. It was Simon's turn to sit stoically under the deluge of snow I was forced to kick down, but daylight had dubious advantages. It made the climbing easier and allowed me to see whether I was about to slip; on the other hand it provided unnerving glimpses between my legs of 4,500 feet of emptiness. Knowing that our belays were anything but secure and that any fall would be disastrous made me concentrate on the way ahead. As I approached the dead end in the gully the angle steadily increased, and it became obvious that I would have to traverse out through the side fluting soon; but . . . which one? I couldn't see over the sides of the flutings and had no idea what I would be traversing into. I looked down and saw Simon watching me intently. Only his head and chest stuck out from the roof of the cave, and the huge drop framed behind him emphasised the precariousness of our position. I could see that the flutings were not as high near the cave, and that Simon might be able to see more of the way ahead than I could.

"Which way should I go? Can you see anything?"

"Don't go left."

"Why?"

"It seems to drop away, and it looks bloody dangerous!"

"What's on the right?"

"Can't see, but the flutings are not so steep. It's a lot better than the left anyway."

I hesitated. Once I started ploughing through a fluting I might be unable to return. I didn't want to find myself in an even worse position. However high I stretched I couldn't see into the gully on my right. I wasn't even sure there would be a gully there, and none of the snow I could see above me gave any idea of what might be awaiting me.

"Okay. Watch the ropes," I shouted as I began to dig into the right-hand side of the gully. Then I laughed at what I had just said. It would do no good concentrating on belaying if the belay was going to rip straight out.

To my surprise, digging furiously with both axes into the fluting was no harder than climbing the gully, and I emerged, breathing hard, on the other side, in an identical steepening gully above which I could see the huge cornice of the summit only a rope's length away. Simon floundered up to me and whooped when he saw the summit behind me.

"Cracked it," he said.

"I hope so, but this last bit looks bloody steep."

"It'll go." He set off up the slope churning huge amounts of freezing snow down on to my exposed belay hole. I pulled my hood over my helmet and turned my back, gazing down at the glacier far below me. Suddenly our exposed stance appalled me. The loose snow was so steep and my belay so precarious that I felt a sickening disbelief in what we were doing. An excited yell tore me from my thoughts and I turned to see the rope disappearing over the top of the gully above.

"Done it. No more flutings. Come up."

He was sitting, legs astride a fluting, grinning manically, when I pulled myself wearily out of the gully. Behind him, less than fifty feet from us, the summit cornice reared up in a threatening bulge of snow-ice which overhung the West Face. I quickly moved past Simon and cramponed on firm snow up and to the left, where the summit cornice was smallest. Ten minutes later, I stood beneath the snow ridge dividing West Face from East.

"Take a photo."

I waited until Simon had his camera ready before planting my axe over the ridge on to the east side and heaving myself over onto the broad-backed col under the summit. For the first time in four days I had a new view on which to feast. The sun bathed the snow sweeping down into the eastern glacier. After the long cold shadowed days on the West Face it felt luxurious to sit there warmed by the sun. I had forgotten that, now we were climbing in the Southern Hemisphere, everything was the wrong way round: South Faces here were the equivalent of icy cold North Faces in the Alps, and East Faces became West. No wonder the mornings had been so cold and shadowed and we had to wait until late in the day before being blessed with a few hours' sunshine.

Simon joined me and we laughed happily as we took off our sacks and sat on them, carelessly dropping axes and mitts in the snow, content to be quiet a while and look around us.

"Let's leave the sacks here and go up to the summit," Simon said, interrupting my self-indulgent reverie. The summit! Of course, I had forgotten we had only reached the ridge. Escaping from the West Face had seemed to be an end in itself. I looked up at the ice-cream cone rising behind Simon. It was only about one hundred feet away.

"You go ahead. I'll take some photos when you reach the top."

He grabbed some chocolate and sweets before getting up and tramping slowly up through soft snow. The altitude was having its effect. When he was outlined against the sky, bending over his axe on top of the spectacular summit cornice, I began feverishly snapping photographs. Leaving the sacks at the col, I followed, breathing hard, and feeling the tiredness in my legs.

We took the customary summit photos and ate some chocolate. I felt the usual anticlimax. What now? It was a vicious circle. If you succeed with one dream, you come back to square one and it's not long before you're conjuring up another, slightly harder, a bit more ambitious—a bit more dangerous. I didn't like the thought of where it might be leading me. As if, in some strange way, the very nature of the game was controlling me, taking me toward a logical but frightening conclusion; it always unsettled me, this moment of reaching the summit, this sudden stillness and quiet after the storm, which gave me time to wonder at what I was doing and sense a niggling doubt that perhaps I was inexorably losing control—was I here purely for pleasure or was it egotism? Did I really want to come back for more? But these moments were also good times, and I knew that the feelings would pass. Then I could excuse them as morbid, pessimistic fears that had no sound basis.

"Looks like we are in for another storm," Simon said.

He had been quietly examining the North Ridge, our line of descent, which was rapidly being obscured by massed clouds rolling up the East Face and tumbling out over on to the west side. Even now I could see little of the ridge, and the glacier up which we had made our approach would be completely covered within the hour. The ridge began where we had left our sacks and rose to a subsidiary summit before twisting back on itself and curling down into the clouds. I saw snatches of frighteningly steep razor-edges through cloud gaps, and some dangerously corniced sections, the East Face dropping away to the right in a continuous flank of tortured flutings. We would be unable to traverse below the corniced ridge at a safe distance. The flutings looked impassable.

"Jesus! It looks hairy."

"Yeah. Better get our skates on. If we move quickly we can traverse under that summit and then rejoin the ridge further down. In fact, I don't think we'll even have an hour."

Simon held out his hand, and the first snowflakes drifted down lazily on to his glove.

We returned to the sacks and then set off to circle around the minor summit. Simon led the way. We moved roped together, with coils of rope in hand in case of a fall. It was the fastest way and, with the deep powder snow hampering our progress, it was our only chance of getting past the minor summit in reasonable visibility. If Simon fell I hoped to have time enough to get my axe buried, though I doubted whether the axe would find any purchase in the loose snow.

The clouds closed in on us after half an hour, when we were on the east flank of the second summit. Ten minutes later we were lost in the whiteout. There was no wind, and the snow fell silently in large heavy flakes. It was about two thirty and we knew it would snow until late evening. We stood in silence, staring around us, trying to make out where we were.

"I think we should head down."

"I don't know . . . no, not down. We must keep in touch with the ridge. Didn't you see those flutings on this side. We'd never get back up again."

"Have we got past that second summit?"

"I think so, yes."

"I can't see anything up there."

The snow and cloud merged into a uniform blank whiteness. I could see no difference between snow and sky further than five feet from me.

"Wish we had a compass."

As I spoke I noticed a lightening in the cloud above us. The sun, shining weakly through the murk, cast the faintest of shadows on the ridge one hundred feet above us, but before I had a chance to tell Simon, it was gone.

"I've just seen the ridge."

"Where?"

"Straight above us. Can't see a thing now, but I definitely saw it."

"Right, I'll climb up and find it. If you stay here you'll have better luck stopping me if I don't see the edge of the ridge in time."

He set off, and after a short time I had only the ropes

moving through my hands to show me he was there. The snowfall was getting heavier. I felt the first twinges of anxiety. This ridge had turned out to be a lot more serious than we had ever imagined while our attention had been focused on the route up the West Face. I was about to call out to Simon and ask if he could see anything, but the words died on my lips as the ropes suddenly whipped out through my gloves. At the same time a deep, heavy explosion of sound echoed through the clouds. The ropes ran unchecked through my wet icy gloves for a few feet then tugged sharply at my harness, pulling me chest-first into the snow slope. The roaring died away.

I knew at once what had happened. Simon must have fallen through the corniced ridge, yet the volume of sound suggested something more like a serac avalanche. I waited. The ropes remained taut with his body weight.

"Simon!" I yelled. "You okay?"

There was no answer. I decided to wait before attempting to move up toward the ridge. If he was hanging over the west side I reckoned it would be some time before he sorted himself out and managed to regain the ridge. After about fifteen minutes I heard Simon shouting unintelligibly. The weight had come off the rope, and I climbed toward him until I could make out what he was saying.

"I've found the ridge!"

I had gathered *that*, and laughed nervously. He had indeed found a lot more of the ridge than he had bargained for. I stopped grinning when I reached him. He was standing shakily just below the crest.

"I thought I'd had it there," he muttered, suddenly sitting down heavily in the snow as if his legs had failed him. "Bloody hell . . . that was it! The whole bloody thing fell off. God!"

He shook his head as if trying to dislodge what he had just seen. When the fright eased, and his body stopped pumping adrenaline, he looked back at the edge of the ridge, and quietly told me what had happened:

"I never saw the ridge. I just glimpsed an edge of it far away to the left. There was no warning. No crack. One minute I was climbing, the next I was falling. It must have broken away forty feet back from the edge. It broke behind me, I think; or under my feet. Either way it took me down instantly. It was so *fast*! I had no time to think. I didn't know what the hell was going on, except that I was falling."

"I'll bet!" I looked at the drop of the face behind him as he bowed his head and breathed hard, one hand on his thigh trying to stop the telltale tremor in his leg.

"I was tumbling all over the place and everything seemed to be happening in slow motion. I forgot I was tied to the rope. The noise and the falling—it just stopped me understanding anything. I can remember seeing all these huge blocks of snow falling with me, they fell at the same speed at first, and I thought, this is it. They were massive. Ten- . . . twenty-foot-square chunks."

He was calmer now, but I shivered at the thought of what would have happened if I had moved up with him—it would have taken both of us.

"Then I felt the rope at my waist, but I thought it would just come down with me. I wasn't stopping, and all the blocks were smashing against me, flipping me over."

He paused again, then continued: "It was much lighter below me, and the blocks tumbled away from me down an enormous drop of space, spinning and breaking up. I kept getting glimpses of this as the snow walloped into me and spun me round . . . Perhaps I wasn't falling by then, but all the thumping and spinning made it feel as if I was. It seemed to be going on and on and on . . . I wasn't scared then, just totally confused and numb. As if real time was standing still and there was no longer time to be frightened."

When he did finally stop, he was hanging in space, and could see over to his left the ridge still peeling away. The cloud on the east side blocked the view slightly, but great blocks of snow were falling from the cloud and went crashing down the face below, as if the ridge was breaking away from him.

"At first I was so disoriented I wasn't sure whether I was safe or not. I had to think it out before I realised that you had held my fall. The drop below me was horrific. I could see right down the West Face, 4,500 feet, clear all the way to the glacier. I was in a panic for a while. The huge drop had appeared so suddenly beneath me, and I was hanging thirty feet below the ridgeline, not touching the slope. The headwall of the West Face was directly beneath me. I could see our route up the ice field!"

"If that cornice had come down we would just have disappeared without trace," I ventured. "How did you get back?"

"Well, I tried to get back on to the ridge, and it turned out to be one hell of a struggle. The break-line left by the cornice was vertical snow and nearly thirty feet high. I didn't know if what was left after the collapse was safe. When I finally got up I heard you shouting from down on the East Face and I was nearly too tired to answer. I still couldn't see an end to the fresh break-line on the ridge. It seemed close to two hundred feet. Funny how the visibility cleared as soon as I fell. Five minutes later and I would have seen the danger."

We were now faced with a very dangerous ridge which, although it had collapsed, was no safer as a result. We could see secondary fracture lines in the snow just back from the edge, and one particular fracture ran parallel to and only four feet away from the crest for as far as we could see.

On the Edge

There was no question of traversing lower down on the East Face for this was a continuous series of large flutings running down into the clouds which had closed over the void again several hundred feet below us. It had stopped snowing. The flutings would be impossibly slow and dangerous to climb across, and to descend lower would see us lost in the white-out conditions below the cloud. There were few choices left open to us. Simon stood up and began moving gingerly along the crest five feet from the edge, along the continual crack-line running away from us. I moved farther down the East Face to wait until he had taken out all the slack rope. At least then I could stop him if the ridge broke away again, but eventually I would have to join him, and we would move together along the ridge.

As I climbed up to rejoin his tracks it occurred to me that I had felt a moment of anxiety only minutes before Simon had fallen. I had noticed this in the past and always wondered about it. There had been no good reason for the sudden stab of worry. We had been on the mountain for over fifty hours and perhaps had become attuned to potential threats; so much so that I had sensed something would happen without understanding quite what it would be. I didn't like this irrational theory, since anxiety had returned with a vengeance. I could see that Simon had also tensed up. The descent was already far more serious than we had reckoned.

I moved carefully. I watched the crack-line, checked I had put my feet exactly where Simon's footsteps were, and continued nervously 150 feet behind Simon, who had his back to me. I might have a chance if I saw him fall in time. I could throw myself down the opposite side of the ridge and expect the ropes to stop us as they sawed through the ridge. He would have little or no warning. He might hear me scream out, or hear the ridge break, but he would have to turn round to see which side I was falling down before he could jump to the safe side. It seemed to me that the most likely accident would involve the whole ridge collapsing, taking us both down in one very long breakaway of snow.

I saw the crack close up, and when I moved past it I breathed a sigh of relief. The ridge was slightly safer at last. Unfortunately it now dropped away steeply and twisted back on itself with each turn, huge cornices bulging out over the West Face. I saw that these difficulties eased farther in the distance so I wasn't surprised when Simon began descending the East Face. He intended to lose enough height to be able to traverse directly across to the easier section and avoid descending the tortured ridge. The easier ground lay a couple of hundred feet below our point on the ridge. I guessed how far we needed to descend before following Simon down.

We hadn't descended far before I realised how poor the light had become. I checked my watch and was surprised to see that it had gone five o'clock. We had left the summit nearly three and a half hours earlier and yet had made little progress along the ridge. It would be dark in an hour and, to make things more difficult, the storm clouds had boiled over us again and snowflakes were blowing up from the east into our faces. The temperature had also dropped sharply and, with the wind building up, it felt icy cold whenever we stopped.

Simon descended a gully between two flutings. I followed slowly, trying to keep the distance between us by moving only when the ropes moved. I descended into a uniform whiteness,

snow and cloud merging into one. After a while I decided that
we must have reached a point where we could now traverse
horizontally across to the easier ground, but Simon carried on
down. I shouted for him to stop, but received only a muffled
reply. I yelled louder and the ropes stopped moving through
my gloves. Neither of us could understand the other's shouts,
so I moved down to get within earshot. I was alarmed to find
that the gully became steeper and I kept slipping. I turned
round to face into the slope, but it was still hard to remain in
control.

I was close to him when I heard Simon shout again and
could hear his query about why we had stopped. At that
moment the snow whooshed away from under my feet and
I dropped swiftly. I had both axes dug deep into the gully
but they didn't stop me. I screamed a warning, and suddenly bumped heavily against Simon, stopping jammed up
against him.

"Jesus! . . . I . . . Oh shit! I thought we'd had it . . . this is
fucking stupid!"

Simon said nothing. I leant face-first into the gully and
tried to calm down. My heart seemed to be trying to hammer
its way out of my chest, and my legs shook weakly. It had
been fortunate that I was so close to Simon when I fell, not too
far above to have built up enough speed to knock him down.

"You okay?" Simon asked.

"Yes. Scared . . . that's all."

"Yeah."

"We've gone far too low."

"Oh! I was thinking perhaps we could descend all the way
into the eastern glacier bay."

"You're joking! Bloody hell! I've just nearly killed both of
us on this bit, and we haven't a clue what it's like below us."

"But that ridge is crazy. We'll never get down it tonight."

"We're not getting off this tonight, anyway. For God's sake, it's almost dark now. If we rush off down there we'll be lucky if we ever get off this bloody thing."

"Okay . . . okay, calm down. It was just an idea."

"Sorry. I was freaked out. Couldn't we traverse out sideways from here and get back to the ridge where it drops down?"

"Okay . . . you first."

I sorted out the tangles from my fall and then began digging into the right side of the fluting. An hour and a half later I had managed to cross innumerable flutings and gullies, and Simon was following a rope's-length behind me. We had covered less than two hundred feet, and by then it was snowing hard, bitterly cold and windy. It was also dark and we were having to use our head-torches.

Stumbling through a wall of sugary snow and into another gully, I kicked against rock beneath the snow.

"Simon!" I shouted. "Stop where you are a while. There's a small rock wall here. It's a bit tricky getting round it."

I decided to place a rock peg in the wall, and then tentatively balance round the obstacle. I succeeded with the rock peg but somehow managed to fall down and round the wall without coming on to the rope. Simon employed an equally basic climbing technique using gravity and body weight, jumping down the wall without being able to see where he would land, but correct in the assumption that, when he did, it would be with such force that he would safely bury himself firmly in the loose snow beyond. The only flaw I could find in his reasoning was that he didn't know whether his landing would be loose snow or rock! We were too tired and cold by then to care.

Once beyond the rock we crossed an open slope of powder, mercifully without flutings. We were heading back up toward where we guessed the ridge would be, and after a couple of rope-lengths found a large cone of snow swept up against a rock wall. We decided to dig a snow cave.

Simon's head-torch kept flickering from a loose or damaged connection. I began digging and soon struck rock. I tried digging parallel with the rock, to make a long narrow cave, but after half an hour gave up. The cave had so many holes in it that it would provide little protection from the wind. It was bitterly cold, and Simon had struggled to repair his head-torch with his bare fingers, fiddling with the copper contacts in the dark. Digging had kept me warm, despite the temperature falling to around the minus twenty mark, but two of Simon's fingers were frostbitten. He became angry with me when I started to dig another cave. Unjustly, I decided that Simon was behaving petulantly and ignored him. The next site for the cave was marginally better and although I struck rock I managed to build it to fit the two of us. By then Simon had mended the torch but his fingers were beyond rewarming. He was still bristling with anger at my lack of cooperation.

I prepared the meal. There was little enough left. We ate chocolate and dried fruit and drank a lot of fruit juice. By then we had forgotten our tired anger and regained a sense of perspective. I had been as cold and tired as Simon, and had only wanted a cave dug quickly so that we could get into our sleeping bags and make some hot drinks. It had been another very long day. It had started well, and we had been glad to get off the West Face, but the descent had become increasingly difficult and nerve-racking. Falling over the cornice had shaken both of us, and the strain afterward had been wearing. We had got angry enough with each other today, and more of the same wouldn't help.

Simon showed me his fingers, which had slowly come back to life. But the index finger on each hand remained white

and solid as far back as the first knuckle. So he had frostbite. I
hoped it would not suffer further damage the next day. However, I felt sure that we were close to the end of the difficulties
on the ridge, and that we would be able to reach base camp by
the following afternoon. We only had enough gas left for two
drinks in the morning, but that should be enough. As I settled
myself down for sleep I couldn't shake off the dread feelings
I had experienced while traversing the ridge. The image of
the two of us falling helplessly down the East Face, still
roped together, had all too nearly come true. I shuddered at
the prospect of such an end. I knew Simon must have felt the
same. The year before he had witnessed just such a terrible
accident at the Croz Spur, high in the Mont Blanc range of
the French Alps. Two Japanese climbers had fallen to their
deaths from close to where he stood, only a short distance
from the top of the route.

For three days there, stormy weather had produced atro-
cious conditions. The rocks were plastered in verglas, a hard
patina of ice covering the holds and filling the cracks. Progress
had been painfully slow as each hold was chipped clear, and
otherwise easy sections had become desperately extreme
climbing. Simon and his partner, Jon Sylvester, had bivouacked
twice on the face, and late in the afternoon of that third day,
another storm was building up—the temperature plummeting,
heavy clouds shrouding them in a world of their own, and the
first spindrift powder snow avalanches sweeping down.

The two Japanese climbers had been following them
closely. They had bivouacked separately, and there was no
communication between the two teams, nor was there any
sense of competitiveness or a suggestion that they might join
forces. Both parties were coping equally well in the difficult
conditions. There were frequent falls, often from the same
points. They had watched one another struggle, fall, and try
again as they progressed up the face.

When they reached the summit headwall, Simon had seen the leading Japanese climber fall outward and backward, arms outstretched in surprise. The awesome 2,500-foot plunge, visible through breaks in the cloud, was framed behind him. To his horror, he had then seen the falling leader jerk and twist and, without a sound, pull his partner into the void. Their belay piton had torn free. The two men plunged down, roped together, helpless.

Simon had struggled up to Jon's stance, which was out of sight of that lower section, and told him what had happened. They stood quietly on the small rock ledge in the gathering storm trying to absorb the enormity of what had just taken place so close to them. There was nothing they could do for the two men, who would never have survived the fall, and the quickest way to get news to the rescue services would be over the summit and down into Italy.

As they resumed the climb they were shocked to hear a ghastly screaming from far below—the chilling sounds of someone in agony, desperately alone and terrified. Looking down, they saw the two climbers sliding down the upper ice field at ever-increasing speed six hundred feet below them. They were still roped together, and various scattered items of gear and their rucksacks tumbled alongside them. All Simon could do was to stare helplessly at the two tiny figures racing down the ice. Then they were gone: disappearing over the lip of the ice field, falling out of view into the horrendous drop to the glacier.

By some desperate quirk at least one of the climbers must have survived the initial fall on to the ice field. Somehow they had been stopped, probably with their rope snagged on some rocky projection—but they weren't saved. It was a cruel twist, both for the victims and for the horrified spectators far above them. Only a short reprieve, five minutes or so, while one of them fought to make himself safe and find some anchor.

Badly injured, he had had little chance. Perhaps he had slipped, or the rope had unsnagged: whatever had happened, the outcome was brutally final.

Simon and Jon, their confidence shattered, minds numbed by it all, had turned and struggled on up to the summit. It had been so sudden. They hadn't conversed with the two Japanese, but a mutual understanding and respect had developed. If they had all got down safely, then they would have talked, shared food on the long walk to the valley, met up in a bar in town, perhaps become friends.

I could remember seeing Simon walking slowly into the campsite outside Chamonix when he got back. He was subdued and looked drawn and tired. He had sat numb, repeatedly questioning why his own tumble had been held on the same piton just before the Japanese leader had fallen and ripped it out. A day later he was his normal self again: an experience absorbed, shelved in his memory, understood and accepted, and left at that.

As sleep crept swiftly through me I tried to shake off the thought of how close we had come to the same appalling end as those two Japanese. There would have been no one to watch us, I thought: as if it would have made any difference.

I had the stove burning away cheerfully by my side, and could look beyond it through a hole in the snow cave. The East Face of Yerupaja was framed perfectly in the circular window I had accidentally built into the cave. The early-morning sun etched the ridgelines with shadows, and danced blue shadings down the edges of the flutings on the face. For the first time in the last four days the tense concentration in my body relaxed. The anxious struggles of the previous night had been forgotten, and the memory of how close we had come to falling to our deaths had faded. I gave myself time to enjoy where I was, and to congratulate myself. I craved a cigarette.

It was cramped in the snow hole, but infinitely warmer than in the previous one. Simon was still asleep, lying on his side close by me, facing away. His hips and shoulders pressed up against my side, and I could feel his body warmth seeping through my sleeping bag. The close intimacy seemed odd despite how together we had been on the mountain. I moved carefully to avoid waking him. I looked through the round hole window at the East Face and felt myself smiling. I knew it would be a good day.

The gas was all used up in the breakfast routine and there would be no more water until we got down to the lakes below the moraines. I dressed and geared up first, before climbing out of the cave and going over to the first cave I had attempted to dig. Simon was slow getting ready, and it wasn't until he joined me on the large platform of the collapsed cave that I remembered his frostbite. My good humour vanished, to be replaced by worry, when he showed his fingers to me. One fingertip was blackened and three other fingers were white and wooden in appearance. Funny how my anxiety seemed to have more to do with whether he would be able to carry on climbing after we got down rather than concern for his injuries.

I started up toward the crest of the ridge which was bathed in sunshine half a rope's-length above me while Simon remained below guarding the ropes. We were both nervous about the possibility of another cornice collapse. When I reached the ridge I was dismayed to see that there was a long section of tortured cornices and knife-edge powder to negotiate. My hope that we might have bypassed it all the day before evaporated. I shouted a warning down to Simon and he agreed to follow me, moving together, once all the rope had run out.

Though we moved with exaggerated caution, we couldn't avoid slipping and falling, only half in control, down the worst sections. I stayed close to the top of the ridge, which kept curling back on itself and dropping suddenly in short steep walls. The possibility of a cornice collapse gradually faded from my mind as I moved, and I became resigned to the helplessness of our situation. The flutings lower down the East Face would almost certainly be a worse proposition. As great a danger as the cornices was the risk of a fall. Any fall requiring a rope to stop it was going to be fatal; neither of us would stand a chance. Yet every time I approached a steep section and was forced to back-climb facing into the snow I usually did so by a combination of falling and climbing. The powder was so insubstantial that, however hard I kicked my legs, I would whoosh down a few feet as soon as I got my weight off my arms. Each sudden, heart-stopping slide seemed somehow to halt of its own accord. Where I would stop would be no more solid than where I had fallen from. It wore one's nerves ragged.

I slipped again, but this time yelped out in fright. The short steep slope I was descending bottomed directly on to the edge of the ridge, which had curved back on itself. I had seen as I turned to face into the slope that a huge powdery cornice bulged out beneath this curve, and falling away below it the West Face plunged thousands of feet down to the glacier. Simon, moving a full rope's-length behind me, was out of sight and would have no warning; no idea which side I was falling down. I rushed down in a flurry of powder so fast that my yelp came out more as a squeak of alarm than an attempted warning cry. Simon didn't see the fall, and heard nothing.

Then, just as suddenly, I stopped, with my whole body pressed into the snow, head buried in it, with my arms and legs spread-eagled in a desperate crabbed position. I dared not move. It seemed as if only luck was holding me on to the slope, and feeling the snow moving and sliding down past my stomach and thighs just made me cringe in deeper.

I lifted my head and glanced sideways over my right shoulder. I was on the very edge of the ridge, exactly at the point of the curve. My body was tipped over to the right so that I seemed to be hanging out over the West Face. All my thoughts became locked into not moving. I gasped fast breaths, scared sucks at the air, but I didn't move. When I looked again I realised that I wasn't actually off-balance, although the brief glance before had made me think I was. It was like discovering the trick behind an optical illusion, suddenly seeing what you had really been staring at all the time. The curve of the ridge away back to my left, and the glimpse of the bulging cornice under its arc, had confused me so much that I had thought I was leaning over the fall line. In fact I found that my right leg had punctured straight through the cornice and, though my other leg had stopped me, it had also pushed me over sideways. This explained why I felt unbalanced, right side down. I scrabbled and clawed at the snow on my left, trying to pull my weight over to that side, trying to get my right leg back on to the ridge. Eventually I succeeded and moved away from the edge, following the curve of the ridge again.

Simon appeared above me, moving slowly, looking down at his feet all the time. I had moved to a safer place and shouted a warning for him to descend the slope further to the left, and realised as I did so that I was shaking violently. My legs had gone to sudden jelly, quivering, and it took a long while for the reaction to fade. Long enough for me to watch Simon face into the slope and descend it in two footsteps and the inevitable rushing slide. When he turned and followed my steps I could see the tension in his face. The day was neither enjoyable nor funny, and when he reached me the fear was infectious. We chattered out our alarm in quavery voices; quick staccato curses and repeated phrases tumbling out before we calmed.

444   JOE SIMPSON

Disaster

We had left the snow hole at seven thirty, and two and a half
hours later I could see that our progress was painfully slow.
Since leaving the summit the previous afternoon we had
descended no more than one thousand feet instead of getting
all the way down to the glacier in the six hours which we had
reckoned. I began to feel impatient. I was tired of this grinding need to concentrate all the time. The mountain had lost
its excitement, its novelty, and I wanted to get off it as soon
as possible. The air was bitingly cold and the sky cloudless;
the sun burnt down in a dazzling glare on the endless snow
and ice. As long as we were back on the glacier before the
afternoon storms I didn't care a damn what the weather chose
to do.

At last the twisting mayhem of the upper ridge eased, and I
could walk upright across the broad level ridge which undu-
lated away in whale-backed humps toward the drop at its
northern end. Simon caught up with me as I rested on my
sack. We didn't speak. The morning had already taken its toll,
and there was nothing left to say. Looking up at our footsteps
weaving an unsteady path down toward us, I vowed silently
to be more careful about checking descent routes in future.

I shouldered my sack and set off again, with no qualms
about being in front now. I had wanted Simon to lead on the
last stretch but had been unable to voice my apprehension
and feared his response to it more than I feared another sickening fall. Deep snow had built up on the wide level saddle,
and instead of anxiety swamping my every move I was back
to the frustration of wallowing through powder snow.

I had run out the rope, and Simon was getting up to follow
when I stepped into the first crevasse.

In a rushing drop, I suddenly found myself standing upright

but with my eyes level with the snow. The shallow fissure was filled with powder, so that however hard I thrashed about I seemed to make no upward movement at all. Eventually I managed to haul myself back on to level ground. From a safe distance Simon had watched my struggles with a grin on his face. I moved farther along the ridge and sank down again neck-deep in the snow. I yelled and cursed as I clawed my way back on to the ridge and, by the time I had traversed halfway across the plateau above it, I had fallen into another four small crevasses. However hard I tried, I could not see any telltale marks indicating their presence. Simon was following a full rope's-length behind. Frustration and the mounting exhaustion maddened me to a fury which I knew would be vented on Simon if he came close enough.

Then, crouching beside the hole I had just made, trying to regain my breath, I glanced back and was shocked to see clear through the ridge into the yawning abyss below. Blue-white light gleamed up through the hole from the expanse of the West Face, which I could see looming beneath it. Suddenly it clicked in my brain why I had fallen through so many times. It was all one crevasse, one long fracture line cutting right through the enormous humping cornices that made up the plateau. I moved quickly away to the side and shouted a warning to Simon. The rolling ridge had been so wide and flat it had never occurred to me that we might actually be standing on an overhanging cornice, one as large as the summit cornice, but stretching for several hundred feet. If it had collapsed we would have gone with it.

I kept well back from the edge after that, leaving a healthy margin of fifty feet. Simon had fallen with the smaller cornice collapse when he was forty feet back from the edge. There was no point in taking chances now that the flutings on the east side had eased into a uniformly smooth slope. My legs felt leaden trudging through the deep snow toward the end of the plateau. As I crested the last rise in the ridge and glanced back, I saw Simon hauling himself along in the same head-down dog-tired manner as myself, a full rope's-length from me, 150 feet away, and I knew he would be out of sight once I began descending the long, easy-angled slope ahead.

I had hoped to see the slope run down to the col but was disappointed to find it rising slightly to a minor summit of cornices before dropping steeply down again. Even so, I could see enough of the South Ridge of Yerupaja to know that the col would certainly lie immediately below that next drop, and then we would be at the lowest point on the ridge connecting Yerupaja and Siula Grande. Another half hour would put us on that col, and it would be easy going from there to the glacier. I perked up.

Starting down, I felt at once the change in angle. It was so much easier than the plod along the saddle, and I would have romped happily down the gentle slope but for the rope tugging insistently at my waist. I had forgotten that Simon would still be wearily following my tracks on the saddle.

I had expected to be able to take a direct line to the small rise without encountering any obstacles, and was surprised to find that the slope ended abruptly in an ice cliff. It cut right across my path at right angles, bisecting the ridge. I approached the edge cautiously and peered over a twenty-five-foot drop. The slope at its base swept down to the right in a smooth, steeply angled face. Beyond that lay the last rise on the ridge, about two hundred feet away. The height of the cliff increased rapidly as it cut away from the ridge. I stood roughly midpoint on this wedge of ice running across the ridge, with its narrow edge abutting the ridgeline. I traversed carefully away from the ridge, occasionally looking over the cliff to see if there was any weakness in the wall, which stood thirty-five feet high at its end. I had already discounted the possibility of abseiling past the cliff, for the snow at the top of the cliff was too loose to take an ice stake.

There were two options open to me. Either I could stay on the ridgetop or I could continue away from it and hope to by-pass the steep section by a wide descending traverse. From where I stood at the end of the cliff I could see that this would be very tiring and risky. We would have to detour in a wide arc down, across, and then back up again, to bypass the cliff. The initial slope down looked very steep and very unstable. I had had enough of slip-sliding around this ridge, and the empty sweep thousands of feet into the eastern glacier bay below the slope nudged me into decision. If either of us fell we would be on open slopes. We wouldn't stop. At least on the ridge we had been able to kid ourselves that we could, with luck, jump either side of the apex in the event of a fall.

I retraced my steps, intending to climb down the cliff at the easiest point. I knew this would be impossible near the crest of the ridge since there it was a near-vertical wall of powder snow. I needed to find a weakness in the cliff, a ramp line or a crevasse running down the cliff to give me some purchase on the ice, which appeared solid to within a few yards of the edge of the ridge. At last I saw what I was looking for—a very slight break in the angle of the ice wall. This part of the cliff was still steep, nearly vertical, but not quite. It was about twenty feet high at the break and I felt sure that at this point a few quick moves of reverse climbing would see me past the problem.

Crouching down on my knees, I turned my back to the cliff edge and managed to get my axes to bite in deeply. Slowly, I lowered my legs over the cliff until the edge was against my stomach and I could kick my crampons into the ice wall below me. I felt them bite and hold. Removing one axe, I hammered it in again very close to the edge. It held fast and solid. I removed my ice hammer and lowered my chest and shoulders over the edge until I could see the ice wall and swing at it with the hammer. I was hanging on to the ice axe, reaching to my side to place the hammer solidly into the wall with my left hand. I got it to bite after a few blows but wasn't happy about it and removed it to try again. I wanted it to be perfect before I removed the axe embedded in the lip and lowered myself on to the hammer. As the hammer came out there was a sharp cracking sound and my right hand, gripping the axe, pulled down. The sudden jerk turned me outward and instantly I was falling.

I hit the slope at the base of the cliff before I saw it coming. I was facing into the slope and both knees locked as I struck it. I felt a shattering blow in my knee, felt bones splitting, and screamed. The impact catapulted me over backward and down the slope of the East Face. I slid, headfirst, on my back. The rushing speed of it confused me. I thought of the drop below but felt nothing. Simon would be ripped off the mountain. He couldn't hold this. I screamed again as I jerked to a sudden violent stop.

Everything was still, silent. My thoughts raced madly. Then pain flooded down my thigh—a fierce burning fire coming down the inside of my thigh, seeming to ball in my groin, building and building until I cried out at it, and my breathing came in ragged gasps. My leg! Oh Jesus. My leg!

I hung, head down, on my back, left leg tangled in the rope above me and my right leg hanging slackly to one side. I lifted my head from the snow and stared, up across my chest, at a grotesque distortion in the right knee, twisting the leg into a strange zigzag. I didn't connect it with the pain which burnt my groin. That had nothing to do with my knee. I kicked my left leg free of the rope and swung round until I was hanging against the snow on my chest, feet down. The pain eased. I kicked my left foot into the slope and stood up.

A wave of nausea surged over me. I pressed my face into the snow, and the sharp cold seemed to calm me. Something terrible, something dark with dread occurred to me, and as I thought about it I felt the dark thought break into panic: "I've broken my leg, that's it. I'm dead. Everyone said it . . . if there's just two of you a broken ankle could turn into a death sentence . . . if it's broken . . . if . . . It doesn't hurt so much, maybe I've just ripped something."

I kicked my right leg against the slope, feeling sure it wasn't broken. My knee exploded. Bone grated, and the fireball rushed from groin to knee. I screamed. I looked down at the knee and could see it was broken, yet I tried not to believe what I was seeing. It wasn't just broken, it was ruptured, twisted, crushed, and I could see the kink in the joint and knew what had happened. The impact had driven my lower leg up through the knee joint.

Oddly enough, looking at it seemed to help. I felt detached from it, as if I were making a clinical observation of someone else. I moved the knee gingerly, experimenting with it. I tried to bend it and stopped immediately, gasping at the rush of pain. When it moved I felt a grinding crunch; bone had moved, and a lot more besides. At least it wasn't an open fracture. I knew this as soon as I tried to move. I could feel no wetness, no blood. I reached down and caressed the knee with my right hand, trying to ignore the stabs of fire, so that I could feel it with enough force to be certain I wasn't bleeding. It was in one solid piece, but it felt huge, and twisted—and not mine. The pain kept flooding round it, pouring on fire, as if that might cure it then and there.

With a groan I squeezed my eyes tight shut. Hot tears filled my eyes and my contact lenses swam in them. I squeezed tight again and felt hot drops rolling over my face. It wasn't the pain, I felt sorry for myself, childishly so, and with that thought I couldn't help the tears. Dying had seemed so far away, and yet now everything was tinged with it. I shook my head to stop the tears, but the taint was still there.

I dug my axes into the snow, and pounded my good leg deeply into the soft slope until I felt sure it wouldn't slip. The effort brought back the nausea and I felt my head spin giddily to the point of fainting. I moved and a searing spasm of pain cleared away the faintness. I could see the summit of Seria Norte away to the west. I was not far below it. The sight drove home how desperately things had changed. We were above nineteen thousand feet, still on the ridge, and very much alone. I looked south at the small rise I had hoped to scale quickly and it seemed to grow with every second that I stared. I would never get over it. Simon would not be able to get me up it. He would leave me. He had no choice. I held my breath, thinking about it. Left here? Alone? I felt cold at the thought. I remembered Rob, who had been left to die . . . but Rob had been unconscious, had been dying. I had only a bad leg. Nothing to kill me. For an age I felt overwhelmed at the notion of being left; I felt like screaming, and I felt like swearing, but stayed silent. If I said a word I would panic. I could feel myself teetering on the edge of it.

The rope which had been tight on my harness went slack. Simon was coming! He must know something had happened, I thought, but what shall I tell him? If I told him that I had only hurt my leg and not broken it, would that make him help me? My mind raced at the prospect of telling him that I was hurt. I pressed my face into the cold snow again and tried to think calmly. I had to cool it. If he saw me panicky and hysterical he might give up at once. I fought to stem my fears. Be rational about it, I thought. I felt myself calm down, and my breathing became steady; even the pain seemed tolerable.

"What happened? Are you okay?"

I looked up in surprise. I hadn't heard his approach. He

stood at the top of the cliff looking down at me, puzzled. I made an effort to talk normally, as if nothing had happened:

"I fell. The edge gave way." I paused, then I said as unemotionally as I could: "I've broken my leg."

His expression changed instantly. I could see a whole range of reactions in his face. I kept looking directly at him. I wanted to miss nothing.

"Are you sure it's broken?"

"Yes."

He stared at me. It seemed that he looked harder and longer than he should have done because he turned away sharply. Not sharply enough though. I had seen the look come across his face briefly, but in that instant I knew his thoughts. He had an odd air of detachment. I felt unnerved by it, felt suddenly quite different from him, alienated. His eyes had been full of thoughts. Pity. Pity and something else; a distance given to a wounded animal which could not be helped. He had tried to hide it, but I had seen in, and I looked away full of dread and worry.

"I'll abseil down to you."

He had his back to me, bending over a snow stake, digging down through the soft snow. He sounded matter-of-fact, and I wondered whether I was being unduly paranoid. I waited for him to say more, but he remained silent and I wondered what he was thinking. A short but very dangerous abseil from a poorly anchored snow stake put him down next to me quickly.

He stood close by me and said nothing. I had seen him glance at my leg but he made no comment. After some searching he found a packet of paracetamols and handed me two pills. I swallowed them, and watched him trying to pull the abseil rope down. It refused to move. It had jammed in the snow bollard that he had dug around the snow stake above. Simon swore and set off toward the point where the wall was smallest, right on the crest of the ridge. I knew it was all unstable powder and so did he, but he had no choice. I looked away, unwilling to watch what I was sure would be a fatal fall down the West Face. Indirectly it would kill me as well, only a little more slowly.

Simon had said nothing about what he would do, and I had been nervous to prompt him. In an instant an uncrossable gap had come between us and we were no longer a team working together.

Postscript: Simon Yates eventually left Joe Simpson for dead, and four days later Simpson literally dragged himself into base camp as Yates was about to leave. After Simpson recovered, he was back in the mountains, climbing.

In 1976 two British mountaineers, Joe Tasker and Peter
Boardman, undertook the challenge of climbing the treacherous West Face of the 22,520-foot Changabang in the Indian
Garhwal Himalayas. Many consider this to be the most difficult technical climb in the entire Himalayas. Joe Tasker's
memoir is a classic of the genre, and a stark reminder of the
horrifying risks encountered by those who reach high places.

SAVAGE ARENA

JOE TASKER

We spent a week carrying food
and equipment up to a camp close to the foot of the mountain.
It was a four-hour walk from fifteen thousand feet to seventeen thousand feet, back along the route I had staggered down
in my delirium from Dunagiri. The loads we carried weighed
between thirty and forty pounds, requiring quite an effort at
that altitude but providing a useful chance to adjust to the
more rarified air, and accustom ourselves to rigorous physical
exercise. It allowed us also to grow familiar with the mountain, and to scrutinise at different times of the day each little
feature.

We came to accept the idea of being alone with each other.
Dick and I had gone onto Dunagiri almost straightaway, so I

had not noticed the isolation so much. I knew Pete less and there were many idiosyncrasies we each had for which we both had to make allowances. I noticed how Pete used to make copious entries into a diary, so many that I could not visualise how he could do or say anything without the awareness that he was going to record that action or word. I had found after Dunagiri the value of recording the days as they passed, in order to keep track of time, and I made one-line notes in the form of a diary. Pete was sceptical of the value of this at all as an aid to remembering events. I countered this by his own tactic of quoting, for greater authority, from other authors, saying that Graham Greene had written that as an author it was not trying to remember things that was difficult but trying to forget them. I could only just remember this saying and Pete was dubious about its authenticity.

We dug a ledge for a tent on the crest of the ridge where it ran into the steepest part of the west face. Above was the inscrutable wall, the first few hundred feet of which was not vertical and looked feasible to climb. Reaching the crest of the ridge had opened up a panorama of peaks, diluting to some extent the sense of confinement we both felt on the glacier, surrounded by steep slopes of ice or rock. I did not mind so much as Pete, who verbalised his frustration at having such a restricted horizon. Perhaps it was that I had surveyed the mountains for so long on Dunagiri and now I could see them in my mind's eye. Pete had read about the mountains, knew more about them than I did even though he had not visited them previously, and felt cheated that he had not even glimpsed Nanda Devi, which was shrouded in cloud when we were walking within sight of it. Partly I was defensive over his complaints, as if he was comparing "my" mountains with "his" mountains, the mountains he had been to before; partly I was apprehensive that his complaints were the beginnings of disillusionment.

We worked from the tent for days, learning more about the climb and about each other. We made progress sufficient to postpone any basic questioning about our overall chances of success. As the wall steepened, we made slower but still steady progress, fixing a line of ropes up from the tent, adding more ropes each day as we pressed on further, and slipping back down those ropes each evening to the haven of the tent. The days were hard but, dressed up in a routine, acceptable because we only had to think a little at a time.

The rock was sound granite, not loose and unreliable as on Dunagiri. Runnels of ice clung firmly to the grooves in the rock. Deciding which way to go was complex, and solving the problems of each section was both mentally and physically taxing. At first I felt conscious of Pete's critical observation when I led a pitch. I noticed an assumption of superiority in his performance and an authoritarian attitude in his climbing techniques and manoeuvres which I put down to his days of instructing. When I paused, working out a move, or summoning up the nerve to commit myself to an unpredictable position, I imagined him champing at the bit and thinking he could have led the pitch so much better or faster than me.

It was when not actually climbing that I noticed his inadequacies. He always took longer to arrange things to make himself comfortable, always found I had something or contrived something that he had not, such as a pillow from coils of rope, or my boots pushed together, and he gave off an air of being badly done by. He was nervous of situations where I relaxed, knowing that we had done all possible to make ourselves safe and dismissing as pointless any further worrying. Pete ended up sleeping on the side of the tent nearest the edge of the ledge and he often voiced his uneasiness at the thousand-foot precipice inches away from him.

We fell into a pattern of defined roles. Pete stirred himself first in the morning and made breakfast; I lingered in sleep, hiding from another day, for as long as possible. At evening I busied myself with the main meal, while Pete flopped into the back of the tent, glad to rest immediately from the day's exertions.

The climbing was mostly a delight, exhausting but enough inside our capabilities to encourage our optimism. We shared the leads, each of us leading four rope-lengths at a time. The difficulties, however, were time-consuming, so we managed only more than four rope-lengths on the first day, and Pete had been in the lead all day. After that it became normal for one of us to spend the whole day out in front whilst the other spent the whole day paying out the rope and following the sections more rapidly once the rope was in place.

I spent an afternoon on a ledge six inches wide and two feet long, while Pete moved upward, ever so slowly toward a barrier of overhangs. The mist came in and he was lost to sight, though no more than a hundred feet away. Hours went by and I had no thoughts left to fill the time. The wind was too strong to let words be heard. I tried to shout information into the mist but heard no reply. There was little rope left to pay out and if he did not halt soon he would be stopped from moving further by the restriction of the rope. I could faintly hear scraping sounds of metal on rock and snatches of words shredded by the wind. I thought I could see a figure near the overhangs when the mist thinned momentarily. I untied the parts of the rope I was using to tie myself to pitons and spikes of rock, freeing a few feet more. Again the rope came tight but I heard the positive sound of a hammer firmly striking a piton and knew he was safe. It was late in the day, Pete arrived out of the mist, having anchored the rope to the piton at his highest point. He told me how hard and worrying it had all been up there in the mist, about the rock becoming increasingly steeper, the cracks getting fainter and how far he had had to go without any assurance of reaching a place to rest, tiring all the time, knowing that he was coming to the end of the rope. That was a worry and fear he was up to, that was when he came into his own, when facing difficulties he could solve by superlative skill and dangers he could ignore in the concentration needed to solve the problem, or put up with in the knowledge that he was committed to a test of skill which he welcomed. He was a different person when climbing from the one who slept uneasily by the side of a steep drop, no matter how securely he was tied in place.

It came about that the two most difficult pitches up to that point were in Pete's rota of leading. I spent three hours next day under the shadow of the overhangs, watching and freezing while Pete struggled, only feet away in the sunlight, to find a solution to the biggest problem we had yet met. The barrier of overhangs spanned the whole area above us. If we could not find a way through then we would have to start all over again. The previous day Pete had moved rightward toward where the overhangs formed a notch at the top of the rounded corner where the wall curved out of sight. He had not seen round the corner, but had been forced in that direction by the impossibility of climbing leftward or straight up.

Now he was exploring the unknown. I could see only the lower half of his body and hear his grunts and imprecations. He could not tell me more than that he could see the next few feet were all right, though difficult. The rest was out of sight round more steps of overhangs. I watched his legs twitch upward out of my range of vision and heard him hammering more pitons in to aid his progress. I dabbled my own foot in the sunlight which touched the slab on which I was standing, a captive tied to the shadows, hoping some of the warmth would creep up my leg into my frozen body. I was disgruntled that it was my turn again to be second on the rope with none of the thrill of breaking new ground and not even warmth from physical exertion, but each of us had to accept a turn in this secondary role every other day. It had been absorbed into my subconscious many years before that physical discomfort was a valuable penance and I sometimes wondered whether our penances and frequent deprival of physical pleasure did indeed benefit our souls and make us better people.

I was frustratingly out of touch with what Pete was doing. No longer able to see any part of him, I became dissatisfied with his uninformative replies to questions with which I could not help pestering him. I longed to have a go myself, unable to comprehend why he was taking so long if it was, as he said, possible.

When at last I could move I was stiff with cold: I was clumsy and awkward in the contortions needed to follow the tortuous line of the rope through the overhangs and up to join Pete at the top of an icy ramp. Justifiably he was proud of breaking through that barrier, finding the vital link to bring us within reach of the vast ice field at mid-height on the mountain. Justifiably he expected praise and pragmatically I thought he had only done his job, much as he made breakfast and I cooked tea; another time it would be my turn and all I could manage was "Good lead, mate." It was an enormous psychological boost to reach that ice field. We were halfway to achieving what we had thought might be impossible, and by the time we had skirted up its left edge and anchored the ropes to its top rim, our thoughts had changed to knowing that we could do it. The wall above the ice field looked equally hard and a huge tower looked more difficult still, but we had found confidence in the progress we had made and no longer had such doubts as we had started with.

It took almost a week of climbing every day to reach the top of the ice field at half-height on the wall. We had brought along a thousand feet of rope at Pete's suggestion to fix on the mountain. This was one of the results of his applying his mind to the problems of the mountain and based on his experiences of the value of fixed rope on Everest.

At the top rim of the ice field I stood drawing in the rope as Pete came up toward me. I had skirted the left edge of ice, which was green and hard, contriving a way up the little ripples in the smooth rock slabs at the side. It was a delicate tiptoe all the time on the verge of insecurity which I revelled in as each gamble of a move paid off. It was nothing like as strenuous as the pitches Pete had led earlier, but every few movements upward had left me panting from the exertion. I watched Pete as he followed up the rope, retrieving all the intermediate anchor points, leaving only the main one at the bottom, since we needed to reuse the pitons and karabiners time and again. I held my camera ready with my eye to the viewfinder, composing the shot in the frame, waiting for Pete to move into a dynamic pose. The pose was not right but I took a shot in case something should prevent me taking a better one, and readied the camera again. He moved up, into a better position this time, I squeezed the shutter, but his head had sunk to his arm as he panted for breath, still not the pose I looked for, but it was real, showing the agony of climbing at altitude. Pete looked up, hearing the click of the shutter, and shouted, "If you take another shot of me like this I'll come up there and thump you," and the day turned black for me. I was sickened at what I regarded as a childish fit of temper; I wondered whether he wanted only photographs to be taken showing him in his best light; he already had pictures of me in similar pose. The fragile, often begrudging rapport which had held us together was for me destroyed; a sense of aimlessness and futility overwhelmed me; we were both far apart however well we had done so far with the climb. What little joy I had felt on reaching the upper edge of the ice field, our halfway stage, the confirmation that we could probably climb this mountain, all vanished. I felt empty and rebuffed. I looked forward no more to the upper part of the mountain, I simply wanted it to be over with.

Pete was repentant and I held back from catalysing the incident further, noting in my diary, "This is no place for an argument." I had had a glimpse of a Pete I had not suspected before, in whom there was anger so close to the surface, and knew that he too, despite the diplomacy and urbanity, was as subject to the stresses and strains of the mountain situation as anyone.

An element of noncooperative, mute hostility arose in things which did not matter such as whose turn it was to make an extra cup of tea, but we were both aware of the strange circumstances in which we were living and of the inevitable tensions which were arising. It became a practice to defuse situations by putting a perspective onto confrontations by a comment relating back to normal life. "Don't worry, it will be all right and won't matter when we get back down to the valley," was a catchphrase we both took to using.

Our days consisted by this time of several hours of tiring, anxious ascent up the hundreds of feet of the single line of rope we had fastened in place. Then hours of taxing climbing, with long, fraught abseils back down the rope, down more hundreds of feet, to the tent at the end of the day. Under these circumstances we could not escape from strain; the high tension which sparked off arguments came from the same highly strung frame of mind which enabled us to keep up the concentration to solve the problems of the climb we had started on with such doubts. The magnificence of our situation, the beauty of the sun setting behind the cloud-wreathed Dunagiri, my old adversary, the deep blue of the sky on a cloudless day and the descent in the rosy glow of evening were all phenomena only partially observed, scarcely appreciated, in a corner of my mind and recorded by photograph for a time when I could view them in comfort.

We had not intended to make a line of rope all the way up the mountain, but thought we might have to prepare difficult sections first, fasten rope in place, and then return for a mobile assault with the hammocks. All the mountain was difficult and we wished we had had more rope to leave in place. We added up all the lengths of extra climbing ropes we had brought with us and found we had nearly two thousand feet. We just managed to stretch this out to reach from Camp 1 on the ridge to the top of the ice field. From there we descended to rest and return with more food and the hammocks.

Our stay at Base Camp was only overnight and we returned to the mountain the next day. There had been a rumour in Joshimath that an American expedition was coming to attempt Dunagiri and would have a Base Camp near us. We had descended in anticipation of meeting them but there was no sign of anyone. The note we had left outside our solitary tent addressed to any passersby was untouched. I rewrote the note, changing the date of departure and expected date of return; I entered details of the point we had reached on the mountain. Of course there were no passersby, our valley was a cul-de-sac ending at Changabang, but if we should disappear forever, without intending any melodrama, we were leaving details of our last location to avoid as many as possible of those uncertainties which make death in the mountains even more fraught for those one leaves behind.

For three weeks now Pete and I had known no other company. A little note from anyone who had trekked up to our camp would have delighted us; the discovery that we had new neighbours in the shape of another expedition would have let

me feel that our partnership, though it seemed to us intense
and jaded, had achieved much and was working well. Meeting more people would have brought more normality into our
closed world.

We took hammocks back with us, having, as we had suspected, spied no trace of a ledge wide enough to take a tent.
On the way back we disagreed about the weather prospects.
Pete had a similar drive to Dick, and seemed untroubled by
any tendency to welcome an enforced delay in returning, so
when we paused to contemplate the heavy cloud and snow
flurries, he won the day, as I knew that at least half of my proposal to defer departure was due to laziness. But bad weather
did come in force. We were caught, late in the afternoon,
hopelessly ambitious to regain the top of the ice field.

We had bypassed Camp 1, with loads much too heavy,
and reached only halfway up the fixed ropes, before dusk and
storm overtook us. It took three hours to produce one mug
each of warm water with the stove perched exposed to the
wind. Conversation was terse and to the point. We abandoned further wretched attempts at cooking in the wind and
snow. It was time for the hammocks to be tried in earnest. We
each attached a hammock by its single suspension point to the
line of rope we had fixed in place over the previous week, and
which we were now following back up the mountainside. Pete
was suspended a few feet below me and I was pleased to
notice that a large flake of rock protruded beneath me; I cherished the notion that if a falling lump of ice should cut
through the rope whilst I was sleeping I might be caught on
the flake or rock rather than fall all the way down.

The hammocks were the full length of our bodies. Three
straps from each side were designed to hold a person securely
in the hammock in a horizontal position. The straps converged on one point so that in such places as mountainsides

where it is rare to find two convenient points to which to attach a conventional hammock, we could suspend the hammock from that single point. The material was nylon with a thin layer of insulating foam. We had brought synthetic sleeping bags to use in the hammocks, as down compresses too much under pressure and is then less effective against the cold. To cover the hammock we had a cape of nylon which draped over the straps and could be clipped in place with elasticated straps beneath the main part of the hammock. In the cold store we had found that we were crushed by the effect of our own body weights which tended to pull the straps together, so we had made some light alloy rods to hold the straps apart, but for our first night of using the hammocks in earnest we did not have the essential rods as they were up at our high point.

It was an awkward and uncoordinated night. Real mountain cold and discomfort made a mockery of using the hammocks. Inserting myself into mine was exhausting. I lay panting on my back, and struggled further to take my boots off. Any time my movements caused the canopy and the base of the hammock to part, gusts of snow-filled wind jetted in from the night. I tied my boots onto the hammock so as not to lose them and, still on my back, pulled my sleeping bag over my feet and along my body. I took a sleeping pill to deaden the discomfort and woke some hours later to find the foot of my sleeping bag hanging outside in the cold and my feet numb. The night stretched endlessly to that point in time when dawn would bring movement and the hope of warmth. Any change seemed desirable. Our situation could not have been worse. Snow squirted in through the slightest parting; I felt crushed by the hammock, and found breathing difficult.

I peeped out when a subtle lightening of the darkness signified dawn. The long journey through the night was over,

but the world outside the red cocoon of my hammock and
canopy was a world of wind, spirals of snow, and heavy
cloud. I shrank from the thought of moving into even-worse
cold.

It was not until 10 a.m. that Pete shouted from below, "Are
you getting up, Joe?"

"All right," and I started the complex procedure of removing my sleeping bag and donning my boots whilst still lying
on my back, in order to emerge fully dressed to face the day.
Pete and I had conversed little during the last eighteen hours.
His silence in the night I took to indicate his greater comfort
over mine. He was calling again, so impatient I assumed he
was ready and criticising my slothfulness.

I was closing the last zips and pulling back on my gloves
when he shouted with real anger in his voice to ask why I was
not up yet. I replied placatingly and pulled apart the canopy
and hammock to step out onto the flake below. Pete was ten
feet lower, still not completely clothed. He was bent double,
his hands thrust into his groin, mutterings of pain escaping
from his bowed hood.

"What's the matter, Pete, I thought you were ready?"

"I've been doing my boots up outside and my fingers have
gone numb."

He showed me his blanched fingers, holding up a hand as
a palsied man might reach in supplication. He could not move
his fingers easily, his face was taut with pain.

Immediately I forgave him his harsh words, my sympathy wiped away any trace of hostility lingering from earlier
confrontations. I felt concern with no reservations, no embarrassment.

"How do they feel?"

He misread my concern for him as concern at the loss of a
partner to climb the mountain.

"They're coming round now, but they're sore. Don't worry, it's not going to stop me."

In doing up his boots outside in the wind he had lost sensation in his fingers, only realising that they were frozen when they failed to obey his thoughts. He winced in pain as the circulation returned and blood filled the damaged cells. His fingers took on a discoloured appearance. They were giving him pain each time he used them.

The incident served to focus our basic intentions in being on the mountain; whatever antagonisms might flare up, when it came to a real test of resolve there was no question but that we wanted to go on. I did not hesitate to let him see my concern, checking to make sure he could cope with each manoeuvre, packing down his hammock to save him bruising further his hands. It had needed an incident such as this to crack the shell of mute hostility which I had felt building up over the last weeks.

We made no attempt at melting snow for a drink, pressing on in the hope of finding a better place for the next night. We knew well that without a plentiful intake of liquid and food we would rapidly lose strength and would feel the cold all the more, but we were deceived by our memories of ascending these fixed ropes in a few hours and preferred to put off the task of melting snow until we had reached the top of the ice field where we promised to ourselves a spacious ledge with room to sit and a place to shelter the stove. But we had not reckoned with the slow pace imposed by our heavy sacks.

The morning cleared and encouraged us on, but it took all the rest of the day for us to reach the top of the ice field and by that time the storm had returned. There was no ledge to be found. I tried to climb further but showers of hail obliterated every foothold and handhold and we resigned ourselves to a repetition of the previous night's miserable performance. We managed again only one mug each of warm liquid and then struggled abjectly once more into our hammocks and sleeping bags. Then there were the tedious hours of waiting, marginally more comfortable, until dawn.

This was the end of a second day with little to eat and drink. Unavoidably we were slipping into a dangerous state of dehydration and starvation, but without a place where we could sit, and shelter the stove from the wind, we were helpless. Inside the hammocks we could not use the stove for fear of burning the fabric or spilling the contents of the pan over ourselves. Pete complained little about his hands.

Our values had become so debased that we only longed for a ledge to sit on, with room enough for the stove as well, not for a bed or our tent below. We wanted only hot drinks, not a feast. The next day we climbed 150 feet beyond the end of the fixed ropes and hacked some footholds from the ice. It was all we had time for before the day was gone and we entered the third night of misery.

It was a blessing next day to wake to the storm; it left no doubt in the decision. In three days we had made 150 feet of progress beyond what we had already done, we had scarcely drunk a pint of liquid a day and had eaten virtually nothing. We were both suffering from exposure and the chances of climbing the remaining 2,500 feet to the summit seemed minimal.

Retreat was welcoming; defeat was sweetened by the relief of escape from such physical distress. I did not think of it as a tactical withdrawal, I just wanted to get out of that misery, descend to warmth, drink, and food.

On reaching the tent of Camp 1, I lay down inside, sheltered from the gusts of wind and lulled by the warmth of the sun which was beginning to make an appearance through the cloud. I was dozing when Pete arrived and he was furious to discover that I had fallen asleep without lighting the stove and melting snow for a drink. There was an implicit understanding that the first one back would always prepare a drink, which was the thing we most looked forward to all day. I knew I was in the wrong but made some feeble excuse about not having a pan and Pete indicated an empty tin I should have thought to use.

The ordeal of the night in the hammocks and days with no shelter from the storms endowed the mountain with a ferocity we had not noticed previously. Glancing back, as we hastened on down to Base Camp, we were as children looking incomprehendingly and nervously at a fire which has inflicted unaccountable pain. The confidence which had grown during the days of steady progress up to the ice field was now shattered; no longer did success seem to depend solely on perseverance. Above the ice field were areas of rock, steeper than below, and with no camp to work from we could not see how we would be able to guard strength enough to climb them.

We spent two full days at Base Camp and it seemed like a week. After three weeks of constant effort, these were our first rest days. We relaxed and ate, losing the furtive mannerisms of those who have come in from the cold. We chatted about home life, about the girls we knew, untouchable idols about whom we dreamed from our self-imposed monasticism. I photographed the ice crystals in the stream at dawn and sparkling droplets on the petals of tiny flowers. We talked about the mountain when the fear had mellowed and Pete suggested taking the inner part of a tent so that we could sit together on the mountain if we could dig out a ledge large enough. I dressed his fingers, now cracked and inflamed at the ends.

They were nothing like as bad as Dick's fingers had been the year before, but Pete was more prepared to admit to the pain he felt than Dick had ever let himself. This I found more comprehensible. His fingers did look painful and I could relate to someone who expressed his feelings of pain rather than subdued them in a stoic acceptance of misfortune. Dick had had no choice but to keep on moving if he wanted to survive. Pete and I were in a situation where we could decide not to go back on the mountain if we thought it too hard or if his fingers were too much of an affliction. At no time, however, did I hear him waver in his intentions of climbing the mountain.

It was implicit that we would try again. Inevitably we would miss our flights home and Pete would be so far overdue on his return to the office that he resigned himself to losing his job. We had come so far and we felt so close to knowing whether the climb was possible or not that we could not bring ourselves to walk away in order to keep to a timetable. Parents and friends would be worried too but we had no contact with everyday life, no external stimuli to alter a decision. The mountain was our main stimulus, and it prevailed.

We packed to leave, altering once again the wording of the note to passersby. Then movement in the little valley out from Base Camp signified life, but it was not an animal, it was a person, and then two more. We were dumbstruck; more humans had reached our planet. They were two members and the liaison officer of the American expedition which we had heard about. Pete and I poured out a medley of questions, hardly waiting for their answers in the excitement of communicating with people other than ourselves. We did, however, gather something from their replies: yes, they were attempting Dunagiri, by the original route of 1939. There were ten of them altogether. The liaison officer was sick and was being accompanied back by one of the expedition who had to return home. The other member was going back onto the mountain to rejoin the rest of the team. Yes, they had seen our note, and when did we expect to go home now? Perhaps we could work together in summoning porters. Yes, their camp was nearby, about ten minutes away but out of sight in a hollow. They told us also the sad news of the death on Nanda Devi of a twenty-one-year-old girl, also named Nanda Devi. She was the daughter of an American climber who had been on the first ascent of the mountain many years before, and who had returned with her for what was intended to be a momentous ascent of a beautiful mountain by a beautiful girl with the same name. But she had taken ill on the mountain and had forced herself on until she had died. It was a disturbing story. We said our "Good lucks" and went our separate ways.

It had been an odd encounter, so casual when it could have been so significant. Certainly, had we been aware of their presence it would have given us some feeling of contact with the rest of the world, reassured us that we still had a place amongst humans. Both Pete and I had found the pair we had met puzzling. They were quite elderly, we thought, to be active climbers on a mountain in the Himalayas and their equipment was all new, as if bought for the occasion, with none of the individuality of tools that are familiar and well used. It was odd to walk down from an Advance Camp anyway to Base Camp carrying an ice axe and crampons, when most of the way was on slopes of rubble or earth. They struck us as people who like the mountains and buy the equipment recommended without a proper appreciation of when to use it. If their whole team was the same as the two members we had met, it emphasised the criteria that the Indian government used to judge expeditions. Age equated with experience and numbers with safety. They had had no trouble obtaining permission.

Pete voiced his puzzlement as we were on the way back up

to our own Advance Camp, thus giving shape to an uneasiness we both shared:

"If anyone is going to have an accident it will be them, don't you think?" We knew, however, that these visitors in their turn probably shared the same view of our efforts on Changabang.

Our own unfinished task menaced every moment we were not on the mountain. We stayed a day at Advance Camp to prospect a possible route of descent. The strain of what still lay ahead imbued me with a depression which made me blame Pete for everything that went wrong. We both overslept and I blamed Pete for not doing his breakfast chores. I blamed him for the late start and late return, resenting the lack of time before I had to busy myself with the evening meal. I felt cheated of the moments I value in which to relax and savour the remaining life before the headlong momentum toward a confrontation with a mountain of which the outcome is uncertain.

Much of the anxiety was due to the apprehension inspired by our experiences with the hammocks. We tried to rationalise our fears, reexamined the progress we had made and the time taken, referred back to the previous year when Dick and I had spent ten consecutive nights on a mountain with much inferior preparation, as proof that we could do at least the same again.

We were delayed at Camp 1 on the ridge by a thunderstorm and the strain was more intense. It seemed as if we were aware of every movement, every action, and even every thought of each other. There were no arguments, few words, a mute passivity, clipped and curt, nonvolunteering responses. For a month we had had to push ourselves to maximum effort and support entirely ourselves the full burden of the physical and mental strain. At no time could we take a day off to let someone else do the work and bear the strain, always the problem was waiting exactly as we had left it. We knew this was our last attempt. We had not food enough for another return. The heavy snow and relentless wind eroded our expectations.

The sky, however, cleared, the wind swept the snow from the mountain and we regained the scene of our ordeal in the hammocks, taking up with us the line of ropes from the lower part of the mountain. We laboured for hours, hacking at the ice, and formed a ledge just wide enough to lie on side by side. Here, at twenty thousand feet, we made our Camp 2. We suspended the thin nylon of the inner tent by two corners, attaching them to pitons driven into ice and rock. It was a tight squeeze for us both to fit into the tent and stay on the ledge and one side of the tent hung off the edge. It was my turn to take the outside position. Only one of us could move at a time, every shift in position required consultation with the other person, and it was a constant worry that we might drop or dislodge some essential item such as boots or stove.

The climbing above was more difficult and very much more sustained. We had disappointments at our slow rate of progress but we were solving a tangible problem. We spent days climbing up steep walls and icy runnels and hours zigzagging round corners. We came to blank spots and strained blindly on the rope to reach other fault lines; we had moments of terror such as when a sharp edge part cut through the rope as I was climbing, and moments of joy at the end of the day as we swung down the ropes fixed as a lifeline back to our cramped and tiny tent on the side of a mountain flaming red with the sunset.

The slowness was frustrating, but each advance added to a state of satisfaction. Each day we were exhausted and at no time were we far from the borderline with danger. Late one night, caught out by the dark, I detached myself in error from the rope and almost fell. If I had fallen, Pete would never have known what had happened. The days became almost routine. I was back first, Pete had lost his descending device and had to use a slower method on the long line of ropes. Back at the tent I would chop lumps from the ice, place them at the front of the tent, then slip inside to have them already melting for when I heard the clatter of Pete arriving and swinging across from the line of the rope.

It took four hard days to climb 1,200 feet above Camp 2, to a point from which we were certain we could reach a broad ramp of snow cutting across the face above and leading to easier ground and the summit. We rested for a day with bated breath lest the mountain should notice we were confident again of reaching the summit. We lay cosy in the sun-warmed confines of the tent, eating, sleeping, relishing the magnificent panorama through the entrance and the splendour of our airy perch three thousand feet above the glacier. Without a hint of the strains from the previous days, I noted briefly on a piece of paper:

> Wednesday 13 October. Today we are both knackered and having a rest day. Can see smoke from the Americans' camp direction. They must be packing up. This expedition seems to have gone on for ages. Be glad to get it over with. Hell of a situation up here. Hope the weather lasts. People must be worried at home now.

Action and confrontation with the problem that had menaced us for so long was more acceptable than the ordeal of waiting. There was neither the constant whittling away of confidence nor the psychological demoralisation of being dominated by the whole problem. We had tackled it in parts

and restored our confidence as we found the solution, no matter how difficult, to each one. There remained one stretch of a
hundred feet before we reached the ramp, and from all that
we could judge there were no more obstacles between the
ramp and the summit.

In the cold of the morning, before the sun reached round
to the West Face, Pete led the way up that last pitch toward the
ramp. He paused often to warm his hands, nursing fingers
that were still painful. He reached the ramp as the sun pushed
a halo of colours over the summit ridge. It was a sign of a
change in the weather.

We did not follow the ramp, but climbed straight up, mis-
calculating the difficulty. It took until evening to gain the bottom of the slope leading uniformly up to the summit.

Bliss was the cessation of movement, shelter from the
wind, food and sleep. We were deadly tired.

I ignored the strict demarcation of tasks in the morning
and produced a warm drink before we left for the summit. We
trailed upward, moving together, linked by the rope. I was in
front and never looked back. If the rope tugged at my waist I
never knew whether Pete was moving more slowly or if the
rope had caught on a fluting of snow. We crawled closer to the
summit, the fatigue and exertion of altitude familiar and not
disconcerting; dimly I was aware that at long last we were
clawing our way to the top of the slope awesomely poised five
thousand feet above the precipice of the West Face. A few
points of metal on our boots and metal tools in our hands
were all that kept us there.

I tried to do the last twenty steps to the summit in one go
but stopped short, panting for breath. I approached cautiously. The summit was a sharp crest dropping steeply away
on the opposite side. Pete joined me and moved along to a
spot which looked slightly higher fifty feet away.

The top was simply an end to the struggle upward. Nanda Devi was clear for a moment long enough for Pete to satisfy his wish to see it. An advancing bank of cloud was bringing the bad weather heralded by the rainbow around the sun the previous day. No anthems played in my head; I only wanted to get down. The summit was just one stage in the process of climbing the mountain. I felt no ecstasy at our achievement nor pleasure at the panoramas on every side. The practical problems of descent and the further days of exertion needed before we would truly be safe prevented me feeling anything more than a relief that we had no more upward movement. For me the exultation and satisfaction could wait until we were back on firm ground. We looked for any remnants left by our friends in case they had reached the top but the snow was deep and we saw none. We were on the summit for less than half an hour, sharing some chocolate and taking photographs, then we started down as the first flurries of snow came and the valleys merged with the grey clouds.

I felt again the superiority in Pete's comments when he saw the piton I had driven in at the start of the long, steep abseil down to the ramp. It protruded for half its length and flexed as I settled my weight on it.

"You're not going down on that are you?"

I was curt in my reply, resenting the implied criticism that he could have arranged something different.

"Can you find anything better?"

He could not, and I sensed he was glad that I was going first. Foolishly light-headed, or with the trust that, having investigated every alternative, faith would add strength to the anchor point, I slid apprehensively down. Having done all possible, we needed now a little luck. The piton held.

It was twilight when we regained the fixed rope at the bottom of the ramp. The rope was our lifeline and I felt reassured when I clipped into it and started the more mechanical manoeuvres to slide back down to the tent. In the thirty-six hours since last using this lifeline, the wind had tossed it about in parts. It had been blown loose from one anchor point and I had to haul myself back onto course and refix the rope securely in place to make it easier for Pete. In the dark everything had to be done by touch and memory. My hands were stiffening with cramp by the time I was making the pendulum toward our tent. I hacked out lumps of ice as usual before tumbling into the tent and lying there, allowing myself to feel more exultation than I had ever permitted on the summit. Halfway down, halfway to safety, I waited for Pete to come jangling in.

Warm inside my sleeping bag, I revelled in the sensual ache of relaxation and started melting ice for a drink. The ice had melted, the water was hot and Pete had still not arrived. I turned the stove down, delaying drinking myself until I could share the pleasure.

I shook myself out of a doze to realise that the pan was still bubbling away and there was no sound of Pete. I peered out into the blackness. Nothing. I shouted. No reply.

I lay back, dredging up from my subconscious any sound from the last hour or two which might have been Pete falling, thus allowing the thought of accident to crystallise. Hopeless despair invaded me as the pan simmered pointlessly for the drink I had hoped to share and now, in spite of a great thirst, I had no taste for it. My mind chased up and down the alleyways of action, ruling out all possibilities of arresting a calamity if it had already happened. I longed to hear the familiar jangle of Pete's arrival which would make foolish all my worries, but I had been back over two hours by this time.

And then it came, the rattle of gear, the scrape of crampons on rock, no sudden rush of catastrophe but the slowness of control. My fears vanished but I could not find again the exultation with which I had wanted to greet him.

"Joe, can you see those lights?"

I looked out and saw nothing.

"Oh, they're gone. Can you hear voices?"

I could hear nothing, and wondered if he were delirious.

"You've been a long time. I thought you had an accident."

"I did. A peg came out and I almost fell off. I ended up upside down, holding on by one hand."

We were accustomed to recovering quickly from shocks; together again we lingered over eating and making hot drinks, without the discipline of another day of upward progress hanging over us. We indulged ourselves a little early in self-congratulations. Even if we died now we had proved that it was not impossible to climb such a route as the West Face of Changabang.

I was unquestionably pleased to be passing down the mountain for the last time. It was true that we had mastered it but all the time I had felt on edge, at every moment the forbidding nature of this colossal wall made itself felt. We were late leaving Camp 2 and it was night once more when we were still five hundred feet from the tent of Camp 1.

I stared and strained with my eyes into the darkness, trying to pick out details below. We were on the mixed ground of snow and rock, groping about from memory to find the rocks in which we had left pitons and marker ribbons. If we were only fifty feet off course in the dark we could miss the tent completely.

It became another bitter ordeal of cold, wind, and fatigue, with my body screaming *no more*. It was hard to think clearly. We could not find one marker and piton and we had differing memories about which direction we should aim. Pete had better vision in the dark and went down on a rope which

I paid out, hoping to take his weight if he fell. After 150 feet he had found nothing. I tied on another rope and paid that out. We had to find the final marker point through the last stretch of icy rock, otherwise we would never find the tent. He had gone three hundred feet down into the blackness when his muffled shouts drifted up with the welcome news that he was on course. My feet were frozen and my legs shook with cold.

I descended, climbing down the snow slope, with the rope hanging loosely from my waist. I kept shouting to Pete for directions. I was thoroughly scared, able to see nothing and relying on my feet to tell of the changes in the texture of snow and ice.

The whole descent had become a fiasco, but I marvelled at Pete's psychic powers in finding the anchor points and markers and bringing us within striking distance of the tent. I slid down the rope, recognising the contours of the slope; my legs folded beneath me as the angle eased. A few steps more and I was home, collapsing on the platform we had levelled out and feeling a suffused elation welling up as I realised we were safe. We had been three hours groping down in the dark.

The urgency had gone from our actions. We did not reach the tent of Advance Camp till late in the afternoon of the next day. There was barely anything to eat there but we stayed overnight in order to retrieve from the glacier the bundles of equipment we had been unable to carry and had thrown down from Camp 1. It was October 18, we had seats booked on a plane for this day and, with no hope of meeting this deadline, we had no more cause to hurry. We went about everything now in the leisurely manner that our weary bodies and spirits demanded.

Later that day we trudged with heavy loads back toward Base Camp. There were only the ties from home to hurry us on but they could influence little our pace. Base Camp itself held little attraction; the Americans had said they would be leaving around October 10 or 12, so there was no welcome congratulation or celebration to look forward to. We stopped often, relaxed with each other as never before, resting our sacks on convenient boulders to save the effort of taking them off. I thought I heard voices but Pete heard nothing. When I heard them again I was not alarmed that hunger and exhaustion might be inducing more hallucinations on this same track that I had walked in delirium the year before from Dunagiri.

We paused at the vantage point from which we had a last view of Changabang before dropping down into the little valley leading to Base Camp. Streamers of cloud drifted past the mountain, revealing periodically the summit cone glowing red in the rays of the setting sun.

We photographed the sight until the colour left it and we stumbled in the rapid dark down the narrow valley, slipping in the dust and tripping over stones.

There was a smell of wood smoke, and voices, this time we both agreed. We saw lights, a campfire. We hurried then, delighted to know there were people to meet. We shouted but had no reply; we approached our tent cautiously; it was dark, undisturbed, and the note unmoved. We dropped our sacks and hurried uncertainly and awkwardly in the dark across to the fire. A large tent loomed up, voices chattered away inside in a strange tongue oblivious of our presence outside.

We poked our heads inside. It was a huge tent full of people, warmth, colour, food, noise. They seemed to know who we were and to be half-expecting us.

"Changabang West Face? Boardman, Tasker?"

"Yes."

Mugs of lemon tea were pressed into our hands and chunks of Parmesan cheese; we were made welcome and indulged ourselves in the glory of their admiration; the inevitable pride we felt in our accomplishment, drinking thirstily of their praise.

They were a group of Italians who had come to climb Kalanka, but having followed mistaken directions had arrived in the wrong valley for tackling that mountain. It did not seem to affect their joyous spirits; they had climbed a small peak, had even gone onto the lower slopes of Changabang, though one had broken his fingers in some stone fall. It was cosy in the tent, there were too many things and too many faces to absorb at first; it did not matter, we were accepted into the comradeship of fellow climbers and swept along in a lively exchange of experiences and climbs.

Pete was closer in to the main group than I, speaking for both of us, and he knew many people in Italy through his work at the British Mountaineering Council. I was light-headed from elation, fatigue, and the return to safety. The warmth of the tent induced a drowsiness. I was content to let Pete do the talking.

I became aware that I was sitting next to the only woman of the group, a tired, drawn-looking woman who, I realised with surprise, spoke English very well. Without having to make the effort of conversing in pidgin English, I started to talk with her.

She told me she was a member of the American expedition and I wondered at the reasons for her staying on alone when the rest of the expedition had arranged porters for their departure several days ago. Then she told me that there had been an accident and I presumed this had caused a delay, imagining someone with a broken arm being helped slowly down the mountain, and that she would be leaving soon with the rest of the equipment.

I grew conscious of the selfish indulgence of Pete and myself revelling in our own success when others had not been so lucky. I tried to show some consideration for an event which had thwarted their ambitions.

"I'm sorry. Was anyone hurt?"

"Yes. Four were killed."

And there it was, a stark non sequitur to my train of thought. A reply as outlandish and different to that anticipated as one would experience in a conversation with someone who was crazy. And it was over to me to adapt to this terrible fact, to assimilate and comprehend. Killed? How could she say killed? Why wasn't such an awful fact apparent on everyone's face, apparent in everything around me? Why wasn't it the topic of all our talk? How could something so awful be said so quietly, so casually? I looked to her for rescue from thoughts I could not contain.

"Was anyone related to you?"

"Yes, my husband."

She said it so unobtrusively, in such a matter-of-fact way, her drawn face registered no change of emotion. For over a month Pete and I had run the gauntlet with death and escaped, to return shouting our triumph. But now I was meeting another side of such encounters. This woman was telling me that her husband had played the same game and lost, as had his three friends. My words, coming from someone who continually played such a game, seemed facile. I fled out of the tent, away from the warmth and chatter, to look at the stars and feel the cool night air.

She had told me that Yasu, my friend from Joshimath, was in a tent outside. I went to find him and he embraced me warmly.

He explained in shocked, subdued tones that Ruth, the woman, had been on the mountain when the accident had happened. Five of the members of the team had already gone home, the remaining five had gone onto the mountain. Ruth went as far as a tent on a shoulder of the mountain and waited there for her husband and the three other men while they made an attempt to reach the summit. The four had reached the crest of the ridge and spent a night out. Next day she had seen them coming down. She did not know if they had reached the summit or not. She was observing them from the tent doorway when she saw two of them fall and plunge three thousand feet to the foot of the mountain. When next she brought herself to look out, the second pair had fallen too and were lying near the two bodies a long way below her. She had tried to descend herself but had been too shaken to get down on her own. She spent a night in the tent watching the Advance Camp for any sign of Yasu, who had been asked to come up to help with clearing the camp on a certain date. When she saw his tiny figure approaching the lower camp she had shouted and waved. He had realised immediately what had happened, being able to see the shapes of the bodies at the foot of the mountain. By that time the Italian Kalanka expedition had arrived at Base Camp and he went back to obtain their help in rescuing the woman. Ruth did not know about the Italians and presumed that Yasu had understood her to be indicating that he should not clear the camp and had gone back to Base to wait until he was summoned. The next day, which was only this morning, Yasu had returned with some of the Italians and brought the woman down from the camp where she was stranded. Theirs had been the voices I had heard as Pete and I walked down the glacier from another direction. Yasu was going back to the mountain next day with his companion, Balu, to examine the bodies.

Pete and I had left gear up at our Advance Camp which we intended to retrieve next day, and I offered to Yasu that we would come over to Dunagiri on our way back. The whole story was shocking and incomprehensible, my

reactions were those of someone stunned; this drama had
come upon us totally unexpectedly and I was unprepared for
the role I should play. The darkness hid any need to worry
about what my facial expressions showed or failed to show.

I was starving with hunger; Pete and I had eaten virtually
nothing all day. Yasu prepared a huge meal over his fire and
Pete came stumbling out into the dark, rightly suspecting that
I would have discovered some food.

Pete had learnt of the tragedy and that night in our tent we
discussed the matter. It was not at all clear whether our help
was needed; unquestionably the four would be dead after
such a long fall, so it was not a matter of rescue. It did not
seem right that the bodies should be left exposed on the
mountainside. On the other hand, the Italians were probably
fitter than we were for going up to the bodies, but they were
not making any plans to do so. Pete and I both knew of the
complications caused through deaths in the mountains, the
endless problems for relatives when no evidence of death is
produced, the long wrangles with insurance companies and
government offices. We resolved to go up there ourselves next
day with Yasu and Balu if the Italians made no move.

We both woke before dawn, restless from weeks of condi-
tioning to hyperactivity, still highly charged from the weeks of
tension. As Pete went off in the dawn twilight to find water, I
went over to Ruth's tent.

She emerged, a tear revealing the pain of her night alone,
and was quietly grateful as I explained our intentions. We
were going to identify the bodies, and I felt clinically callous
as I asked for any means of identifying them. I had to tell her
that it was possible after having fallen so far that the bones
which gave shape to a person's face would be damaged and
the faces unrecognisable. Identification from their passport
photographs might not be possible. She said her husband had

a gold ring and that so far as she was concerned it was more appropriate that his body be left to rest on the mountain.

We left with empty sacks and long ice axes borrowed from the Italians. Pete and I trailed far behind Yasu and Balu, pushing on limbs which protested their need for rest.

Yasu indicated details of the Americans' route on the way to their camp on the glacier and when we reached it he pointed out the dots which were the bodies high up on a shelf above an ice cliff. We inspected them through binoculars and hoped that the many objects scattered round them were not their dismembered limbs.

We climbed up a steepening slope of the glacier. I could see the ridge, not very far away, on which Dick and I had spent so long the year before. It was impossible now for me to conceive of what had gone on. Now I felt strong and capable, with enough in reserve to go to the assistance of people less fortunate.

The bodies lay on an ice shelf, in a direct line three thousand feet below the ice slope from which they had fallen. From what I could judge at a distance, that ice slope was very similar to the one on which Dick and I had both fallen the year before and, though the two places were thousands of feet apart, I suspected that both incidents were due to the same cause—fatigue and hard ice.

As we climbed up, Yasu and Balu, who had been so fit at the start, dropped back, Balu complaining that he was feeling ill. They were out of sight when we arrived on the sloping shelf at twenty thousand feet close to the foot of the mountain. Fortunately the bodies were intact, the objects scattered around being items from their burst rucksacks. Some objects clung to a rock buttress above us, showing where they must have struck in their headlong fall.

We examined all four. They were joined together by ropes

in two pairs. A fractured ice axe near to one body indicated a possible reason why they had not been able to stop each other from falling. We cut open their frozen pockets and searched inside, looking for a means of positive identification. But no one carries his passport or wallet on a mountain. We looked for cameras to retrieve the film so that we would know if they had reached the summit, but found none. We found Ruth's husband with his gold ring. I forced myself to photograph each body, aware of the morbid misinterpretation that this action was open to. To obtain a death certificate a body needs to be identified by a relative and certified as dead by a doctor. We were neither, but there was no way we could take the bodies back for identification, and our only sort of proof that they were indeed dead, apart from our word, was a photograph.

Pete told me he felt sick. I was as if anaesthetised; I let myself feel nothing in order to cope with the job in hand. Pete was uncertain about burying the bodies, concerned that we were acting beyond our responsibilities. I had no time for the bureaucratic formalities which would leave the bodies exposed as food for the crows for weeks before anyone could return here if anyone ever should. I insisted that we bury them and we took a rope each, drawing the bodies in pairs to the edge of a crevasse. They were frozen and awkward in shape. I sensed Pete's wordless sorrow and saw the tears in his eyes. I slid two of the bodies into the depths, resting them on a bridge some distance below the surface. I took over from Pete, who seemed in a daze.

"Watch out, Joe, on the edge of that crevasse."

I slid the second pair in to join the others and scrambled away from the brink to sink down beside Pete.

"Do you believe in God?"

"I don't know, do you?"

"If the prayers are for anyone, they're for those left behind."

"Prayers don't need words. Let's just stay here silent for a while."

In a few days the winter snows would start and cover the bodies completely. In time the crevasse would close and the bodies would become part of the mountain glacier forever.

We gathered up all the equipment we could squash into our rucksacks, responding to an unformulated notion of tidying up any loose ends. Descending, we could see the summit of Changabang poking over a small peak in the foreground—that dome we had been privileged to walk on and return from.

Back at the camp on the glacier we found Yasu and Balu warming water over a stove and we drank gratefully. They were visibly relieved to see us back and we understood now that they had been terrified of going any further and glimpsed something of the awe with which they regarded us now for having gone up to have dealings with the dead.

They loaded themselves up with all that they could carry—Yasu wickedly asked if we had found any watches or cameras—and we plodded down together.

It was night as we reached Base Camp, noisy hordes of people making movements round a campfire. Porters for the Italians had arrived and a singsong was taking place. Ruth was in the circle and Pete and I pushed in to give her a report, feeling the unwanted bearers of bad tidings in the midst of a happy throng.

We both felt too estranged from such merriment to partake in it and we left to find our own tent and make a meal. I borrowed a large tin can from the Italians and went off to fetch water. It was much colder now than it had been all those weeks ago when we had first arrived. The stream near our tent was dried up. I went off up the hillside in the dark, tracking down the sound of trickling water. It was a long way before I found a flow substantial enough to scoop up into my bucket. I tripped and staggered all the way back, spilling water down my legs, longing for the rest I felt we so much deserved. Implicitly I imagined Pete getting the stove going and waiting impatiently for my return.

I heard no sound as I regained the tent. Pete was inside warmly clad and settling down into his sleeping bag. I presumed he had had trouble starting the stove.

"What's the matter with the stove?"

"Nothing. I've just been getting myself settled in."

"Settled in? And I've been running about in the dark for the last half hour to find water!"

I was really angry that I had postponed relaxing until all was ready, assuming that Pete would be similarly motivated without need to discuss what we each should do. It was a jolt to realise that my impression of us complementing each other and working as a unity was an illusion. The paring away over the last few weeks of all superfluous niceties made me blunt and forthright in my indignation.

"I suppose you were waiting for me to cook you a meal as well?"

He grabbed the stove and worked furiously at it. In a while he had some water heating in a pan and the evening meal was in progress.

Yasu and Balu had come over and sat in front of our tent round a small fire. I sat with them. It was a simple life. Time passed; a little warmth was thrown up by the flames and we were three shadowy figures sharing it.

Yasu looked up: "You know the monkey god, Hanuman? They say he has servants who are also monkeys and who rush about doing everything for him."

He looked over at our tent.

"Just like Pete does for you," and his eyes twinkled.

There were not porters enough for Pete and myself, so we agreed between us that I would leave with the Italian party and Ruth in order to send back five porters. Meanwhile Pete

would go back up to our Advance Camp and bring down the
rest of our gear. I was glad to be the one to leave. I had spent
too long the year before on my own waiting for porters to
want to go through that experience again. Pete for his part
was glad to stay on because his feet were sore and he could
have a couple of days' rest before having to do anything.

I packed a few essentials into a rucksack for my journey
and raced after the main party who had left an hour before.
The day was beautiful. I felt fit and strong, confident and satisfied. I crossed a plateau of grass browning with the arrival of
autumn, and delighted in my effortless progress. I wanted the
sensation of strength and capability to go on and on. I crested
a hill and came upon Yasu and Balu, waiting for me. The spell
was broken, I was amongst men again.

I fell into step with Ruth, the Italians chattered in their own
little groups, and I sensed that they felt inadequate at communicating in their imperfect English with someone whose sorrow was so deep. She was unsteady on some awkward steps
where the track led over precipitous ridges. I slowed my pace
and stayed with her. She never asked for help but I felt I
needed to stay with her and I talked about anything to bring
her away from that solitary vigil she had endured for two days
and nights looking down on her husband's body and not
knowing whether she herself would die too. I could not keep
repeating how sorry I was at her loss. I just talked about anything to give her a person, out of a crowd of strangers, to
whom she could relate. I talked about my past and my ambitions, I told her about my training to be a priest and what a
different life I now had. She told me something of how she
had passed the time alone in the tent, reading a book until
help should come and how she had despaired when she saw
Yasu turn back. She told me of the things she had done with
her husband and the plans they had had to travel round India
after the trip, how she needed to return before it was in all the

papers and burglars would raid their home because they would know she was absent. I wondered at her calm and control and told her how important it was to inform immediately the relatives of the other three dead before the merciless press should seize the news and broadcast it without thought for the hurt it might cause.

We stumbled together late at night through the woods into the clearing at Dibrugheta and I climbed with her next day up to Dharansi Pass and across the plateau. I told her the story of Dick and myself on Dunagiri the year before but felt guilty at the end of my tale as I realised that we had survived where her husband and friends had not.

I left her when we reached a broad path and it was all downhill. I met Jim Duff from the expedition to the south side of Changabang and his girlfriend, Sue. They had stayed on after the expedition to trek around the hills. His team had reached the top of the mountain a week before we had, by a route which had taken them two days, and clearly the snow had covered all trace of them before we had arrived on the summit. I asked Jim and Sue to take care of Ruth and rushed down to reach the road for the bus which I knew went past at 4 p.m.

I saw the bus, the only one of the day, when I was still some minutes from the road. I did not reach Joshimath until the next day and sent the telegrams which I hoped would appease the anxieties of all at home. "Changabang West Face climbed. Both of us safe and well. Joe."

I sent one to each of our parents. I knew that Pete's parents would wonder why my name was at the end of the telegram, but I decided against making it seem as if Pete had sent it. He still had to reach here from Base Camp and until he did I could not bring myself to pretend that he had.

Two days later the first snows of winter whitened the tops of the hills, and my anxieties grew with the knowledge of the struggle I had had to escape from Base Camp at the same time twelve months before in deep snow. I was thankful that I had not telegrammed any pretence. But Pete was safe and came striding into the rest house late in the afternoon some days later, still carrying with him the wildness of mountain life and the aura of one newly returned amongst people.

We had by this time run out of money. Anticipating this possibility we had cabled home for more but it had not arrived. Bhupal Singh, proprietor of the motel, loaned us Rs 1,000 on the promise that we would send it to him as soon as we reached Delhi. But his trust in us was so great that he said it could wait till we reached England. Rs 1,000 was approximately £50 but in that small hill town it was the equivalent of £1,000 and he lent on trust alone. In my two encounters with him I had come to regard him as a close friend whom I admired and respected.

We used the money to purchase bus tickets back to Delhi and returned there in a twenty-four-hour, cramped, and bone-jarring journey which was made unpleasant by the onset of the usual stomach pains and diarrhoea on coming out of the sterile hills.

In Delhi we made statements about burying the bodies and saw the stress on Ruth's face as round after round of questions from officials and press and acquaintances wore down the control and calmness she had managed to achieve for herself.

We made our good-byes and boarded a plane. Pete, forgiven his long absence, to return to his office and myself, with no other ambition to fulfil, to look for employment. The adventure was over.

For nearly two years I had been totally absorbed with climbing three mountains. Each one had represented something different, each one had been at that moment, in its own way, the greatest test I could conceive of. Each test had been passed and I was left bewildered. I was alarmed to have succeeded; in a way it would have been more reassuring to have failed. Instead, success left me with an uneasy, unsettling questioning about where to go next; something harder, something bigger? Where would it all lead? What had I gained from the last two years if all that was left to me was an indefinable dissatisfaction? Was I destined to be forever striving, questing, unable to find peace of mind and contentment?

We had met death and lent a hand in coping with the accident practically, as if it were an everyday occurrence in our sport, and I blocked out the questions those bodies had raised. As I had shut off all emotion in order to complete the task of burying them, I shut out all the doubts and uncertainties about my own involvement in a game which courted death in order to continue playing that game. I was certain that I did not want to die but I knew that the risk in climbing gave it its value. The sensation of being stretched to the limit mentally and physically was what gave me satisfaction and if there was danger it was another problem to solve, it made me more careful, made me perform at my best, and added a special uniqueness to the experience. If there was courage needed it was only the same courage required to meet all the everyday problems of life, to go for an interview, to bring children into the world, to propose to a girl, to take any new step. If we had shown courage in going up to bury four fellow climbers, the only difference was that our everyday problems were located on the side of a mountain and we were on the spot and suited to the task.

If I had died, I would have wanted no sorrow. I would have been achieving my ambitions, would have been exercising the drive and vitality which made me friends or enemies in ordinary life. If I did not do something to the limit, if I had not channelled my energies into climbing, I would not be a person liked or disliked, but someone mediocre. When a friend was killed in the mountains I could only regret that he had not fulfilled his dreams; when a friend was killed drunk and driving as usual too fast, my sorrow was selfish, I wished

I had seen more of him. He lived fast, he lived at the limit, and his absence made the world a little less fun for those who knew him, but he died in the way he lived and in a way which he had escaped from only by a hair's breadth many times.

Four people had died and we knew how painful this loss would be for their relatives and friends. For them we had buried the dead and to them we wrote to let them know it was not all loss, that they had our sympathy, that they had contact with us who had last seen their loved ones.

Pete and I were united as one person, if need be one spoke for both; we had emerged from the trial of six weeks of confinement together with a friendship which needed no words. The animosities and estrangements of that period sank into insignificance, seen for what they were, products of particularly trying circumstances. Through it all the unity had prevailed, and the cooperation which had been needed to succeed had always outweighed any differences.

No longer strangers, there was now no need for the small talk which Pete had felt at first; we knew each other so well there was also less need for more serious discussion. I could guess Pete's views and reactions so closely I was sometimes unsure whether we had actually talked about a matter or whether I had mentally resolved what would be his opinion. A girl complained to me once resentfully about Pete, "The thing about you two is you don't need to talk to each other."

He offered me a place in his house until I found a new direction in life, and I set about looking for a job.

Postscript: Joe Tasker and Peter Boardman continued to climb high peaks together until their joint disappearance on the northeast ridge of Mount Everest six years later.

NOTES ON THE CONTRIBUTORS

FELICE BENUZZI was a lawyer and a career diplomat for the government of Italy. He died in 1988.

WALTER BONATTI pioneered new routes in the Alps, Himalayas, and Patagonia, and is the author of *On the Heights* and *Magic of Mont Blanc*.

ART DAVIDSON is a journalist and the author of *Light on the Land* (with Art Wolfe).

HEINRICH HARRER (1912–2006) was an Austrian who escaped imprisonment by the British and spent most of World War II trekking through Tibet and Lhasa, where he became a friend of the Dalai Lama. From these experiences he wrote *Seven Years in Tibet* and *Lost Lhasa*.

MAURICE HERZOG brought worldwide recognition to high-peak mountaineering, and his account of the Annapurna expedition went on to sell eleven million copies—more than any other mountaineering book ever published.

THOMAS F. HORNBEIN is a physician and a professor who has published widely in the field of anesthesiology and the physiology of breathing at high altitude.

NANDO PARRADO is a television personality and motivational speaker living in Montevideo, Uruguay, where he also helps run the family's hardware business.

PETER POTTERFIELD has written more than a dozen books on outdoor adventure, including *Classic Hikes of the World* and *Selected Climbs in the Cascades*.

DAVID ROBERTS is a writer who has written many books on mountaineering, including *Escape Routes* and *On the Ridge between Life and Death*.

JOHN ROSKELLEY has summited Everest and is the author of *Stories Off the Wall* and *Last Days*.

JOE SIMPSON has written five books on his climbing adventures, including *This Game of Ghosts*, *Dark Shadows Falling*, and *The Beckoning Silence*.

JOE TASKER (1948–82) climbed throughout the Alps and the Himalayas, and he died ascending Everest with his close friend Peter Boardman.

PERMISSIONS ACKNOWLEDGMENTS

JOE SIMPSON: Excerpt from *Touching the Void* by Joe Simpson, copyright © 1989 by Joe Simpson. Reprinted by permission of HarperCollins Publishers, New York, and Jonathan Cape, The Random House Group, Ltd., London.

JOE TASKER: Excerpt from *Savage Arena* by Joe Tasker, copyright © 1982 by Joe Tasker. Reprinted by permission of Curtis Brown Group Limited.